RUTH MAIER'S DIARY

A young girl's life under Nazism

EDITED BY

Jan Erik Vold

TRANSLATED FROM THE GERMAN BY

Jamie Bulloch

Harvill *Secker*

LONDON

Published by Harvill Secker 2009

2 4 6 8 10 9 7 5 3 1

First published with the title *Ruth Maier's Dagbok* in 2007
by Gyldendal Norsk Forlag, Oslo

First published in Great Britain in 2009 by
HARVILL SECKER
Random House
20 Vauxhall Bridge Road
London SW1V 2SA

www.rbooks.co.uk

Addresses for companies within The Random House Group Limited can be found at:
www.randomhouse.co.uk/offices.htm

The Random House Group Limited Reg. No. 954009

A CIP catalogue record for this book is available from the British Library

ISBN 9781846552144 (hardback)
ISBN 9781846552151 (trade paperback)

This book was published with the financial assistance of NORLA and has been
selected to receive financial assistance from English PEN's Writers in Translation
programme supported by Bloomberg

The extract on pages 55–6 from Thomas Mann's *Enttäuschung* (found in Thomas Mann,
Der Wille zum Glück und andere Erzählungen, 1966, © Katia Mann) is reproduced by kind
permission of S. Fischer Verlag GmbH, Frankfurt am Main

The Random House Group Limited supports The Forest Stewardship
Council (FSC), the leading international forest certification organisation. All our titles that
are printed on Greenpeace approved FSC certified paper carry the FSC logo. Our paper
procurement policy can be found at www.rbooks.co.uk/environment

Mixed Sources
Product group from well-managed
forests and other controlled sources
www.fsc.org Cert no. TT-COC-2139
FSC © 1996 Forest Stewardship Council

Recommended by pen

Printed in Great Britain by
Clays Ltd, St Ives plc

CONTENTS

III
War

EPILOGUE
... who disappeared

TRANSLATOR'S NOTE

The literary qualities of Ruth Maier's diaries and letters have been widely acknowledged. In a lucid, yet often highly lyrical style, Ruth displays a skilful talent for narrative and drama, and rounds these off with a sharp wit. Given her unquestionable flair for writing, it is easy to forget that we are reading spontaneous material in its first and only draft, never intended for publication. When translating the diaries this raises the issue of how much revision and editing is justifiable. Can we possibly improve the text, or does such an approach detract from the authenticity and immediacy of the work?

As would be expected, we have removed orthographical and grammatical errors, while the punctuation has been cleaned up for reasons of clarity. Stylistic polishing is a more contentious issue, and applied indiscriminately can ruin the colour of the original text. In this instance, the approach has been to reproduce Ruth's voice as faithfully as possible, while eliminating or modifying the occasional idiosyncrasy that could jar with an English-language audience. I have endeavoured to adopt a style that might not have been totally alien to a girl growing up in 1930s Britain with a similar social background to Ruth. At the very least I hope I have managed to avoid howling linguistic anachronisms.

In his introduction, Jan Erik Vold explains the editorial procedure undertaken for the Norwegian edition of the book, which involved being very selective with the first volume of Ruth's diary while reproducing the later ones in full. We have implemented a few more cuts of our own; these do not affect the diary entries or letters, only the poems dotted throughout the text. A larger proportion of the poetic material written towards the end of Ruth's life has been kept in, as this reflects the balance of her diary output at the time: fewer descriptions of day-to-day life, and more short prose pieces.

Finally I should like to express my warmest gratitude to Ruth Maier's sister, Mrs Judith Suschitzky, who has taken the trouble to look carefully through the English proofs. This is the first time she has seen a lot of the material reproduced here, and her contribution to the finished book has been invaluable. Many thanks are also due to Jan Erik Vold. Both he and Mrs Suschitzky have helped clear up issues we could never have worked out for ourselves, highlighted errors and offered suggestions which have improved the quality of the text.

Jamie Bulloch
November 2008

One of us

Ruth Maier was a refugee from Austria. She arrived in Norway before the war and stayed for four years before being arrested as part of a large round-up of Jews in late autumn 1942. Together with hundreds of other Jews she was put on board the ship *Donau* and deported. Ruth was born on 10 November 1920 in Vienna and died on 1 December 1942 in Auschwitz.

Ruth kept a diary throughout her life. The earliest surviving entries were written when she was twelve. The final volume was completed two days after her twenty-second birthday. Eight books of diaries and fifty letters survive from the period 1933 to 1942: the daily, weekly and monthly observations of an enquiring and educated young woman with artistic talents in many fields. Her friend Gunvor Hofmo, the Norwegian poet, kept these diaries for more than fifty years.

Around 1,100 diary pages and 300 pages of letters have been found, and these have been turned into a 400-page book.

At the end of January 1939, Ruth arrived in Norway from the German Reich as an eighteen-year-old schoolgirl, settling in the small town of Lillestrøm, close to Oslo. In 1940 she took her school-leaving exams and then met a group of Norwegian friends while working in the women's labour service. One of these was Gunvor Hofmo, with whom she travelled across Norway for two years, taking odd jobs in various places. In September 1942 she moved into a young women's boarding house in Oslo, where she attended courses at the arts and crafts college, and earned money painting souvenirs.

Ruth left behind diaries, letters, literary texts, as well as many water-colours and drawings. She also left good memories among those who survived her, a handful of whom are still with us today. From the very start

Ruth had a profound influence on Gunvor Hofmo's poetry (even if her name is not actually mentioned):

> On a rainy night like this
> you feel her close presence,
> a Jewish friend they killed,
> she whose body they burned,
> among thousands of others.

Of Ruth Maier's last journey we know this: 188 women, 42 children and 116 men unfit for work aboard the *Donau* were taken to the gas chambers immediately upon their arrival in Auschwitz. The bodies were burned in the open air. No death certificate exists for any of these 346 individuals.

Ruth Maier's name appears in two places in Oslo: on the memorial for Jewish war victims in the eastern cemetery, and on a plaque commemorating students from the arts and crafts college who were killed during the war. In Döbling cemetery in Vienna her name is engraved on the tombstone of her mother and father.

Here are some details about her family background. Ruth grew up in a secure and comfortable middle-class home in Vienna, which she shared with her father, mother and younger sister, Judith. The family belonged to the well-established community of secularised Jews in the Austrian capital. Ludwig Maier was a senior official in the Austrian postal service, and Secretary General of the Postal, Telegraph and Telephone International (the PTTI). He held a doctorate in philosophy and spoke nine languages. Ruth had a close bond with her father. The relationship with her mother, Irma, was more ambivalent. When Ruth was thirteen her father died of the severe bacterial infection erysipelas. Ludwig's brother, Robert, a bank manager in Brno, Czechoslovakia, now became the family's 'guardian'. Irma's brother, Oskar, a dedicated communist in Moscow, was another uncle with a strong character.

Ruth and Judith had a happy childhood. They travelled a lot: to Yugoslavia, Italy, Switzerland, France and Hungary, but the most frequent holiday destination was Moravia, then in Czechoslovakia: their father was born and raised in the small village of Zarošice. Every summer they spent a few weeks there. The good years came to an end when Hitler's troops marched into Austria in March 1938. The 200,000 Jews of Vienna — previously an integrated part of the middle class — immediately became social outsiders and declared enemies of the state. The Maier family was forced to move from their modern apartment into a ghetto. Jewish children were no longer permitted to attend regular schools. Public bullying and the looting of shops were everyday occurrences. Hateful slogans against Jews appeared everywhere. Arrests and murders were commonplace. These atrocities culminated in the so-called *Reichskristallnacht* in November, which happened to coincide with Ruth's eighteenth birthday.

Ludwig Maier's two brothers and four sisters all perished in concentration camps, as did Irma's only brother. Ruth and Judith Maier were two of thirteen cousins, six of whom survived the war. Among them was the philosopher Stephan Körner (1913–2000), a pupil of Wittgenstein and a Kant specialist. In December 1938 Ruth's sister Judith fled to England, followed within six months by her mother and grandmother, Anna.

Before the Nazi takeover in Vienna, Ruth enjoyed a happy time at school and with her friends. She had a distinct talent for acting, played the lead roles in the annual school play and loved going to the theatre. She had problems with Maths, but was gifted at writing. The earliest surviving diary entries were written in a normal school exercise book. The later volumes were better quality books and more substantial.

From the volumes that have survived we can assume that Ruth kept a diary on a fairly continual basis. The gaps that do exist are probably due to the fact that some volumes went missing. There are many instances where such volumes are referred to in her diary entries. The extant diaries have been numbered and cover the following periods:

Volume 1: May 1933–October 1934
Volume 2: November 1935–October 1936
Volume 3: November 1936–April 1937

Volume 4: April 1937–July 1937
Volume 5: September 1937–December 1937
Volume 6: September 1938–December 1938
Volume 7: April 1940–July 1940
Volume 8: January 1941–November 1942

The biggest gap is the first fifteen months that Ruth spent as a refugee in Norway. In this instance we are fortunate that around fifty letters have survived that she sent to her sister Judith, who was living at the time in Brighton. The German invasion of Norway on 9 April 1940 interrupted their lively correspondence; only a few letters arrived after that. From this point on, however, we have Ruth's diary entries again, which begin on 10 April and go through to the summer.

Her last notebook, 'Ruth Maier's diary 1941, 1942', runs to almost 350 handwritten pages and is the most substantial – as well as important. Gunvor Hofmo quoted from this diary for her article 'Ruth Maier', which she wrote for the literary journal *Vinduet* 2/1948. Gunvor Hofmo used extracts from this volume to try to persuade her Norwegian publishers to bring out Ruth Maier's diary as a book. Her suggestion was rejected, however, as they considered the material too private. In response, the poet concluded that her grief for a 'Jewish friend they had killed' was something she would have to live with alone, sharing it with nobody. This, in turn, led to a period of mental instability; it was twenty-two years before Hofmo was able to break away from psychiatric institutions.

The lines cited above come from the poem 'Møte' ('A Meeting'), which appeared in Hofmo's debut volume of 1946. It ends with the words, 'Why shouldn't we suffer when there's so much suffering?' From a letter that Hofmo wrote to Ruth's sister after the war, we know that this sentence – written in German in the Norwegian poem – was copied word for word from a letter Ruth managed to smuggle ashore from the *Donau* to Hofmo back on land. Ruth also wrote in this letter that she left all her belongings to Hofmo.

In correspondence with her publishing house over the possible publication of the diaries, Hofmo underlined the importance of Ruth Maier to her own life:

I can only hint at what Ruth meant to me, even though I 'only' knew
her for two years, from 1940 . . . Since my childhood I'd followed
the persecution of the Jews in Germany very closely. 'Followed' is
actually the wrong word; I was totally obsessed by this human
degradation and by the Nazi regime itself . . . It was only when I
met Ruth in the voluntary labour service – I was nineteen at the
time – that my involvement and struggle with these issues could
come out into the open. In the beginning she was this: a Jewish
refugee, a victim of human atrocities which I had detested for so
many years without ever having been able to lift a finger to help.
Then it transpired that she was a like-minded individual, my
spiritual twin, despite the fact that we had grown up in entirely
different surroundings and had sharply contrasting childhoods.

The chronological arrangement of this book, which is in three parts, was self-
evident:

> I: Diaries from Vienna, five chapters, 1933–1938
> II: Letters to her sister in England, five chapters, 1939–1940
> III: Diaries from Norway, ten chapters, 1941–1942

Each of the twenty chapters has a short introduction summarising the
biographical and thematic content of the entries. References have been
provided for all the quotations and comments included. The book concludes
with an epilogue describing Ruth Maier's last day in Norway.

The material from the Viennese period is divided up according to the
individual diary volumes, apart from the first chapter, which covers the first
two volumes. This chapter is composed of samples from the early diary
entries rather than the text in its entirety. The other four chapters follow
diaries three to six – here, too, some entries have been abridged and others
omitted.

The letters to England have undergone more substantial editing. Save
for a few exceptions, only those to Judith are included, even though Ruth
occasionally wrote to her mother and grandmother. Passages that openly deal

with Judith's private life have largely been cut, as have those that discuss friends and relations driven out of Vienna, as well as Ruth's observations about her future, where these are repetitions from earlier letters. Although most of the letters have been abridged, we have attempted to preserve the informal tone.

The diary entries from Norway have been reproduced as extensively as possible. They include some short lyric texts, most in the form of prose poems. These are printed in italics and arranged chronologically in the text. Ruth had integrated them in her diary entries, but there are also some fair copies on separate pages.

The writing in this book is also complemented by pictures that relate to the diary entries. These have been included in the places where they are to be found in the original. There are photographs, drawings, newspaper cuttings, and other documents and articles, as well as some of Ruth's watercolours and facsimiles of her handwriting.

The editorial work consisted of assembling, translating and editing the texts so that they were in publishable form, providing titles and introductions to the twenty chapters, as well as selecting the pictures. Only a couple of the literary quotations in the diary are reproduced in full.

I am grateful to many people for the fact that this book has finally appeared after so many years.

First and foremost, Mrs Judith Suschitzky, Ruth's sister living in England. I have been in contact with her since I sent my first letter to Manchester on 15 May 1997 and paid my first visit six weeks later. She had kept all Ruth's letters and other correspondence with Norwegians. Much of the information about Ruth and her family background comes from conversations and correspondence with Judith. Two of Ruth's early diaries were also in Manchester. For a decade Judith and her husband Hans Suschitzky have been the invisible driving force behind this book. Ruth Maier's diaries, files, letters, watercolours, drawings, photograph albums and other documents will now be donated to the Holocaust centre in Oslo.

Thanks are also due to Gunvor Hofmo's nephews, Tor Guttormsen and Svein Ole Guttormsen (who died in 2005), as well as her cousin Inger Hofmo. The war historian Kristian Ottosen (died 2006) provided invaluable assistance and through his friend in London, David Lane, he enabled us to find the address of Ruth Maier's sister.

Many thanks also to Walter Baumgartner, head of the Scandinavian department at Greifswald University, who kept an eye on the progress of this book. Thanks to Carola Biederstaedt, the departmental secretary, who typed up some of the diaries and all the letters; also to the two Scandinavian studies students, Karen Dworatzek and Beate Bruß, who produced a draft translation of the letters and of two of the early diaries. Sabine Richter typed up Ruth Maier's diaries from Norway. Oliver Møystad looked through the translations of the original German text.

Additional support was provided by Karen Voldsgård Jensen and Liv Width, the two surviving friends of Ruth Maier and Gunvor Hofmo. Nunna Moum and Marry Mikalsen gave details of the day of the arrest, 26 November 1942. Edla Nygaard worked as a maid for the Strøm family who accommodated Ruth in Norway. Turid Strøm was the daughter of the household. Jan and Nina Ström from Stockholm are her children. Stein Opjordsmoen from Ullevål hospital and Kari Bøe from the Riksarkivet supplied a number of documents. Trygve Lange-Nielsen, Fernanda Smith and Johan Fredrik Thaulow were Ruth's classmates at the Frogner school in Oslo. Other sources of information were Nils Messel, Martin Nag, Einar Rædergård, Guri Skuggen, Espen Søybe, Thor Sørheim, Gro Varden, Bjørn Wetslie. Thanks to all of them.

Ruth Maier, the eternal Jew. The eternal refugee. The eternal intellectual. The eternal artist's soul. The eternal androgyne. The eternal outsider.

Strong and homeless. One of us.

Jan Erik Vold
June 2007

I

Ruth turns eighteen on *Kristallnacht*

DIARIES FROM VIENNA

1933–1938

Ruth the schoolgirl

1933–1936

This first chapter contains the writings from the two earliest of Ruth Maier's diaries that still exist: May 1933–October 1934 and November 1935–October 1936. The entries from the intervening period have been lost. The first diary begins when Ruth is twelve years old and finishes when she is almost fourteen. The next one begins when she has just turned fifteen. At the time Ruth was a schoolgirl in Vienna.

The first diary is a school exercise book (17 x 21 cm – quarto size), which is missing the first few pages. The first complete entry is for Wednesday, 17 May 1933: 'We got our French test back today. I got a 2. I'm good friends with Käthe and Fritzi. Now I'm going to Vulcan's. Vulcan's was jolly fun. We went on the swings, played dodge ball and Vulcan showed us the kittens. They were so sweet.'

The entries for the rest of the month document the everyday life of a schoolgirl who runs around the park, goes on outings to the woods, has piano lessons, plays cops and robbers, eats cherries, collects stamps and has fun with her friends. At school Ruth gets 1s in History and Nature, a 3 in Arithmetic (her worst grade), and 2s in all other subjects: 'Mama was very satisfied, apart from the 2 for Conduct.'

The first time that less routine material appears is in the entry for 2 July 1933. A holiday that had been promised has not materialised: 'We didn't go to the Wachau. I'm so angry I could smash everything to bits. I'm so angry, angry, angry, angry, angry, angry, angry, and once more, angry. Angry and angry again . . . Because I can't go to Obernholz. Angry, first angry, I could be angry, no, no I am so aaaaaaangry! I could scream with anger and rage. I was in the garden, I was angry, very angry, livid.'

The entries from the second half of June are written in Zarošice, the village in Moravia where Ruth's father was born and where the family spend the summer holidays each year. The children collect eggs from the chickens, fetch water from the fountain and sit with their grandfather under the acacia tree. Ruth sleeps in a hammock. When

The Bauhaus-style apartment where the Maiers lived from 1929.
The father's office was on the floor above.

it rains they play cards. Some entries are written in runic letters. 'That's my secret
language' (14 July 1933).

Later that summer they have a holiday back home in Austria. In Piburg they swim
in the lake; in Kühtai the Alpine sun is scorching: 'Pupi got sunburned on his legs. We
stayed the night in the Dortmunder Hütte.'

In September the family is back in Vienna. That autumn Ruth only writes a few
entries in her diary. On 29 October she notes, 'Uncle Robert and Auntie Aranka have
arrived. Auntie Aranka gave us two giant sweets.'

After a short illness Ruth's father, Ludwig Maier, dies on 28 December 1933 from
erysipelas.

The first diary entry after her father's death is on Tuesday, 13 February 1934:
'The Social Democratic Party has been liquidated. (We got a new uncle about a
fortnight ago.)' And the following day: 'The house is going to be searched. I'm pretty
frightened.'

In the winter and spring of 1934 there are short descriptions of a skiing course in
the mountains, a sprained foot and worries about a Maths exam. Ruth's fear of burglars
causes her to hide with her sister in a wardrobe in her room late one night when their

mother, who had forgotten her key, knocks at the door. On Saturday, 21 June there is the following entry: 'The meanest thing of all: the children in 3a found my diary at school and read it. So mean! And now they're making fun of me! Stop it!'

In summer 1934 they return to Zarošice. Ruth does not write much about the time spent there. The last major entry in the first diary is from autumn, when they are back in Vienna. It is reproduced below in full. The issues preoccupying the soon to be fourteen-year-old girl are the changes in her body, the desire she feels and the question of how life starts.

THURSDAY, 16 OCTOBER 1934, VIENNA

It's all over!!! How happy I am! Yesterday I found Mami cutting a pair of panties. She said to me, 'These are panties for when you have your period. So that we don't get such a surprise.' I'm going to get *lots* of praise at school today for my composition ('My Holiday'). Pany says its poetic, etc. I feel very flattered. I'd love to become a writer or an actress, but not a career where you can't achieve greatness. I think I'm obsessed by greatness. I'm always pulling such silly faces in front of the mirror. I must have told myself a hundred times that I'm going to write something etc.

Käthe and I, we talk a lot about such things (sexual). Anyway, that thing about homosexuality is all in the past now. Auntie Ada was so kind to explain it to me. It's somebody who is very disappointed by love (when two people are not right for each other) who then starts to make similar sexual advances towards people of the same sex. When I think how ghastly it all was, how I used to think about it. I used to look in dictionaries. And I couldn't help thinking about it all day long. I also asked Mutz, but she said I wouldn't understand. Thank God it's all over now! Making problems where there aren't any!

That other thing was awful, too. When I woke up at night I was so afraid that I could barely move. I really believed I had persecution mania.

Ugh!

PS I looked up 'embryo' in the dictionary, it's so interesting. *Pourquoi Maman ne dit pas moi ces choses?* I often wonder what it would be like for a child who didn't have such a lovely Mumi and Papi and Auntie Ada. They would be

— well, I just don't know. If you think how the boys in the street talk! And
what Gerda says. And if you don't understand that love is something great and
sacred! You go insane and think that people are bad. But if they can love each
other like that, they can't be bad after all. The most important thing I have
read is this: The world is not bad, for if it were bad then we would ask,
'How does goodness come into the world?' I'd like to be famous. I don't
want to just drop off like a screw from a machine. I can't imagine living in the
shadow of unfame, so to say. People vanish. I want to live! And leave something behind, a document saying that I was there. A great, beautiful work. In
bed I often imagine I'm helping, I'm embracing the whole world and kissing
it on the mouth, and everything is good. So beautiful!!!

When I have written something in my diary I feel as if a weight has been
lifted from me. And I see the diary as my friend. I can't believe that it's only
paper. Just paper.

Pen and ink drawing: 'Zarošice', summer 1936.

*The second diary is a larger format (19 x 25 cm), with a hard red cover. It is 140 sides
long and there are no blank pages. There are also a few drawings and watercolours. The
first entry, from Wednesday, 13 November 1935, begins thus: 'I'm very dissatisfied with
myself. Something inside me wants to get out; I don't know what it is. I would like to
write. Plays — something I've experienced myself.'*

*Over the course of the autumn Ruth writes about various ambitions and issues
relating to her body:*

I'd love to write a novel. I've got such a strong desire. I spoke with Uncle Rudi about the Social Democrats and the communists. He's been a great influence on me! On the other hand I still have my doubts as to what is better (20 November 1935).

It's my time of the month. I'm very happy. I always think: I can have children now; life now has a purpose. I'm very happy (30 November 1935).

I'd like to go to Russia and visit Uncle Oskar! I'd like to work there, do nothing but work. I'd like to write something about various children, or a diary. A novel. Other times I think I'd like to be an actress, or focus on helping people and study medicine, or go and work in Russia. Or I'd just like to love somebody and have children (1 December 1935).

There follows a selection from the entries for 1936. In term time Ruth is in Vienna; in the summer holidays she is in Czechoslovakia – in Zarošice, Rosental and Brno. The entries from the late summer in Hungary have been omitted.

END OF JANUARY 1936, VIENNA

I'm very unhappy. I don't know why, sometimes I think I'm not going to amount to anything. I don't want to admit it to myself. But that's how it is. I definitely think I'm going to become a stage actress. But the other thing, the writer, what I long to be, I'm not so sure about. If I read a book which echoed my thoughts, I wouldn't be so unhappy. I'd think there's somebody there who has the same ideas. After all, there are similar ideas in some mawkish books; they're just badly expressed. Sometimes when I come across a good idea in a poem or a bad novel I can sense something that wants to get out of the person but it's so badly expressed. Perhaps it's like that with me. It's just that sometimes when I'm writing, I don't even know myself what I've written afterwards. I'm so in love with Lizzy Kantor. It's too much! Last night I dreamed that she gave me a kiss. I'm curious about love. And yet I want something to come out of me! Perhaps one day I'll write a novel although I'm much better at writing very short things. Ideas! But that's all nonsense!

SUNDAY, 2 FEBRUARY 1936, VIENNA

Now I'm confident of victory again! At school we're performing a play and I've basically written the script. They praised me.

FRIDAY, 7 FEBRUARY 1936, VIENNA

There is something strange about love! About all the frills that go with it. Not just the love between a man and a woman, but also the love between girls! I'm lonely but I'm proud, proud that I'm lonely! I'd like to have a great friend and as I don't have one I console myself with pride. I'd like Rosa Schall to be my friend, or Lizzy Kantor. I'm so full of ideas, of love, and of something that wants to come out of me. Po cried today. It was terrible. First her lips quivered, then her eyes were full of tears (we told her that she never explains anything). I feel sorry for her.

I have this craving for love, for boys. I'm looking forward to dance school. My whole life has been dominated by jealousy recently. I'm jealous of Lori when Weissberger and Lori hold hands. I'm jealous of Marion when I see that Marion likes Gertie. I'm jealous of Lizzy, of Anny – that's what happens when you're lonely. I'm going to try to get rid of this jealousy. It is frightfully ugly. Now I want to write the story of my friendships.

WEDNESDAY, 12 FEBRUARY 1936, VIENNA

Nothing came of my story of friendships, perhaps another time! Last night I dreamed of Papi. I was lying on his chest and he said, 'Don't cry!' I've been dreaming about Papi a lot. Once we were sitting under some birches. Another time he wasn't being brave, his teeth were chattering and I said, 'Look here, Papi! You have always told me to be brave, not to cry, and now I'm having to tell you this.' Once I stroked him. Once he was lying in bed, and everybody came and squeezed Mama's hand, and I said why are they doing that!? I'm very happy when I dream about my Papi! I found a sort of diary belonging to Papi. There's so much in there that reflects how I think. Poems, too. I'm going to copy them out. I will never forget Papi. He's always beside me. I often think that I must have something good inside me because I have my Papi for a father.

When I dream of my Papi every night I also often think that the night is the day when he's with me, and the day the night when he sleeps: perhaps he can see everything that I do.

I am very much in love with Lizzy.

SATURDAY, 22 FEBRUARY 1936, VIENNA

I'd like to write lots now but unfortunately it's already evening. Blanka has been here with me. Because of the script for the academy. Apart from five words I did the whole thing myself. It is quite good.

I'm not so in love with Lizzy any more.

I've had a discussion with Gretel about communism and social democracy. Although I defended social democracy, deep down I sympathise with the communists.

There was an Indian at our school today. He was just like I'd imagine an Indian to be. A little unshaven and very dark brown. He had very beautiful eyes and told us about India. He put a turban on his head, then he wrote some Persian and Indian on the board, and spoke a sentence in Indian (Persian, too). It sounded beautiful, like music. He said, 'India is the most beautiful country in the world. It is like a garden and the Indians are the nightingales that sing' (that's a quotation from a poem). He was very handsome. I'm *really* looking forward to dance school (although that doesn't really fit with my other, serious opinions – perhaps it does!). I'm already looking forward to being together with boys, or rather with a boy whom I will love dearly.

Unfortunately I've got to lie down now.

THURSDAY, 27 FEBRUARY 1936, VIENNA

I've been to the pictures. I'm in a very good mood. Something is wrong. Uncle Rudi is arriving tomorrow. I'm fond of him. I long for tyranny (passive). I've never been so sure of myself. I'm reading *Etzel Andergast*. A magnificent, great work. I'd like to write more about Etzel Andergast. I *will* study medicine. I fooled around on the way home from school, it was *such* a hoot. Mama gave Dita a clip round the ear. There are two sides to her. One Mumi is refined by Pupi, the other is not.

My whole being longs for the one who will dominate me. I'm afraid I must sign off now.

TUESDAY, 3 MARCH 1936, VIENNA

I want to write a few lines before I go to sleep. Now I want to have another friend: Gertie Weissberger. She's really lovely. The two of us (Lori, too, afterwards) went into that shop pretending to be Englishwomen, and demanded green nail varnish in a perfumery and evening wear from a gentleman's tailor. All with an English accent. We acted as crazy as possible (all of this during gymnastics — we were wagging from school). We also went to a music shop to enquire about violin repairs. The owner was a young chap. He said he also knew a little English and he was *very* nice. Then we went to a gramophone shop, a school (!) and the Volksoper to ask about wigs. At another hairdresser's they did really show us wigs, but of course they were far too ugly for us. It was a real hoot. I'm afraid I've got to sleep now. There's still so much more I'd like to write. Goodnight!

SATURDAY, 14 MARCH 1936, VIENNA

Tomorrow I'm going to the Burgtheater to see Goldoni's *The Liar*. With Hermann Thimig. Since *King Lear* I've worshipped him as a . . . well, you can't describe it. I'm quite crazy about him. I often dream about him. I wish (it's stupid) I could kiss his white hands. He was brilliant as the fool. I've often written letters to him in my head.

WEDNESDAY, 25 MARCH 1936, VIENNA

I've been at my new school for a week now. I don't like it. I feel very lonely there. I don't have a single friend. Nothing! Sometimes I want to weep. And yet I feel drawn to so many people. Lizzy! She is bright, not beautiful, although her eyes have a profound sparkle. I think she's lonely, too. Lots of girls go around with her. She doesn't look at me, and I'd love to pour my heart out to her and ask her for advice. Oh God, it's so terrible.

We're talking about the Emperor.
>   RUTH: Do you want an emperor?
>   KURTI: Oh yes! Then I could see him going around in his golden
>   carriage full of flowers.

We're talking about *The Thousand and One Nights*.
>   RUTH: And the King's wife was unfaithful to him.
>   KURTI: What does that mean, unfaithful?
>   RUTH: The wife loved another man more than the King.
>   KURTI: Why? Surely a King is better?

We're talking about a missing plane.
>   RUTH: And they never found the plane.
>   KURTI: Why not? Can't they X-ray the sea?

We're talking about war.
>   RUTH: And many, many people die, and it's not nice.

KURTI: How come? My dad and my uncle were also in the war and nothing happened to them.

War again.

KURTI: What about if the others start it?

War yet again.

RUTH: And many people become crippled.

KURTI: Well, they don't have to die.

SATURDAY, 28 MARCH 1936, VIENNA

I made a right fool of myself during rehearsal. I'm curious to see how it will go during the actual performance.

SATURDAY, 4 APRIL 1936, VIENNA

The performance! It was magnificent. Me, the hero! They clapped and clapped! They congratulated me. I want to say what happened, bit by bit.

I wasn't excited at first. Then it all began after break time. We put on make-up. I was jolly dashing in a black wig and helmet. The curtain went up. Then, when I stabbed myself, how the audience laughed! And there was great applause. Martha Lifschütz threw the violets on to the stage (we'd given them to her beforehand). A few fell next to the stage, so Sachs and Reichel picked them up and threw them on. Fischer said, 'Maier is a rascal of the highest order!' and then I exited. They all congratulated me and I gave Fritzi a kiss out of sheer joy. Nelly said, 'Because you were so good you get a kiss!' I was so happy! Sachs came and almost stroked me . . . Gerti was jealous because everybody congratulated *me*. I felt sorry for her.

Thinking about it now it was indeed very lovely, but so insignificant next to the Great One. And then again I think: Perhaps it was the first step. At some point they'll all surround me again and shout, 'You were great, wonderful. Congratulations!' Sachs threw flowers on the stage! . . . Maybe! Now for something else! Lori's sister, Marion, is very affected and stupid; she used to be much sweeter. She's still nice, though. At break time yesterday she said over and over again, 'You're going to get a slap!' and I said, 'Do you know what, Marion? You don't say "You're going to get a slap!" But if you feel you must say it, then don't go on and on!' Then she stroked me. (Marion really likes Gertie, I'm not jealous!)

I *really* like Sachs! I believe it is the most beautiful love; I worship her! She's often made me feel hurt. But still! I know she's fond of me. First I cheated in the test, then I told the tiniest of lies and at the end I told her I'd lost the book rather than forgotten it! How cross she was! She said she'd overestimated me and that upset her. Perhaps she did overestimate me, perhaps not. But the fact is that in the presence of somebody whose expectation of me is greater than my own, I can feel the strong encouragement and support she gives. Also, you sometimes really do achieve more. (That's the case with Etzel Andergast.)

Hans was there today – he's a nice lad. Very lazy. A keen mathematician (!). I also give him a bit of tutoring (unpaid, of course!). His intellectual horizons do not extend much beyond mathematics. But he's nice. (I couldn't love somebody like that.) Perhaps he likes me a bit. Perhaps, but only as an object suitable for a Maths ace. His second passion is skiing. I'm going to rope him into English after the Easter holidays. (Willi is no longer having lessons from me.)

(There are two groups of people that write diaries. The first really are moved to write by an inner spirit. The others in the secret hope that their diary will one day be discovered by an unknown muse and become a sensation as – I don't know – the classic sentiments of a chaste and modest young girl. Sometimes I'm in the first group, at other times in the second one.)

SUNDAY, 19 APRIL 1936, VIENNA

I'm a little in love. With Hans. It's ridiculous. But it's true. Perhaps because he's the first boy with whom I've been in a *slightly* closer relationship. But maybe I'm just imagining I'm in love. All I know is that I'm always a little happier when I think of him! He's lovely. We talk together. And that's it! No more! And yet! He took off his glasses and he was so . . . insignificant, so small and hairless. I'd love him to come to me and weep. And I'd love to stroke him. (I'm not writing these lines with hot, glowing cheeks like a lover; everything to do with Hans is restrained.) He's not in love with me, not a whit. (I can't imagine him in love at all; he's *far* too restrained.) At best he sees me (apart from the Maths) as somebody to have a good chat with. He hasn't the faintest idea (I don't think) that I might like him a little (I'm not that fond of him). He could calmly tell me his tales of love (if he had any at all) without thinking that it might cause me embarrassment! He doesn't see me as a woman (!), but as something else. Maybe (?) as a friend. But then that's much nicer, too.

FRIDAY, 8 MAY 1936, VIENNA

I don't like Hans at all! On the contrary! I'm off to English now. Just for a change there's been a bit of a hullabaloo. You see, I bought a squirting flower and squirted Fischer with it, only a little bit of course. She didn't notice it was a trick. As I told Mama, she made a huge fuss about it. (I've already got two warnings for conduct — I really don't know how.) She'll tell Uncle Rudi. I *hate* Uncle Rudi! He's a philistine. I'm going to write more about this. I'm *definitely* going to write a play. I've just got to let it ripen inside me. Like a fruit. Alas, I've got to go to English. I'm also going to write more about Hans!

SUNDAY, 24 MAY 1936, VIENNA

At the moment I don't really feel the need to write in my diary. Frau Stern just telephoned: Hans is ill. *Quite truthfully*, I don't like him at all. He's ghastly. When he's not wearing his glasses I can't look at him. I'm definitely going to write the play, but not quite yet. We had German homework: 'Old / Young'. Uncle Rudi: I really don't like him. He's so stuffy. When he looks with his dreadful eyes or with his glasses perched on his nose and talks very deliberately about communism etc. Then I find him soooo ridiculous.

FRIDAY, 29 MAY 1936, VIENNA

I'm in a good mood at the moment; I don't know why! I did my homework. I made a good job of 'Young / Old'. I'm going to copy it out. The play might be quite good. I don't know the title. I'll get going on it soon. (I'm doing badly in Maths, might get moved down.)

WEDNESDAY, 17 JUNE 1936, VIENNA

Swimming. Went home with Lizzy. She's a bright girl. We talked about anti-Semitism and education. Saw a blind man on the train. He was reading a Braille book. It impressed me. It showed the human will and also goodness – I don't know how to describe it. I managed in Maths.

SATURDAY, 20 JUNE 1936, VIENNA

Yesterday I was in a park. A lady sat next to me. With grey hair, sour-looking mouth. A worker's wife. Four children. One of them, Dita, a dark, fat girl, came over and said, 'I've looked all over, can't find him anywhere. The smaller they are the cheekier.' The lady said, 'I've told her, "I'm not like you – you filthy Jew!"' The lady kept on threatening her youngest, Otti, a lovely blond boy. She said, 'Look! The young lady's got a bag. She'll put you into it.' Then: 'Right, I'm going to fetch the park-keeper. That man's going to take you with him, he'll put you in his sack' etc. Poor little chap. When a person kills another out of hatred and with justification, it's not his conscience that weighs him down, but the fear of being punished (for example in Gorky's *Three People*). Gorky is dead. Such people shouldn't die. (Mumi said that, too.)

MONDAY, 29 JUNE 1936, VIENNA

I saw an elderly man on the tram. He had a shrunken mouth and a brown face. A beautiful girl with a large bosom was standing next to him. The type you see by the thousand. I only heard a part of their conversation. The big-bosomed girl with beautiful eyes asked him how he liked it here. The man said, 'I feel *verrry* lonely. I've got nobody at all.' He made a very sad, strained face. Then he started to ask questions in a childish way. He smiled: 'So, did you miss me, too?' The girl, who didn't seem to care much about the old man, said, 'Yes, we've often spoken of you.' Suddenly the old man was very happy. And each time the girl wanted to go away he took her hand and asked very cheerfully, 'Did you really think about me, really?'

That same day I saw lots of people being handed food. They looked poor. One lady was wearing a newspaper on her head, a faded dress, ripped stockings. An old man with red cheeks who made jokes, a blue pot in his hand and rags wrapped round his legs. And many other people, too.

Winter aid, alms, these are symptoms of an unwholesome age. People don't need alms, offerings, or winter aid if you give them work (in decent conditions) and enough to eat. Winter aid, offerings for hungry children etc. etc. are temporary measures and create a false impression. A government that starts to make such collections doesn't know how to cope any other way, can't create any job opportunities.

I'm a communist already. In Russia they've now introduced the right to vote.

The entries from the rest of summer 1936 are not dated, but the place where they were written is noted. First Ruth and her sister travel to Zarošice, where they stay in Uncle Victor's house. After that, they stay on the Rausch family's farm in Rosental, a neighbouring village. Then they travel to Brno, home to Auntie Ritschi, Auntie Ada, a widow, and Uncle Robert, a bank manager with his own chauffeur. Uncle Robert became the family's guardian and supported Irma Maier financially after Ludwig Maier died.

Uncle Viktor's shop in Zarošice. He took over the business from his father, Simon Maier, whose name can be seen on the sign above the door.

JULY 1936, ZAROŠICE

We're now in Zarošice. It's beautiful. I prefer it to Vienna. It's like home to me. I'm going to write. I've got to have a good look while I'm here. And take inside me all the beautiful things around. Then when I'm back at school I'll be able to use it again, live off it. Like a camel does with its fat.

JULY 1936, ZAROŠICE

It's beautiful here. The fields and the people. I like peasants. They're not fake or sentimental. They're real people. They say that all peasants are healthy. That's not true. A quarter of the population of Zarošice has tuberculosis and another quarter is poor and has nothing to eat, which is surely a disease, too. It is peculiar how many village idiots there are in small villages. The children laugh at them, they smile stupidly, and sometimes they weep. In Vienna they call them cretins, they say they're mentally ill and put them in fancy lunatic asylums.

Yesterday I wanted to photograph Zarošice cemetery. Then a little old lady came out of the cemetery. She was hobbling and had a shrunken mouth. She spoke to me. Czech. I didn't understand much. She said that she lived on her own. She had nobody. She was just taking a look around the cemetery. So she hobbled along the road beside me. And said, '*Ti dretzka*' or '*Ti troitki*' (I don't know whether I've written it correctly). I feel I've read somewhere in a book that an old lady walks through a village, occasionally mumbling, 'Yes, the children!' or, 'The flowers!' or, 'Yes, the sun!'

I imagine that dear God must love peasants above all other people. They don't talk a lot about things that concern them, but they still feel these things. They don't start crying at every opportunity. But sometimes they're very sad. They don't kiss each other, or only seldom, and yet they love each other. For example, they don't even tell us how much they love their homeland. But they certainly love it, and far more than some other person who doesn't stop banging on about it at every suitable and unsuitable opportunity.

I don't want to write any more because I'll feel I'm writing such frightfully soppy stuff. If I write any more it'll be meaningless. Sometimes I think I'm in a fairy tale. In Zarošice, when I walk through the village. Everything is peaceful. The sun is shining, children are playing, peasants working, geese shrieking, women coming and going with water. It's *so* beautiful.

JULY 1936, ROSENTAL

I really don't know what I want to write. I could write so much. But I don't want to write my personal feelings in my diary any more. Because I think one should deal with these oneself. And anyway, they're mawkish. I could write, 'Yesterday I was sad, I like a boy, I know he's stupid,' etc.

But I don't want to. Because it's jolly boring.

So we're staying with the Rausch family. A big farm. Cows, piggies. Herr Rausch, the father, is a quite normal peasant with a long moustache and he's already a bit frail. His wife is a peasant, too. The children. Fanda: a pretty girl with pretty, round eyes. Anna: a skinny girl (in other circumstances you might call her a tart), anaemic. A poor blonde thing who does the cooking, washing etc. Vena, a handsome lad – I think he's horrid. Dita likes him. Jenda: I like him. Now he's really not a weed. He's not handsome. His mouth is nice. I like him.

JULY 1936, ROSENTAL

It is wonderful to sing love songs when you are in love!

JULY 1936, ROSENTAL

I really can't bear it. I have to write about how much I like Jenda. I *do* like him and it's lovely that I like him. Yesterday I was so happy. I danced and sang. Not today. I'm feeling bad. Yesterday I lay in the hay cart and looked up at the sky. I thought about death and what it's like. The nicest thing would be if we kept on returning to the world, if we kept on feeling life because it's just so lovely to *be* here. But if that's not the case, if that goes against all reason, then it's also wonderful to have lived *once*. Because if you have seen everything, the sun, the flowers, the woods, and also if you've loved somebody, then you've seen everything and it's not necessary to live any more. I've decided that I'll

Pencil drawing of the farm where Ruth and Judith stayed in summer 1936.

commit suicide when I feel that my life can't get any nicer. But perhaps this is just my megalomania talking and who knows how I might cling on to life later on (more than ever). But I do not want to die as a little old trembling woman.

I watched Jenda cutting in the field. I saw the stalks falling and Jenda striking broad swathes with his scythe. Then it struck me that the idea of death being associated with the scythe and cutting people down is as ancient as humanity itself, ever since man has tilled, sowed and cut the fields.

JULY 1936, ROSENTAL

It's wonderful. If you want to write something about Rosental and Zarošice you can only do it in pictures.

I go into the field with Jenda and his father. Jenda is handsome and fit; he stands in front of me. He has a brown back. The sky above him is quite blue. The cart rocks! I look at Jenda.

We're in the field. Jenda toils. It's lovely to watch him working. He bends and stretches himself. He's quiet. There's no sound, just sun and fields.

I'm in the barn, it's dark. The cows breathe. I lie in the maize. It's beautiful.

I bring a lunch bag to the field. There's nothing but sun. The women work. Then they sit and eat. They drink beer and talk.

I always used to want to love weak, sickly people. Not any more. I want to love someone healthy.

It's wonderful that this peasant, now so old and bent, has brought two such handsome and fit people into the world.

Yesterday I heard the father, the mother and the two sons praying. I imagine prayer to be something more beautiful. Prayer is beautiful, to thank a greater power for work, for the sun and everything! But they rattle through their prayer as if they'd been forced to do it. If they're not doing it because they really want to, then they shouldn't bother praying at all.

JULY 1936, ROSENTAL

Vena likes Dita and Dita Vena. They've even written each other love letters. He's very much in love with her. And yet they're highly embarrassed when they're together. What? Don't they say that they're fond of each other? Do they go into the woods together, both of them happy?

I like Jenda. He likes me, too.

At the moment I feel as if I could compose many poems. About fields and the sun.

Family picture from Zarošice Simon Maier (arms crossed) and his wife Eugenie (hands on her knees) with four of their seven children. Behind (from left to right): their sons Viktor, Ludwig, Robert, with his wife Aranka to his right, and the Maier's son-in-law Moritz Hamlis, who was married to their daughter Ritschi (on the far right). Viktor's wife Thea has their son Rudolf on her lap; her daughters Lisa and Gerda are sitting at the front. Robert and Aranka's two sons are standing in front of their parents. From this photograph only the Maier's granddaughter Lisa, who was deported to Auschwitz, survived the war. Their daughters Ada, Erna and Vilma (not in the picture) were also deported and killed.

JULY 1936, WITH AUNTIE ADA IN BRNO

We've left Rosental now. I didn't think that I'd be so unhappy. I long for Jenda. I'd like to be with him, or at least have a letter. I'm sad. I'm thinking of him, and also of Vena and all the others. It was so lovely. We loved each other. As we left Vena gave me a goodbye kiss. We also went for a walk together. Just as friends. I'd like to be with Jenda.

Ruth's father Ludwig Maier, Secretary General of both the Austrian Postal Union and the International Association of Postal Unions, held a doctorate. In addition to German and Czech he knew French, Italian, English, Turkish, Modern and Ancient Greek, and Latin.

JULY 1936, WITH AUNTIE RITSCHI IN BRNO

Yesterday Mama said something very sweet. Once, before Mumi was married, she was going for a walk with Papa and she saw that Pupi was not walking in rhythm with her. So Mama took a small step that looked like a hop. When Papa noticed it he said, 'Rascal!'

That's very sweet. I find it so charming. They're walking through the woods. It's autumn and there are spots of red and yellow in the woods. Papa is being very serious and Mama is walking beside him, very jolly and in love. Then she hops. Papa looks at her, laughs softly and then says, 'Rascal!'

Many of the things Mama has said make quite an impression on me and when I recall them later it's as if I'd read them in a book. For example: Mumi is sitting in a small office. She's wearing a very pretty, sheer blouse. Made out of angora wool. Her hair is black and she's tied it into a bun on her neck. She looks lovely, as if straight out of a glass case. She's working at the typewriter. Her boss is sitting beside her in a large reclining chair. He looks very much like Hugo Thimig.* He looks at Mama in total delight. As old men look at young people. From time to time he says something. 'Fräulein, that's a very pretty blouse you're wearing!'

JULY 1936, BRNO

Jenda wrote to me. I don't know if I love him. If so, then it's not the Jenda Rausch part of him that I like, but something else, something more beautiful. It's queer, I can see him before me, standing in the field, sitting on the cart, but I can never recall the times he talked to me. If Jenda were to come to Vienna, perhaps I wouldn't love him at all. He's only suited to fields, lots of sun, cows and water. I believe that there are people who, once taken out of their surroundings, no longer make such an impression on us.

    Uncle Oskar is arriving tomorrow!!!

JULY 1936, BRNO

Yes, Uncle Oskar has been. He's nice. He also brought along my new aunt. She's nice, too. Slim and blonde, a German. She told us about her past: she's been married once and imprisoned twice.

    Grandmother behaved like a young girl. She very much likes Uncle Oskar, too.

* Hugo Thimig (1854–1944), Viennese actor and theatre manager, father of Hermann Thimig.

*Large pen and ink drawing found between pages
in the 1935–1936 diary.*

JULY 1936, BRNO

Jenda has written to me again. I think I don't love him *that* much. It's so funny: the Jenda who stood in front of me on the cart and scythed in the field, and the one who writes stupid letters – they're two quite different people.

Mama also asked when we're going to finish with this letter-writing farce. She said it was a pity about the money and the stamps.

Rather tasteless!

Man exists in the world and lives in order to achieve and create something. But I will die waiting to find out *what* I am to achieve and *what* I am to create.

JULY 1936, BRNO

People going here and there
*   and knowing not what for.*
People going here and there
*   and knowing not for what.*
People getting weary.
*   For dust is in their lungs.*
People getting saddened.
*   For their children are unwell.*
People getting so gloomy.
*   For they do not know the sun.*
People getting angry.
*   For they really long for the light.*

AUGUST 1936, BRNO

Yesterday we went to the pictures with Uncle Robert. Bank manager. The film was utter rubbish. But two images in the weekly newsreel made an impression on me.

The first one was a mining accident in England. The people, mothers and children, waiting for their fathers in the rain. It was terrible. The coffins were loaded on to the carts.

Robert Maier, the railway manager, then said, 'That's quite enough!' A sympathetic heart! God bless him.

The second was from the civil war in Spain. Women firing rifles. Armed young men and adolescents. A dead man lying on the ground. Tolosa in ruins.

So what is the point of all of that?

The communists want world revolution. What will that be like? Millions of people would die! Perish! Keel over!

But perhaps it's not so wretched if I know I'm doing it for freedom?

FRIDAY, 11 SEPTEMBER 1936, VIENNA

I've now read my other two diaries. They're so corny it fills me with horror. I don't think I'm going to begin a new one when this is finished. At the very most I'll just note down observations and ideas. If I really feel the need to write I can do it on notepaper; that can be burned afterwards. To think that I've lived sixteen years and the results are: a few quirky habits and some more or less idiotic scribblings. And I've done absolutely nothing. It makes me miserable.

When you're alive you should learn as much as possible. I'd like to learn a lot: biology, medicine, law, botany, astronomy and, above all, natural sciences.

A photograph of Ruth from the family album.

Ruth as a baby with her mother Irma. From the family album.

Mummy, have you forgotten me?

NOVEMBER 1936 – APRIL 1936

The diary that covers the period from late autumn 1936 to early 1937 is a small, attractive notebook with 160 unlined pages. It has a red trim and a soft imitation leather cover. There are more than 130 pages of writing, followed by some blank pages and then sixteen sides of literary notes on books such as Tolstoy's The Kreutzer Sonata, *Jack London's* Martin Eden, *B. Traven's* The Death Ship *and a volume of Heinrich Heine's letters.*

Ruth is now on the verge of womanhood. The entries begin the day after her sixteenth birthday. She attends dance school. Christmas is different from usual. She gets angry about a murder trial and writes a dialogue between Ruth and the court. In February she goes on a ski course in the mountains. She writes about her friends. And tells their fortunes. She also writes about her Latin tutor, who begins giving her private lessons this spring. Sometimes her diary crosses the boundary into fiction.

This volume of her diary is dominated by her relationship with her parents. On New Year's Day she remembers her father who has been dead for three years. The way her mother now makes herself up looks different from before. Ruth accidentally overhears a private conversation. It troubles her. Ruth idolises her father, whom she calls Papa, Papi or Pupi. And she has a more strained relationship with her mother, whom she calls Mama, Mutti, Musch, Mumi and Mutz. Or Muscherle. Her mother calls her Dorrit, Lore and Claudia. Ruth's sister, Judith, who is a year and a half younger, is often called Dita. Or Dittl. Sometimes Ditterle.

WEDNESDAY, 11 NOVEMBER 1936, VIENNA

It's an awkward feeling starting a new diary. You have to get used to it first.

There's a boy I really like. He's from the dance school but he's really nice. I've now turned into two Ruths. The first one who's very much in love and only thinks of 'him' etc. And the other Ruth who knows it's a load of nonsense and thinks: it's just a soppy adolescent fantasy. I mean, I shouldn't be wasting my time. I mustn't. I've got so much to do. I often feel like someone who has a pile of work pending, but who taps her finger impatiently on the desk, saying, 'Just a moment, just a moment, gentlemen, I'll have to think that one over.'

I saw a blind woman in the tram. Blind people smile a lot, more often than sighted people.

A young man was sitting in the Meridianpark.* In front of him was a pram which he peered into carefully.

A destitute man was sleeping on a bench under a magnificent tree. His hands were covering his face. He was still young.

SUNDAY, 15 NOVEMBER 1936, VIENNA

Today I'm going to meet the boy at the Burgtheater. Perhaps I won't meet him. *Saint Joan*. I'm so looking forward to it. I'd love to become an actress.

Ruth designed a title page for 'Diary of a Young Girl'. She followed this with an introduction: 'The heart of a young girl is a strange and beautiful thing. It is full of dreams and wishes.'

---

* Meridianpark was in fact renamed Joseph-Kainz-Platz in 1931, after the famous Austrian actor (1858–1910) whose statue is also there.

SATURDAY, 21 NOVEMBER 1936, VIENNA

I've got to wait! I'd like to give up the diary and turn the whole thing into a book, a 'Diary of a Young Girl'.

THURSDAY, 26 NOVEMBER 1936, VIENNA

I walk through the streets in the evening. And it's completely dark. The windows glow softly. And I cannot believe that there is so much heartache behind the windows, for they glow so softly and cheerfully.

SUNDAY, 29 NOVEMBER 1936, VIENNA

It's cold. I can see feet. Sore feet, shoes that are torn and full of holes. It's cold and the feet touch the ground, and go round in circles. They are sad, sore feet, they go round in circles like caged birds, always in circles, the sad, sore feet!

SATURDAY, 12 DECEMBER 1936, VIENNA

It's the Dirndl* festival today. I'm so excited!

TUESDAY, 15 DECEMBER 1936, VIENNA

There's a major change happening inside me. It's quite revolting. I'd like to write something like a 'Diary of a Young Girl'. Or a Christmas novella, or a

* A traditional Alpine dress worn in southern Germany and Austria.

story of our everyday life. But you need so much courage for this. I used to think myself capable of it. For the moment, perhaps, I'll write something nicer instead.

CLAUDIA

Christmas has come again. The sky is frozen blue. The streets are covered in snow. The smells of Lebkuchen and spun sugar fill the air again. The plump, rosy-cheeked women are already standing on the corner, selling their Christmas trees. There is an odd sparkling in the air.

And yet! Strangely, Christmas used to be quite different from this. Much nicer! Much more mysterious! It used to be so delightfully mysterious, so wonderfully cosy at Christmas. It was as if it were ringing in the air: Christmas, cling, clang, bam, boom.

It used to sparkle everywhere. And in my mouth I would have the strong taste of meringues and cake mixture, which was both sweet and strange. I often thought I saw angels descending to earth with candles in their hands.

And now! Mother is still scurrying around the place very secretly and closing doors behind her. Mutti says that the baby Jesus is coming.

In bed I want it to be like last year. I want my eyes to glint and to say softly, 'Christmas!' and I want to hear angels singing. But it's not happening. It makes me sad and I think, 'Come on, Christmas comes only once a year. You've got to be jolly at Christmas. I'll pray to dear God, he'll make me happy again.'

And then Christmas arrives and Mutti asks with red cheeks, 'Guess what you've got, Claudia?' And I'm sad because I'm not really interested.

Mutti looks at me in a strange way, as if she wanted to say, 'You're not enjoying yourself.'

And evening comes. The stars are in the sky and the snow on the streets is totally blue.

And for a moment, a tiny moment. Now I feel it. Now! And I'm full of joy and I want to sing a Christmas carol.

And then the moment has passed.

And then the door opens and I see Mutti's face. She looks at me with such expectation. Then I see Auntie and the Christmas tree. So many candles! And I say, 'Beautiful!'

And I feel so terribly empty. I want to lie under the Christmas tree and weep.

TUESDAY, 29 DECEMBER 1936, VIENNA

When I grow up I don't think I'll need to write a diary any more.

FRIDAY, 1 JANUARY 1937, VIENNA

Two days ago I bumped into Herr Hermann on the tram. I have a penchant for older men.

Yesterday was New Year's Eve. Dr Brauchbar was there, too. I like him a lot. His eyes were completely red because he hasn't had a proper night's sleep for a long time. I feel sorry for him.

I've been going to dance school for some time now. It's just how I had imagined it. Dance school air, tango lighting, dance school jokes. I even have someone who hangs around me all the time. He's the intelligent Jew type. Glasses. Prominent cheekbones. Sometimes unshaven. Just how I used to imagine my ideal man. Only this one adapted for dance school. He pushes himself close to me. He talks like they do in novels. So hackneyed! With his eyes raised. In blue tango lighting. Declares his love. Makes you want to vomit.

Some time ago I saw a wonderful film: *The Story of Louis Pasteur.*

One ought to just read . . . read! And learn.

SUNDAY, 3 JANUARY 1937, VIENNA

Papa is dead – not 'dead'! It's quite simple. One word: d-e-a-d. I don't want to think about it. It ought to be peaceful. The religious studies teacher said that one should suffer everything. Suffer. I don't like it. Anyway, it's not true.

First because it can't be. That's obvious, isn't it? You can't just be gone like that and then there's nothing. You don't feel anything. All over. I must ask Papa. I'll go to him and say, 'Papa, it's not true, is it? I'm right, aren't I?' And then he'll have to get up. He'll have to hear, won't he? He has to. It just can't be. I dreamed it. Suddenly someone will open the door, and I'll refuse to believe it, and it'll be Papa. Everything will be OK. And I'll say, 'I had a bad dream.' And Papa will caress me.

I often wait for Papa to come. And then I want to scream and smash everything to bits, and then I'm a bird in the blue sky, flying through the air. Then it's like mill wheels churning inside me, my God, my God, and my eyes are hot. I long for the cold. My God! Please! It's not true. I've made a mistake. Please! Please! Please! Everything used to be so lovely. Papa is here. Here. Here. Here. And he says, 'Liese, let's go for a walk.' He says, 'You're my pride and joy.' Everything is fine. What am I to do when I'm feeling sad? What am I to do when there's something I don't know? Then there's a hole inside me. And the hole is always there. I can't believe it.

TUESDAY, 19 JANUARY 1937, VIENNA

1, 2, 3, 4 . . . Lots of dolls appear, ping, pang. First leg. Second leg. Third leg. Fourth leg. They have little pink skirts and red cheeks. They open and close their eyes and have long lashes. They swing their legs from right to left. They bend their arms and smile.

DANCE SCHOOL

Dusty air. Young, adolescent girls in short skirts, hand-knitted jumpers, red lips. Lanky, anaemic young men with moustaches and trousers that are too baggy. Sweet, vulgar music.

Young lady, you have such a beautiful . . .

THURSDAY, 21 JANUARY 1937, VIENNA

When it snows everybody is quiet and walks softly. The flakes fall gently. Whenever a hurdy-gurdy plays it's like a fairy tale. An elderly lady is freezing. People have snow on their clothes.

There's a drunk on the tram. His eyes stare and weep. He rants and curses and harasses the conductor. People laugh. One person holds his stomach, another gives a huge smirk, a third laughs gaily. The conductor, a fat-bellied man, says, 'What I have to put up with from the public!'

Another man with glasses, who had been talking with his wife about the drunk: 'For goodness sake, you can't take a drunk that seriously.'

The conductor replies gravely, 'But look. Even if you're not so smart you don't have to behave like an idiot.'

I'm on the tram. A young chap in a threadbare green velvet suit gets on. He's wearing grey woollen gloves and there's a hole in his coat. He must be a little short-sighted, for he screws his eyelids together when he peers at something. He gets off and looks at me through the chipped glass window. I laugh and he waves. Then he waves again. And then we're off already. I'm very happy, I start singing and can't help smiling like someone who has seen something particularly beautiful.

How strange! I saw him, made him look at me, became fond of him, then he had to get off. At the end he waved.

Whenever I walk on my own through the Meridianpark I always stop at the Kainz statue. It has snowed. A lot of flakes have settled on the statue. I look at it again and again. Yesterday, two children appeared. They made snowballs and laughed. One stopped.

'Look, it's the Kainz statue.'

Then they went.

SUNDAY, 24 JANUARY 1937, VIENNA

There's a trial on at the moment. The defendant is an unemployed man accused of robbery with murder. There's nothing really unusual about the trial. The motive for the crime: poverty.

Newspaper photograph of a courtroom which Ruth had stuck in her diary.

The only difference in this case is that the defendant is an intelligent man. He was sentenced to death by hanging.

R: Why was this man sentenced to death?
C: Because he killed another man.
R: That's why he was sentenced to death?
C: Yes. And?
R: The motive makes no difference?
C: No.
R: The death penalty is a good thing?
C: Yes.
R: What does it achieve?
C: It rids society of one of its harmful elements.

When a case like this comes to court. When the defendant cries, 'I wanted to work. Why wasn't I given the chance to work?' When someone who is deep down a good man, a young man who wished to lead a nice life. At that moment the whole of society deserves to be hanged. The whole of society is then so corrupt and rotten that there is no other solution than to wipe this society out.

But what does writing all this in my diary achieve? It's not going to change anything. But I'll remember this case when I start to fight for a better world.

The people in the courtroom cried and blew their noses. But they didn't see what it all meant: an *intelligent* man fell into such hardship that he was forced to commit murder. An *intelligent* man, even if he was crushed by poverty.

I've exaggerated this a bit, of course, but seriously! And this society, this society which has driven this man to commit a murder, this society dares to sentence the selfsame man to death.

The awful thing is that it's not an isolated case. Many, many people are suffering the same sort of poverty, many people. It's just that they're too downtrodden, too deadened (and too unintelligent) to commit murder.

(I sense I'm exaggerating again.)

In writing this I don't want to give my support to any further murders. No. But the fact that such a man commits a murder shows that something is not right. *Something is not right!*

I can't stop thinking about the following:

You can say, 'I am being hanged, I will be hanged.' But you can't say, 'I was hanged.'

SUNDAY, 31 JANUARY 1937, VIENNA

We went skiing. It was fantastic!

One ski ran away from its owner. There's no more touching or tragic-comic sight than that of a ski descending a slope. All on its own. It would make a good fairy tale!

Today I lay in the snow and looked up at the trees. The trees stood out gently against the sky. The sky was grey. I thought, 'That's a lovely view.' The black branches and the grey sky. There must be something behind it. Behind all the grey sky and black branches and snow and air that prickles the face. It's all got a purpose. And I've got to get to the bottom of it.

Käthe was also on our trip. She's not really my friend because we're such different people. She's become very pretty, but not desperately intelligent.

But she's determined to achieve whatever goal she's set. At the moment she's building the foundations of a library. She always tells me, 'Do you know what? I'm going to buy some Heine, then Goethe and Schiller.' I like that. I think that nice thoughts and the impulse to strive for something better disappear with age.

I like spending time with little girls. They have such pretty eyes and they smile cheerfully when you look at them. That's how I smile when I look at a boy I like. In exactly the same way. It really surprised me when I realised this.

THURSDAY, 4 FEBRUARY 1937, VIENNA

Life is like a gramophone record. It starts, comes to an end, then it's put away!

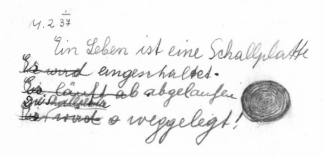

FEBRUARY 1937, VIENNA

At about five o'clock this afternoon I was sitting on the sofa. In the dining room. The light was so beautifully faint. Dusk came and dark golden streaks filled the room. I closed my eyes and thought about nothing. Like swimming in a black sea. I curled up into a ball. It was silent.

Then I heard Mutti's voice. Mutti's voice has such a lovely tone. I always call it a musical voice. And it was so peaceful: the dark golden streaks, the black sea, the piano was open – our piano that Mutti bought for a lot of money – and its ivory keys had a dull gleam, and Mutti's voice fitted the mood perfectly. I didn't mean to eavesdrop. Because I never do, and because it's not right. I just wanted to hear Mutti's voice because I love listening to it. I thought how lovely Mutti was. And how I'd like to lie like that for ever. Mutti's voice.

Then I heard it. Mutti's friend, Frau Timt, with her thick red lips and white teeth, said, 'Are you going to tell Lore?' (That's me.)

And with her beautifully bright voice Mutti said, 'No!'

When she said 'No!' I was still in a daze, in the middle of that peaceful tranquillity. But I suddenly felt uncomfortable. I can't remember how it was. Just all of a sudden. And I thought, 'How and why? Mutti, my Mutti, why should she hide something from me? How can that be?'

And then I started to listen properly. I wouldn't have thought myself up to it, because eavesdropping is dirty and disgusting. That's what Mutti always says.

Then I heard Mother saying, 'I don't know how Lore would react.'

Frau Timt said, 'Irrespective of how Lore reacts, don't let that influence you. The key thing here is your happiness.'

Then Frau Timt, the revolting Frau Timt, paused and said, quite assertively, 'Are you sure you're not letting yourself be taken in? Is he serious?'

I could sense Mutti smiling, her good smile. Mutti said, 'Yes, Hedwig, he is serious. If you could only see him.'

'You really like him, then?'

Then I sensed Mutti smiling again; how she spoke was so strange and yet familiar that I felt very queer. She said, 'A little.'

And then they talked about other things. But I could no longer hear so well. For I had to think.

This 'he' that they'd kept talking about – what did it mean? Who was the 'he'? Where was the 'he'? What was the 'he'?

From the way Mutti said 'A little' I got the impression that she didn't like him a little, but actually rather a lot. I immediately felt something swell up inside me – like a blood-red wave that renders one defenceless. And it was hatred. For this 'he'.

Who is the 'he'? Where is the 'he'? And why does Mutti love him more than me?

And suddenly I felt something akin to an understanding. Something inside me, very close. And just as swiftly it was gone again. I felt only hatred. Very dark red! For this something. This something!

It's so slimy and yellowy-green. You come across him wherever you turn.

I know Mutti thinks I'm stupid. But when I want to know something, I really want to know, and I *will* know it, too.

Absolutely, and I *want* to know that. I want to know what it is.

I know what Frau Timt said. 'Is he serious? And do you love him too?' These words are tied up with lots of other things that adults keep quiet about.

Even the fact that children are produced by a man and a woman loving each other, they even want to keep that a secret. They all seem to believe that I don't know what love is. But now I'll get to the bottom of it. I want to know it in all its details.

Mutti's been so strange recently. She dresses much more beautifully. She now goes around wearing a Venetian pearl necklace.

Two days ago she took it out of her jewellery box, placed it round her neck and said, 'Does it suit me, Lore?'

And she looked so strange. At the moment, in fact, Mutti looks strange all the time. It's a mixture of how she looks when she's laughing and when she's crying.

Sometimes she sits there for half an hour without doing a thing, her hands in her lap. Then she looks beautiful.

Overall, Mutti is much more beautiful now. Her cheeks are redder, her eyes are sparkling and her hair is always shining.

Mutti is getting queerer and queerer. She's frequently going out in the evening, and then the next day she's quite absent-minded. She looks at me and she's thinking of someone quite different.

That's not what a mother should be doing!

When she looks at me she should be thinking of *me*.

She's forgetting me completely. Yesterday evening she didn't give me a goodnight kiss. I called out, 'Mutti, kiss!' And she said quite stonily and tersely, 'Yes, OK, Lore. Goodnight!'

She doesn't stroke me any more. And she doesn't say, 'My golden child, my comfort.'

I feel so terribly lonely and isolated. I can feel Mutti getting ever more distant from me. I'd just love to cry out, 'Mutti, Mutti, you used to love me so much. Now you're forgetting me altogether.'

But why? It's me, for goodness sake. Lore. Your Lore.

I often cry at night. Then I bite into the cushion. I don't want Mutti to hear me crying.

But she wouldn't hear it anyway. I could cry as loudly as I wanted to. Mutti wouldn't hear.

When I think back to how she always used to stroke me and say, 'Lore, if I didn't have you.'

Yes, if I threw myself out of the window, Mutti would cry then. Oh yes! What a pleasure that would be! Then she'd be sorry. Ha ha!

Mutti doesn't even cry about Papa any more! She hasn't worn her black clothes for ages. Even if I don't mean anything to her any more, at least she shouldn't forget Papa.

Mutti's turning into an independent woman! She goes out somewhere different almost every night.

I know I'm becoming ever more neglected. But I ask you! It's not my fault at all. Whenever I ask Mutti where she's going she looks at me in such a queer fashion and says, 'To the hairdresser. You know that.'

But I will find out *who* is behind all this. I mean nothing any more.

Mutti doesn't even notice how dreadful I look.

It was only yesterday that she said, 'You look terrible, Lore. You should get some more air!'

It's as simple as that! Oh, well.

The above entry continues further back in the notebook, perhaps written a few days later.

. . . Lore this, Lore that.

But I ask you! No, no! Not until I'm dead, then she'll bring flowers to my grave, then the howling will start.

But I'm not going to have Mutti imagine that it's going to kill me. I'm going to survive.

But I will find out who's behind it, because there is someone.

Why does Mutti telephone so often? I heard her saying, 'Bye-bye, Darling!'

That really hurt me. *Darling!* Mutti only used to call me 'Darling'. So now somebody else is Darling. I'll find out who they are, this other Darling.

I still don't know who this other Darling is.

I think about it at night.

Perhaps another child, or . . .

I don't know anything. Not a thing.

I hate Mutti. I never thought that you could hate your mother.

Yesterday I heard Mutti saying on the telephone, 'So we'll meet at the opera house at half past four. Bye-bye!'

At half past three Mutti started putting on her beautiful clothes. I watched her very carefully.

Her silver dress and the beautiful fur coat. Then she walked up and down in front of the mirror. Put on lipstick, powdered herself – she hasn't done that since Papa died. And started getting excited about something. Then she was ready to leave.

I said very seriously and stonily, and it really hurt me, 'Aren't you going to give me a kiss?'

Mutti noticed immediately that I said it in a strange way. She stroked my hair. I could feel her cool, slender hands.

And then I became sad.

Mutti was astonished and said, 'What's wrong, Darling?'

As I heard this word I remembered everything and fell into a frenzy. I'd love to have lashed out. I wanted to pitch my entire icy hatred into Mutti's face so she'd scream.

Full of rage, I cried out imperiously, 'Don't call me Darling!'

Then I saw Mutti recoil. And I could see that Mutti was old. All of a sudden. I could see it. It was like a revelation. I could see Mutti's face, blurred by my tears. Mutti's lips were coated with a garish red, her face completely white with powder. And small wrinkles around the eyes. I'd said, 'Don't call me Darling!'

She'd winced as if I'd hit her. Now she was crying.

And suddenly I thought, Mutti looks like a harlot! A poor harlot!

I felt sorry for Mutti. *So* terribly sorry. And then a large tear ran down her cheek. And where the tear ran it carried specks of powder with it. Underneath, the skin was all wrinkled. And I saw that Mutti had grey hairs on her temples.

Now Mutti is a child. A tiny child. I thought she looked so vulnerable, I wanted to take her in my arms and sing.

It all happened so suddenly.

And I said, 'Sorry, Mutti. I didn't mean it.'

I ran into the children's room.

I'm so big. So big. So far from Mutti. I fear for Mutti for she is small, so very small. And I know that Mutti is hiding something from me. It's all connected to the telephone calls, and the large amount of flowers she brings home, and the fact that she goes out a lot in the evenings, and that she smiles so much, and that she puts red lipstick on.

I cry at night, about the fact that I don't have a Mutti any more. But I'd like to have a Mutti. I'd like this Mutti to comfort me and wipe away my tears, I'd like to be very small again and know nothing.

But it's not going to happen. I'm big and I don't have a Mutti. And I get the impression that it's more like I'm the mother of Mutti than she my mother. Mutti is small and titchy. Mutti cannot comfort me. Mutti is far away.

And I'm big and alone. That's the most horrible thing of all – that I'm alone, so terribly alone. I'm like an old lady. I look in the mirror and check to see whether I've got a few wrinkles or the odd grey hair. I'm so hurt. Sometimes I'm so openly hurt. When I see a tree or a meadow or a balloon, it's as if these are cutting into something sore, something naked. I cannot describe it.

Sometimes I imagine I'm standing on a cliff, I'm made entirely of ice, and below the people are as tiny as ants. And I smile again so oddly. It's horrible.

At night I dream that I'm an old lady and I'm dying. Mutti is standing by my bed, and where the tears run down her cheek they drag a small pile of powder with them. I can see it down to the tiniest detail. Mutti is crying and says, 'So young and yet she has to die already.'

Then I lay my hand on Mutti's head and say, 'I bless you, my child.'

I have horrible dreams like this. When I wake up in the morning tears are flowing down my cheeks.

I often cry in my dreams.

Two days ago Mutti woke me and said, 'Claudia, you were crying in your sleep. Did you have a bad dream?'

And I thought that in the past I would have crawled into Mutti's bed. I would have gone to sleep there, no fear, no tears.

When I crawl into Mutti's bed now I feel even more afraid.

I think that Mutti feels safer and more protected with me than I with her.

I'm very lonely and I don't know what to do.

I buried my head in the cushion and it was all dusky again! I could feel Mutti next to me. She gave me a kiss. I was so happy as I felt her wrinkled lips touch mine.

I'm happy now. Mutti needs me . . . I understand now, little Musch!

If I understand, then . . .

MONDAY, 15 FEBRUARY 1937, VIENNA

Why can't the people in the city see that the clouds are moving?

SUNDAY, 21 FEBRUARY 1937, STEINHAUS

I'm on a skiing course. It's lovely. I'm sleeping in a room with Gretel Mihocovicz. She has a calm, rustic face. She sits on her bed and writes. Her face is full of devotion. It's totally quiet. There's nothing lovelier than a girls' bedroom.

WEDNESDAY, 24 FEBRUARY 1937, STEINHAUS

The nicest thing is going up on your skis. When you get the sure feeling that you're climbing towards the sun and you stop for a moment and see the snow and countryside below you. And then the descent is lovely when the wind blows, tingles and drives the snow into your face. Then you get a blissful feeling. A thirsty feeling. Perhaps that's what life is.

I'm really fond of Lizzy. There's a boy she likes. It was a silly fortune-telling game. She was told that she liked a boy and that he loved her. We told her his name. It was true because we'd found out beforehand. She believed us, and she was nervous and excited.

I took pity on her and felt as if I were her mother. I like it when she puts her head on my shoulder. I would be a good friend to her.

The maternal feeling is the loveliest and most profound feeling.

You could write novels about the souls of young girls.

THURSDAY, 25 FEBRUARY 1937, STEINHAUS

Here at Steinhaus problems are unfurling.

1. I love Lizzy. I really do. I sat with her in the bar today. They were playing jazz. It was so dark and cosy. We chatted.

2. I used to think that Lizzy was unintelligent and above everything. I don't believe that any more. There's an Achilles heel in her life. It's a boy (it all goes back to the fortune telling). As soon as the topic crops up she lets out a dreadfully forced, nervous laugh.

3. Today Irma (a lovely girl – sometimes she says she wants to become a nun) came up to me and said she'd heard I can predict the future. I made it quite plain that I wouldn't do it because I'd had enough of all this nonsense. Then she came up a second time. She begged me and looked at me so sweetly. Finally I said, 'All right then, tomorrow.'

This made her happy. She said, 'Tomorrow! Definitely!'

She's obviously got love worries.

(I'll tell her that she's very lovely and that there's someone who is pining for her.)

When Lizzy heard about this she laughed again so strangely. I wanted to stroke her.

I've got so much material now for stories and tales. You could write a book about the conversations girls have before they go to sleep.

Every person has pains and worries.

Everything is so mysterious and large. People really ought to help each other and be nice to each other.

FRIDAY, 26 FEBRUARY 1937, STEINHAUS

I like Lizzy more and more each day. I can't find any faults with her. She is lovely and good. True?

I told Irma's and Renate's fortunes. Irma was born out of wedlock. She's having a terrible time at home and she can't see any way out other than to enter a convent.

I feel very sorry for her.

I just told her good and nice things: somebody loves her, she will have children and a nice life.

She was *very* happy. It's nice making other people happy.

THURSDAY, 18 MARCH 1937, VIENNA

I don't know whether I should write about it. Yes I should. After all, it doesn't matter.

I've met somebody new.

I find it so rare that one meets new *people*. His name is

Herr Professor Herbert Williger.

And I like him.

It's what I knew already. That there's somebody you can tell everything to and who 'looks after your education'.

He gives so much. More in one hour than another could in a year. He's already quite old. (Gretl said, 'He's a starving old man.' That's an exaggeration, of course.)

He's very lovely and he says so much that I'll always remember. I hope and believe that I'll have the pleasure of his company for a long time yet. (Not just in Latin tutorials.)

He likes me a little, too (in the same way that you could like a 'frog').

Otherwise he wouldn't have said that he missed me.

I think he's *frightfully* intelligent. And nice.

He talked to me about homosexuality. Not directly. But he told me about pederasty in Rome.

He said he hoped we might at some point read *Hannibal* by Grabbe? together.

He said that we might at some point read Plato's dialogues together.

He said that he'd missed me.

That you don't start living until you're sixteen.

That he'll look after my education.

He asks me what I'm reading. Who my favourite author is and whether I write as well.

He often laughs at me. I get annoyed when other people do that, but not Herr Professor Williger.

He smokes heavily, has little money and he's very nervous. He laughs a good deal and is very helpful.

I'd love him to tell me lots, for me to be able to talk to him and for him to read me nice books.

FRIDAY, 2 APRIL 1937, VIENNA

That Williger! He is so lovely.

I don't think that murder goes against human nature at all. Otherwise, 100,000 people that murdered others in the war must be tortured by remorse. But this is not the case. These people don't harbour the slightest remorse. They watched these individuals dying before their very eyes.

I can't understand that. But I do understand one thing: murder is not 'inhuman'.

I believe that's why murder is *allowed* in war, and *not allowed* in peace.

I believe, 1. You could say that taking human life means nothing to some-one if he kills for a purpose. Even the person who murders in peacetime does it for a purpose.

2. You can say that someone who murders another person in war doesn't feel any regret about it afterwards, because he's carrying out this murder for a *higher* purpose. Even people who are conscious that they are not killing other people for a *higher* purpose don't feel any remorse.

You could argue that if people were allowed to murder in peacetime, they would feel regret each time they took a life.

Why? Because they'd got to the stage where they saw murder in peace-time as murder, whereas they didn't consider murder in war to be murder.

How come? Isn't *murder* just a word? The moment they recognise murder in peacetime as a sin, they must instinctively recoil from all blood-spilling, all taking of human life. Irrespective of whether they see it as murder or not.

I'll think about this and ask somebody.

When I write something like this, I don't do it because I enjoy splitting hairs or composing essays, but because my thoughts become clearer when I write them down.

SATURDAY, 3 APRIL 1937, VIENNA

Either Williger is a *really mean fellow* or he is *very nice*.

SUNDAY, 4 APRIL 1937, VIENNA

There's so much I've still got to write. Later!

THURSDAY, 8 APRIL 1937, VIENNA

It's funny, the thing with Williger.

He must be very lonely; perhaps he's sad as well. Perhaps he already feels old and I'm something like a pleasure to him.

I love him. Like a father.

Sometimes he fills me with horror. Then I get the feeling that he has a physical desire for me. That would be horrible. It disgusts me!

I don't want to have any relationship of dependence with him.

Ruth Maier grew up in a cultured household. The photograph shows Ruth's father, Ludwig Maier, in his study. According to her sister Judith, Ruth used to enjoy sitting in this room on a ladder and reading books.

Thoughts come and go

APRIL – JULY 1937

The diary from spring and summer 1937 is a sixty-four-page lined quarto notebook, entitled 'Ruth's Diary'. Fifty-eight sides of the book are filled with writing, partly in pencil and partly in ink. We see the existential reflections of a young girl: 'If you expect too much from life you're bound to be disappointed. But if you look at life without any expectation or hope, then you see wonder everywhere, in the smallest and slightest things.'

Thomas Mann's short story Disillusionment *is carefully copied out in cursive old-fashioned German handwriting. Other than that, most of the entries are in Ruth Maier's speedy, fluid style, where the long strokes soon disappear. On the last pages are some musical notation, a doodle and several addresses, including that of her Latin teacher, Herbert Williger: Währingerstraße 12. Ruth no longer takes lessons from him, but she never forgets his saying: 'Child, you don't start living until you're sixteen.'*

The diary does not give any details about places, but it was probably written in Vienna.

FRIDAY, 30 APRIL 1937, VIENNA

I don't have a pen, so I have to write in pencil. I intend to write *as much of this diary as possible* without any sentimentality. It all depends on what the diary's binding and paper etc. is like. If the pages were handmade laid paper and the binding made of red leather, then I'd start writing in such a solemn tone that only rubbish would come out. But if I write in pencil in a perfectly normal notebook, then there's the hope of avoiding writing sentimental drivel.

First: Williger. Until now I've written about him as little as possible. But it's no good. I'd like to describe in detail how the whole thing began etc. (Herr Professor Williger no longer preoccupies me.)

Background:

I was weak in Latin. I did two tests just by guessing and was convinced I'd be moved down. As a result, Mama found me some help. This help was Herr Professor Williger. Herr Dr Brauchbar told me just what a genius, what a luminary, how intelligent this Professor Williger was. OK then.

I went on Monday.

I climbed up six floors, arrived at the top. There was a note on the door.

Ring 1x for Ingenieur Glas

Ring 2x for Ingenieur Mos

Ring 3x for Professor Williger

I rang three times. A blond man with marine-blue eyes came out. Herr Professor Williger wasn't at home. But I could go in. Herr Williger's apartment was all over the place, or whatever the term is. Just like student lodgings and quite eccentric. There were a few pictures on the walls, a photograph, a portrait . . . Hmm, him perhaps? Excellent! A picture of the ruins of some Greek temple, stuck on to white wrapping paper.

The bust of some woman. A few amateur drawings. On the desk, a bust of Caesar with a very long inscription.

In any case . . . the focus on Antiquity. Temple ruins, bust of Caesar, detail from a painting.

The library . . . pathetic! *Alice in Wonderland*, English dictionary, a volume of Shakespeare, Stefan George's poems . . . '*Wie herrlich leuchtet mir die Natur*' . . . Ibsen . . . and Tolstoy's *The Living Corpse* . . . Nice.

What else?

The desk (the size of a table-tennis table) is littered with all sorts of paper, pens, pencils, rulers, a triangle, a pipe (yuck!) etc. The room is very large and bright with big windows. Like a studio. In the corner is a small table with a spirit burner, tea, milk, coffee, biscuits, etc.

I wait.

Finally the Herr Professor arrives. He made a very strange impression. I'd imagined someone more masculine.

He looked like a scholar. He had his hat on, which meant you couldn't see his bald patch, only some grey locks of hair or something similar. He had a shrunken mouth and deep-set eyes. (At the time, of course, I wasn't thinking such mundane thoughts. I didn't dare to make any criticisms in the presence of a god like Herr Williger. Thank goodness!)

I started coming twice a week. That's quite often and in due course I got to know the Herr Professor better.

To begin with I got myself into such a stew over him. I wasted a lot of precious time. Now it's all calmed down. At first I thought, He's a decent human being, a man of substance. He'll turn me into someone decent, too. We'll read beautiful things together, books, he'll discuss things that are important for me to know.

I was fond of him. Although it was eerie that he had such a liking for me.

I thought, He's an old man. He is very lonely. I'm something he can get close to, something lovely and beautiful. He likes looking at me. He always looked at me so affectionately, with such a smile. (At the beginning he only ever said, 'Sweet!') How lovely!

Then the Herr Professor paid us a visit. It was ghastly. I thought he looked like a toad. He brought chocolate. And he kissed my hand quite furtively. He stroked me and said that he was so happy to see me again. It was terrible . . . He put on an affected voice (like Herr Weiß from the dance school).

After this visit Mama warned me, 'Don't forget, Ruth, that Herr Professor Williger is a *man*.'

I felt better!

I reflected that it may have been carnal feelings which caused him to behave like that. I went to see Ella and poured out my heart to her.

It would be dreadful if he saw me as a woman. I thought about it a lot. The Herr Professor invited me to the theatre. I didn't go.

I don't need to love a bald-headed man with a shrunken mouth. I need someone really young, *really* young that I can love. The Herr Professor was offended that I didn't go with him. He became ironic.

The time before he was nice. He was sad that I wouldn't be coming back for a week. He accompanied me to the tram and said, 'Now I feel as if I'm standing at the station and you're going away – to Paris.'

How odd. I had exactly the same feeling. It was raining. I stood with him at the stop. All those people and I was so alone with the Herr Professor. When I looked at the Herr Professor I couldn't help laughing, and then he laughed and said, 'Do you have any idea *how* much I love you?'

And I got the feeling again that he liked me as something lovely and young.

(But once he told me something he never ought to have said: 'Somebody who's never met you said that you're the only woman who knows how to handle me.' I think I went very red. He really ought not to have said that if he considered me to be a child.)

Sometimes Herr Professor Williger also thinks his relationship with me is quite odd. Once he said, 'Do you know, Ruth, the thing I have suffered from most of all is that women understand me so badly. I've never said that to anyone before.'

And suddenly he said melancholically, 'Why does it have to be a little girl?'

When I write about this, the Herr Professor seems to me very likeable. But when I reflect that he's got a shrunken mouth, a bald patch and that he smokes a pipe, he horrifies me as much as a toad would (perhaps that's an exaggeration).

SATURDAY, 1 MAY 1937, VIENNA

I believe that many of our ills and evils are due to the fact that we have such a frightfully poor relationship to nature, the sun, the earth, flowers. We're too little in tune with the earth. If there were no towns, human beings would be much happier.

I sense myself becoming deadened by the boring, commonplace, every-day things in life. I intend to battle against this.

I've read a wonderful short story by Thomas Mann. I'm going to copy it out.

The following fifteen pages of the diary contain the short story Disillusionment

Ich habe eine schöne Nouvelle von
Th. Mann gelesen. Ich werde sie abschreiben.
      Enttäuschung.
Ich gestehe, daß mir die Reden dieses sonder=
baren Herrn ganz und gar verwirrten,
und ich fürchte, daß ich auch jetzt noch
nicht imstande sein werde sie auf eine Wei=
se zu wiederholen, daß sie andere in ähnlicher
Weise berühren, wie an jenem Abend mich
selbst. Vielleicht beruhte ihre Wirkung
nur auf der befremdlichen Offenheit, mit
der ein ganz Unbekannter sie mir äußerte.
      Der Herbstvormittag, an dem
mir jener Unbekannter auf der Piazza San
Marco zum ersten Male auffiel, liegt nun
etwa zwei Monate zurück. Auf dem weiten
Platze liegt nun etwa zwei Monate zurück
Auf dem weiten Platze bewegten sich nur
wenige Menschen umher, aber vor bunten Wim

The manuscript is interrupted twelve lines before the end, with the following note:

. . . etc. While I was copying this out it occurred to me that what's written here is quite wrong.

TUESDAY, 11 MAY 1937, VIENNA

Now I want to write about the Herr Professor for the last time. I think I'll write him a letter, in the holidays.

I've read letters of condolence (sent to Mama). It is so shocking that people can write such tasteless and cretinous things. When you think that the time will come for all these ghastly, tasteless letter writers, too, it's so sad. I find it downright pathetic. For all those people who write these letters do it so pompously, so sympathetically, but with a hidden sneer, glad that it's not their turn yet. And to think that other people will write *their* bereaved ones exactly the same sneering, pompous letters!

When you consider that all that remains of a beautiful, rich life is a handful of condolence letters, it makes you want to vomit.

THURSDAY, 13 MAY 1937, VIENNA

Papa had such a beautiful life. Like a fairy tale. Papa travelled around many foreign countries and Mama waited at home. Papa wrote love letters and Mama thought about him fondly. I'd like to have been Mumi. I'd like to have been Papi. I won't accomplish anything. I won't have so many friends. It must be wonderful.

What's written in the short story is not right.

You must *search* for what's beautiful, what's good in life. You mustn't wait until it comes to you. You must be prepared for beauty.

If you expect too much from life you're bound to be disappointed. But if you look at life without any expectation or hope, then you see wonder every-where, in the smallest and slightest things.

It doesn't necessarily have to be divinely pure or devilishly vile. I believe that wonderful is sufficient.

I believe we can take an example from Leonardo da Vinci.

You must keep your eyes open and mustn't dream.

FRIDAY, 28 MAY 1937, VIENNA

Each individual is a many-faceted, complex being.

Anni

Anni is a bright girl, and nice. She's not pretty. She's got uncombed hair and a pinched mouth. She has no feminine charm whatsoever. She's unrefined and withdrawn. For her the time has not yet come where the body opens out and blossoms. She's still at the stage where it's plain and uneven, and where it prickles under the skin. Her body has no form. Her face is austere and closed. She is the girl of tomorrow. (However silly that may sound.) She is a person choked full of problems, unresolved questions, puzzles. A person who broods and *reflects*.

Heidi

Heidi is a girl with a single gesture. Hollow and empty. Affected. She hides her hollowness behind frenzied histrionics and makes out as if she is above everything. She cannot be as brainy as she pretends, because really intelligent people do not behave like that, they don't *need* any gestures.

For example, she dismisses anything to do with men with a lofty smile. Today I found out that she went walking with a boy in Cobenzl park, their arms all around each other. I cannot believe it.

In Leo Tolstoy I've read about a boy who lives only according to his principles. He develops an opinion on this or that and then lives according to that opinion. That is excellent. He even forms opinions on trifling matters.

I want to do that too. But I want to begin with the trifling things, for I want to figure out the big ones gradually.

Do I want to drink alcohol?

No?

Why not?

Because it is harmful and unhealthy.

I don't deny that, but if it gives you pleasure, then can't it be just a little bit unhealthy?

Quite apart from the fact that it doesn't give me any pleasure, I don't want to drink alcohol because I consider it inhuman to reel around in the street and behave like an animal.

Inhuman? Why? It is only too human for somebody to want to offload his torments and worries, to long to free himself, to get drunk because then he hopes that everything will look more beautiful and golden.

But it is also human in another sense. The sense in which you want to understand the word human – with this meaning you want to excuse all the mistakes, lapses, crimes that human beings commit. But I understand the word inhuman as something which is unbecoming a human being.

You're quickly becoming a moralist. Don't drink alcohol, *it is unbecoming a human being*. Don't put lipstick on either. *It is unbecoming a human being!* In short: apply yourself to those tasks which are worthy of a human being.

You think you can undermine me with your jokes and mockery. Honestly. I say it is unbecoming a human being, so I understand *very* well when someone does anything unbecoming a human being. I (to put it nicely) pardon you.

You pardon me. That's nice, very nice indeed, that you pardon me. You forget that one has to have a certain entitlement to pardon.

All right, I concede that. I don't pardon, I *understand* it.

Are you trying to say, O super-being, that you haven't succumbed to these unbecoming things?

Oh no! I never said that. I have succumbed to them. But I want to fight them, and the very fact that I'm saying 'I don't want to drink any alcohol' shows that I'm not above it all.

It's a good thing that the individual can exert his will over his own life. That he can say, 'I want to live,' and that he can say, 'I don't want to live.' Every desire I experience comes from my will.

TUESDAY, 1 JUNE 1937, VIENNA

There is something delicate and coy between myself and Lizzy. Something guarded. I cannot describe it accurately, I don't even know if she feels the same. I feel something warm and maternal.

The maternal longing or urge in me (I don't know what it's called) is very powerful.

I've already had this feeling towards many people. Bibi, for example, and then towards almost all children, Kurti etc., then Harri. He's the son of somebody we know. He's gentle and I feel sorry for him. This maternal feeling is very warm.

One of Grete Salvender's principles is to raise children in the community and take away the mothers because they raise children selfishly (communism).

In my opinion that's quite ridiculous . . . For it's the mothers who give their children so much love, and mothers who give them so much that is good. So much that it's impossible to do without. I think of the many great men, of Goethe, Petzold,* Rembrandt and many others, and what riches their mothers gave to them.

I think about Papa and how empty it would have been without him.

MONDAY, 14 JUNE 1937, VIENNA

Our neighbour's daughter, Steffi, is always getting me to translate letters into English etc. He (of course it's a 'he') is from India. Steffi has a yearning for the unusual.

TUESDAY, 22 JUNE 1937, VIENNA

Before doing something nasty or unpleasant to somebody else, you should consider that he is a human being and that it will hurt his feelings.

---

* Alfons Petzold (1882–1923), Austrian writer.

MONDAY, 5 JULY 1937, VIENNA

Yesterday I felt love for everybody. Dr Robert Knöpflmacher is a swine and a fool. He was rude and mean.

I believe that one of the greatest evils of our age is that we have too little time; we hurry too much, and when we do have time we don't know what to do with it.

At school we acted out *Death and the Fool*. I was the young girl. I acted it well. And that made me very pleased. Maybe I'll become an actress.

I'm drawn to everything that's sick and helpless. Blind people, for example. Yet after some time I find these things repulsive. I can imagine really loving a blind man, caring for him, but after some time he would start to disgust me terribly. For this reason I don't think I'd make a good doctor.

THURSDAY, 8 JULY 1937, VIENNA

I wonder whether Jack London might not be right in *Martin Eden* when he says that, in essence, socialism is nothing more than sentimentality. Jack London contrasts socialism and Darwinism and, like Darwin, says that the capable and talented in life will always be superior to the untalented. That the talented will always triumph and dominate the untalented. That the laws which operate among animals also apply to human beings and cannot be suppressed.

   1. August Bebel says that advocates of this opinion forget that human beings have the understanding to exclude themselves from these laws. I don't know whether that's right?!

   2. My question is: do those among the untalented who share this opinion understand? – the unemployed who don't even have anything to eat. Do those among the talented understand? – the millionaires who began as newspaper boys!

Can the talented person get anywhere today?

An adolescent girl is a contradictory being.

On the one hand this is when all the emotions and feelings begin that draw a girl to a man. But these feelings express themselves very childishly and awkwardly. I think it's all quite usual, even the so-called girly giggling, the gentle laughter.

On the other hand everybody at this point in life must start thinking about the world, about good and evil, about God and so many other questions.

And then comes the contradiction. You have to think about so many questions that great men before you have racked their brains over and obviously you think that everything apart from these earth-shattering questions is unimportant etc. (But I think so too!)

Now I'm just wondering, 'Why are adolescent boys so different from us?'

I think it's because boys don't want to please girls quite so much as girls do boys. Girls are much more vain.

SATURDAY, 10 JULY 1937, VIENNA

I saw a *very* nice film. *Tanz unterm Galgen*. I despise myself *very much* because I don't have the courage to *die*. It is terrible. I dream about it often, too. Fine! I wouldn't have the courage to commit suicide! But I don't know. I wouldn't have the courage to die for a good cause either. For freedom, or something like that! An average person should always follow the example of the person who is above average. I'm waiting. It's so terrible that I don't want to die. But perhaps it will come. It doesn't really matter whether it's a second earlier or later. I want to die for a good, noble cause. It is not nice to arrive at the realisation that you're not capable of achieving anything. That you can't do a thing. That's the mistake – that there are so few people who are capable of something. Why can't I stand up and say, 'We want to be free'?! Why can't I stand up and say, 'There shall be no war'?! Why can't I if I want to? The loveliest moments are when I'm sobbing! It's when I'm listening to beautiful music, when I'm reading a wonderful book! When I'm full of enthusiasm. That's when I start to sob. Why do I look just like other people?

It is so stupid. I don't know what I'm writing. But I want to write, which is why I'm writing – it flows! If I can't be the type of person who's capable of achieving something, I'd like at least to pretend to be the talented person!!! If I were a maid and my master said, 'Kiss my feet or I'll kill you,' I'd kiss his feet to avoid having to die. And that is what I call *cowardly*. Someone who acts like that is a worm. And it's terrible to know that one is a worm. It is terrible to want to, but not be able to! I could murder myself. I will not stand up and I will not even follow the one who stands up. *Because nobody is going to stand up.*

TUESDAY, 13 JULY 1937, VIENNA

Erna Prokopee is a quiet and gentle girl. She is eleven years old. I think she's going to be one of those rare girls who are spotless and quiet, even when there's a lot of filth around. She writes. She wants to become either a writer or an astronomer. She has written a poem about the stars and about how the sky is bleak without the moon and stars.

There was an article about Käthe Kollwitz in the newspaper. It said Käthe Kollwitz believes that everything originates in sorrow, everything that happens has its roots in sorrow . . . I believe that too sometimes. But to believe this is fruitless, joyless and no fun at all in my opinion. Yet I cannot help myself. It just comes straight from my feelings. I don't want to at all. I see people on the streets, unemployed people with children, old women with terribly wrinkled faces. And I think about it. I feel that everything I'm writing is very unclear. I can't do anything else.

I think that if there comes a time that is full of peace and beauty, then I won't love people any more. I love people when they are miserable. When people are miserable they are at their most beautiful. When people are happy they become snobbish and ugly. I don't mean happy in spirit but in life over-all. If they're successful in everything, if they have everything they wish for, etc.

I'd like to write more about misery. I'd like to give an example. Let's say I'm looking at a proletarian family. They're poor and have three children. They're thin and unhappy. They've had much bad luck. They push their children around in the pram. The mother laughs. The children play. I can't describe it that precisely.

Now I imagine the same family, but happy. They've had a lot of good fortune in life. They go around in fine clothes. They have a haughty look. They don't love each other as much. They're content. (Perhaps I should be using the word 'content' instead of 'happy' throughout.) When I see them like this I don't love them. The whole thing is very superficial. It's not at all rational either. Perhaps it's just tied up with what's on the outside. I prefer a person when he looks awful and has bags under his eyes, to when he is round and fat with a large stomach. For the same reason it is also nobler to fight for a cause than to enjoy the cause that's being fought for. For the same reason?!

Yes! Because if I enjoy the cause then I'm indolent, lazy etc. etc.

If I read back over what I've written then I get completely muddled. These are just very untamed thoughts, which come and go.

The shadow of death

SEPTEMBER – DECEMBER 1937

The diary from autumn 1937 is a 150-sided, unlined quarto notebook with a hard cover, which has been almost filled with writing. Ruth begins the diary in Vienna after the summer holidays and the entries finish at Christmas. We must assume that all the entries were written in Vienna, although the location is not always identified. Some afterthoughts were added shortly before Ruth's departure from Austria in early 1939.

During this period, the last six months prior to Anschluss, when Hitler annexed Austria, there are frequent thoughts about death and thoughts about her own father. Throughout the diary there are also many disturbing sketches.

The previous diary from the summer of 1937 in Château de Salorges, where Ruth and Judith stayed in a holiday house run by the French postal union, has been lost. In this diary from autumn 1937 Ruth writes about the children she met from several countries.

She also writes affectionately about the popular actor Hermann Thimig, then at the height of his career, and an up-and-coming pianist, Jean Hubeau (1917–1992), who would later become famous, but at this time is studying in Vienna.

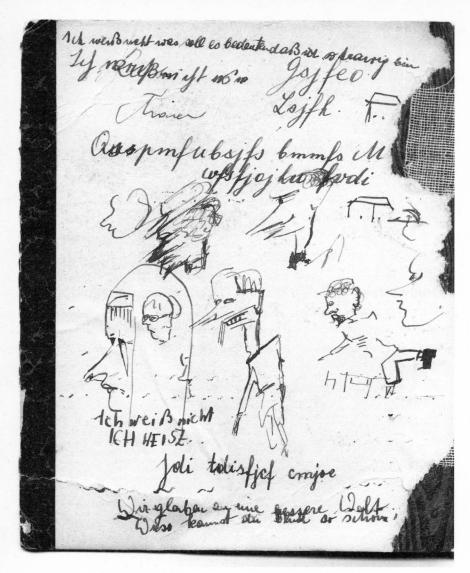

Inside cover of the diary from autumn 1937.

TUESDAY, 21 SEPTEMBER 1937, VIENNA

Now we're back in Vienna.

SATURDAY, 25 SEPTEMBER 1937, VIENNA

I wrote a diary in Château de Salorges. I lost it. There's nothing I can do about it.

In front of a florist's we saw a butterfly. It was large and brightly coloured.

I think a lot, perhaps I think too much.

SUNDAY, 3 OCTOBER 1937, VIENNA

Time is passing quickly. You cannot stop it. You die, and nothing will remain of us but muck.

TUESDAY, 5 OCTOBER 1937, VIENNA

I'm longing to write. I believe I have to write down my exquisite thoughts. Even when I do write I know nothing. Then there's nothing inside me but emptiness.

I don't know if this is right, but I've noticed something, particularly in Austria.

1. That the enemy does not become great by ruling tyrannically, but through his friendliness (the emperor speaks to the people). Hence resistance is disarmed.

2. That people are tricked by small promises of freedom and are deceived about what the whole thing really means. They say: Look, we're decorating our windows with red flags, we're singing the 'Internationale'.

Of course, it's only the really mediocre people who are duped by such nonsense.

One day I'd like to write an intelligent diary without aphorisms.

One day I shall be through with writing.

School has started. We've got Betty for German. Follender for French. Follender is an elegant woman in black who is very particular about conduct and speaks good French.

School is rather dulling my mind at the moment. I've read a young boy's composition about the 'Jews of Zinsdorf'. It's not bad.

A. It's the job of the teachers to introduce pupils to various fields of knowledge. They could do this in such an elegant and wonderful way. They could open up for us all these hidden wonders. This is, after all, a life's vocation. What do they do? Nothing, absolutely nothing. We have to swot up on the most banal rules and we get absolutely no insight into the wonders that must lie behind these.

B. You forget that it's not just the teachers but the pupils who are absolutely incapable. The teachers are incapable of teaching. All right. I admit it. But the pupils are just as incapable of taking in what's taught them. Not everybody can see like you into the world of wonders.

A. I know what I'm talking about. When I was at school I remember how we pricked up our ears when the teacher hinted at something other than dusty old rules and formulae.

B. I admit that teaching today is perhaps somewhat too dry. But surely there's still a difference between banal rules and wonders.

A. Wonders or no wonders. That is not the crux of the matter. Forget the wonder of things. What they teach in German is grammatical analysis – medieval opinions on everything. Hartmann von Aue. Then there are dates, dates and more dates. No notion of fundamental issues, or discussions that at least attempt to provide clarity. Then there's history: Middle Ages, modern period. Also crammed with dates and details, without any real importance. At the end of the lesson you might know when the Battle of Salamis was, but there's no overview of the whole of history, no talk about deeper causes. So you learn about the succession of emperors! But let's move on!

And then there's no mention in history of current events. That has to be the latest irony. While I know that China and Japan are annihilating each other, we're discussing the Thirty Years War. While the civil war is going crazy in Spain, we're discussing the Glorious Revolution in England. I can see that you shouldn't ignore the past completely. But you can show its connection to the present, albeit not in such a narrow-minded way.

Of course, you'll always have a few perverse people who know all about the Council of Constance, but have no idea when the revolution in Austria was. Should the Council of Constance or the Peace of Westphalia make us forget the present completely? The past is, after all, only paper for us. But if the reverse is true then it's even worse.

There are people who have no connection to politics, who express opinions even though they have no idea where these come from. Why don't they teach us again how National Socialism, socialism and communism evolved?

But we don't need to spend so much time on history. Let's take a look at natural history. The way of teaching this is very peculiar indeed. A secret shadow covers knowledge about the human body, about reproduction. And particularly about reproduction from sexual intercourse. School could do so much good work here. Later on, of course, there is some coy talk about embryos (but nothing about the process of reproduction itself). There are even girls in the seventh year who do not know about it. Why can't we just go to the teacher and say quite frankly: Frau Doktor, I don't know anything about this or that.

And then the seventh year itself: sixteen- and seventeen-year-olds. The period of not knowing how or why ought to be long past. Just think what confusions, improprieties, doubts, etc could be prevented if they gave a detailed account of sexual intercourse already in the third year.

B. You're forgetting one thing: unfortunately this suggestion is unfeasible for thirteen-year-old girls. If you start jabbering on about this topic, you'll come up against an embarrassed silence, then perhaps a wink of the eye, gentle laughter. You forget that the mention of the word 'breasts' makes girls snigger.

A. Yes, and whose fault is that? It's yours, and yours again. You present everything to do with sex in a devious and ambiguous way. Treat this subject as any other, as you do cell division in algae. Why don't the teachers speak about this? Why do they say very matter of factly: cell division is non-sexual etc.? They must talk about everything, about the reproduction of bracken, of algae, of greenfly, not just about human reproduction. Of course people think there's something forbidden, ambiguous about it. The result of such an education is that when they want to talk about this subject to young people, the response is a quiet snigger. We, the young people, want a school that helps us out of uncertainty. Not a school that serves us up formulae and rules, but one that connects us to the present, a school that, at the very least, makes us into able and efficient people.

THURSDAY, 7 OCTOBER 1937, VIENNA

We've received a letter from our Spanish friends at Château de Salorges.

They've got to go back to Spain, to the war. '*Mucha pena.*' Much sorrow! Why? These beautiful, healthy Spanish children should not need to know war. When I think that Fernandito, that handsome boy whom everybody called 'Mimos', could also be one of those 100,000 children who will die. That it's already happening in Japan. I beg you!

I feel as if all the worries of the whole world are upon my shoulders. Please tell me, explain to me why they have to be on me. If they were to gobble each other up I'd live in happiness. Even if in the month I write this

Refugee children from the Spanish Civil War in a makeshift camp.
Ruth and Judith met them in France in summer 1937.

1,000,000 people in China were to scream in pain. Our task, the task of young people, is to remember these screaming individuals, to think of the many children who are being torn apart by bombs. Tell me of the sort of people who wish to fight with us. Tell me how we can be triumphant!

I'd love just to lie in some clear water now, or talk with a gentle human being. No politics, China, Japan, Spain. Just water! In truth, I'm sad.

SUNDAY, 10 OCTOBER 1937, VIENNA

We had an excursion. It was autumn in the woods. There were leaves on the ground. The trees were red and yellow.

Yesterday we went dancing. At Dick Roy's house. He looked like someone from a ruined castle. Sweat. Heat. There was a boy there I liked. He looked like a virtuous schoolboy. He had a high forehead, glasses. He was

American. When he talked, it was strained and unnatural. I danced with his friend. Stupid etc.

I want to write about some of the children I've met so that I never forget them.

Hansi

I was very fond of Hansi. I met her in Brno and I liked her immediately. She was small, delicate and had eyes that promised fun. She was staying there with her grandmother and grandfather. She would always say: let's sit down, let's play. She said: 'Neboise is sooo small. 'Neboise. That's where she lived. She was vain. And she was terribly fond of me. I told her stories. *The Happy Prince* by Oscar Wilde. In the evenings we used to go for walks together. We played hospitals, shops. We made a little house in the bushes.

I'll probably never see her again.

Karli Simonek

He was a small, cheeky boy. A frightful scallywag. I met him in Alpland. The first time I saw him he had very red cheeks. I was very fond of him, too. We also built ourselves a little house in the woods. There he told me stories he'd made up himself. Later we wrote them down . . . I told him we'd have them published. He was amazed. He was very intelligent. He could draw beautifully. He drew such a stunning magical garden; twelve-year-olds couldn't have done anything better. We taught him how to add and subtract, and he grasped it very quickly.

We played out scenes in the street. For example, our meeting again in the future. He would be a famous writer, a married man. We played police and lots more besides. He gave me a kiss twice. Once he said, 'I want to tell you something, Ruth.' And then he gave me a peck on the cheek. Then once at night. I can't remember exactly. We were saying goodnight before going to bed. It was heavenly. There were times when we small children were very close. That's how it used to be. Like a warm surge in my heart. It's true.

Later on, Karli wasn't so nice. He blathered on about an invisible hand, and then he pinched and scratched me.

One summer in Austria.
Ruth is sitting on the left in the middle row; her sister Judith is beside her.

Ricardo

He is a small, sun-kissed Italian boy. Just as you would imagine. Playing with a ball in the street, the juice of melons dripping from his mouth. With ripped clothes and such a joyful, sunny laugh. The street golden with lots of dust. I was very fond of him. Even madly fond. As I might be of a man. He was twelve. He had small brown hands and I wanted to look after him. He spoke a lot of Italian to me. I couldn't understand a thing. With every sunrise he said '*Allora, una volta*'. He would say it with a cheerful glint in his eye, open out his hands and look up to the sky. I really liked him a lot. I would often stroke his hair and kiss him. The last time I saw him it was raining. He didn't know that I would be leaving. I saw him through a window as we moved off, his small childish face.

Ren

That's his sister. She was sun-kissed like her brother. Her entire being radiated the sun. She was like a strawberry. Her eyes were like when the sun shines through leaves. The first time I saw her was at the station; she kissed her mother on the hand. She was wearing a blue dress with a red collar. That's how I picture her.

Or I picture her making pretty figures with string. She looked absorbed, a small vertical furrow on her forehead. I can see her in my room. She's laughing and saying, 'Angelo, Angelo!'

The last time I saw her she looked anxious, as if she wanted to weep. I gave her a quick kiss. I felt miserable.

Serge

A small French boy. When I first saw him I thought that this is how David Copperfield must have looked when he was young. He undertook long journeys on his own. Milky-white skin, pink fingernails, thin red lips, black frizzy hair, small brown eyes. Serge was gentle and shy. He definitely needed somebody to help him. He wasn't very bright. A really lovely boy. I'd be curious to know what will become of him.

Ly

Ly is Melitta's daughter. She's quite a chubby girl. She's very sweet. She wants to hear stories all day long. She used to love me terribly. I know. I went for a walk with her in the Türkenschanzpark and she said, 'The reason why it's called a weeping willow is because the willow looks as if it's crying and sad.'

I love children.

WEDNESDAY, 13 OCTOBER 1937, VIENNA

I was at the dentist's today. I was drugged. It was so funny. I have to write about it. The dentist asked me if I wanted to be anaesthetised, for the treatment was going to be very painful. I said yes. A girl placed a cloth over my mouth and the dentist said, 'Breathe in deeply! Breathe in deeply!' in a calm and clear voice. I breathed in deeply, and got a dizzy and sweet feeling in my mouth.

Immediately, suddenly, it felt like a . . . mass of air in my brain. As if my brain had been filled with a large ball. I was astonished. And I didn't need to think. I thought about Hedy Türk and life is a puzzle. I thought: S...t...r...a...n...g...e I c...a...n...n...o...t t...h...i...n...k.

I thought in slow motion. My thoughts rolled along very slowly. Then I heard the doctor far in the distance, as if through a thick veil. He said, 'D...r...i...p D...r...i...p A...r...e y...o...u l...o...o...k...i...n...g a...t t...h...e j...a...w...b...o...n ?'

Then I felt a pain and I held on to something creased. And I thought: T...h...a...t i...s t...h...e H...e...r...r D...o...k...t...o...r...'...s c...o...a...t.

Then the doctor said, 'Right, we're finished. Are you still under anaesthetic? Emma, open the window.'

I saw everything as if in a dream. As if through a glass bowl. Emma went over to the window. The doctor said, 'Rinse out your mouth.' I rinsed. I was trembling. Then the doctor said, 'Just look how long that's lasted with you. You only breathed in four times, didn't you?' Then he drilled again. He said, 'I'll make the most of it.' I could feel a twitching in my tooth. Then he stopped. More cool air on my forehead.

Gradually I started to see everything as normal. He did something else. Then I left.

I thought how death is also that simple. You cannot resist it, you die and then have no more consciousness of yourself.

THURSDAY, 14 OCTOBER 1937, VIENNA

I think I'm only able to write in the first person. Perhaps it's got something to do with the fact that I've a talent for acting. But I will write a novel one day. I could write a novel like Dostoevsky's *Poor People*.

SUNDAY AFTERNOON, 17 OCTOBER 1937, VIENNA

Yesterday I was in Laxenburg with Ernst, Willi, Marianne, Peppi and Dita. It was very lovely. Everything is autumnal. We went in a rowing boat on the pond. The pond is totally grey-green. And the oars dip very softly into the water. It was dark and there were white swans swimming very slowly. The palace is green and grey. I could do a good painting of it. The area around Laxenburg is poor.

The earth is bright brown. Sugar beet, the sky is grey. The people stooped.

I've seen a wonderful film: *The Life of Emil Zola*.

THURSDAY, 28 OCTOBER 1937, VIENNA

Il pleut sur la route
Comme il pleure dans mon coeur.

I like that. It's so sad. I have to think a lot, because everything is so short and because what I know of life today presses against my heart, to be gone tomorrow. And murdered in a ditch. That's a terrible thought. It makes me sad. It makes me fearful. And one ought to love all people because it's short.

Today I saw an ambulance drive past. They carried out a tall, pallid individual. In total silence. The servant closed the ambulance door. Then the engine started up. They drove away. I've realised that nobody can experience suffering that is alien to them. You don't know how death is before you experience it. I have a beautiful body and in the evenings I sit in front of the mirror, stroking my naked skin. I delight in every part of my body: my breasts, my legs, my arms. And I long to offer up this body, pure as it is, to somebody I love.

Just as one offers up a crystal-clear bowl of a delicious drink. That's exaggerated . . .

I long to feel life in my body. To produce life is one of man's tasks. And certainly not the worst.

Ruth loved the theatre and was a keen visitor to the Vienna Burgtheater,
where Hermann Thimig was one of the major actors. Judith was also a big fan
of Hermann Thimig. She used to write him letters, and he sent her a photograph
with the dedication: 'To Miss Judith Maier — a souvenir'.

SATURDAY, 6 NOVEMBER 1937, VIENNA

Do I worship Hermann Thimig? So old and still so crazy. I could write so
much. In my head. But in truth I always lose the inclination and the thread.

I sent him violets, Williger, and then I called him several times without
saying it was me.

These are the afterpains. The whole thing's rotting away already. I'll send
him something at Christmas. Because he's on his own. And because one ought
to make people happy at Christmas.

I often think, 'He'll die soon.' I find it very harsh and mean to think that. But I think it nonetheless.

When he dies I'll visit him, I know I will. Then I'll be very sorry. Oh well. That's all romantic nonsense. It's almost completely over.

So, what else? Oh right! Thimig. We know already. I worship him etc.

Then there's Jean Hubeau. A charming Frenchman. He's a musician and very lovely. He blushes easily and ignores me. There's nothing I can do.

Actually I don't care about anything: 1. school, 2. life in general. It sounds silly and pretentious. But it's the truth. I often think: Why should I torment myself? It doesn't help. The best would be if I committed suicide. These are passing thoughts. But that would be the best. I often think: I'm seventeen now. Should I not rather die before this repulsive life makes me come unstuck? While I still have some belief in all that's beautiful. Before I've become Frau Klein or Frau Silberberg.

It makes me sick. One ought to be able to write books, or be able to act wonderfully on stage like Thimig.

It's raining outside, drops tapping on the window.

Would it not be lovely to be able to say: My heart is like a blooming bunch of violets?

(Bunches of violets do not bloom.)

SUNDAY, 14 NOVEMBER 1937, VIENNA

What was it that I wanted to write? Oh yes! That it's lovely to walk through the streets and look. Just to look and meander. To wander around, enjoy life with one's hands in one's pockets.

Men are playing hurdy-gurdies. A grandmother is waiting with a child for its mother. She's a shabby-looking grandmother. The child has a blue bow tie and is laughing at me.

At that moment I started thinking. This child, with its flat, blissful and innocent face has been born to shoot other people – his brothers (as it's so nicely put) – dead. This child with its soft face, free of wrinkles, will be goaded into murder and bloodshed. And this child will be killed by a shell, and when it's dying it will call out for its mother. This child with the blue bow tie.

It was all so clear. In a flash.

I can only compare it to the time in Brno with Uncle Oskar. There was an open-air concert. Muggy and steamy. Lots of people. Hot and oppressive. Bloated faces, material and sweat. Lovers. Soldiers.

Uncle Oskar said, 'Just like the atmosphere in 1914 when war broke out.'

And it was clear then, too.

War. Yes! In a flash. Special edition: War.

Sweat, heavy air, soldiers, lovers.

And again in Brno. Through the window of a barracks I saw strong-looking men march past. Bare chested. They were singing a valiant Czech song. And there it was again: cannon fodder . . . brothers!

Brothers!

Tomorrow I'm going to *The Sunken Bell* by Hauptmann. With Thimig. Thimig is playing Waldsratt. I'm looking forward to it. I like Thimig tremendously. I recall how marvellously he acted in *The Thomson Brothers*. How he came and said, 'I'd just like to work.'

He said these words so brilliantly. I sensed that he understood people who want work. He understood them so profoundly. He said, 'I'd just like to work.' He said it with a gesture. So noble.

I think it's quite unnatural that life only lasts as long as it lasts, fifty, seventy years. Perhaps I'm living all lives.

Perhaps I'll achieve something one day. I'll act and write, or I'll live. Live nicely, or I'll paint. Pictures of the sky and the earth, the water, woods and meadows.

I'm lying in bed, breathing. Perhaps somebody will read this after I'm dead. I wish him luck.

Why do I think so much about death? Perhaps because I fear that I will not have done anything.

Strange, isn't it?

Well then. I will achieve something. I'll have children. I'll write a book, paint a picture.

Dying does not matter. I will fight for your good world. *I promise. I will keep my promise.*

WEDNESDAY, 17 NOVEMBER 1937, VIENNA

In bed.

I went to *The Sunken Bell*. Thimig was in it. I love Thimig. On Sunday I'm going to see *Talisman*. Thimig's in that, too.

I don't want to go to school any more. I want to do . . . what should I write?

. . . Goodnight! . . . Best of luck!

SUNDAY, 28 NOVEMBER 1937, VIENNA

I've been to see a beautiful work of art: *La Grande Illusion*.

I think that people are good if they want to be.

There were so many beautiful things in this film. It's all said so delicately.

It's a war film. And again I think that I will fight for a better world. It's better to think through all of that than to write it down.

MONDAY, 29 NOVEMBER 1937, VIENNA

I like walking through the streets. Two days ago there was a motorbike accident. A man was bleeding from his forehead. The policeman pushed the man's hat away from his face. It was dark. And looked at the man's bloody forehead. It was a nice gesture. Perhaps it wasn't meant as nicely as it looked.

On the tram there was a lady with a child on her arm. The child was wrapped in a pink flannel cloth. Fastened with a safety pin. The child had a yellow face and was terribly thin. Its eyes were tiny and sad. It was sucking a lollipop and coughing wretchedly. It was a child, a little worm. A lady gave the mother some money and said, 'Buy something for the child.'

Father and daughter.

MONDAY, 6 DECEMBER 1937, VIENNA

I cannot get my mind around the fact that my father is dead. Sometimes I feel it when I'm alone, doubtful. Then I want to go to him. I miss him so much on those occasions. Such a support. Something wonderful. No, I cannot. Really cannot. I feel it when I see the books, see the photographs. Papa was handsome. I'd like to marry someone like Papa. As a young man. It's terrible not to have a father. But I will do Papa proud. I want to. Without a doubt. I have the feeling that Papa was a Frenchman. In France. The charm, the elegance — it's all French. Papa once said that an Italian had told him, 'He who thinks like that dies laughing.' That's beautifully put. I want it to have happened like that. I'd give everything for Papa to be here with me. Just when I could have done with him, he's gone. If Papa had died today, I think I would have liked to have died with him. Death is everywhere.

Everybody who lives will die. Grandmother. I love her. She's an old woman. And she's been through so much. One should never be hard with her. I mean upset. I like Uncle Oskar.

I'm fond of Jean. Because he's nice. He's virtuous. There's something childish, handsome, gentle about him. I think he'll always be like that. Some woman will be disappointed. He ought to find a girl who is as virtuous as he. Jean plays the piano. Like pearls. Each sound drips into the heart. The heart gets wet. I'd like to kiss him on the forehead. He has beautiful, delicate, white hands. Fine wrists. He's a child. I'd like to mother him.

It's strange that I'm not in love with him. He's so distant from me. He has beautiful blue eyes. Whenever I meet people like that I think: I really would have fallen in love with him. It cannot work with Jean. Another opportunity gone. I feel that perhaps something ought to have come of it.

I think I believe in reincarnation.

Strange that we only see death in front of us. It's behind us, too. Everything that's happened before one's own life is death. Did you suffer back then? Yes? Before your life was death. Think about it. Who can prove to you that there was life before you? Don't accept anything dead. Always create something new. Create from within yourself. Don't believe in alien things. *Believe yourself*. Before you there was death; there will be death behind you. You alone are life. So live! Have a nice life! Make life your life.

That's very muddled, isn't it?

FRIDAY, 17 DECEMBER 1937, VIENNA

People always write in diaries when they're misunderstood. A boy (Friedl) who was at our Matura party has invited me to go with him and another boy and girl on a six-day skiing trip. It costs twenty schillings. No further expenses. When I tried to discuss it with Mama, she said, 'Please don't go on.'

That's very funny. Mama always does that. With the result that I don't talk any more about the things that concern me. With the result that: 'My God, my children don't tell me anything! Am I not their mother, for goodness sake?'

Well, I grant you my reason for wanting to go is not very lofty and cere-bral. But perhaps it's important for me.

I'm fed up with ancient relatives. I like young people. I feel at home with them. We talk about things that even interest young people. We're gay, we have fun ... Old people talk about things I couldn't care less about, etc.

As any discussion between Ruth and Mama was rejected, I resolved to put together a written dialogue. (I'm absolutely certain Papa would have talked to me about it.)

A. I was invited on a ski course today. I'd be going with a boy I danced with once. And another boy and girl. For a six-day skiing trip.

B. You're not going to say yes, are you?

A. Why not?

B. Well, you don't even know the people.

A. So?

B. It's not suitable for a young girl . . . with completely strange people!

A. It may well not be suitable, but as I'd like to go, and as I feel the need to spend a few fabulous days with young people, the impropriety has already taken place, wouldn't you say? Its execution is just a minor point.

B. I'm just afraid that you'll be terribly disappointed. You probably imagine these young people to be wonderful, ideal individuals, who are refreshed by nature, who discuss philosophical problems. Are you not afraid of being disappointed?

A. First, I think what you say about ideal individuals is totally incorrect. Young people are young people. And they've definitely got more in common with each other than young people do with old people. Don't you think? . . . I have a horror of ancient relatives, old fogies. They talk about the most tiresome, uninteresting things. At length, asthmatically. Ghastly! . . . Maybe it's because I only know old people that I love children so much.

B. You're forgetting school, I think.

A. Oh yes! School. But you don't get close enough there. Four young people in nature, on the other hand. You do get close. Without doubt.

B. So you don't think you'd be disappointed at all.

Ruth and Judith often went skiing. This photograph shows them with a mutual friend, Grete. Judith is on the left and Ruth in the middle.

A. There's a fifty per cent chance of disappointment. But disappointments are enriching. I will learn that young people are not always young. That nature in itself is not enough to bring young people close. But right now, at this moment, I want to see it as it is. I want to be in the mountains with young people. Skiing. Maybe the disappointment will come afterwards. But why should I agonise now about whether I'll be disappointed or not?

Of course Mama was proved right. Always the same. Mama wasn't expecting anything different. And it would have been better had I said nothing at all to her. Ugh! Isn't it the same as confiscating someone's post? The girl from a good home, ugh!

THURSDAY, 23 DECEMBER 1937, VIENNA

Christmas! Lovely, so lovely. But actually not.

I really have no idea why I'm sad. Perhaps because yesterday Frau Dr Brauchbar said, 'Do you see Williger occasionally? He really likes you.'

I felt so miserable.

I've sent him an ill-mannered letter. A common letter that he'll read and be hurt by. I don't know if I'm sorry. Maybe it's a good thing.

But the fact is that Williger is an intelligent and good man, and one should not ignore that. Maybe he's a very estimable man, and I've behaved like a downright base and common girl. Perhaps I haven't sensed or thought that one mustn't repel the love of another person like that. That it might cause great pain.

I've been working very hard. I know why. Because of my horror of disgusting old people.

On Sunday I'm going skiing with Friedl, a young boy. My dream! And now I'm thinking about just how much more the disgusting old man can give me than the young, dim-witted boy.

I heard something very good: young people fancy themselves to be original and reckless; often they're nothing more than tactless and ordinary.

That's me exactly. It's sad. But what can I do?

Now is a time when I want to talk to somebody, a time when I'm very alone.

Maybe that's why I'm thinking about Williger. I'm sure it is.

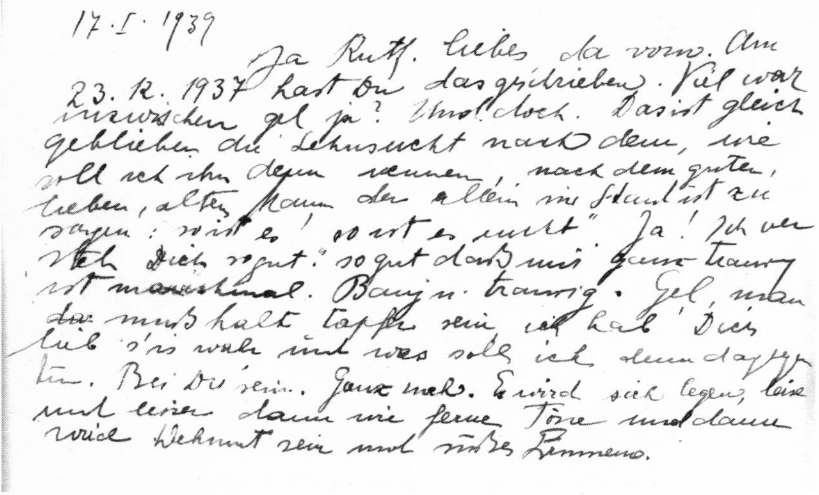

[handwritten diary page in German]

Before she left for Norway in 1939 Ruth read her diary from autumn 1937 again and added this paragraph.

AFTERTHOUGHT – TUESDAY, 17 JANUARY 1939, VIENNA

Yes, Ruth, my dear, that's what you wrote on 23.12.1937. A lot has changed in the meantime, hasn't it? And yet. That has stayed the same, the yearning for – what should I call him – the good, lovely old man, who alone can say, 'That's right! That's wrong!' Yes! I understand you so well. So well that I sometimes feel terribly sad. Anxious and sad. One just has to be brave, I love you, it's true. What can I do to resist it? To be with you. Very close. He will lie down, gently, then there will be distant sounds, heaps of melancholy and sweet tears.

The last autumn in Austria

SEPTEMBER – DECEMBER 1938

The diary from autumn 1938 is a completely full, eighty-sided, unruled quarto note-book. On the front is a note in Ruth's hand: 'Do not burn!' She took the notebook with her to Norway. The previous diary was lost, as was the one (or ones) that followed.

Austria is now a part of the German Reich. In autumn 1938 the family is forced to move to Obere Donaustraße 43, part of the Jewish quarter in the centre of Vienna. They now live an austere existence in a small room and share a lavatory with the Singer family. From now on Ruth and Judith attend a Jewish school.

This diary begins with a summary of the political events since Hitler's annexation of Austria in March. Then there is a discussion of the Munich Conference in the autumn, where the British foreign secretary agrees to Hitler's march into Czechoslovakia. During the night of 9–10 November throughout the German Reich, there were attacks on Jews, murders, burglaries of Jewish shops, and the smashing of windowpanes. This Kristallnacht *coincides with the eighteenth birthday of the schoolgirl Ruth Maier.*

Autumn 1938 will be the last that the Maier family spends in Austria.

Ruth's sister, Judith, leaves Vienna on 11 December and travels to Britain. Her mother, Irma, and grandmother, Anna, follow her during the course of the following year.

Ruth becomes aware of her identity as a Jew. She is horrified by the brutality she witnesses. She draws extreme pictures of Christmas celebrations in Nazi Germany, of which Vienna is now a part. And she quotes from the Sermon on the Mount.

Ruth also describes her Jewish friends who are about to be scattered across the globe. She writes fictitious letters of admiration – to the Russian author Maxim Gorky, who is dead; and to the Jewish actor Ernst Deutsch, who is living in exile.

The cover of Ruth's last diary from Austria.

TUESDAY, 27 SEPTEMBER 1938

I've given up writing my last diary where I talk about my fear, then my cowardice, then my hope etc. Fear of what? Fear of what the German language knows as the beautiful word *Krieg* (war).

I'm going to try to describe the situation as unemotionally as possible.

When Hitler annexed Austria in March there was no talk of war. All the Austrians were celebrating and jumping about in excitement. Flags were hoisted; people hugged and kissed each other out of sheer joy.

The former leader, Schuschnigg, abandoned by England, France and Italy, was held prisoner in the Hotel Metropole and then the Belvedere Palace. Cardinal Innitzer gave his blessing to Greater Germany. The Jews were downgraded from their existing status – which might not have been one of equality, but was at least tolerable – to that of non-humans, pigs etc.

Soon after the *Anschluss* some angry voices made themselves heard. They had imagined it would turn out very differently.

But these dissenters were soon sidetracked by Jew-baiting and suchlike. In May, two months later, Hitler marched into Sudeten Germany. The reaction of the Czechoslovak Republic was to order a general mobilisation.* Agitated and annoyed, Hitler now started to campaign against Czechoslovakia. The Sudeten Germans were oppressed, he said, German children were not allowed to be educated in German schools, women were being abused etc.

The issue became ever more complicated. An English adviser, Lord Runciman, talked to the Czechoslovak government. Negotiations began. Konrad Henlein published the ten Karlsbad points: he demanded a separate army and foreign policy for the Sudeten Germans. A few days later German radio broadcast a proclamation by Henlein: We want to return home to the Reich. The international situation became ever tenser. England and France don't know what to do next. Soviet Russia promises to give assistance to Czechoslovakia. Chamberlain goes to good old Berchtesgaden and discusses with Hitler a peaceful solution to the international situation.

* Ruth is mistaken here: The Czechoslovak government mobilised the army in 1938, suspecting that a German invasion was imminent, but no offensive took place.

Soon afterwards the Hodža government 'painfully' accepts the German demands, but resigns straight afterwards. General Syrový, who was trained in the USSR, takes Hodža's place. The tension increases. Martial law is imposed over more Sudeten German areas. Syrový mobilises the entire country. More and more refugees arrive from Sudeten Germany and start campaigning actively for war.

On 26 September Hitler hands Prague a memorandum: the surrender of purely German areas. Plebiscite in the other German–Czech areas. In his speech of 26 September Hitler promises that this is Germany's final territorial demand in Europe. He understands that to thirty million Poles the Polish Corridor, i.e. access to the sea, is a matter of survival. He's never had designs on Alsace-Lorraine. The German population there, he says, is at its happiest when nobody is fighting over them. He says nothing about the South Tyrol. A line has been drawn at the border there. Mussolini and he have always been in agreement. But his love of peace stops at Sudeten Germany. He says the German-German people cannot and will not continue to look on while German blood is being subjugated. The German memorandum has been handed over. Czechoslovakia must say 'yes' or 'no' by 1 October. 'Herr Beneš, it is your decision.' Those were his last words.

That's the situation at the moment. Today is 27 September. And what happens in the future will . . .

War and peace will be decided on 1 Oct.

Now this afternoon, Brno radio announced the resolution of the British government not to bomb the civilian population should war break out. At the beginning of hostilities France says it would undertake an offensive to relieve the Czech front.

Perhaps I'm just trying to persuade myself that we're on the verge of a great turning point in history. On the verge of a bloody, gruesome spectacle, yes, certainly. Perhaps after this will come light, sun and freedom and *peace*.

I couldn't start loving these people again until they've washed away what I hate about them with blood. Perhaps they'll rise again, purified by grief and misery – but hold on! There must be another option. I do not want to experience the grief, unhappiness, pain, death and horror.

Jean! Why do I think about him so often at the moment? Because he will have to murder, too? He, the Frenchman with the pale, narrow hands, the child's face with his thousand melodies played with those fingers which know only how to sweep over the ivory piano keys. Jean, whom everybody loves. Who sees the world so childishly with such trustful eyes, who shies away from close contact with girls.

Susi, whom I really have loved very much with his brown, sinewy arms, and Williger, and Egon. Better not to think about it.

And when I think of them all. Williger, Egon with a rifle. Then I think it mustn't happen. It mustn't and will not happen. Of course it won't happen for the simple reason that it just doesn't exist.

And when I think that Papa . . .

But I don't have to think about them all individually. About their lovely faces, their lovely habits.

I want to think about the French with their *esprit*, their charm. About their language, which I love so much. About the Russians with their Dostoevsky, their Tolstoy, their Gorky. Their Russian peasants with their wives and children, beloved mothers. About the Italians with their sunny language with their *Divina Commedia*.

I don't want to think about all of them. I just want to think that they are all people, that together they have the capacity to fight for a better goal, that they are not capable of annihilating each other. I want to believe that one human being doesn't necessarily have to feel horror, fear and hatred in the presence of another.

They are playing popular songs on the wireless. It is a funny, ghastly world.

❦

WEDNESDAY, 28 SEPTEMBER 1938, VIENNA

1 October, the ultimatum that Hitler has set, is getting closer. There is tension, nervousness in the air. Or am I just imagining it?

Chamberlain made a speech yesterday. He said he had done everything humanly possible to maintain peace. Now he cannot see any further way of helping the cause of peace. The last thing the British people wanted to do was to go to war for such a far-off land as Czechoslovakia, but if one power on earth believed it could use terror to spread panic and fear throughout the world, then . . .

Roosevelt delivered a message of peace to all European countries. Hitler answered that *because* he knew the consequences of a European war, he could not accept the responsibility for such a war.

And me, I've been looking at the wonderful picture of Papa when he was young. It looks so peaceful, it gives off confidence and peace . . . The sweet, white skin, the hands . . .

I envy Mama! I would have loved Papa so much as his wife. We would have got on so well, Papa and I. Ludwig and Ruth.

My child will be called Ludwig.

THURSDAY, 29 SEPTEMBER 1938, VIENNA

Mussolini, Daladier, Chamberlain and Hitler are meeting today in Munich. They will be discussing war and peace.

I'd really like to join the Red Cross.

SUNDAY, 2 OCTOBER 1938, VIENNA

Threat of war is over. Hitler got what he wanted.

I was with the blind people yesterday. I really enjoy visiting them.

Today I was at the Chajes-Gymnasium* for the first time. This school is so wildly nationalistic. It is a danger one cannot underestimate and, who knows, perhaps it's just because I'm opposed to this that I'm no Zionist.

The headmaster gave a guarded and compelling speech full of Jewish national consciousness. He is a small, browbeaten man who moves his head from one side to the other. He lectured us on our responsibility, on 'acting with dignity', and he expressed his conviction that we would all end up in

* A Jewish grammar school in Vienna that Ruth and her sister now have to attend.

Palestine. He hoped that even those who were 'christened and godless' would enter the Jewish community.

It was a strange feeling us sitting there, us young people, boys and girls, everything around us hostile and horrible, on our own . . .

Yes, that's exactly what the danger is: 'the Jewish community'. My community used to be the human race; is Jewishness now suddenly supposed to replace humanity?? There is a path leading from humanity through nationality to bestiality!!!* Sinister words, I don't know who said them first, but they've proved to be utterly accurate.

Today the headmaster said, 'One can explain and excuse National Socialism, but still condemn it.' Now, I can explain, excuse and *understand* Zionism (clearly linked to nationalism), but I condemn it. Precisely because, as Anny Schermann. said quite rightly today, I permanently feel the consequences of nationalism in my own body.

Yes, I am quite convinced that national consciousness is the last thing on my mind at the moment. And yet, is there not something completely negative, unwholesome, about always wanting 'assimilation'? One's own demise, the demise of one's individuality? So at the moment I find myself swaying between socialism and, however I *dread* having to write it, nationalism.

And perhaps it is this, this very swaying from one to the other, which has become a symbol of the Jew, the Jewish person.

But, to bring this point to an end, the truth is that 75 per cent of the young Jewish intelligentsia has moved over to Zionism.

And the blind people. What are all these problems, admittedly critical ones these days, compared with the blind people up on Hohe Warte . . .

The young boys, the girls, the old people, but most of all the children. I often think that if I had the power to give sight then I would start with the children. Because they are the most innocent, the purest, the most eager for sunlight and life. Yes! I'd start with the youngest. With Silvi. She is so young, so milky, full of bright red blood. And yet she's blind. You can often forget this, you look at her dark eyes, and then when she wants to show you a doll and has to feel along the wall. When she can't find the doorway, when she asks, 'Who are you?' When . . .

* The line comes from the Austrian writer Franz Grillparzer (1791–1872).

It's so sad. And she's so grateful for all the nice and good things you do for her.

And Janek! With his lovely compositions and his poem, 'The Sunshine'. 'Dearest sunshine be/Ever close to me.' You do really feel this little, this tiny child's fear of the eternal darkness. And how he loves to put his hand in mine, and how he loves to have his spiky hair gently stroked. Recently, without being prompted, he told me about a dream he'd had. 'I'm always dreaming that I've got a little brother, his name is Mozu, I really love him, I always protect him and look after him and we share everything with each other.' How sad that this blind child, who often bangs into ledges, boxes and doors, and who writes 'Dearest sunshine be/Ever close to me', this child dreams about a little brother whom he protects and looks after. Janek! I love him so much. Last time he played me his compositions. They are so sweet and lovely: 'Birthday' and 'Farewell to my parents'.

Yes! Parents! They all long for them. One fifteen-year-old boy, Ludwig, told me a poem: 'Dear Mother'.

This poem is perhaps one of the saddest and, I suppose, most moving of all. The longing for a dear, kind mother, all these sad, lonely feelings that everybody knows and that the blind people, the blind children and young people, must feel particularly strongly.

Perhaps this is the place to describe a little scene I was part of.

Holding Silvi's hand I open a door, it's dark, I can't see anything, not a glimmer of light, a boy is sitting at the piano and playing, alone in the dark, and singing... 'When the children are in the dark'.

TUESDAY, 4 OCTOBER 1938, VIENNA

DEAR MOTHER

You do all the best for me.
How I love you!
We will not see each other for a long time now.
I am getting sad and frightened.
My heart is pained.

You have always sat by my bed.
If only I had you by me always!

Ludwig, blind.

WEDNESDAY, 5 OCTOBER 1938, VIENNA

It's early, nobody on the streets. A Jewish man, young, well-dressed, comes round the corner. Two SS men appear. Both of them hit the Jew, he staggers . . . holds up his head, moves on.

I, Ruth Maier, eighteen years old, now pose the following question as a human being. As a human being I ask the world whether it should be like this . . . I ask why it is allowed, why a German is permitted to hit a Jew for the simple reason that he is a German and the other man a Jew!

I'm not talking about pogroms, outrages against Jews. Window smashing, looting of homes . . . These don't express so clearly the incalculable brutality.

It's here, in this punch. If there is a God . . . I don't believe in one and I don't like to utter his name . . . but now I have to say it to Him up above . . . if there is a God: This punch, it must be . . . it must be paid for in blood!!!

And I want to tell you, all of you, you Aryans, Englishmen, Frenchmen who condone this: all of you must bear responsibility for this punch, for you have allowed it to happen.

And there's so much sorrow. Never anything but sorrow. What illustrates that better than the Jew who staggers and then . . . moves on?

Susi told us about Wehrgasse. There was a policeman screaming at some Jews. He got into a rage and shouted things like 'Jewish swine!' and much more besides. He stood in front of the Jews, bawled them out. Susi thought: What happens . . . if he hits me? There's nothing I can do about it . . . nothing at all . . . But it's good . . . very good . . . the more the better . . . the more the better. Do you want any more, you swine, you monsters, you beasts? Oh, I could just spit at the lot of you. Or perhaps I should describe the picture from the 'Eternal Jew' exhibition. Shall I describe to you the faces of the Jews, the Jews from Dachau? Those starving, emaciated faces. Intelligent, transparent, full of spirit, shaved bald, with high foreheads, and underneath: 'The Doctor', 'The Shopkeeper'.

Shall I show you? They've sewn a small yellow patch on to their clothes because we are Jews.

Or shall I list the many, many men who are Jewish: Heine, Börne,* Schnitzler, Marx, Lassalle, Zweig and many others. Just take a look. These are men of the people you are persecuting because it is of a different race.

In the past people used to believe in evil spirits, in masters. Now they believe in race.

And us, are we not all martyrs of race?

I could weep for the Jews now, for my childhood dreams of humanity and its redemption.

I don't believe in this any more. No, it's true, I've lost my faith.

Today is Yom Kippur. The long day, the Jewish day of fasting. The SA have devised a joke for it. They've informed the Jews that they have to leave their homes within three days and leave Germany within one month. 'Or you'll be beaten up.'

Is that the golden Viennese heart, or the apex of bestiality? We're used to being bullied. But what's unheard of is this enjoyment of toying with one's defenceless victim. It's the urge to torture which civilisation has suppressed. A frenzy of sadism.

I despair, yes I despair . . . Recently there's been a spate of Sudeten German refugees from Czechoslovakia coming into Austria, or should I say the Ostmark.†

Allegedly they've been tortured and martyred over there because they're German. Now they're arriving in Vienna, moving into Jewish apartments and demanding – that's to say taking – bedlinen, clothes etc.

So these people who have been tortured and martyred are taking the first opportunity to torture and martyr others . . . And the Jews, what a great object of martyrdom they are!

You can take it all out on them, all your suppressed tendencies, urges, your feelings of inferiority, your bestiality. Whatever you want! We have no

* Karl Ludwig Börne (1786–1837), German political writer and satirist.
† The official name given to the former territory of Austria after *Anschluss*.

weapons and, by God, we cannot defend ourselves. You can send our fathers to Dachau, poison our mothers with gas, and our sons have to crawl across the border like animals!

I think of an episode outside the tax office in Porzellangasse. It was raining. We Jews had been standing there in the rain, soaked to the bone and freezing cold, since seven o'clock that morning. A street sweeper appeared with his broom and bellowed at us, waved his hands in the air, shouted. He was foaming at the mouth: 'If you don't go away, you bastards, I'll drag you all away.' How delighted he was, the street sweeper, that he could take out all his fury on us, the inferior race. The street sweeper!

An Aryan woman went in before us, although we'd been standing in a queue for hours and she'd only just arrived at the last moment. When she tried to apologise somebody said, 'But my dear lady, you do not need to apologise. We're second-class human beings.'

He said it without any pathos. It sounded so dreadful even though we're not second-class human beings, we are . . . what are we in fact?

SUNDAY, 9 OCTOBER 1938, VIENNA

There's never been an event in history so full of misery, sorrow, humiliation, shame and brutality.

I'm amazed that we can *endure* it. That in spite of everything, we don't turn on the gas tap or jump into the Danube.

Three days before giving birth, a Jewish woman crosses the border illegally. The family is torn apart . . . the wife a cook in England, the husband in Belgium illegally, the mother still in Germany, the brother in Dachau, the sister...

It's too hideous for us to imagine. On Yom Kippur, SA men went into flats in the 18th, 19th and 17th districts and ordered the inhabitants to pack up and leave within twenty-four hours. You can imagine the terrible scenes. Not the finest of people. A few people turned on the gas taps. They were at the Ehrlichs' place and Frau Kamil's. Hildegard's parents wanted to go to the Vienna Woods . . . in the twentieth century . . . No, I beg you, it was a joke, a hoax . . . Jewish women and girls had to clean up the temple with soap and brush . . .

SA men enter flats, commandeer books, say, 'Look, the Jews read Heine.' They burn Heine, Zweig, Schnitzler. 'International riff-raff.'

Some people just cannot take any more! Frau Herr's mother killed herself!

To be away from here!

SUNDAY, 16 OCTOBER 1938, VIENNA

Pogroms!

They are beating up Jews and want to hang them from street lamps. They shout, '*Hepp, hepp!*'* The emergency services have a lot of work to do. The temple is being destroyed. They're tearing off the beards of old Jewish men, they're bashing the women. They're smashing windows. Make a note of this, Ruth. It's seven o'clock in the evening and now it's starting up again. In the small alleys: Schiffamtsgasse, Leopoldsgasse etc.

Käthe has blue rings round her eyes. It's gruesome. You can't say anything. You press your lips tightly together. Medieval. Those dreams, my childhood dreams, my love of people, these wretched beasts . . . They want to murder me because I am a Jew. No, that's how it is and I have to ask, 'Are we cattle, animals? Are we people?' 'Yes,' Herr Goebbels says, 'in the same way that fleas are animals.'

1938 was a very dark year on earth!

And I love the Jews, that's the one positive thing. I love them because they are suffering. I love them from the bottom of my heart. Yes, I almost love them physically. These intelligent faces. Let them cry, '*Hepp, hepp!*' I am a Jew! And let them all know it, let them hang me from the tallest spire of the church tower, kick me, spit on me, beat me black and blue – I am a Jew . . . What more do you want? Cut open my veins, so my Jewish blood flows. Howl and scream! You swine! And if you ever read these lines, then grab my hair,

* A rallying cry first used in anti-Jewish riots in early nineteenth-century Germany.

hit me. I'm at your disposal . . . Afterwards you can play jazz music and enjoy yourselves. Because it really is a pleasure.

Yes! I'm even forgetting that there are still fields, golden ears of corn, sun, gentle wind, stars, blue sky. It's all so distant now . . .

If you really want, I'll paint it for you – a picture. Above his face the Jew has a red streak, you've put out his one eye and ripped off his beard. Do you enjoy that?

And you students, you sentimental do-gooders, socialists, communists, dreamers, enthusiasts with your white hands. Why do you let it happen? Why?

I can imagine everything. Everything! And I would let it happen because I wouldn't be able to do anything else. If I were still conscious I would think, 'The more the better.' But if you touch my father, I don't know what I'd do. I think I'd go for a revolver. Because you mustn't touch my father. I'd drop to my knees before you, ask you, beg you, 'Don't harm my father! Don't harm my father!'

And I'm consciously becoming a Jew, I can feel it. I cannot help it.

I apologise – my mind is all over the place. My writing is so incoherent!

OCTOBER 1938, VIENNA

It's evening again. October! On 10 November I'll be eighteen. So young! Still. And yet! I'll never be seventeen again. Never fourteen again. Every age is different for us girls. From one to twenty. And I'm pure, untouched. Aren't I? My body is very beautiful.

It was yesterday that they attacked another Jewish home and there are many young Jewish boys in bandages. Beating up Jews is a sport. The director of the home said, 'It is a peculiar morality to beat up Jews' and he's right. It is actually a peculiar morality . . . Yesterday I walked past a Jewish shop. The glass windows had been cracked. A tiny hole and sharp lines. It looked so wicked.

I may go to England as a nanny. Maybe. What do you think?

TUESDAY, 1 NOVEMBER 1938, VIENNA

Dear Herr Gorky,

I know that you are dead, but I must write to you. I *must*, to thank you from the very bottom of my heart for your two stories: *Children*. I wept while reading them – that is irrelevant – but I felt so good, so grateful. You are a writer; perhaps it is only writers who can have such pure and clear feelings. All the Jews in the whole world, in England, France, Germany, Palestine and the USA, all of them weep when reading your two stories: *Children*. They are all grateful that there is somebody who empathises. There is so much sorrow, but now there is hope. We thank you!

WEDNESDAY, 2 NOVEMBER 1938, VIENNA

I was with the blind people yesterday. One of them wanted to commit suicide because . . . well, because of the current situation. He's blind now. He has a fine Jewish face, a bright forehead with a scar on one side . . . Now that he's blind he loves life. He walks around uncertainly, his hands stretched out in front of him . . . He's forty years old and is *sooo* in love with Silvi. Sooo in love! He presses her to himself and says, 'My darling girl, good girl.' He likes to feel her head close to his chest, he strokes the back of her neck and says, 'You ought to have a whole lot of happiness, always have an uncle to look after you.'

'What does that mean, "look after"?'

'If somebody loves you very much, gives you food, buys an apartment . . .'

Now he's blind and he wants to die – can that be allowed to happen?

THURSDAY, 3 NOVEMBER 1938, VIENNA

I've had a letter from Williger. Mrs Wellum, with whom I might be taking a position, has made an enquiry to him about me.

Dear Ruth,*

This morning I was asked by a Mrs Wellum, Essex, to supply her with a report of a certain Ruth Maier she is contemplating to take into her employ. I did my best and I hope you will get the job.

I was pretty surprised at you still being in Vienna. Some weeks ago I learnt from a letter, I think from Mrs Brauchbar, that you and your sister were leaving for France.

Now I have the prospect of meeting you here.

One thing I want to tell you in advance. You will be admitted to this country only for domestic work and many Austrian girls of your education were a bit bewildered at the computations they were subjected to. But I think that the most humble position in this country is to be preferred to your present life.

My love to your mother and all the best to yourself.

Yours sincerely

You see!

FRIDAY, 4 NOVEMBER 1938, VIENNA

Well, it all brewed up again yesterday, it just appeared again like a ghost, and yet I felt it so closely . . . I know precisely why I cannot forget it: everybody, every single normal person who longs for a little romance, for a few golden moments in his life, for stupid, really stupid, useless things, cooks up a short novel, a little secret of his life, a corner where he assembles everything that is sweet and dear to him, and everything that is buried deep within him. He loves this corner, he doesn't want to separate himself from it, it's where he takes his disappointments, yearnings, his tiny dream. And if (like me) you're small and a nobody, you dwell on these dreams instead of trying to achieve something, irrespective of whether it's a bald professor who's taught you Latin, or a beggar standing at the street corner with pale hands. It's the same if you think: That's the fulfilment, the dream etc.

*Williger wrote this letter to Ruth in English. The stylistic and grammatical errors have been left as in the original.

I recognise it when I think of him, of Williger, literally – I mean in great detail – when I see people who pass by make the same small movements he does, or use the same words. Then I'm filled with horror because I cannot imagine him physically, in the flesh so to speak.

Everybody has their Williger. Even Grandmother. In her case it was a forester, a Christian she was not allowed to marry. Isn't there something Williger-like about one's first love?

TUESDAY, 8 NOVEMBER 1938, VIENNA

A small, seventeen-year-old emigrant made an attempt on a German diplomat's life. He's a Polish Jew.* My God!

The mood of despondency has returned; the air is full of sadness. The Jews are sneaking along walls like baited animals. Now it's dead. No Jew goes outside. We're all scared that they'll beat us up because a Polish Jew wanted to kill a German.

FRIDAY, 11 NOVEMBER 1938, VIENNA

We've been attacked! Yesterday was the most awful day of my life. Now I know what pogroms are, I know what *human beings* are capable of; human beings: made in the likeness of God.

At school the headmaster told us they were burning temples, making arrests and beating people up. There's a lorry by the school gate . . . they've arrested three teachers . . . then we're called to the telephone in turn . . . like in an abattoir, we didn't dare go out into the street, we laughed . . . cracked jokes . . . we were nervous . . . Dita and I took a taxi home – it's a hundred

---

* On 7 November 1938 Herschel Grynszpan shot Ernst vom Rath in the German Embassy in Paris. Rath died of his wounds two days later. The assassination served as the excuse for the nationwide pogrom known as *Reichskristallnacht*.

metres. We raced through the streets, it was as if war had broken out . . . People stood and stared, the air was cold, figures were dotted around and in front there was this lorry full of Jews, standing up like livestock on its way to the slaughterhouse! I'll never forget this sight – I must never forget it: Jews like livestock on their way to slaughter . . . People stood and stared.

We slipped into the house like hunted animals, panted up the stairs. Then it started. They hit people, arrested them, smashed up apartments etc. We sat there at home, so pale, and from the streets Jews came to us like corpses. I asked, 'What's it like outside?' – 'Ugly.'

They took forty-six reichsmarks from Grete L; they yelled; they hit a seventy-five-year-old woman and she screamed that they'd smashed up her apartment with a hammer etc.

I walked through the streets today. It's like being in a cemetery. Everything destroyed with desire and pleasure, Jewish shops closed up, nothing but shutters. Then, a note: The owner of this café is Aryan. Do not damage.

In the *Volksruf* it says, 'Where is the yellow badge?'

And even if we have to wear a yellow badge, they cannot take away our customs, what's inside us, our world that we carry around with us. And that's why they take out all their rage on windowpanes, beat us up and scream, 'Death to the Jews!'

Down below an Aryan said, 'I gave the Jew a shove and he stumbled right into the corner.'

Human beings, the likenesses of the gods! And then: 'Blessed are they which are persecuted for righteousness' sake.'

SUNDAY, 13 NOVEMBER 1938, VIENNA

Next door a Jew is playing the violin. Sweetly, albeit with the odd mistake . . . So in spite of everything, in spite of pogroms, beatings etc. If the Jew next door plays the violin I'll look at Michelangelo pictures with my heart pounding.

Actually, I just feel an emptiness inside me at the moment: I'm neither especially sad, nor especially jolly. Everything is so dreadful that I cannot grasp it any longer. I sing, make jokes, and yet. It's misery the like of which I've never seen before.

We've just been to Gildemeester, a Jewish aid organisation. There was a pretty young woman there with deep, dark eyes and a fine line round her mouth. She had two children with her. The husband is in Dachau and there's been no letter from him for four weeks. She must love her husband very much; you could see that from her eyes. Her children were so small; she walked with them from door to door.

Then there was an older man. A locksmith from the provinces. Been expelled. All those from the provinces have been expelled.

They're even beating up men with war decorations, medals.

On the streets . . . nothing but removal lorries, massive and simple lorries full of bedlinen, crates, rocking chairs, coffee mills – everything in a heap: a Jew's home, just a Jew's home.

And the newspapers! Full of 'Jews out!', 'Jewish sods!'

We're so defenceless and they do what they like with us. The headmaster says, 'We must find the path within ourselves.'

FRIDAY, 25 NOVEMBER 1938, VIENNA

It's so sad!

SATURDAY, 26 NOVEMBER 1938, VIENNA

Dear Herr Deutsch!

I do not think you will ever receive this letter. I know nothing at all about you, save for the fact that you are a great actor, a wonderful actor, and that you have left for America. But I want to write to you. Yes, I do!

I am so happy that you have left. Left here. For you, too, would have been beaten as we are being beaten and they would have sent you to Dachau, just as they are sending our fathers to Dachau. They would have sewn a yellow badge on to your coat and you would have had to work outside breaking stones. And it is so painful to see people that you love and worship look sad. That is why I am happy that you are no longer here, but far away in America, that you can act again.

That people can enjoy your performances again.

That people are laughing and crying again at your performances, that you will often be able to forget us here in Germany. I am not envious, but just happy that you can act again outside this country.

I want to keep writing for a bit. Yes, I know that I am saying a lot. I want to do it for you, because you have beautiful hands . . . I went to the Eternal Jew exhibition and saw so many handsome photographs of you. I was so happy that you had not been forgotten. I only saw handsome and wonderful individuals there: Heine, Schnitzler and all the others. And you were among them; I was so happy. Do not think about what is happening here. At the beginning it was said that you had committed suicide. Nobody told me. I only found out about it later . . . Your acting in *Ghosts* was so marvellous. And I honestly believe I will see you act again, often. I do! I hope so, with all my heart . . . Back then I sent you hellebores – once it was violets – and that was my way of saying that I worship you. If *those* violets still have a hint of their fragrance and have not totally withered, then . . . that would be so lovely . . . I used to wait so often outside the theatre with flowers and whenever you arrived . . . well, I just did not have the nerve. You had such beautiful white hair. Whenever I pass the theatre now I close my eyes, think about the past and imagine you there again . . . Then I'm so happy that you went away from here and are acting. Please believe me.

Please write to me – no, not write – just think about me for a second before you throw this letter in the waste-paper basket. My name is 'Ruth'. Please think about me, 'Ruth'!

Ernst Deutsch (1890–1969) was a Jewish actor, born in Prague, who also worked in Vienna, Dresden and Berlin. He left Germany in 1933 and emigrated to America in 1938. Deutsch (right) is shown here with Joseph Cotten in Carol Reed's The Third Man *(1949).*

SUNDAY, 27 NOVEMBER 1938, VIENNA

This evening – no, late afternoon – we said goodbye to Uncle Rudi, Papa's friend. I noticed his eyes suddenly welling with tears. I was brave. Mama wept. We gave each other a firm handshake, Goodbye! Uncle Rudi the socialist also says I ought to think about going to Palestine, because as a Jew it's the only place I'd feel at home. It's this feeling of being at home, secure, human – that's what I imagine the Promised Land to be. Because the life I'd lead in England, France, maybe even in America, would only be that of an 'emigrant'. How tragic, how distressing this 'emigrant life' is. We, the German Jews of 1938, we know it. No house, no home, me dependent on you, you dependent on me, united by our destiny, by our sorrow. It sounds melodramatic, but that's how it is. Through our *sorrow* we're all holding on to each other tightly.

Is it not understandable that we're looking at Palestine for the first time with tears in our eyes? Think about it: we who are outcast, pale, deathly tired and battered, will we not, as children do, finally find our way back to our mother? And this mother is Palestine: the 'Promised Land', Erez Israel. The land: Erez. And will you hold it against us that our eyes glint, that we shudder when we think of 'the Land'. Of *our* land where we are at home. Yes! It's true, Uncle Rudi has fortified my belief in this, he *said* it, said out loud what until now had been stifled *within* me: we Jews are only at home 'in Palestine'. To that I'd like to add, 'today'. For tomorrow, tomorrow socialism will come. Then our home will be humanity, the world. Then we'll be able to live as human beings among human beings.

Well! I wanted to write about people who have secretly vanished. One to Palestine, one to New Zealand, and another to Bombay or Shanghai.

Ruth describes eleven friends. Four of the portraits are reproduced here.

Anny Schermann

I'm still attending the Chajes-Gymnasium with her. She wants to study medicine and she's a socialist. She's one of those progressive, 'emancipated' women. She reads Turgenev, Rilke etc. Apart from that she views *life* with open eyes; it's just that her intelligence makes her go on at length. This continual 'Oh, I've got something to discuss with you' at break time. Sometimes it really gets on my nerves. She has the habit of whispering constantly and the nauseating tendency to labour issues to death. Listen, I understand the need of immature people to fathom serious things by means of conversation and discussion. But this continual 'What do you think about . . . ?', is repellent. There's no doubt that Anny is bright, lovely, has a nice laugh, but . . .

And we've also had many nice and friendly chats. I remember the time we were going home along the Ringstraße together after the opera. It was autumn, there were yellow leaves on the ground, the sky was bright blue. We laughed so much and it was lovely . . . as perhaps it can only be when you're young.

If I were a boy I'd hate her, because there's something dreadfully coquettish about her. *Ghastly*! Perhaps I'm being unfair on you, Anny, but . . . but I don't mean it in a bad way.

Lizzy Kantor

She was the only girl I ever loved. It was perhaps the purest, most tender love in my life. A single word, a half-smile, a small gesture with the hand – all of these meant *soo* much to me . . . Right to the end, shortly before Lizzy went away, there was something wounded, something cautious in my behaviour towards her . . . I would speak nicely to her, always mindful of the love I'd had for her before . . . What it was about Lizzy that was so special, what attracted me to her, I don't know. She's not particularly bright, nor beautiful. She was always patronising, condescending. Often she was hurtful and tactless. Her observations were frequently stupid, so stupid, and yet she was thought of as bright. Her body was very delicate. I can remember it precisely. At the school doctor, in gymnastics . . . She gave me such happy times. Unconsciously natural. On the way to school! When it rained, in spring on Sternwartestraße. I always felt warmth in my heart, even just being able to walk beside her. The nicest time was on the skiing course. We sat there all together in the front bar. Soft music came from across the room. It was warm and I felt so happy . . . It was one of my best times . . . It's not that unusual for a girl to love a girl. *Love*, without any sensuality, but otherwise with the same tender feelings. In *The Magic Mountain* Hans Castorp speaks of his love for a boy whom he has only seen once. My feelings were very similar.

She's Jewish, of course. Now she's in Grenoble, continuing her studies. I loved Lizzy throughout my schooldays. Lizzy Kantor. This name still has such a heavenly ring for me. Lizzy never knew about my love. I told Dita and Anny Schermann about it.

Irene Epstein

A 'Polka' as the 'natives' like to call them these days. Very Jewish. Black, frizzy hair, pimples, no sharp lines, everything blurred, nothing taut about her body, as if it were made of plasticine. Satisfactory at gymnastics . . .

She really wanted to be my friend, she begged me, but in the longer term I couldn't abide her . . . Her intellect was very limited. In her stories she had a way of blathering on about an innocent episode and *that* annoyed me. I think she'll end up a garrulous, fat woman. That's what I thought. And I went with a person like that to see *Ghosts*, with Ernst Deutsch as Oswald. My teeth were *chattering* afterwards. My whole body was trembling . . . Irene said, 'If you listen to conversation in the street now it sounds so *banal* . . . ' I'd have loved to hit her there and then.

Nelly Freudemann

Typical Jewish dance school girl. Hair curled under at the ends, made up. Enterprising, with a little wit and brains to add. Sexually excitable. The sort of girl that has a very powerful effect on a certain type of man. Through her easy charm, her wit etc. She's always prepared to flirt, always has a clique of similar girls around her. Has the idea for a party etc. Where gossip thrives etc. I had a nice time with her on the skiing course. The two of us separated ourselves, got lost and clambered over a tree . . . Afterwards she said, full of astonishment, 'This Ruth Maier's a really nice girl!'

WEDNESDAY, 7 DECEMBER 1938, VIENNA

My God! Will I never, ever be able to forget!? I still have such a warm feeling in my heart when I think of him . . . Is there something weird about me? Must I always think of people I love wherever I am? Let's dissect your feelings. Think, Ruth. *Why*? Why don't you forget? I know why. I think I'll find something there that doesn't exist, yes, I think he'll give my life some *substance*. Nitwit!

You have to give *substance* to your life yourself. I *cannot*. Idiot! All this that I'm writing here is so mawkish. Forgetting, not forgetting, substance.

Mustiness is sticking my words together, and yet the ink is still fresh and I'm writing about living feelings.

THURSDAY, 8 DECEMBER 1938, VIENNA

Well, what on earth was wrong with me yesterday? I felt so pained and sad. These feelings from yesterday are now alien to me, as if I'd never felt them. Who is it that says 'everything flows'? Inside you and around you. Sometimes I'm ghastly. Shameless. I hate that about me, the shameless, forthright wallowing; greed without any sense of honour. And then always staring at certain pages from my diary, getting angry and going into raptures. Disgusting! I'm prostituting myself to myself.

FRIDAY, 9 DECEMBER 1938, VIENNA

Dita's leaving tomorrow. For England. To a camp for Jewish refugee children. Away from here! I can only feel it occasionally. At this moment, perhaps there's some cold, fresh air somewhere over there. You lean back in the compartment, close your eyes and then you look out of the window. The train sings and your hair wafts. Abroad, a foreign land. Then being Jewish no longer means being tortured and martyred. I can hardly believe it any more. It must be wonderful, marvellous!

So Dita is going to England tomorrow. One's so rarely able to collect one's thoughts these days, events are happening so quickly that only seldom can I snatch a few ideas about how I'd like to do it. When Dita was washing her stockings and the washing line was hanging the length of the dining room, it was then I realised: 'emigrant'. The clothes box is empty now as well . . . She's so sweet and competent, Dita. Mornings in bed, totally buried in a dozen pillows, her hair glimmering, all warm from sleep, such a soft mouth, hair, skin! I've read both her diaries. Sweet! Anyway, Egon loves Dita – I don't need to waste my time on her other observations. A new life is beginning for her.

And nothing has changed for me. Absolutely nothing. I'm still sitting *here* at my desk and my pen is scratching away. It's funny when you think about it. Why do we feel the need to daub a few white pages with blue ink . . . and then get so childishly excited about it? I think this is going too far. All I wanted to tell you was that nothing has changed for me. Well, perhaps my sensibilities have become more blunted. Things that used to *horrify* and torment me now leave me cold. It's true. When I first saw 'For Aryans only' on the benches, or 'No Jews' in cafés, the broken windows, I could hardly believe it. Now I just pass by and scarcely notice it. It's only occasionally, for example when I hear from Herbert that a boy of my age, handsome and lovely, is now in Dachau, that it flares up in my mind again. Or when I go to Wehrgasse. I still see Jews there. Where are you going? To Shanghai. Christ! It amazes me that this continual misery exists. There was a blind Jewish man and one who is stateless. He came out looking so pained, so tired: 'There's nothing else for it. I've just got to wait until I'm expelled.' Not long ago two people – admittedly they were only Jews – committed suicide. They wrote a note before they died: 'This is how you get over the border in twenty-four hours.' Perhaps they were straining for effect. It's possible. But most things don't matter before you die and anyway: how can this be happening?!

It's the same as ever! First I can feel a distant prickling, then it gets stronger and stronger, and finally one evening I can't resist it any longer: I just *have* to write him a letter – full (I say this mercilessly) of sentimental nonsense, yearning etc. The letter is my outlet, then it gets weaker, easier, more wistful . . . gone, it has slunk away again until . . . until . . . one day, I can feel a distant prickling and rumbling again.

I just know that Zionism is not compatible with socialism. I saw it today. I'm a socialist and I'm striving to conquer, develop this socialism I feel inside me.

SUNDAY, 11 DECEMBER 1938, VIENNA

Nine o'clock in the evening.

Dita has gone. She's now on the train, at this very moment. She's laughing, unpacking her food, or perhaps she's feeling homesick.

It's terrible keeping a diary. Ghastly. On the previous page it says: Dita is going away tomorrow. And today: Dita has gone. And so it continues. One ought to feel ashamed.

Yesterday: the fast train at eleven o'clock. There's now a void in our 'home'. Mama says 'Dittl' to me, and Grandmother weeps and Mama weeps. 'Separation, separation, separation, who on earth devised this separation?' That's what it says in *Danton's Death* . . . It's a banal truth that life is nothing more than saying goodbye. Perhaps saying hello and goodbye. To every minute, every second! . . . Come on, Ruth, don't get sentimental! It doesn't help.

Yesterday was just like a scene from a painting. Out there in Hütteldorf it was dark and black. The Jewish stewards lit the place up with torches. As did children under seventeen. Boys and girls with rucksacks and suitcases. Endless kisses. One more kiss, and a final one. Next to me a woman was crying: not just discreetly to herself; she was wailing, groaning, sighing deeply. Her whole face was shaking . . . Small, four-year-old children were screaming. Madness! They had to be carried away. And the mothers! The fathers of the young ones are in Dachau. A young woman leaned back, her husband leaned forward towards her. Somebody whispered, 'Both together, both'.

'Mama,' I said. 'Mama, look. Those are our young people, young Jews. They'll get through this, they've done their schooling, they've suffered tremendously and they're going to build a new life with their own hands.' Some of them, the young ones, will have blood on their hands, I think to myself. The little ones who've been wrenched away from their parents, perhaps they'll cry at night. They will. I saw them. Jews. You Jews, whose children were wrenched away from you before you were able to have your fill of kisses, this is what I think: The Jews must have something special about them, mustn't they? They have to suffer so much sorrow. So much sorrow! Because they're Jews! That's why. It sounds so lovely when you say, 'There

were heartbreaking scenes as they said their goodbyes.' No, the heart doesn't
break so quickly. Mama said, 'If one of them had yelled, just a single one, then
all of them would have started.' No, nobody yelled, cursed. They just wept.
Only tears, all I saw was tears. Dita stood there with a few others in a small
huddle, in the dark. All I could see was her white scarf. As we walked past this
small huddle of Jewish refugees, she called out 'Mama' once. And waved.
Then they were gone. Just like that! Dita and Mama had wanted to give each
other a final kiss. Their lips were so close when the steward thrust them
apart: 'Don't make it any more difficult.'

Jewish refugees. They are going to be allocated to different English
families. Dita will write soon. She shall live an upstanding life. She shall
prove herself worthy. It sounds old. And yet: '*I* will strive to lead a worthy
life.' And Dita will too. I won't see her for a long time. What will she look like
then? In a year's time! We'll already be in America then. Because we've got
affidavits. Who was it who said recently: 'We've got a permit to travel to
Affidavit?' I'm letting myself be driven by my thoughts, I'm not exercising any
restraint . . . Yes, the image is appearing again. A tall railway embankment, a
slope grown over with grass. Above, there are railings. Over there the train
with bright windows. Boys inside, the Jewish children. And the parents
standing there behind the carriages with their children inside. (We weren't
allowed on the platform, so they were creeping around like animals.) Shouted
over, and the children inside pulled the windows down, whistled, gestured.
One shouted, 'Mama!' Everything suddenly became clear to me. In the
dark, out there in Hütteldorf. We were standing together. Dita had number
258. 'You see,' I said, 'now you're no more than a number.' 'Oh no, I'm
still Judith Maier.' . . . Yes, and when number 258 was called. In there like
a flash – quick, march! Life is beginning! For us young people the transition
to life is normally a gradual one, cautious, no surprises. But now! We're
chucked out. Today still at school; tomorrow housemaid. But let's not
kid ourselves. Mama always says, 'But then you'll belong to a house; at
least they'll know who you are.' I don't give a damn! I'll be a housemaid. A
proletarian! Why not? Then at least I'll belong to them. Completely and
utterly!

The sky was so clear and there was no end to the kisses. And the woman
next to me trembled and wept. And in the dark small children were weeping.

It was cold and wet. Dita marched past us. The blue-white scarf shone. Brave. And the young people, they will fight.

Jews, Jews, Papa, Heinrich Heine.

SATURDAY, 17 DECEMBER 1938, VIENNA

No, it's not because of any silly yearning or other ridiculous feelings that I want to write this now:

Recently I read something particularly beautiful about Heine, my beloved Heine. The poems, his dream images are written about a girl he loved called Amalie. In truth there wasn't very much behind this love, so occasionally it seems that there are too many words used to describe something as commonplace as an unhappy love. But we have to understand Heine. At the time he was wrestling with an *inner story*.

That's so beautifully put. He was wrestling with an inner story. The things one can read into that! The inner story.

Who do you think came to mind when I read that? Yes, of course! The Herr Professor. That's the only sensible thing that can be said to – hopefully – conclude the matter. In reality there's not much behind it. I'm wrestling with an inner story. My feelings, what I'm putting and writing into this little nothingness is experience. This is where my most secret feelings can romp around, be given free rein. My poor tiny feelings. Heine! Yes, Heine was able to write a *Book of Songs* about his 'inner story'. Me? Oh my God!

Do you think that on silent evenings . . . and that's it.

Go to bed, Ruth!

SUNDAY, 18 DECEMBER 1938, VIENNA

I dreamed about Papa last night. So wonderful!

THURSDAY, 22 DECEMBER 1938, VIENNA

In a fit of weakness, shall we say, I wrote to Dr Brauchbar, yes, Dr Brauchbar, Prof. Williger's friend. I explained a little about what I'm feeling: that I cannot escape him, that I find the whole thing unhealthy. Today I received a lovely, sweet reply. He said so many nice things, even if his expression was often childish and clumsy. He said, 'I'm not surprised that you often think of W. I'm certain he often thinks of you, too. I knew that you mean something to him, but not that he means so much to you.' Doesn't that sound comforting? Then: 'You ask whether it's worth it. My dear, love is always worth it. For W. is a spiritual man and it may be that the spiritual element of his person is having an effect on you. That would definitely delight him. So, you cannot escape him. Now, I'm sure you'd only like to escape the torment, not those things that are permanent.' Excellent!

But on an intellectual level and in one's emotional life, the age difference can make the meeting of two people easier and afford it greater substance: you have more to impart to each other, more to help bridge the time span between you. What did he bring to you? The love of a brilliant man for something which the genius of creation has shaped, both internally and externally, into a young girl like you.'

Yes, a lot of truth in that, although I don't like the 'genius of creation' being dealt with in a letter in such summary fashion. And yet it's right. But that's precisely what *I don't like* about this love; I wrote about it to Dr Brauchbar. I want to be loved *for my own sake*, for my personality, not because I'm a young girl. There's also Käthe, Dita and Polina. He would have loved Polina the same as me, as the emergent girl. It was a coincidence that it was *I* who crossed his path. I gave him my youth, that's what he loved about me, nothing else. I'm absolutely certain of this. That's why I find this love degrading. It turns me into a slave. Because I'm not being loved for my own sake. There'll be English girls and he'll have forgotten me the very moment he finds somebody else.

Dr Brauchbar's letter was good. I was unusually happy the whole day long. It snowed today and things seemed so lovely to me, stuck in my mind . . . Snowflakes were dancing, the snow, the sky . . . everything was good. I wandered down the street and talked to myself like a madwoman . . . It was lovely. A full day.

We have such an excellent logic teacher . . . He gives a lot in one lesson . . . life could be good . . . so good!

FRIDAY, 23 DECEMBER 1938, VIENNA

Yesterday evening I remembered that it's Christmas now. Because there's been nothing but silence over these Christmas days. Last year Mama was lighting the Christmas tree. I remember the bright candles, the fragrance of fir needles, sweet things. When I went into the room, I thought: Beautiful! So beautiful! Earlier I'd rung the Herr Professor. There was pale snow outside . . . I leaned back, listened to the voice on the telephone . . . Afterwards a woman came and said, 'Are you feeling ill, young lady?'

There was a peaceful glow to those Christmas days. They've stolen that from us, too. Peaceful glow . . . This time we're not celebrating Christmas.

Dita wrote from England to say that she'd lit some Hanukah candles.

There was another thing I wanted to say. The light, the golden light!!!

Our logic teacher says that every one of us must overcome these problems. We have to fight, we mustn't deceive ourselves . . . I don't know how to tackle these problems; they slip away from me the moment I think I've got hold of them.

It's as if I'm in a prison. It's true. Sometimes I walk in the street when I go to school. Then I'm aware of it. White snow, the bridge over there that is lit up in the evening. The Danube canal . . . There is still life out there, there's more than just swastika armbands and *Heil Hitler*! Then things get very close, get right into my heart . . . A square of sky. The houses, steep, reaching upwards . . . I was startled the first time it snowed. Really startled. I was sitting by the window and flakes suddenly started falling to earth . . . I realised that it was winter. The year has passed. In spring there was a bright pink tree on the way to school. Summer, autumn: a few withered leaves on the Ringstraße. Winter, December: snow is falling. From my window I can see a tree, another tree, a distant roof. It's a greeting to me from afar, from a beautiful world . . . It was so long ago that the tree was green and so recently that the snow arrived . . . If I had one real person, a *human being*.

I don't like people. If only I knew what was behind it. What is it all about? It's evening. In the room next door Mama is talking about carpets . . . Herr Singer is teaching the budgerigar to say, 'My name is Bobby Singer and I live at Obere Donaustraße 43.'

Bleak . . .

OH, THE SUN WAS SO BRIGHT

Oh, the sun was so bright
and the trees sticky and wet . . .
In the evening stars quivered . . .
It was spring

Oh, the sky was blue
Flowers blazed
. . . your lips smelled sweet . . .
it was summer, autumn, leaves withered,
and in winter I sat at the window . . . it snowed

And Ernstl, little Ernstl comes to us in uniform with a swastika armband! . . . Today we said goodbye to each other. Ernstl kissed Mama's hand . . . We'll see each other again in America . . . He laughs again through the chink in the door, bows, raises his hat. Ernstl!

SATURDAY, 24 DECEMBER 1938, VIENNA

Half past ten at night.

So it's Christmas. I've been for a stroll through the streets . . . snow . . . the streets empty . . . The wireless is blaring out Christmas carols, sweet, languorous. Opposite, the broken windows of the Jewish shop are gleaming, Hebrew inscriptions. How false the world is! So false. A car goes phut . . . couldn't that have been a shot? . . . A shot on Christmas Eve . . . Bells ring through the air . . . on one shop it says *Jew*, nothing else. On another . . . Get to Dachau, Satan! . . . In the window above, Christmas candles are burning . . . Christmas in Nazi Germany. I had to kiss this daubed '*Jew*'. Kiss it, yes. To be Jewish, how full of sorrow, how sad, and yet . . .

*Irma and Ludwig Maier with Ruth and Judith in their attic apartment
in Peter-Jordan-Straße. The family lived there until 1929.*

SUNDAY, 25 DECEMBER 1938, VIENNA

Ten o'clock in the morning.

Everybody loved Papa. Everybody, everybody! If only I can be worthy of
him. That's the only thing I wish for myself. To be worthy of him! I love Papa
so much. Soooo much. If I had my father I wouldn't need a Williger. Nobody
but Papa . . . And Mama was allowed to love Papa, too. He kissed her. He and
she gave birth to us two: Dita and me . . . I can discuss anything else with
other people . . . just not Papa. I've told nobody else about him, it's within
me. I'll tell my children about him.

Five o'clock in the afternoon.

I don't know if it's Dr Brauchbar's letter. I'm just so full of desire. I don't
feel drained or ill. No, it's warm inside me. Something warm, a glow, a faint

smell. And sometimes I just smile for no reason; I dream to myself. I feel peaceful inside. I see everything from behind this glow, more clearly and purely . . . I have such lovely thoughts, I walk through the streets and everything falls into my heart, as if through a crystal. Strange! Nonetheless, I still feel the same misery as ever. I'm just sad.

MONDAY EVENING, 26 DECEMBER 1938, VIENNA

This diary fills me with dread. I know it, yet I don't want to rip the thing up. For beneath all this mess perhaps there's a lovely, genuine idea that deserves to be written . . . I'm currently reading Goethe's *Correspondence with a Child*. Yes! At this time, in this torment and misery. Bettina is a wonderful figure. Who was it that recently said: Woman has reproductive power rather than creative power? . . . Bettina is so earnest, a child. A ray of sunshine, a withered leaf: that is her world. A snowflake that melts on her hand . . . If she were living today, there's no doubt she would have been unable to tolerate this life; she would have perished.

TUESDAY, 27 DECEMBER 1938, VIENNA

A classic example of modesty and shamelessness. Bettina von Arnim writes, 'And by morning it is *he*, before whom I veil myself when I dress.'* I think, 'And by morning it is *he*, before whom I *unveil* myself, *he* to whom I show my body, stroke my breast, swing my hips, and say, "This is me. I'm here for you. You *can* possess me if you desire me."'

I went to see the blind people. They were singing. One of them, a little woman who looks like an ugly duckling, has a jubilant voice. Another one who is totally blind, young, as young as a girl, with a peaceful face and an inner smile, sang intensely and fervently. They sang pieces from Haydn's

* Translation by Bettina von Armin, 1837.

Creation, *The Marriage of Figaro* etc., and a song with the words: 'Nobody who could comfort me' . . . Two candles were burning on the *piano*. The flames were flickering and my mind was filled with all sorts of thoughts. For example, that there are Jewish blind people or, if you like, blind Jews (I don't know which is more wretched) singing – one jubilant, another intense and fervent. It was the same feeling I had when the violin was being played next door, two days after the pogrom of 10 November. I kept on thinking of the Jews in Dachau. And of Williger, too.

A different people would not be able to suffer this. A different people would perish, numbed. The Jews *migrate*. They went to *Shanghai* with small children. The Jews migrate.

Sometimes I think about what's written on the bench in front of me. Smeared in white: 'Aryans Only'. 'No Entry for Jews'. What does that mean? What does Jew mean? J e w. Three letters. You can comfortably say that this word is one of the most frequently uttered, whether it's for or against Jews. They don't want to believe that we're completely normal people. Understood! People who have suffered a lot. Granted. But people who just want peace, finally. Peace. A patch of earth. Sky, sun, and just for *once* not to be reminded of our lineage. Every day, every second. We are human beings just like you and we're downtrodden. You can bend us but cannot break us... The Jews migrate. That's the refrain, the traditional motif! They migrate. When will it end?

The Jewish question is a lie. They should leave us in peace for three to four generations and the Jewish question would be resolved. You don't want to? All right! So we have to help ourselves. Self-emancipation. That's the word. Isn't that precisely what the workers did? Do we now have to deny socialism?!?

II

1940 sounds so ... horrible

LETTERS TO HER SISTER
IN ENGLAND

1939–1940

*Until 9 May 1940, the day of the German invasion of Norway, Ruth and Judith
Maier — one a refugee in Lillestrøm, the other in Brighton — remained in regular
letter contact. The letter shown here is stamped 26 May 1939.*

Irma Maier with her two daughters Judith and Ruth. Taken in a Viennese photographic studio.

Refugee in Norway

JANUARY—MARCH 1939

The middle section of this book is made up of letters that Ruth Maier wrote to her sister Judith in England when she was a refugee in Norway. The text has been abridged, especially those parts which deal with Judith's private life, and family and friends in Vienna, many of whom by this time are in exile. The opening and closing addresses ('Dear xxx') have been omitted.

Ruth arrives in Norway with a three-month permit to stay from the Norwegian authorities and an English visa. The telegraph employee, Arne Strøm (1901–1972), has declared his willingness to be her host and guarantor. He is married to Dagmar and they have a seven-year-old daughter, Turid. Their maid, Edla, is the same age as Ruth. The contact between the two families developed from Arne Strøm having met Ruth's father, Ludwig Maier, at an international postal and telegraph conference.

The first two letters to Judith — sometimes referred to as Dita or Dittl — are written in Vienna. Ruth takes the train to Berlin, then to Sassnitz, then catches the ferry to Trelleborg, from where she travels via Malmö to Oslo. She arrives in Oslo on the evening of Monday, 30 January. The Strøm family meets her at the station. They live at number 7 Storgate, two floors above the telegraph office. He is an active member of the Social Democratic Party and editor of the Telegrafbladet journal. Ruth takes over Turid's bedroom. The family is kind to her.

In spite of this, Ruth is nagged by doubts about the future, worries about her permit to stay, uncertainty over her education, and the thought of her mother and her grandmother who are still in Austria. Most of all she is preoccupied by the hope of being reunited with her loved ones, whether in England or the USA.

THURSDAY, 19 JANUARY 1939, VIENNA

Today I am very happy. We received a telegram from Norway: 'Visa arranged, travel tickets sent, letter to follow.' Dita, I'm so happy, so happy!!! The only thing that's sad is that I won't be seeing Williger. Yes, of course. Don't smirk. I called a short while ago. Where he used to live there is now an architect, Schöppler. He was grumpy. First I asked whether I could speak with Herr Professor Williger. He said, 'Who knows where he is? He's been in England for more than a year now.' What a queer feeling that was, Dittl. Why can't you understand that I love him so much? The whole thing is quite simple. I never forget; it's just the way I am. Dittl, Dittl. Sometimes I'm quite afraid. Can you understand that? At the moment I'm reading Goethe's *Correspondence with a Child*. Dittl, there are sentences in this that I could have written, so heartfelt. I shall tell you something, something very personal. A secret. From one of Bettina's letters: 'And what shall I then? Relate how the glorious friendliness, with which you met me, now exuberates in my heart – all other life at once repressed? – how I must ever yearn towards that time, when I first felt myself *well*?'*

What do you think of that? . . . And yet, I am so happy, so happy that I have permission to go to Norway. Yes. But enough of that. One must know when the right moment to stop is. I'm in the mood to enjoy life to the full, shall we say.

Did I tell you that Grandmother has been a little poorly? She's already feeling better now.

SATURDAY, 21 JANUARY 1939, VIENNA

We received your letter today and we're frightfully happy that you've finally reached your destination. Yes, Dittl, and soon I'll have reached my destination, too. In Norway! My visa is already in my passport. Dita, my happiness truly knows no bounds. It's this week that I'll be travelling to

* Translation by Bettina von Arnim.

Ruth Maier took a large collection of books with her to Lillestrøm, including Bettina von Arnim's Goethe's Correspondence with a Child *which Ruth often refers to in her diary. Bettina von Arnim (1785–1859) corresponded with Goethe when she was sixteen. She published the letters in 1835 after his death.*

Norway. All I'm waiting for now is the tickets that Herr Strøm is sending to me. Yesterday we received a letter from him. You can't imagine how lovely he sounds. I'm so looking forward to it . . . The silly thing is that I can't speak Norwegian; I'll just have to concentrate very hard on learning Norwegian when I'm there, so that I can continue my studies after a couple of months.

Dittl, I would *sooo* love to see you again, even just for a bit. But now it's going to be a little while. But you know, time goes so quickly. Too quickly, I think. It's this week that I'm going to Norway. Herr Strøm wrote that Turid will be at the station even if it's very late.

WEDNESDAY, 1 FEBRUARY 1939, LILLESTRØM

Although it's already eleven o'clock and I'm already in bed, I must write you a few lines . . . I feel as if I've been in Norway for a month already. All of them are so lovely and friendly to me: Turid, Dagmar and Herr Strøm. Turid is a small, blonde girl, her mother is still very young, and she and Herr Strøm are a really happy couple. In the evenings we sit by the fireplace, Herr Arne reads the newspaper, the wireless is on . . . Do you know, I'd just like to be able to do something, you understand; I don't like idling around. But the time will come.

Actually, Dittl, I wanted to tell you about my journey. It was like something from a fairy tale, you know. A tall, blond Norwegian man was very kind to me. Well, let me start at the beginning. Taking my leave of them all was not easy. Grandmother wept a lot. Then in the train I sat with a Yugoslavian sportsman. He was a very nice man. Twenty-eight years old (Willi Hüber). In the evening it was all a bit awkward. He and I alone! Well, in fact another man did come into our carriage and so I could go to sleep reassured. Then in Berlin we had to change trains etc. Our train was loaded on to the ship. Before that was the border control. My suitcase was examined by a nasty piece of work. With revolting white hands. He read pages from my diary. Williger's letter from start to finish. He stared at the Ernst Deutsch picture and said something about him. I don't know what, I only heard the words in the distance and thought: It's all over. When I think about it now I get a burning sensation somewhere inside me and it's most unpleasant. Afterwards I howled with anger and locked the door. The border guard found this highly suspicious. Oh well! Very stupidly I also smuggled through twenty Reichsmarks. I can't really explain it. At any rate, the Norwegian gentleman told me afterwards just how dangerous that was. I don't think I need to describe how I felt when I was over the border. Suddenly (over the border) the Norwegian hauled me into his carriage and showed me a gold watch and Iron Cross that he had brought out of the country for Jews. He was very jolly and very friendly to me. We went for a walk together on board the ship; the wind and the sea. He was your type (this just occurs to me now!). Tall, slim and awfully polite. Helps you put on your coat etc. And then you get the feeling with him that you don't have to worry about anything; he's there. Dita, just the man you'd wish for. Then he laughs at you and you feel very small. Up on deck, you know, he put his arm round me and pulled me tight against him. But it wasn't bad. After all, I was so happy and he said he was keeping me warm. Don't giggle.

I did not fall in love with him. I would quite happily tell you if I had. It was just so lovely. We drank coffee together, he told me about himself and I told him about me. Dittl, don't think that I've forgotten those who are still in Germany. Mama and Grandmother should get out *jolly fast*. Now that I'm out, I can finally see just what a pigsty Vienna is. I'm so happy to be away from there.

I'll write more to you today. You must be so happy that you can *go to school*. Yes, Ditz, now you'll take your Matura before me. I'm idling here and I haven't got any bright ideas as to what I should do. After all, I can't just learn Norwegian all day long. Everybody is so kind here. Herr Strøm always talks to us in German. Turid (Türid) is also kind but I would just love to do something, achieve something. I know it's only my second day here, but still.

MONDAY, 6 FEBRUARY 1939, LILLESTRØM

Oh Dittl, I can't begin to describe Herr Strøm to you. He is *sooo* nice. Smokes a pipe and always wanders around the place as if he hasn't quite had enough sleep. In slippers. His laugh is very friendly and he talks German to me. Yesterday he even danced a waltz with me to the music on the wireless. Nice? Frau Dagmar is also *sooo* lovely. She wears spectacles and looks very young. Their apartment here is quite modern and tasteful, too. A small étagère with books. Jack London, Sigrid Undset, Henrik Ibsen etc. Very nice pictures, too. Everything is bright and friendly. 'Just as if these were young people.' My room is quite small and narrow. A tiny piece of Norway looks into the room through my window. I've very little space for my clothes and underwear, etc. . . . I'm learning Norwegian, that's my only real pursuit here.

Did you read in the newspaper that Else Wohlgemut killed herself? She was a Jew!!!

Is there much in the newspapers over there about Spanish refugees?

Ruth was a compulsive writer of letters, and often accompanied these with short notes. This drawing, which shows the view from her room in Storgate 7, Lillestrøm, was on a small piece of paper sent together with a letter.

SATURDAY, 11 FEBRUARY 1939, LILLESTRØM

I'll have you know that your letters have caused me the greatest embarrassment. Herr Strøm brought me a letter from you. (He's just so nice!) Of course I was delighted and I think he's so nice that I had to say to him, 'You can read the letter, too.' And then you write, 'You should give Herr Strøm a lot of pleasure (does he deserve it?).' . . . When he got to this part I had to quickly look away. Honestly: does Herr Strøm deserve it? What do you mean by that? He is sooo nice. Today he went with me to a Jewish children's home in Oslo. One of my school friends had asked me to visit her brother there. Herr Strøm was *very* kind. Perhaps I can tell you: he is a male substitute. That means he *is* a man, but only in *one certain* respect of course. Yesterday evening he went with me to the pictures. We had a little walk afterwards. And, you see, he doesn't treat me like a baby. Of course he says '*du*' to me but, for example, he lets me go first, walks on my right, helps me put on my coat etc.

I find all that very nice. You mustn't misunderstand it. It's so sweet when he walks with me in Oslo, for example; he's very paternal.

I know what I'm writing is all nonsense. But, you see, I'm that sort of 'woman' or 'lady' (if you prefer) who likes such tripe.

You're thinking, 'She's got worries!' But *you* can talk, I say. You *crave* a bit of that: tango lighting, being helped into your coat, etc. An amateur can notice that. Yes, Dittl, learning is wonderful, but why do you think you wear a blue flowery dress or silk stockings? Dittl, you're sixteen. Williger used to say, 'You don't start living until you're sixteen.' Don't forget that. Anyway, don't believe that I'm still thinking of Williger even just a tiny bit. I could write to you about it in a letter. *Finis amoris*. I admit that in Vienna I had all sorts of feelings. I believe it bordered on madness. Although Musch never noticed anything, she really doesn't have a good eye for such things.

I want to tell you briefly about the children's home. I understand you *sooo* well. In the camp you saw a little of the Jewish spirit. Jewish spirit! Chajes-Gymnasium etc. Thinking about it makes me feel so warm. Not the ghetto spirit but . . . ! Well, we understand each other. I only need remind you of Trann and Goldberg. Skullcaps off and . . . Judaism!! I think that only . . . well, only we can understand this. If I were to tell Herr Strøm about it, he would just give me a stupid stare. There are certain things that 'Aryans' just don't understand. It's true! I wanted to tell you about the children's home. An old Jew was sitting outside the house. He was reading a Hebrew newspaper! Right outside we met a young Jewish boy from the home. Sigi Korn. Very, very sweet and lovely. He could hardly speak German any more, only Norwegian. The home itself was not very cosy. Jewish housekeeping. Dirt. Chaos. (The other side of the coin!)

Dittl! Now a third thing: my future. I can't picture anything. That's the best. Next week we will extend my English visa. I'm always asking Herr Strøm, 'And then?' He laughs, says, 'Why are you so impatient? Later . . . we'll talk about it later.' Am I to let myself get into a pickle over this? I think it's impossible for me to tell Herr Strøm that I want to go to England. Learn nursing – that's if I wanted to. *But I don't know if that's what I do want*. It would be absolutely splendid. It all depends on what plans Herr Strøm has for me. If he found something nice for me to do, then I would like to stay in Norway. But if not . . . then I want to come to England.

By the way, do you know that Williger wanted to give me a part in the chorus of his play? This Williger thing: I talk about him so much that you must believe I still think about him. I prefer Herr Strøm one thousand times over. Even if Herr Strøm is just an average man and the other a 'brilliant man' (quoted from Dr Brauchbar's letter). My purpose has been achieved, you see. You think the brilliant man is still haunting my mind. Ha ha! . . .

Dittl, I feel like I'm an old woman, all this nonsense I'm writing. There's no end to it, Dittl. I'll sign off today feeling quite ashamed.

FRIDAY, 17 FEBRUARY 1939, LILLESTRØM

What am I doing here? To be honest, time is slipping away without my noticing it, slowly but surely. Herr Strøm is doing wonderful things for me. He so intoxicates me with his lovely smile, etc., that I become incapable of resistance. The idea of just running away is not a bad one.

My Norwegian? Now I can speak Norwegian a little better than Czech and I understand it quite well if they speak to me as if I were an idiot . . . that's to say in slow motion . . . My future is all up in the air. Perhaps I will go to school here and do my Matura, although I *really* can't imagine it. Here in Norway (to top it all) there are two languages, and I would have to know them both. That's crazy, obviously. Moreover, school begins in August; I wouldn't be able to wait so long!

There's nothing at all new to report from here . . . I go for walks with Herr Strøm and he is very nice. The great thing is not Herr Strøm but . . . how should I put it . . . the wonderful thing is that there's a man in the house. Perhaps that sounds a little exaggerated and excessive. But a man in the house! That's not to be underestimated, you know. When he's there everything suddenly appears different. Everything revolves around him. You hear him singing in the morning. Very badly, but he does it with great confidence. Today was the first time I've seen him help out with the housework: he vacuumed. I immediately had a laughing fit. So beguiling! He whistled while he vacuumed, and when I came and took the vacuum cleaner out of his hands he gave me a look of relief . . . I'm developing a psychology of the male and then I've got my own ideas about marriage: for people who want to watch how 'the other thinks' it's ideal, but . . .

Anyway, I've been rummaging through the books to find Schiller. I felt very warm when I read *The Ring of Polycrates*. It's been such a long time since I read any German. Nothing but Norwegian newspapers . . . These are not just to be scoffed at . . . It might interest you that almost every day they report on acts committed against Jews etc. (And in a country like Norway!) Acts is of course the wrong word; these are just sharp little diversions to remind Jews that . . . well, you know . . . that they're Jews.

Dittl, I notice to my horror that I've forgotten to answer the following questions:

1. What is a fjord like? . . . A fjord is like the sea if you don't know that it's a fjord. That's to say that it's not exactly like the sea, but the sea with a narrow beginning. I've only seen the Oslo fjord. Very beautiful.

2. What is Oslo like? Oslo is a very pretty city – not a large city (like Vienna) – as if it had just been daubed there. Lots of sky everywhere and trees, too. The streets are very narrow and there is not much traffic. The nicest things are the fjord and a few streets. It's particularly lovely when the sun is shining and there's blue sky. In front of the university, students go back and forth and while away time in the sun. (Idyllic!)

FRIDAY, 24 FEBRUARY 1939, LILLESTRØM

Yesterday Edla handed me your letter in bed. Well, I was so happy! You know that . . . and I'm replying to you, as you can see, at great speed.

Dittl, today I was in Oslo (Uschlo) with Herr Strøm to extend my English visa. There was an English woman there who spoke dreadful Norwegian and . . . who didn't extend the visa. Herr Strøm is such a sweet optimist; he believed it would be sorted out in next to no time. First we have to complete an application. The process will take about two months . . . Herr Strøm will submit it to the 'Passport Office' in Oslo.

Anyway, it was very, very beautiful in Oslo today. We went for a walk along the harbour, the air was quite salty . . . I like Oslo very much. Such an airy, pretty city . . . The only thing that rankles with me is that I'm not work-ing. Today I said something quite unassuming about it to Herr Strøm. He went a little red, I think, and said, 'Yes, yes.' Anyway, it's delightful that you can picture Herr Strøm so well. To get a more complete idea of his person you should also know that he has a lock of hair or something similar that always falls over his forehead. Today, Herr Ruud (he's also from the telegraph service) pulled him affectionately by this lock of hair . . . It was simply enchanting . . . Otherwise, he is as nice as ever. I mean it! What would you do in my place? Today I'm going to ask Frau Strøm what she imagines I'm going to do. Perhaps *a woman* has more understanding . . . In all probability the Strøm family will decide to let me do some courses: typing etc. But that's not my dream, either. I'd like to learn a profession, even if it were only . . . what? . . . business school or something similar. My Matura is all up in the air.

You say that I don't write anything about the country, its people and customs etc. So: Norway is a kingdom. Where the king has nothing to say. Herr Strøm finds this very important (as do I). In government at the moment is the Arbeiderparti, another name for the Social Democrats. Herr Strøm is of course an Arbeiderparti supporter. There are also the 'Liberals' and 'Conservatives'. Supposedly there are no Nazis here . . . (?) Herr Strøm is very, very proud to be a Norwegian and once he told me, 'If I were not a Norwegian I'd like to be a Swede.' The Swedes, Norwegians and Danes feel a very close connection to each other, as if they were one country, so to speak. Swedish and Norwegian are very similar (Danish, too). Almost every Norwegian owns the complete works of Ibsen and Bjørnson. Did you know, by the way, that Hamsun and Undset are Norwegian? Bjørnson, especially, is very popular. In fact I saw his son today. He looks so much like his father.

SATURDAY, 4 MARCH 1939, LILLESTRØM

At the moment I only exist to put on weight . . . The Strøm family say that I must wait until my Norwegian residency is arranged. We made an application for an extension to the 'Passport Office' in Oslo and I hope that the decision will soon be made as to whether I am to remain here or have to go to England.

As far as my knowledge of Norwegian is concerned, at the moment I am quite satisfied with my progress. I can speak it quite well already and I'm sure I read Norwegian better than I do English. (Especially newspapers.) Mostly I'm reading about Norwegian literature, art history and other similar subjects.

Of course I'm happy when I go for walks in Oslo. But that happens so seldom. I like Oslo so much and it's so beautiful to go walking by the fjord . . . Last week Tobben (Frau Strøm's brother) invited me. That's to say he took me out in Oslo. It was delightful. Tobben is thirty years old, laughs rather a lot and smokes a pipe (as all Norwegians do). And yet he's got the beginnings of a bald patch! . . . Apart from that he's very nice. We went to the pictures, took a walk (by the fjord!), then went to a café. He must have spent a hell of a lot of money – the meal itself cost twenty-three kroner! He made no advances towards me whatsoever. Pity. I was up for it. The day before I had raced home and spent hours racking my brains as to what I should wear . . . so provincial . . . As far as the 'boy' is concerned, I'm in the same position. Edla (seventeen and a half!!!) sings love songs all day long and she has a *kjæreste* (lover). Turid is asking me whether my *kjæreste* is in Vienna etc . . . Well, I'm not going to let myself get involved in any discussions of this (hmm!).

The 'Strøm clan' in Norway is very well informed politically. Herr Strøm is a social welfare councillor, etc. Frau Strøm's father is a *Stortingsmann*, that's to say a deputy in the parliament. That's very, very important here. You can listen to the parliamentary debates here . . . Is that the case in England, too? Yes, Dittl, you're right: Norway is a healthy country and the Norwegians are proud of their Norway . . . But in spite of all of this . . . If I knew how my future were mapped out I'd be happier. Here they're all nice, nicer, the nicest. I eat and sleep, yesterday I was at the pictures . . . but, but!

WEDNESDAY, 22 MARCH 1939, LILLESTRØM

You won't believe me when I tell you that there's so little I can do here to help. I really despise myself. Do you know, my own stay here is waiting to be decided. A parliamentary deputy is going to argue my case, and perhaps I'll

Pippa Sirotkova, a communist and Uncle Oscar's girlfriend in Prague,
managed to escape to Britain from Czechoslovakia. When Judith and her mother
left Brighton in 1940, Pippa found them somewhere to live in London.
Pippa later married the artist Jakub Bauernfreund in Britain.

get an extension to my visa beyond 1 April. If that happens, I'll attend a typing and English stenography course until August (start of the academic year). In August I'll go to school and in June 1940 I'll take my *examen artium* (Matura). That's quite definite. And I'd have to go to school in Oslo, which would mean endless to-ing and fro-ing. That doesn't matter.

I don't know what's better: to stay in Norway or go to England?

Dittl, I've been thinking so much about Mama's business at the moment. Couldn't you do something to speed it up? War could break out at any moment. Perhaps you don't read the newspapers that much. I'm very worried and I've written to Musch that if it gets that bad she should leave illegally. It's really terrible.

It's unbelievable: Zarošice in Germany. And then concentration camps, persecution of Jews. I wrote to Pippa straight away. Perhaps something has happened to her. Look, couldn't Pippa study nursing in London? (I'm always thinking about her, it's *her* we should be helping first of all.)

You can't imagine how incensed I am with Chamberlain. Is there no prospect that Eden will become prime minister *soon*? (At this moment there's a speech on the wireless about Czechoslovakia, the drama in central Europe and Germany's drive eastwards.)

Norwegian opinion might interest you. Here they are totally committed to a 'policy of neutrality'. Apart from that there are two parties, one of which (on the right) is in favour of re-armament and the other in favour of national defence but without party political agitation (what they mean by this I don't really understand). So your average Norwegian is rather aloof from the events in central Europe. Edla has no clue about politics; not long ago she asked me whether they were at war where my mother lived. Frau Strøm is not at all informed and she prefers to read her family magazines rather than the newspaper. Herr Strøm is the only one who understands anything, but only with 'Social Democratic' sympathies. Turid, on the other hand, is the only person who shows compassion. I can't repeat her political utterances. She hates Hitler from the very depths of her soul and tries to comfort me by saying that he's sure to die 'tonight'. Sometimes she expends all her energy in highly detailed descriptions of the terrible diseases that he is going to die from. She asks why the *Jews* don't hound the *Germans* out etc. She deserves a kiss for each of her observations . . . Sometimes I read her Andersen's fairy tales in Danish. (I can understand Danish very well and read it particularly well!)

It is completely idyllic here. I've already told you that Edla is happily in love. Herr Strøm continues to be very kind . . . I have the feeling that the whole of Lillestrøm knows me already. At any rate they all stare at me when I cross the street. They look at me as if I'm some sort of mythical beast and it infuriates me.

Dittl, sometimes I have this uncontrollable desire to see you, or Musch, or Grandmother. I last 'looked' at you at the station. I'll remember your blue-and-white scarf for a long time . . . Because of where we are. Do you know what we did with Grandmother after you left? It was as if she had all of a sudden lost her mind. That's to say, she couldn't remember a thing. It was

Ruth's drawing
of the Strøm's dining room.

terrible, I can tell you. We thought that was it. Dittl, why am I telling you *that*? It has only just occurred to me now.

I can't draw it. This is what's happening: Herr Strøm is talking Norwegian on the telephone! Frau Strøm is busy in the kitchen. Turid is sleeping in the *soveværelse* (bedroom). Dinner is in front of me on the table. The pen is scratching. I'm going to bed.

Dittl, it's Turid's birthday on 30 March. Send her a card. A lovely children's card. It will give her such pleasure . . . Now Herr Strøm has started singing!

FRIDAY, 24 MARCH 1939, LILLESTRØM

You know very well that written congratulations have always been my weak point! I've never been able to understand why people congratulate each other on their birthdays! Forgive me, Dittl, I'm not a pessimist; far be it from me to say that 'condolences' would be better on such an occasion. There are still a few little 'pleasures' that make one's life worthwhile. Don't you agree? Condolences are a touch exaggerated. But to wish each other happiness is also a bit too rosy! Why should I congratulate you? Because you made an appearance on this earth? Because you're seventeen years old? (Hear, hear!) Because you appeared on this earth as Judith Maier and not as a dwarf *Affenpinscher* or a . . . well, it's not relevant!

Well, anyway. After registering my protest against congratulations in general, let me now offer them to you from all my heart. Seventeen years! Dita, tears are running down my cheeks: 'How blissful, how blissful to still be a child!' (Where's that from? I don't even know myself!) No, Dita, be quiet for a moment . . . yes, yes, seventeen years! The well-known characters, Williger, Ernst Deutsch . . . Well, that's just a digression. Seventeen years. Full stop. No, even better, colon. The time of young love, sexual ripening or precociousness, ripeness, or riping – whatever you want to call it! Again: the time of young love, the first kisses . . . (what a prospect!) the shy embraces, the first longings. (Dear Moon, you go so quietly! I see the moon. You see the moon. Both of us see the moon!) In short, in your seventeenth year you enter life, as it were. I admit that the last sentence was wrong, but you will really have to forgive me, I am overcome with emotion.

Dittl, if I'm supposed to wish you something decent, something substantial, then I really can't do it. Happiness, good health, all of that is nonsense; and that we'll be together soon etc. etc., well we know that already. Something substantial would be to wish for you (and for all the others, too) that the whole of Germany, Hitler and his consorts would suddenly explode somehow, blow up into the sky. But there's not much chance of that happening! Or perhaps a more appropriate wish that Chamberlain would finally go and Eden become prime minister! But perhaps you're one of those who would like to award Chamberlain the Nobel Peace Prize. If you are, then I beg you humbly for your forgiveness!

Tomorrow I'm going to Holmenkollen (I only have a vague idea of what that is) with Herr Strøm. Something to do with a ski race and foreign guests: apparently world famous (i.e. insignificant). In Norway, you see, everything is world famous, even if nobody outside Norway has a clue of what it is! At any rate I'm looking forward to it immensely and I'll send you a Holmenkollen badge that Tobben bought me. (Hmmm!) I'm particularly looking forward to it because Herr Strøm is going with me. He sleeps persistently almost all day long (when he is at home), then he goes to meetings and to the telegraph office. He's heavenly. Recently he said, 'Well, in spring I'm always so tired and I need lots of sleep.' A secret. He has – sweaty feet. But his sweaty feet do not bother me. Dita, that's true love. This is how I think: 'Sweet little one, do you have sweaty feet? Sweet little one has sweaty feet. Little one should wash his feet, but little one is much too lazy, little one is bad. Sweet little one has sweaty feet.'

Is that true love? When the smell of his sweaty feet reaches my nostrils I can't help *smiling*. I ask you!

WEDNESDAY, 29 MARCH 1939, LILLESTRØM

There is such a large heap of letters piling up in front of me that I feel quite giddy. So now I'll get down to work and it's your turn first. But, alas! I don't know where I'm going to find the money for stamps. Frightfully tragic! I'll have to go begging to Herr Strøm and whisper to him that I've no money left. You should know: last week I got ten kroner. That was the money I had smuggled through. I changed it, of course . . . Well, these ten kroner have literally vanished. It's Turid's birthday tomorrow, so I went shopping today. I'm a confidence trickster. Me, a poor emigrant, a filthy German Jew hounded from home, I buy: 1. magic leaves, 2. transfers, 3. sweet Easter paper napkins, then 4. a sweet chocolate nest with eggs and a duck (of all things!), 5. chocolate too, 6. (and this is what finished me off) a Walt Disney book . . . three kroner, ninety-six øre.

By the end I didn't have enough money for the return fare to Lillestrøm and . . . with admirable skill I managed to locate Herr Strøm in Oslo. He had a meeting, you see, and I found out *where* the meeting was. I simply went into the telegraph office and asked. A very nice man telephoned around twice to find out where he might be and he actually got hold of Herr Strøm. On the telephone he said, '*En ung dame* (a young lady) is looking for you, Strøm!' Well, 'the long and short of it' (where's that from? I don't know!) was that Herr Strøm arrived in his sweet blue suit and saved me. I was allowed to wait for him until the meeting was over. Well, the whole thing turned out all right in the end, as . . . I really like Herr Strøm! . . . Recently we went for a walk together . . . so lovely. Today he stroked me. I'm sorry! I'm acting like a . . . I don't know what . . . like a thirteen-year-old baby . . . An

Watercolour: 'Behind the church', April 1939, Lillestrøm. On the back Ruth
wrote to Judith, 'Please give me your honest opinion. Don't you think it has some
atmosphere? Don't throw it away.' That August Ruth writes, 'Dittl, I find it
touching that my drawing is on your desk.'

eighteen-year-old girl writes to her sister: he stroked me! Like a dog (now I know). I think this is all down to my chronically unfulfilled need for love.

Meanwhile nothing more has happened as far as my Norwegian residency is concerned. Today is 29 March; on the day after tomorrow my permit expires. I'm going to wait until 12 April (expiry date of my English visa). Hopefully I'll be able to stay here. It would be just wonderful to be able to do my Matura! . . . Today I was at the German consulate in Oslo with Herr Strøm. Well, I don't have to tell you about what I felt when I was there . . .

Norway is only separated from Germany by a small stretch of water. That's by the by. I read something frightfully good in the newspaper today. A Frenchman, Georges Duhamel, called Hitler's tactic of 'protecting' one country after another the 'White War'. Not bad at all.

Did I tell you that I read *Hunger* by Knut Hamsun (Knüt Hamsün) in Norwegian? In Norwegian it's called *Sult* (Sült). Not so difficult.

THURSDAY, 30 MARCH 1939, LILLESTRØM

Last night I was lying in bed, all drowsy, when Herr Strøm knocked at the door and asked in such a beautifully soft and unassuming voice, 'Rütt (!) are you asleep yet? Because you can see the Northern Lights outside.' Well, here that's not particularly unusual, but I slipped quickly out of bed and then stood with Herr Strøm at the window for a long time, just looking . . . The Northern Lights is a totally white, milky light that gets weaker and stronger. In some places it sparkles and then dulls again . . . I was very cold, so Herr Strøm fetched a blanket and placed it over my shoulders . . . Dittl, I'm slipping into a romantic fantasy. It's not good for me. Today is 30 March. There's no word yet from the passport office.

FRIDAY, 31 MARCH 1939, LILLESTRØM

Your letter arrived for me yesterday as good as gold, along with the birthday greetings for Turid. It was not quite the right card, as Turid was eight and not seven, you see? Well, I don't have to tell you just what sort of a bash it was here yesterday. All the friends and relations. Today a birthday card from Muschl and one from Grandmother arrived for Turid!

I'm still not working. But this situation is going to change soon. Very soon. Everything will be resolved by 10 April. You know my situation . . . Herr Strøm is so kind that I feel warm all over whenever I think of him. He's so close to me . . . perhaps it's also because he's the only person here that I speak German with. Today we went walking together and now I know that he also . . . loves me. Well, well!

Sometimes I think I'm going crazy. I don't know whether you understand. I often think that it's as if you were all dead . . . Yes, my dearest, your sweet Dita heart starts to thump when it hears the word 'dead'. And says, 'I'm better off being Judith Maier.' Whether *I'm* better off being Ruth Maier is debatable . . . Yesterday, as we were sitting by the fire and burning paper, Turid said, 'Just imagine I were a piece of paper like this and had to be burned.' I liked that. But I don't know whether it fits here.

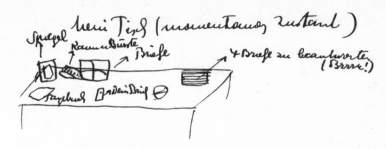

A drawing enclosed with the letter of 31 March.

O Dittl, what else can I tell you? Today I received a letter from Otto in Palestine... After I've finished this letter to you I'll read Ibsen (*Rosmersholm*) and then I'm going to the pictures. Dittl, despite Norway, the cinema, despite all the sun and beautifully blue sky here, despite Herr Strøm etc. etc. I'd rather change places with you. You are able to help, you are able to study! Everything else is? Meaningless.

Whenever I say anything to Herr Strøm he replies loftily, 'Yes, but first your affairs have to be put in order!'

I'm just back from the pictures. (I was alone.) It was called *The Adventures of Marco Polo* with Gary Cooper. I'm just amazed that they're allowed to film such rubbish. It's a quarter to midnight. I'm going to sleep.

Goodnight.

Sleep well.

Sweet dreams.

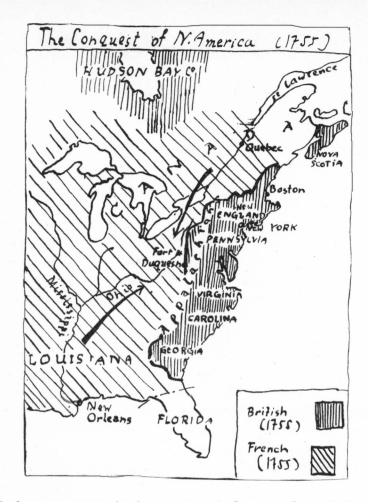

Ruth was very interested in history. Among the few pieces of paper she kept from her time at school in Norway were maps she drew, such as this one: 'The Conquest of North America (1755)'.

The dream of America

APRIL–JUNE 1939

Ruth's worries are growing: her visa expires; she has not yet been able to start at a school; and it may be years before she can be reunited with her family — and that would be in America. In April her mother, Irma, obtains an entry permit for the UK. Ruth is concerned about her grandmother, Anna, who is still in Vienna. Kurt Pollack, who is mentioned from time to time, is a friend from Vienna who has managed to emigrate to the USA.

Spring has arrived, Ruth goes on long walks — along the quayside in Oslo, through the streets of Lillestrøm and out in the woods. The evenings are long and, for her, unusually light. Strøm walks together with Ruth; he is kind to her. Is she in love with him? Is he fascinated by her? On one of their excursions he kisses her. He apologises the following day, but the trust between them is broken. Ruth confides in her sister the following month.

The visa extension is arranged. Ruth can now sit in on penultimate-year classes at the Aker Gymnasium. The school is in Pilestredet, in the centre of Oslo. After the spring of 1939 it is to be closed down and the pupils will be allocated to other schools.

Every school day Ruth takes the train into Oslo. She is praised by her Norwegian teacher for a good essay. She discovers the Deichmann library. She attends meetings of the Workers' Youth League and joins the International Peace League. She gets to know a few young people including Åse, with whom she walks arm in arm through Lillestrøm; and Øyvind, whom she befriends at a political meeting.

The Strøm family plans a touring holiday for the summer, camping in tents. Ruth is excited.

WEDNESDAY, 12 APRIL 1939, LILLESTRØM

I've been in a really foul mood recently. Your letter cheered me up . . . You are sweet, Dittl, to believe that we'll see each other again soon . . . But my matter is now settled: I'm staying in Norway. Today my English visa expires. That means that we probably won't see each other again until America. Please don't think that I'm spluttering this out, my voice choked with tears. I'm not. It's just a fact . . .

The reason for my foul mood is that I have my doubts as to whether Herr Strøm really intends to let me study and learn something. Until now he has used the excuse that my stay here has not yet been properly settled. So now every day I'm waiting . . . and this endless waiting is not fun at all, believe me. I'm already quite nervous.

This is what Herr Strøm said today: 'Today I'll talk to someone from the educational authorities about how you might be able to sit in on Seventh Year classes until June.' When I think of what's going to become of me! Oh well. I tell you, I'd rather not think too hard about my future.

I'll probably arrive in America just having obtained my Matura.

But I'm whining on at you and that's not my normal style. Is it, Dittl? . . . And after all! I mean it's so beautiful here and, save for a few things, I'm very happy. Save for a few things.

Could you get me a registration form for America?

SATURDAY, 22 APRIL 1939, LILLESTRØM

A quarter to ten in the evening.

Right, first of all I give you my highest esteem, thanks, and veneration that – believe it or not – you sent me nineteen kroner, seventy øre. I needed it so badly and shall *never* forget this sisterly favour. Yes, my dear, it is not wholly beneath my dignity to say that I was delighted by the two paper notes (hmmm!). Instead of two paper notes I could also say 'vile Mammon'. But that's overdramatising it. Just one question: where did you get this sum of money from? From Miss Griffith, generosity personified? Or are these your hard-saved groschen, or what is the equivalent of groschen in English? Oh yes, penny, plural pence (I hope that's right). Well, thank you so much in any case. Straight away I gave fifteen kroner to Frau Strøm to put away. She first advised me to deposit it somewhere, rather than carry it around in my purse or it would vanish. Edla was paid back and I immediately bought my 'weekly ticket'. All in all I feel like a multi-millionaire!

Now a question for you, Dittl, which I'd like you to answer by return. Is Mama in England yet? It's a real pleasure to be able to write this sentence: 'Is Mama in England yet?' No really, you must allow me the pleasure of asking it just once more: 'Is Mama in England yet?' I don't intend to comment on my feelings.

I also think about Grandmother. I had a good idea yesterday. If Grandmother is at the stage that she can go to England and all that she needs is someone to escort her, then we have to send an Englishman from England to Germany in order to fetch her. Am I right?

You write that the trip to America will probably happen at the beginning of next year. I'd like to register my strong protest. If I do manage to get into the Eighth Year, I'd want to do my Matura here, of course. That's obvious, isn't it? 'If I manage!' . . . But I'm starting to doubt this . . . You see, my case is currently back down to zero. My Norwegian residence permit has not yet been approved. My English visa has expired. I don't know any more than that. Herr Strøm has also written to the Ministry of Education requesting an exemption from the Middle School Exam. We're now waiting for an answer. That means impasse.

Do you know that Musch called me? I spoke to her and was very happy!! Herr Strøm and Turid also said a few words to Musch.

Dittl, there was a very sweet little episode (with Herr Strøm) . . . But now everything is sort of back on track; it's just that I'm still miserable. It was sickening. Oh well . . . Anyway, you've taught me how to shroud myself artfully in veils and secrets. 'I never disclose everything.' Well, that's enough for today. I'm going to take a bath, then have a read and then . . . sleep, and tomorrow . . . tomorrow, the same again as always. It's wonderful that Musch is there with you!

Excuse me: tomorrow is Sunday. We'll be having soft-boiled eggs for breakfast.

On this postcard Ruth wrote 'church' and 'This is where I live'.
The view is of Storgate, looking north.

POSTCARD TO HER MOTHER – FRIDAY, 19 MAY 1939, LILLESTRØM

On the picture you can see Lillestrøm, Town of the Gods etc. I live in this street. I know this street as well as you know . . . Hockegasse. I live in this street etc. etc. Funny, isn't it? Write soon, Musch. Listen to this! Today I had the *best* composition in our class. In Norwegian. 'The composition might be printed in your newspaper.' (The words of my Norwegian teacher.) Eh? I've a lot to learn and I plan to visit England soon.

SATURDAY, 20 MAY 1939, LILLESTRØM

!!! For Dittl !!!

I'm going to tell you everything! It'll give me great pleasure. The only silly thing is that I told Mama about the whole business and it's so long ago now it sounds a bit banal to me. Anyway, you tell everything quite differently to a sister.

Look: Herr Strøm, I like him a lot, kissed me – wait, I've got to check my diary – on 11 April. Writing this down feels so stupid. We were walking together. You have to know, at the time he was *frightfully* nice to me. He would often stroke me and there were lots of 'caresses'. And sometimes now, when I'm feeling a bit soppy, I long for his caresses. (Doesn't this sound like a schoolgirl novel?) Because, as I'm sure you can imagine, after the 'kiss' there is no question of any more physical closeness. Well . . . Of course, I've got to tell you about it in greater detail.

So, we were walking together and then we took a rest . . . a lovely, sunny spot. We spread out our coats and were so happy . . . both of us. He laid his head on my arm and it felt . . . uncanny . . . I closed my eyes and blinked in the sun . . . Well, then he bent over me and . . .

When I think back to it now it was lovely. But at the time! . . . I went crazy. Wanted to run away. I wrote Pippa a letter: 'You must sort me out a visa right away!' But it was quite serious. Do you know, that night I put an armchair behind the door and a pair of scissors beside me in bed. I don't have to say any more . . . For a day and a half I raced around like a lunatic. In my mind, of course! Outwardly I developed an intense fear of Herr Strøm's hands, his legs, in fact of his whole body. I was so uncertain in his presence. You know, when you live together with a man under the same roof, there are always 'situations', even if it's just his touching my fingers when he hands me the bowl of potatoes . . . But Herr Strøm smelled something immediately. He understood that it was a crime, what he had done. It *was* a crime, against me, against my very self. Well, the next day. Even when I think about it now I still feel a bit ill. Just think, the next day he gave me a talk. That's to say, he apologised . . . and promised that he would not do it again. He gave his assurances that he was not a bad person, that he thought I no longer saw him as a friend and . . . For a long time he stuttered and stammered as we . . . wandered through the streets of Lillestrøm. (He was definitely sweating!) So . . . what was the upshot? No more walks in the sunshine, no more kisses on the cheek, no more hair stroking . . . Of course! Can you imagine that these things would still be possible after everything that happened? Well . . . at some sentimental moments in the evenings, I long . . . for him to be so nice to me again . . . with his hands . . . I think how I sat at the window, looking at the Northern Lights, I was cold and . . . he warmed me up . . . Perhaps you can't even explain these things to your sister. You see, I know that it was brilliant, no I don't mean brilliant, but good and right that it came to that. Don't you think? You understand what I mean. It didn't go any further. After all, you can get ill from such . . . Perhaps, you know, he meant the stroking etc. partly in a paternal way, and it was *me* fooling myself that I liked him and that all this sentimentality was proof that he 'liked' me *too*.

Well, perhaps you're starting to wonder. I myself think that Herr Strøm is taking up too much room in my brain. The day before yesterday I seriously agonised over whether I was in love with him, but in the end I managed to convince myself that I only 'quite like' him. I feel, however, that now he's retreating further and further from me, emotionally as well. He used to be fonder of me . . . in the past . . . when he still used to stroke my bare arms and ask, with a soft smile, 'Are you cold?'

Well, I think that the subject of 'Herr Strøm' has now been exhausted. I have to tell you, though, that he's in fact quite ordinary, sometimes very stupid — no, not stupid, but really not very bright. Nothing 'special' at any rate, not anybody from whom one might be able to learn something. I fancy that I know him terribly well.

I'm going to become a member of the AUF (Workers' Youth League). It's a socialist organisation and my first meeting is on Thursday. I'm already very excited about it. I always need stimulus from others to deal with my inner 'problems'.

The (one) nice thing about living with the Strøms is that they allow me my freedom. And yet, if I tell Frau Strøm that from now on I'll be going to Oslo every Thursday to attend meetings of the Workers' Youth League, I can't be 100 per cent sure of the reaction I would get.

There's so much more I could tell you; after all, it's been so long since our last letters to each other. I just want you to know that I think I'm soon going to have something like a 'friend'. Isn't that great? At the moment I've only felt the labour pains. (Nicely put, eh?) The name of the girl looking for friendship is Åse. (See mother of Peer Gynt, pronounced Oße.) We don't really have anything in common; it's just so nice to go around with her arm in arm and to talk Norwegian with her. She also has a lovely laugh and looks after me. I don't know her surname.

Have I told you about 17 May? It was just so wonderful. 17 May, you see, is Norwegian national day. Processions, flags. I marched alongside them, you know, and sang '*Ja, vi elsker . . .*' (the national anthem). The King was sitting up in the palace with the Crown Prince and Crown Princess. A meek smile on his face. That quite spoiled the atmosphere for me.

THURSDAY, 25 MAY 1939, LILLESTRØM

You know, I think it's just so silly and pointless that we can only 'write' to each other rather than talk face to face. You over here with me and I there with you. Whenever I think about how long it's going to be before we see each other again I get quite melancholic. But think how wonderful it will be to be 'together again'. Close to each other. Anyway, I don't want to get sentimental. But it's a quarter after nine in the evening and through my window I can see that it's as light as in the afternoon. And spring! Norway! I was really happy to receive your letter. You always write so much to me . . . and it's so lovely.

Well, I also knew that you had imagined how the whole thing was with Herr Strøm. How? Well, just from tiny hints in your letters. Once you wrote something like, 'Everything has its limits' etc. Of course Herr Strøm isn't a 'Great Love'. Although I don't know what you understand by 'Great Love'. Look, I think that everybody one likes is a great love. I'm no enthusiast of ordering things by rank: great – greater – greatest love, small – smaller – smallest love. I'd like to try to explain this to you. If I like somebody in the sense of 'love', I like him in a particular, unique way that I cannot compare to anything else. I like Herr Strøm in a very particular way and Williger in a completely different one. So if I like somebody then I just like them. And now I realise that, on account of this 'theory', jealousy is simply impossible.

I'm still 'sitting in' on classes. On average I have two free periods a day. I don't find the school wholly satisfactory. In my free periods I go into the

Deichmann library. It's free. I can sit there and read . . . (I've just started a book on the Russian Revolution!) It's magnificent.

I'm fine at the moment. There are often little things I can look forward to. On Sunday, for example (today's Thursday!) we're going on an excursion in the car that Herr Strøm has just bought . . . Have I told you that I was at a *party* on Monday? A real party with crystal chandeliers, different types of wine and the most elegant evening wear. I smoked cigarette after cigarette, and danced a Rheinländer with Herr Strøm. Yes I did! I was even rather pretty . . . I think. Blue taffeta dress, quite long (Musch sent it over), with red and white make-up, and eyelashes . . . black. But my youth, my eighteen years, was wasted on swine. All the men were wearing . . . wedding rings. The occasion for the party was the 'National Assembly' of the union of telegraph employees. One man (who had a three-year-old son) spoke very kindly to me. He knew Papa, but then everybody knew him. This man also had similar eyes to Williger. He was really so nice to me. At half past two we drove back from Oslo to Lillestrøm. At half past two in the morning it is *so* light here!! As it is at ten o'clock in the evening . . . There were an astonishing number of speeches at the party. One for Herr Strøm! He is, you see, the editor of the *Telegrafbladet*. (Herr Strøm is so versatile!!! Welfare Councillor, editor etc . . . And now he's correcting compositions from the school in Lillestrøm.)

Is my handwriting illegible? I'll write better next time.

THURSDAY, 1 JUNE 1939, LILLESTRØM

At the risk of becoming a nuisance to you, I'm writing straight away. (I'm only writing about 'becoming a nuisance' so that you can protest in a kind and saintly fashion in your next letter etc.) No, honestly, I really do look forward to your letters so much. Just write often. After all, I'm just a poor being abandoned in Norway, who doesn't even know what 'emigration' means. What should I do? Should I run to my window and throw myself out? (Although it's less than one storey high.) Should I slit my wrists to prove to 'the world' that I know what emigration means? Ugh!

Oh yes, the love theory! Look. I don't in principle believe in the idea of a great love. Out of a feeling of purity and self-confidence. Ugh, how ghastly these pining women are, who within themselves are only half a person, and who believe that *he* will redeem them from their innate stupidity and weaknesses. Do you not understand that you have to *work* on yourself? You need to obtain clarity and battle your way through life. 'Battling through' is a nice phrase. It's just that I don't know exactly why we have to battle through. After these sorts of ideas I always think about 'finishing it'. Of course, 'finishing it' would be the last option; an option only to be taken if I no longer knew where I was going. Now I've got carried away and I apologise.

But it's true that this clamour for great love stems from a lack of self-confidence, of independence. And Dittl, get this straight: what do you imagine this great love to mean? Look, I'd like to meet a man with a fit body, as aesthetically pleasing as possible, with whom I could have a child as quickly as possible. And if there's to be no child, then at least I'd like my various needs satisfied; I don't give a damn about the rest. Don't care a bit! Dittl, of course I know that it sounds indecent, but I'm telling you something that I've never told, and will never tell, anybody else. Of course, you don't make any hints in your letters. You might wonder, no, not too much. This 'satisfying needs' is, in my case, somewhat degenerate. Anyway, the business is settled now. Completely. I've pulled myself together. I had a recollection that there is something else apart from high-minded thoughts about socialism and Jewish persecution . . . There is something and this thing is your body.

Dittl, you should get to know Edvard Munch . . . the picture by him is called *Døden i sykeværelset* (Death in the Sickroom). I can send you a copy of it if you like.

WEDNESDAY, 7 JUNE 1939, LILLESTRØM

Half-nine in the evening.

The main thing on my mind at the moment is school. It's all such a mess. I finally got the letter of approval from the Ministry of Education allowing me to do exams in autumn in Maths, Chemistry and Geography. I can study for

Geography by myself, but for Chemistry and Maths (really easy!!) I have to take private tuition. But I can't start private tuition until after our holiday. Oh, you don't know – we're going on a trip! With a tent, I mean camping etc. I'll see the fjords and the high, high Norwegian mountains. I'm so excited already. I'll write to you about our tour, of course.

Well, Dittl, I'm reading through your letter at the moment. Hmmm . . . you completely misunderstood my 'secret'. Do you think I don't know that every girl indulges in a little 'debauchery of the mind' now and then? No, Dittl, I was talking about debauchery of the body, I mean fiddling around in a disgusting way, if you want to know the details. You're not to refer to it in your next letter. But as I said, I've pulled myself together and it's all over . . . completely finished (since 11 April).

Your dream, by the way, is so sweet. Guess what *I* dreamed last night! Grandmother was here, she came to visit me in Norway and told me that I'd been too friendly with Herr Strøm. It can't be fair on Frau Strøm that I, a young girl, smile at her husband at every opportunity etc. I thanked Grandmother profusely and was jolly happy that she'd made it clear to me.

Anyway. I was quite astonished when I woke up that I could have dreamed such a thing. It's really . . . the limit . . . But my relationship with Herr Strøm has . . . cooled off . . . completely, in fact. Of course I'm still looking forward to our snacks and evening meal when we sit together at the table. But that's a tradition (the pleasure, I mean). Have I told you that I'm most fond of him when he's washed his hair? When I think that he once . . . in May, no in April . . . kissed me on the mouth . . . it seems like a . . . just like a fairy tale.

Anyway, Dittl, Herr Strøm has been relegated to the background by a young boy called Øyvind. I met him last week on an excursion with the International Peace League. I don't know if I should detain you from your study with a detailed account of this excursion. What happened, you see, was that I wandered away . . . from the cabin, the meadow, our picnic. He followed me and . . . nothing happened. Åse, Øyvind and I then went for a walk in the woods. It was about a quarter to twelve and so light, you know. We talked the whole time. We went arm in arm together and . . . well, as a chaste maiden I'm not used to that sort of thing. It was really lovely. I hope I will see him again some time.

It's not because he's anything special, but . . . because . . . he's a boy. He has a wonderful, slim body and I also think that his smile is lovely (similar to Kurtl Pollack's). He is twenty-two years old and is studying philology. He's very naïve . . . On the way home (from Oslo) I was so happy . . . as if I were in love . . . but it has passed now.

Dittl, I'm enjoying playing the brazen girl. So: I'd like to see him again . . . because he is a boy, etc. No, things are not going so terribly badly for me. I sometimes start to think a little along these lines. But . . . in moderation. 'And . . . nothing happened' – that was a really cheeky sentence, too, wasn't it? Isn't it daft that I write such stuff? Me! Dittl, you must excuse me. As I said, I'm revelling in the role of the scorned woman, craving . . . physical . . . bodily, not . . . intellectual . . . union. It is personal, it is singular. But sometimes I have these pains when I see a man caressing a woman.

That also happened on the same excursion when I 'met' Øyvind! I saw it . . . I mean I really *saw* it . . . ! I mean, do you really believe that these boys and girls get together there because of peace? Of course!

I think it's so funny that nobody outside Norway has a clue about what's actually happening here and what the Norwegian people are like. Let me tell you something: ceremony, etiquette etc. . . . these things just don't exist here. The Norwegians (that I've met) are all intent on being comfortable and cosy. When anybody comes to visit (*selskap*), you ought to see it . . . Candles on the table (have I not told you about this already?) and . . . they put on the finest clothes. They're very hospitable here . . . and . . . you feel at home immediately . . . Whenever Norwegians get together there's always an 'atmosphere'. They laugh and sing etc. Not like that . . . that particular 'intellectual' mood you get in Jewish company. Heated debates and highbrow attitudes. No, here their discussions are . . . how should I put it? . . . harmless . . . and they laugh together. But behind this 'harmlessness', you know, there is something more profound than you might think . . . I don't think I could tolerate this charming 'cosiness' for ever. But atmosphere, the Norwegians really know how to create atmosphere. Of course, what I've told you is nowhere near the sum total of the Norwegians' character. They have to battle hard here, you know. Norway is a hard country. Nature, etc. but to be honest, I can't tell you much about that from *personal experience*. But have I told you what people say to each other when they meet again after a (nice) evening together? They say, '*Takk for sist*' ('Thanks for last time'). I think that's nice. Although I find the *Takk* obsession over the top.

I'm only smoking when I dare accept cigarettes that people offer me!!! Hmm.

I'll manage alone. Don't you think?

LETTER TO HER MOTHER – SATURDAY, 17 JUNE 1939, LILLESTRØM

First of all, Musch, I'd like just to tell you that it's Frau Strøm's birthday on 23 June. Do send her a card or . . . if you feel the irrepressible urge . . . a letter.

Musch, please tell me what you've done with my diaries. I do feel like a bit of a joke always . . . asking for my diaries . . . as if they were my greatest treasure etc. I'd like to have my little blue diary . . . the one with Kurtl's dedication. As far as I'm concerned you can burn all the others.

The loveliest thing of all here is that the nights are so light. I'm horrified when I think that in . . . America it's already pitch black around nine o'clock. It's so light, you know, that I have *absolutely* no desire to go to bed. You can't go for a walk until the evening. I must say, the area around Lillestrøm is pretty. It really is.

Musch, I've had a brilliant idea. If grandmother is to buy something with all the money she has saved, then she should buy me a bicycle.

Please!

The German bicycles are so cheap, you know. You can get one for fifty Reichsmarks. It could even be a *second-hand* one. I'd much rather she bought me a bicycle than a spring coat. Please think about the bicycle! Quite apart from the fact that everybody here has a bicycle, I really need one. There's absolutely no traffic here, so you shouldn't be worried about *that*! Turid has one, too, and I am, after all, *eighteen* years old!!

Please!!! I just can't accept the idea that Grandmother might *leave* money behind in Vienna. And just think what a pleasure it is in *America* to have a bicycle. No need to spend money on travelling.

Musch, I've sent these photographs to Dittl, too. In an outburst of extravagance I've made far too many copies.

That's us in front of the National Gallery in Oslo. A bit to the left is my school. What do you think about those grinning faces? And don't I look as if I'd like to . . . *at the very least* seduce the chap next to me . . . or . . . that's quite enough!

This is our class in front of the statue of Wergeland. (Wergeland is

In this photograph of the Latin class at the Aker Gymnasium Ruth is standing behind on the far right. In the picture above she is sitting on the far right.

probably the greatest Norwegian poet; it was down to his efforts that Jews were allowed into Norway.) The girl in the middle at the front is called . . . Solveig.

MONDAY, 19 JUNE 1939, LILLESTRØM

Until now I've been sitting in on the second Latin class at the Aker Gymnasium . . . And in autumn I was supposed to join the third Latin class as a regular pupil, but take exams in those subjects the others have already passed. You see, the system here is that each year you complete one or two subjects, which means that you only do two or three subjects for Matura (*artium*). Do you understand? So in October I'm supposed to be taking exams in Chemistry, Geography and Maths!

'You're eager to know what the complication is.' Yes! Right, the first thing is that our class is being disbanded. There are only eight of us in total. Then the school is being torn down, or something like that. So at the moment I'm back to square one. Of course, the headmaster will place me somewhere else, but he cannot guarantee that I'll be accepted straight away as a regular pupil. School begins in September already and I've got examinations in October. Now we've got to apply again to the Ministry of Education . . . etc. etc. I know that this endless muddle bores you.

I must tell you about what's been happening with Øyvind, that young Norwegian. Ha, ha!! I haven't seen him since. On 23 June (St John's Eve, summer solstice, celebrations etc.) the IPL, of which he is a member, is organising a trip to the Oslo fjord. To a little island . . . bonfires will be lit, dancing etc. I'm sure it would have been great fun. But I don't want to give myself heartache. 1. The evening would get very late and we are starting our tour the next day. 2. I don't have any money . . . Really, I'm totally penniless. 3. It's Frau Strøm's birthday on 23 June. Herr Strøm said, 'She might think it important that you stay at home.' Oh well, adieu St John.

All the people I know are about thirty to forty. 'Young couples' visit the Strøm household, but these people are no longer young . . . they just look it at first glance. I've only been together with really young people once: that was with Øyvind. It was wonderful. Øyvind may not be a soulmate, but . . . nonetheless.

Every month I receive ten kroner from Frau Strøm. It's quite tight. Just imagine! And then there's Frau Strøm's birthday, I ought to buy her something but I've *absolutely* no money. I'll borrow some from Herr Strøm. Very convenient.

The nights are now really quite light. I don't think I'll ever be able to get used to dark nights again.

I go for walks at night and generally retire to bed about eleven o'clock.

TUESDAY, 20 JUNE 1939, LILLESTRØM

Right, Dittl, the first thing I've got to do is to give you our *temporary* summer address: Ørevik, Figgeskjær, Langesund (pronounced: Örevik, Figgeschär, Langesünd). Pretty good, eh? On 24 June – Saturday – we're setting off with the car, tent, spirit burner, rubber mattress etc. etc. Langesund is on the Skagerrak coast. Actually it's also on the Oslo fjord. Like this:

From Langesund we are going to continue over the mountains to the fjords on the western coast. By the way, I think it's about time you made the effort to look at Norway on the map. Hmmm. You might even find Lillestrøm.

There is an atheistic atmosphere here. Not in Lillestrøm, but specifically in the Strøm household. Herr Strøm is *absolutely* anti-religious. He doesn't even like going into churches . . . I think his attitude is a bit childish. He's not a fanatical atheist. The Strøms are (I'd almost like to say Thank God!) *never* fanatical. But he has a quiet aversion to everything to do with 'Christ thou art our saviour' etc. Frau Strøm acquiesces in her husband's opinion . . . as she does in everything.

Seeing as I've embarked on another discourse about this godlike figure, I ought to tell you that I had a very depraved dream about him last night . . . He made love to me! It was jolly fun, I can tell you. He switched between gently caressing me . . . and then all of a sudden grabbing me roughly and . . . I can't say exactly . . . Then we sort of . . . 'rolled about' in the bathtub. In short it was idyllic. I haven't been burdening my mind with him at all recently, so this dream came something like a thunderbolt out of a clear sky.

In your letter you write so wittily about how the 'power of youth disappears when singing hymns', while I write grovelling (why grovelling? Think about it!) descriptions of my dirty dreams. Yes. 'Change of policy!'

You have to tell me whether you have a good idea of how *I* live in Norway. My days just pass between breakfast, lunch and dinner. Eating here is a sort of ceremony. People don't see eating as simply the act of 'eating', but also as being together, talking, laughing etc. in a convivial atmosphere. Here they don't have anything like 'gobbling down' food...

What am I reading? At the moment I'm actually reading bits from Eduard Bernstein's *The Strike as an Instrument of Political Struggle*. I bought it myself (thirty øre, about the same price as a stamp). And then I'm reading Ibsen. *The Master Builder*. You know, you really ought to learn Norwegian, too. Just think about it! Maybe in America . . . we'll read Ibsen together.

Well, then I'm reading a book by Trotsky. (Norwegian translation from the Russian) *Mitt liv* (My Life), and in the Deichmann library (now closed!) Trotsky's *Russian Revolution*, too . . . I'd just love finally to have some clarity about my political views. I find it ridiculous that an eighteen-year-old still has no idea of her convictions...

This is a Social Democratic household. Through and through. Only once have Herr Strøm and I had a political argument. I lay on the ground and he was perched by the fire. He gave me a lecture on the Norwegian Workers' Party. He was quite astonished when I asked him what he had against communism . . . Apart from that I did not contradict him. I could still kill myself for this.

If there's anybody one might envy it's Herr Strøm. He's so sane, you know, so contented. Here's an example: whenever you talk with him for any length of time, the 'conversation' changes into a lecture on his part. Whether it's about . . . Norwegian herrings . . . or the . . . workers' movement . . .

Frau Strøm . . . is really sympathetic to the 'Left'. She's also afraid of thunder and lightning . . . But isn't it a universal feature of all happy marriages that *she* is 50 per cent below his level? Or can you imagine that a wife would feel happy if she *couldn't* look up to him?

Oh well, if I'm to come back to this world again, then there's no way I want to return as a girl.

And yet, not even I would wish that my man had to look up to me . . . The best would be . . . that we were equals. Yes, nothing is going to develop from my meeting with Øyvind. There's nothing to be done. Very stupid.

Something else you'd notice is just how enthusiastically they celebrate their parties . . . or . . . perhaps it's just me who enjoys them so tremendously . . . You know, I've got used to enjoying the least thing. At the moment: summer holidays, Langesund, mountains . . . I don't know what's coming next. Or: that's right – now I can really start to look forward to America . . .

After all that I've written you must think me totally daft. But I'm not yet.

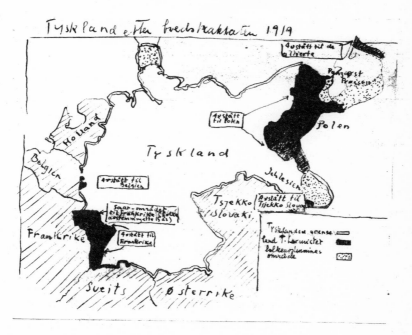

A map drawn by Ruth: 'Germany after the Peace Treaty of 1919'.

*Ruth Maier on a trip to the Tyrifjord with Arne
and Dagmar Strøm in August 1939.*

Summer holidays

JUNE–AUGUST 1939

Ruth goes with the Strøm family on a two-week touring holiday: Herr and Frau Strøm, their daughter Turid and Frau Strøm's brother Tormond (Tobben). First they drive to the family's cabin in Langesund and stay by the coast for a few days. Ruth goes fishing for cod.

The holiday continues on to western Norway. Ruth mentions Geirangerfjord and postcards show the mountain road Trollstigen in Romsdal. They cross the fjords by ferry. Their tour makes its way back home via Gudbrandsdal and the Rondane Mountains. Ruth writes to her mother, 'Outside there is snow on the mountains. Norway is magnificent. I'll tell you more about it when I get home. I mean: I'll never return home.'

In summer 1939, Ruth also starts to write about brief encounters with a few young gentlemen, as well as describing the preparations for, and realisation of, a successful meeting with Miss McLachlan, her sister's gymnastics teacher in Brighton. The letters frequently reveal how she is caught between her desire to be reunited with her family in England and her efforts to take her Matura in Norway the following spring. The newspapers carry reports about the threat of war.

Dr Williger, Ruth's former Latin tutor, has fled to London. Ruth's mother, Irma, has arrived in England; her grandmother, Anna, is on her way there.

WEDNESDAY, 28 JUNE 1939, LANGESUND

Between Lillestrøm and Langesund there is so much sea, sun . . . and gramophone records etc . . . Right, so I'm sitting in our cabin. Before me is
Langesund and a tiny bit of open sea. You know, Norway really is a wonderful
country. I'm just talking about the landscape now. Here the sea is not like in
all those seaside resorts, Grado etc. – you know, just with sand. No . . . here
there are mountains and woods, all quite green . . . No, you have to be here.
Today we went on a fantastic sailing trip. Not in the open sea, but between an
endless number of islands, and woods and rocks. As in a fairy tale. Langesund
is a tiny seaside town. With fishermen's huts and the smell of salt water,
chunky Norwegians with pipes and the obligatory blond youngsters in the
streets...

It is very beautiful here. We've been here for three days, by the way. Today
is Wednesday and on Saturday we'll be moving on.

I love the sea. I really do. A short while ago we drove in the car out to
a place where the sea lies before you, so open and wide. I sat on a rock in
my brassiere and panties . . . the waves came right up to me. It was so
wonderful.

After this uncivilised outpouring about Norway's scenic beauty, of which
you must now have an excellent idea having read these lines, I shall carry on
regardless.

I must tell you that we're doing an awful lot of fishing. Cod mainly. It's
just brilliant. The day before yesterday we got up at three in the morning. You
mustn't think that fishing here is a tedious affair. Ha ha! We caught twenty
fish! . . . The feeling when you get a bite . . . Oh well.

I don't read any papers here and so my worries are few. There's another
positive thing! I've 'seen through' Herr Strøm. I've never come across such
self-confidence before . . . He knows everything. He knows how to navigate
sailing boats, steamboats, motor boats; how to catch fish; identify seabirds;
the name of this and that flower; what the weather will be like tomorrow; how
to use a spirit burner etc. Other people know these things too, obviously, but
there is such a broad understanding in the way he conveys the various facets
of his knowledge that I feel quite unnerved whenever I listen to him. He
makes philosophical observations at every turn, all terribly shallow. He

carries most of his convictions around with him on a tray . . . In a nutshell, he's slowly but surely getting on my nerves. I feel very happy here, nonetheless. In the evenings when I smoke a cigarette (!!!) in the company of Turid, Tobben, Herr Strøm etc. everything is fine. Yes. I still have to describe Tobben to you. Frau Strøm's brother. Bachelor with an unhappy love life. I'm obsessed by the idea that he's being eaten by a silent grief. He's starting to develop a bald patch and he sleeps like a newborn baby. He laughs a lot and is in a constant verbal sparring match with Herr Strøm. He offers me cigarettes, but otherwise sees me as just a little child. My relationship with Turid is very good at the moment. For some unknown reason I feel awfully tearful whenever Herr Strøm strokes Turid or sits her on his lap. I always have to look away and I start to feel very miserable.

Did you know that I'm drawing? A silent craze. What can you do?

Seagulls are screeching outside. It's fantastic to listen to, you know. Seagulls are wonderful . . . If I were an animal . . . I'd like to be a seagull (original?). If I were a boy, I'd like to be a sailor. Sometimes I get the feeling that I've seen all this before . . . the wonderful Norwegian coast . . . and sometimes I think I'm dreaming.

Pencil drawing: 'Evening', Langesund 1939.

Besides the 'natural' pleasures, I'm leading the existence of a nun. Ha! I've reached the point where every male being is a sensation and I think, 'If you want it, then I want it too . . . Please!' Isn't that tragic? But it can't remain like this. Either I'll soon become a total man hater, or the object of my desire will appear on the horizon. On two occasions yesterday a couple of males appeared before my eyes. One of them might be a possibility. He owns a sailing boat (see above), but he's chosen for himself a beguiling Norwegian girl. He's blond, smiling and radiates youth. Well! The other one, brother of the above, is a peachy baby.

Now a few more lessons about the Norwegian psyche. Ha! Isn't that just typical? Tonight we're having a 'party'! We're going to light a bonfire, and Frau Strøm is darting around the place to make it nice and *koselig* (cosy). We'll play gramophone records and our conversations will not be much more than prattle. I'm actually far too dependent on these people here. I can't really explain it to you, but I feel very comfortable when I'm 'allowed' to be with them. Do you understand? All in all the Norwegians are a very friendly race and yet a Jewish face . . .! Whenever I see a Jewish face here, I feel a terrible urge to go over – without embarrassment – to go over to the Jew and ask him questions, talk to him etc.!

In all honesty, swimming around on one's own in Norway is no joke. It's just a 'blessing' that I'm allowed to be here with them . . . listening to gramophone records, fishing . . . Sometimes I forget, you know, and I think that I really am one of them. Then one of your letters arrives, or a Jew crosses the street . . . or Herr Strøm strokes Turid . . . or someone says something provocative to me . . . and then the feeling of belonging vanishes.

God be with you, Dittl. No, I can't stand the word God.

I'm quite sure that I'm a socialist! Quite, quite clear. And I think I'm a Zionist, too!

FRIDAY, 30 JUNE 1939, LILLESTRØM

We're moving on in an hour's time: into the mountains. Dittl, I'd like to be in England . . . I don't want to be in Norway if there's a war. Christ! Do you think I should write to London about my visa? I've read the newspaper. Write straight away to Lillestrøm.

If you, with your greater understanding of the conditions etc., think that my coming to England is exactly the right thing to do, because of the war etc., then do what's necessary. Go to the Coordinating Committee (Nursing Department), Bloomsbury House, Bloomsbury Street, London WC1. Tell them you're the sister of Ruth Maier to whom they've promised a visa. That it's got to this stage. I would have had my visa already. The application had already been made to the Wallnerstraße,* but then I wrote to them to say that I wanted to do my Matura first and make use of the visa afterwards. They wrote to tell me that was all right. Dittl, I think it's absolutely the right thing to do to come to London if there's a war. After all, I have to help. Norway will remain neutral. I'm very much at peace when I write. Do what you think you have to. I'd like to come.

POSTCARD TO HER MOTHER, EARLY JULY 1939, RONDANE

Ha! Isn't it wonderful here? (Actually, I was not at this spot exactly. Only nearby.) My mood might plummet if I read the newspaper up there. Oh well . . . for the meantime I'm happy.

Outside there is snow on the mountains. Norway is magnificent. I'll tell you more about it when I get home. I mean: I'll never return home. I . . . well. I don't want to think about the future. (Last night we slept in the tent.)

* The address of the British Embassy in Vienna.

Postcard showing the Rondane Mountains.

POSTCARD TO HER MOTHER, 8 JULY 1939, RONDANE

Ten o'clock (evening).

We're sitting in our tent in bluey-grey mountains, 1,000 metres up. I'm brown all over, I've just smoked a cigarette after a huge dinner, and we sang. I'm so happy, it's a real disgrace. It's foggy outside. The mountains here are so . . . you can't describe it . . . You know, I've never seen so many new and beautiful things in a fortnight. Fjords, sea, mountains you wouldn't even dream of. Snow, waterfalls, sky. Sometimes it's really lovely to be alive – When you get this letter I'll be back in Lillestrøm already. Pity! (Interesting sign-off!)

Norway is soo beautiful. (They've started singing again.)

Postcard showing the 'Trollstig' — a mountain pass to the east of Ålesund, opened in 1936.

SATURDAY, 8 JULY 1939, LILLESTRØM

Midnight.

We arrived back in Langesund when Herr Strøm asked suddenly, 'Have you read the newspaper? . . . War's coming.' I read it and war looked so certain that I became terribly afraid . . . and wrote you the letter.

Because, Dittl, if war comes and I'm in Norway, then I'll be one of the unhappiest people in the world. You can cite this as an argument *against* my staying in Norway. Dittl, today I'm *not* writing with any 'cheer'. Another letter arrived with yours saying that I've been accepted as a regular pupil at the Frogner school. I have to do a Maths exam in German first. Then I'll do my Matura in June 1940. Now I have to ask you and Musch and Pippa again, and it's very, very urgent: do you think it would be a good idea for me to stay in Norway and do my Matura? I'm forgetting all my English; I've got a piece of paper in my hand that doesn't even have a mark for English on it. I also have this sweet vision of having to have my Matura certified (is that what you call it?) in America. What a joke that would be. I torment myself here for a whole year with three kinds of Norwegian, yet there I'd be in America, with my freshly printed school-leaver's certificate and not a word of English . . . How sweet!

You see, Dittl, today's letter is just like the last one. You have to help me and tell me what you think. Please reply to me as quickly as possible. I have to take private lessons for my exam, you see, so I'd like to know in advance exactly where I stand. Another thing: if I start school and we get permission to go to America this year, then you simply have to go without me. Because it's quite clear that if I stay in Norway I'll remain here until I've taken my Matura!!! That is a very important point. But if I come to England, then we'll go together, and I'll have a little time beforehand to swot up on English . . . I do believe that there are more reasons in favour of England. I just think that until June 1940 I should toil away at the *Norwegian* Matura. But perhaps I'm very much mistaken. You know I'm very open to all counter-arguments. Dittl, I'm not thinking at all about my desire to see you, but what is more sensible? If I come to England then one thing is clear: I will have to work as a nurse in a hospital. Do you think that's a counter-argument? I really can't say that I *want* to become a nurse.

Dittl, I imagine that my lengthy debate has set your brain whirring. But be so kind as to consider what's best. Dittl, I really do think about you often.

Dittl, our camping trip was so lovely. Magnificent. Norway is incredibly beautiful. I've seen so much over the last few days. When I think back on it now it's as if it were a dream. It was all like a picture book. It was new, you know, so, so new. The fjords are more than just small bodies of water, after all. When I think that I want to leave Norway . . . I am also sooo fond of the Norwegians.

This morning I woke up at 1,000 metres. In the tent. There was a fine drizzle. It was foggy outside, the mountains were so . . . yellowish and blue and green . . . every colour, in fact. A lot of reindeer moss, no trees. We made coffee inside the tent (coffee drinking is an obsession here in Norway!!!), it was so cold outside. Herr Strøm and Tobben shaved (very sweet!). We sang, too. Norwegians have beautiful songs. (Grieg was Norwegian, perhaps you knew that.) Yesterday evening we sang Solveig's (Sulvei) song and other songs. I also smoked a cigarette with great pleasure.

We were in Dovre (you know, from *Peer Gynt*). In Vestlandet, that's to say the western coast, we crossed the fjords by ferry. There you are at sea level and you can see mountains above you, very tall with snow and everything else that mountains should have. The valleys are very narrow, you know, and mountains so terribly jagged like . . . bone lace . . . so high up . . . massive waterfalls gush down from the very highest peak. Simply ridiculous.

Everything I'm telling you is so unconnected because I can only see images before me! Images, do you understand? When I saw the Geirangerfjord for the first time I had this very unreal feeling. The water in that fjord is so, so still, like glass...and to the left and right there are mountains, high up, with snow. And seagulls above the fjord. Do you like hearing gulls shrieking, too?

Really, Dittl, I describe nature very badly. I give up . . . But I've also got to know Norway's people a little. Everybody waves when you pass them in the car. And they laugh as they wave. A Norwegian laugh, if you like. Some of them call out '*heia*'; that's like the English 'Hello'.

Dittl, I've got something very important to tell you! If I gave in to my lethargy I would remain in Norway. If I think about it, if I shake myself, then I'll understand that I should go to England. Yes, and then there's the yearning.

THURSDAY, 13 JULY 1939, LILLESTRØM

Oh yes, your gymnastics teacher. Well, I could meet up with her on Sunday, 6 August. I'll put on my blue suit, besides I don't have a coat! (Makes a 'plain, modest and yet . . .' impression.) Blue stockings, blue shoes. And red lips, obviously! She should meet me at the Karl Johan Grand Hotell. (It's as I've written it.) Anyway, Karl Johan is Oslo's boulevard which is *bound* to disappoint her. (You can only really *like* Oslo when you get to know it better.) Of course I'd love to show her Oslo. That's to say, the things I know! What is she interested in? Herr Strøm and I will draw up a so-called plan of what I ought to show her. And he'll come over all desperately important. But, oh God! Did you know that during our holiday Herr Strøm made frantic efforts to teach me how to be practical? That's to say he tried to turn me into somebody who might notice when one of the wheels on the car was loose, etc.

We had a nice, friendly argument at Rondablikk, 1,000 metres above sea level. Ha, ha! I'm turning into an *åndelig snobb* (an intellectual snob). This statement only goes to show that he doesn't know me at all. But he fancies that he does. Totally . . . Anyway, the only repercussion of that 'blissful April' is that both he and I are frightfully reluctant to touch each other's hands.

Am I thinking of acting? (Hmm.) I'm on the floor, frantically searching through the box of books for a volume of Goethe's plays, which I will attempt to read. I want to see whether my 'talent' hasn't already evaporated. I've already given up the idea of becoming an actress myself. That is further proof for you of how I'm 'turning towards real life'. Look, when I read *Danton's Death* on the loo I was certainly a great actress. Afterwards I was awfully hoarse, and Frau Singer was so desperate because she'd really 'needed to go'. (Nice expression?)

FRIDAY, 28 JULY 1939, LILLESTRØM

If you've ever doubted that you have a model sister, then you should regret it now. Outside it is brilliant sunshine, and my heart – I mean my body – is craving a nice sunbathe on the roof; yet I'm sitting here in my room writing to you . . . Dittl, Dittl, what will become of me? It's more than three days now since I learned a single thing . . . I'm prancing about in the sun and going swimming. What's more, I made two 'swimming acquaintances' today. Two youths by the name of Herman and Åge; each one as stupid and disagreeable as the other. But that's no reason for my not meeting up with them tomorrow. I shall, so to speak, pounce on these two with all the fervour of a dedicated virgin.

I'm sure I already told you that the Strøms never challenge me on anything. When I get back home from Oslo at about half past midnight, I don't even get a reproachful look…What am I up to in Oslo until half past midnight? . . . You see, that is my secret . . . I stroll . . . stand by the shop windows . . . and I'm endlessly reaching for my purse to buy this or that . . . but then I decide that this or that is wholly unnecessary. And then of course I go walking in the harbour by the fjord. The shouts from all the tall, blond Norwegian boys 'spirit me up', or to put it in our language, put me in good spirits.

There's so much I actually wanted to tell you about today. But my mind is coming to a standstill. Honestly, you really don't have a clue about Norway. There aren't any castles here, you know, nor are there any villages. Not like Zarošice, for example. No! Here the farms are widely spread among the fields.

So not like Zarošice. Each farm has its own barn and a house where the family lives. The barn is red and it shines . . . Dittl, I've turned stupid, telling you all this boring nonsense. Norway is of course quite foreign to you, and I don't know where to begin. Does it interest you to hear that only 30 per cent of the population live in towns? That for this reason there are very few towns? Oslo only has 250,000 inhabitants. Look, there's a change in the Miss McLachlan business. Unfortunately I told Frau Strøm that I would be meeting one of your teachers in Oslo. She told her husband . . . and her husband . . . has now offered to drive her round Oslo in his car. It's so typical . . . I can picture it right now . . . I'll go along with them, but of course he'll do all the talking. His English is painfully bad, but still. He'll explain everything. One of his passions.

Very sweet. (When I ask him at lunchtime, 'What sort of fish are we eating today?' I'm only doing it to please him.)

I'm struggling with Herr and Frau Strøm. And I'm going crazy. I'm happy at the moment, you see. I'll go up to the roof and read a book about the political workers' international . . . Yesterday I listened to Moscow! Herr Strøm listened in too.

Look, of course it's mean for me to keep on writing horrible things about him. He's a socialist, you know, more a democrat than a socialist, that's all there is to it. But he's not hungry, so it's often the case that I cannot bear him. I can only love hungry people . . . on a long-term basis. But as I said, that's no reason for my not meeting those two boys tomorrow.

Couldn't you ask Pippa to pay a visit to Williger? Dittl! Don't be mean, trying to thwart my plans! Honestly! I pined for him again a few days ago. But now that has all passed and you should simply ask her to visit him. She should contact him regarding English lessons. Please be so kind as to write that to her. She should tell him she's a refugee and then he won't ask for very much. Of course, she could always go away again without taking any English lessons. She should just go there and make enquiries! And she's to say nothing about me, of course. Not even that she knows me!!

Dittl, a sweet 'performance' from Herr Strøm. His lip quivering, he's just told me that I mustn't go and sunbathe on the roof any more. By sitting on the crown of the roof I attract attention: 'In my attracting all this attention I should take more consideration of him and his wife.' That's what happens when you live in a town of 8,000 people. For goodness sake!

When I left Germany I'm sure I told you that there was a chap from the Balkans in my carriage. I lay there with my hands behind my head and stared into thin air. And he said, 'What are you dreaming of . . . is it happiness?'

I've just thought of that, I don't know why.

I really must tell you that the Norwegians adore the Swedes. I must have told you that already. And yet, you know, the Norwegians almost went to war with the Swedes in 1905. And now every Norwegian becomes rapturous whenever you mention the word 'Swede'. I think the Norwegians are much friendlier than the Swedes, they look up to them,

Ugh! How boring! Be good and write soon.

The postcard shows Storgate in Lillestrøm.
Ruth has marked the Strøm's house with an arrow.

POSTCARD
THURSDAY, 3 AUGUST 1939, LILLESTRØM

Now I'm taking my revenge with an incredibly flattering card of Storgate where I live (stor = large; gate = street). Supposing we compare Brighton (Front) with Lillestrøm (Storgate). Well, this is where I promenade my dear etc. etc . . . You can see that there is plenty of woodland here, and sky. Actually I ought to give you a detailed description (see above) of the various shops and other sights. We live at the crossroads. Just think, my child, that Lillestrøm is among the second group of largest towns in Norway. First, of course, you have Oslo, Trondheim and Bergen . . . I await your letter and hope that you can appreciate the sacrifice that such a card costs (thirty-five øre).

FRIDAY, 4 AUGUST 1939, LILLESTRØM

(Hamsun is eighty years old today!)

Dittl, I find it touching that my drawing is on your desk . . . I really do
. . . But how can you put up with such awful pictures in your room. If it were
me, I would of course make short shrift of it and throw the lot of them out
in one go. I've also had ghastly prints like that; they're now lying on the floor.
Beauty, my dear, beauty etc.

I'm not speaking any German at all, you know! Although our 'neighbour', who's called Gulbrandsen, sometimes makes poor efforts to refresh his
German in conversation with me. He pauses for about five minutes after each
word, which I think is a bit exaggerated. The result of this is that the tips of
my toes start to itch et cetera (isn't it nice to write out etc. in full?). So I speak
Norwegian all day long. At the start I was a genius . . . but I'm slowly hitting
a limit, do you understand? It's very difficult to proceed beyond a certain
limit . . . The ability to move around a language with total freedom must be
something quite different. I can pretty much read everything by now. I'd like
awfully to buy Norwegian books, but they're so expensive it's a joke.

I am going to tell you about Norway. I get the feeling that I'm a living
geography or history book, but that doesn't matter. Right, first a little geography. I'll endeavour not to bore you, but if you do get bored you must clear
your throat or something like that. The capital is Oslo! . . . (is that not fitting?). Oslo is the largest port in the whole of Scandinavia. There are always
many large ships there, and gazing at them for some time arouses a distinct
yearning. Most of these ships go to England and America etc. Overall,
Norway has a disproportionately large merchant fleet, in fifth place after
England, Germany, Japan and America . . . At the beginning, you know, when
you're here, you sort of look down on Norway . . . from the heights of your
central European culture or erudition. You have the feeling that these
Norwegians, Swedes, Danes . . . ought really to be pitied. You think that they
are dwarfs who want to join in. It's not a conclusion you arrive at immediately.
To begin with, of course, you affirm just how tremendously you appreciate
the 'free north', but basically (see above) 'you' are superior. You only realise
gradually that, by comparison with Scandinavian culture, you're inferior
rather than superior. I can remember that when Herr Strøm said the

Norwegian merchant fleet was ranked fifth I felt very ashamed . . . I have to admit that I would not have believed it of them. You laugh when they turn Ibsen and Bjørnson into a cult here, something we don't even do with Goethe or Schiller. And when they start talking about Ibsen, you think, 'Well, why shouldn't you lot have some of the off-cuts from our great men?' . . .

And that's completely wrong, you know.

These 'prejudices' are simply the fault of our upbringing. I mean the education we received at school. In literature we only hear about Goethe, Schiller, Heine, Grillparzer etc. In history, about Barbarossa, the various Charleses, Henrys, French Revolution etc.

And when you come here, everything is so new that you instinctively put yourself on a 'pedestal' and observe the goings-on around you . . . But I've reached the conclusion that Nordic culture is unique, certainly in Europe. For example, there is real democracy here. Press freedom and all those things that our ancestors fought for 'heroically' in various revolutions. You know, I think the best way of gauging culture is by the quality of the newspapers. In my opinion, Norway holds its own with the best of the Western democracies. When I think of Germany and small newspapers like the *Wiener Journal*, which kept on changing their political line within a couple of years.

Dittl, I don't know how I could let myself get carried away and gush like that with such grave solemnity. And a quivering undertone at the end. Ugh! Mind you, some of it is right, the bit at the beginning about feeling 'superior'. Norway is incredibly large, you know, as large as England: 324,000 km². When you talk to a Norwegian, Norway is always the small country: 'We've got a good life, we're a small country.' That's because only 2.5 million people live in the whole of Norway. Imagine! That's about as many as in Vienna!! Isn't that absurd?

I'll stop now, Dittl! I've already heard you clearing your throat several times. The end.

I've heard nothing yet from Miss McLachlan.

SATURDAY, 5 AUGUST 1939, LILLESTRØM

A quarter past nine in the evening.

Just picture this, Dittl, I'm sitting at the typewriter, torturing myself trying to copy something from Maxim Gorky for Pippa (I've completely ruined the typewriter, by the way), when the telephone rings and who is it? . . . Miss McLachlan. First of all I can hear two female voices whispering in English, then among the whispers I can clearly make out a voice . . . it's Miss McLachlan's. She's got the letter and wants to know whether I'd like to come at a quarter past nine tomorrow. A little later, I say; so I'm going to the Hotel Regina at ten tomorrow. I'm very much looking forward to it, but I don't know what to show her, or whether I'll be able to keep up a conversation in English! I'm now (quarter past nine, see above) furiously going to revise my English grammar. Luckily, when I was on the phone it occurred to me to say, 'I am very glad to see you.' (I missed out the 'tomorrow', unfortunately.) Then it occurred to me that one ought to say 'Goodbye'. She said, 'It is very kind of you.' What have you got to say to your sister then, eh? I'll put on my suit tomorrow, apply a discreet covering of lipstick, and . . . well. I really must learn English.

Detailed description of Miss McLachlan, my performance etc. in my next letter. Goodnight.

SUNDAY, 6 AUGUST 1939, LILLESTRØM

You are in *total* suspense. You've got my intriguing card from the Karl Johan and you want to know what it was like. Yes you do. Well, it was really very nice. These three English ladies were all waiting for me together in the Hotel Regina lounge. First I took them to the fjord and then we went to Bygdøy by ferry. Miss McLachlan really is delightful. On the ferry I only talked to Miss McLachlan, and for the most part I was very happy. Really I was. She did ask me rather sanctimoniously whether I went to church and whether the people I lived with went to church, but I was in good spirits and her questions only made me more artful. Twice she tried to elicit something from me. But the fact that she couldn't disguise her ulterior motives only showed her naïveté. Look, first she asked whether you wanted to become a nurse: 'Miss Griffith would like to train Judith to become a nurse, you see . . . she only needs her Higher School Certificate . . . Judith does think this is a good idea . . . doesn't she?'

Then she asked whether you were going to come with us to America. I sensed that Miss Griffith had given her the task of finding this out. Do you know what else she said? She said it wasn't good that you spent (or 'spend') so much time together with Pippa. I mean, she is a political refugee! I asked ever so carefully whether she thought it might do you harm. Oh well. On Bygdøy (a sort of public park, like the Praterauen) we just had a look at the Folkesmusem (Folk museum). You can well imagine that I was really happy the whole day. I asked about you, Miss Griffith and everything, everything. She said that you were working very hard and were very nice . . . The two other ladies then vanished and the two of us had 'lunch' alone. Fish and fruit salad, and I do believe that, apart from a few pauses, we made conversation the whole time. I felt so independent. There I was, an emigrant alone in Norway and I wasn't uncertain or embarrassed for a single moment. Really, I mean that. After all, I have lived a bit, I'm not a child any more, I'm surviving on my own (even if I'm dependent ultimately) in Norway. The other thing was that I felt so incredibly Norwegian, born and bred. Just imagine, I was able to speak Norwegian with the natives. (I honestly think I've never spoken Norwegian as well in my life as I did yesterday. It was as if Norwegian were my native tongue.) I really ought to tell you more. It was lovely on the ferry: Oslo behind us with the ships and next to me on the bench someone who knows you, who's seen you every day. Bygdøy was very beautiful. We raced between the various farmhouses and looked at a wonderful *stavkirke*.* Over lunch Miss McLachlan even gave me a half-full bottle of perfume and although a dog tore my orange scarf to shreds it was quite idyllic. There was music playing on the wireless and I let on to Miss McLachlan that you liked dancing. She was astonished. She also told me that Miss Griffith likes you very much and would like to do everything she can to make you happy. She said this quite genuinely and I became convinced that you ought to be very nice to Miss Griffith. You see, everything I'm telling you is so fragmentary.

You must try to imagine how I stuttered, how dishevelled I was and how

---

* A wooden (*stave*) church, of medieval origin and particular to Norway.

softly she smiled at me. I asked her whether she thought I looked like you and she answered, 'Yes.' It's just that I'm much thinner (hmm!). So, after lunch we went back to Oslo. I showed her Karl Johan (the main street), the university, the palace, the statue of Ibsen. Finally I bought you an absolutely fantastic . . . that she'll bring you. At four o'clock Herr Strøm + wife + car were waiting for us outside the hotel, and that was the start of the second act of the drama . . . or tragicomedy, shall we say. You . . . you just can't imagine how terribly fond I am of Herr Strøm and his wife when strangers turn up. I get this very tender feeling for them . . . and everything about them appears new to me. Do you understand? Well, it was like that yesterday. Herr Strom was wearing a new collar and a red silk tie, his hair was so beautifully combed and he was soo self-conscious. I noticed that Frau Strøm is actually quite pretty and she has a very sweet laugh . . . I really wanted to tell Miss McLachlan that she should tell you about these two and I whispered to her, 'Very nice people!' Herr Strøm spoke English . . . of course, but I didn't just remain silent, not in the least. I was so happy, really I was. We drove out a long way from Oslo. To a fantastic lake (Tyrifjord). Miss McLachlan kept on saying 'beautiful, lovely' etc., but she was very nice. Just think how lovely it was that she met the Strøms! We had dinner together and . . . I smoked a cigarette . . . (wonderful). Miss McLachlan looked jolly surprised and said that Miss Griffith would not give you permission to do that. Well, we went for a walk. She exclaimed how similar it was to Scotland here. I was happy, truly happy. I loved Norway and was so grateful for everything. We drove back home via Drammen (a town). It was already dark. We stopped occasionally and got out of the car for a stretch . . . I told her about a dozen times (no exaggeration) that I spoke bad English, very bad English.

SUNDAY, 13 AUGUST 1939, LILLESTRØM

Uncle Oskar very sweetly sent me some things to read. Two tiny books about Jewish persecution, one book (*The Pogroms*) and six booklets of Austrian news. Plus a little Reclam edition of Schiller. I think that's so frightfully nice of him.

You don't know that I've a 'rendezvous' tomorrow, do you? A German emigrant, communist to the core, from Hamburg. I 'met' him purely by chance. I was in Oslo, walking past a building where some Viennese were standing outside. Inside the 'building' there was a socialist youth meeting and I paid the entry fee with my last krone. There were real Viennese just milling around. One of them even knew Papa . . . But the funny thing is that I've got a second 'rendezvous' on Wednesday . . . at the Wergeland statue (remember?) with a Norwegian. I'm absolutely sure he'll turn up. Whether I'll go or not, I don't know. I think it's a bit much to flirt with two of them. But I was born a slattern. Anyway, it's not certain that the chap from Germany will make an appearance tomorrow. But I would be happy (if he did). Just think, I've spoken German for the first time in half a year. An emigrant from Sudeten Germany even confirmed that I had an accent (hmm) . . .

Yes, Dittl, I'm going to sign off now. Tomorrow I'll be able to tell you whether he turned up or not. Then it'll be time for a detailed description.

Anyway, I find Øyvind (blissful times) a thousand times more likeable even though he's not a communist nor an emigrant.

Now it's 14 August.

Dittl. Hell! Studying Maths all day long has its disadvantages, I can tell you. Not the studying itself, but the fact that you 'set out' to study Maths for a whole day, yet every so often or so you get these ridiculous impulses. After the first minute I have to go to the loo . . . then I notice that in the right-hand corner of my decent cupboard there's a torn silk stocking that needs to be mended. Then I just have to dance and . . . now I feel the need to burden you further with a second letter. It's catastrophic. School begins on the 23rd. And yet I want to go to Oslo on Wednesday to meet up with someone who's not very nice. For goodness sake! What's more I had this dream last night . . . you were in it too as a warning voice. So.

Frau Strøm really is an angel. She's got me a theatre ticket to see *A Doll's House* on Thursday. I'm in ecstasy. A plague has broken out on ships carrying emigrants.

I know that Hamsun is a fascist. Hitler sent him a telegram on his birthday. But I've got to buy *Hunger* in Norwegian. It's really fantastic.

Write and tell me just how much I 'enthralled' Miss McLachlan. That anybody could be enthralled by me is such a rare phenomenon that it deserves closer examination.

ANCHOR-DONALDSON LINE—Turbine Twin-Screw Steamship "ATHENIA"

On 1 September 1939 the British liner Athenia left Glasgow for Montreal,
Canada, with 1,100 passengers on board. More than 300 of these passengers were
Americans wanting to escape the impending conflict. On 3 September Britain and
France declared war on Germany. German submarines were given the order to attack
any enemy ships equipped for war. Taking the Athenia for a troop transporter,
a German submarine commander ordered it to be torpedoed. This was the first
torpedo attack of the Second World War. Among those killed was Hildegard Ehrlich,
who had been in Judith's class at school. She was on her way to the USA
to meet up with her parents who had taken an earlier boat.

At school in Norway

AUGUST–DECEMBER 1939

Ruth has been accepted by the Frogner school in Oslo. She will join the Latin track in the final year, which leads to her Matura. She is unhappy at school. Her snobbish classmates find her strange. She spends her break times in the loo.

On 1 September Nazi Germany invades Poland, precipitating the outbreak of the Second World War. There is outrage in Norway and Sweden at the attack by the Soviet Union on Finland on 30 November. Relief efforts are set up.

Ruth becomes more and more desperate about obtaining the necessary visa papers. To travel to the USA, where some of her Jewish friends have already fled, she needs an 'affidavit' which she tries to obtain. The document is necessary as a confirmation of her identity.

Ruth's relationship to her host family in Lillestrøm has become complicated. Her sole pleasure is when Frau Strøm's brother, Tobben, offers her a cigarette.

She likes to walk along the quayside in Oslo, where she gazes at the large ships. She fantasises about travelling to England as a stowaway. In her letters to Judith she discusses literature, politics, Jewishness and personal matters. She quotes from Heinrich Heine's poem 'Abroad'. She writes enthusiastically about Leo Tolstoy's prose and Arthur Schnitzler's dialogues.

News of the death of Hildegard, a mutual friend from Vienna, sparks thoughts of martyrdom, suicide and senseless death.

Ruth is unsure about how the war will end.

SATURDAY, 26 AUGUST 1939, LILLESTRØM

It's Friday night, but in fact it'll be Saturday in five minutes' time and I'll be able to wonder, 'What will the coming day bring?' Yes, Dittl, on the one hand it's an advantage to be in a neutral country, but on the other . . . It looks pretty wretched, doesn't it? If I could just be 100 per cent convinced that England would be 'victorious'. But . . . don't you think that the chances of this are slim?

You're experiencing this all very differently; in England there is nervousness in the air . . . I know from our time in Vienna. Here it is quiet. The newspapers carry stories about the economic arrangements that have to be put in place, the population is being advised to keep their heads should it come to war, the foreign minister is making a speech on the wireless . . . Edla, the maid, dreams of war, and I think that's a very bad omen, because she normally doesn't show the slightest interest in politics and doesn't read the newspapers either.

Personally, I'm 99.9 per cent certain that there'll be war. And rather war than Munich, you know! Because war has to come at some point and I think that the sooner it comes the better. We just have to be clear in our minds and look to emerge from it as best possible. After all, you look to have an operation over and done with as quickly as possible. This operation might cost us our lives . . . that doesn't matter . . . just get it over with . . . that's roughly my point of view.

If Germany 'wins' (strange word for mass murder) in the end, then at least we'll know where we are. But this doubt, this uncertainty that prevails at present, it is unsustainable . . . As I'm writing the war may have begun, Dittl. In some small corner of Danzig they've started shooting . . . I'm writing about operations and such rubbish . . . I worry that we're deceiving ourselves, that even this war has nothing to do with human rights etc., but that the various fathers, sons, lovers etc. will merely perish to preserve for England her colonies and a variety of other appetising morsels.

But I don't want to think about it any more now. Against Hitler, against the 'For Aryans only' mentality – all that's fine . . . but with the best will I cannot summon up any enthusiasm for war . . . Outside a cheery soul is whistling the latest song, and happily it's now Saturday . . . You know, we really must try to survive it as best possible. Make yourself very, very small – inside, I mean – show the enemy as little of us as possible, that's how you escape with the least damage. Close our eyes, or no! Open our eyes and experience . . . *see*.

I am in a neutral country. You've got to write to me a lot now. Especially if war breaks out. Then I'll have cause for concern. Dittl, will you be joining the Red Cross? And Musch will be performing National Service, too. You've just got to be very careful . . . *I* have to learn Latin vocabulary. We've air raid protection exercises here tomorrow.

Goodnight. I have to write Latin vocabulary. Strange! No – maddening.

SUNDAY, 24 SEPTEMBER 1939, LILLESTRØM

How I long for company, Dittl. Just a single person I could talk to. Do you not understand that I'm so lonely it's as if I were living on a fig tree in the jungle? That gets on your nerves after a while, I can tell you. Each day the Strøms are another thousand kilometres more distant from me. I exchange on average about ten words with them per day. If I were living alone it would be all right, but to wander around like a shadow beside the others!

And at school! Do you know, we are under strict orders to spend break times in the playground. I creep secretly into the loo so as not to have to traipse around on my own . . . There is, of course, no hope that this state of affairs will change. And in the end it really doesn't matter. After all, I do have books. You know. Trotsky!

The only danger now is that I may become too 'proud'. It's even a miracle that I'm writing this to you . . . After all, one never really *wants* anybody to get too close.

But enough of that . . . Yesterday I went walking by Oslo fjord. I pictured what it would be like if I crept on to an English ship and sailed to England. Ugh, what nonsense.

I've also got something sweet to relate to you. Yesterday we were sitting at the table for dinner. Turid snuggles up to her father and says to me with a proud, gloating smile, 'He's not your father!' I find that charming – fitting.

If only I were a man! . . . I thought the following: I would 'give my life' immediately if I could save an English merchant ship from being torpedoed. I would give my life immediately if I could make petrol rationing in Norway unnecessary. Why? Because viewed from a higher level an English merchant ship is worth more than Ruth Maier . . . But here comes the punchline. If I were forced to choose between an English merchant ship being sunk or failing my Maths examination, then I'd be quite happy to see two merchant ships sunk if it meant I passed my Maths exam.

It's a tragedy, you know, if emigration can't at least save you from Mathematics. I feel as if Mathematics has been hounding me ever since I was born. To as far away as Norway. My examination is on 7 October. The anguished cries of the entire population of Warsaw fade before this event . . . Rubbish!

Dittl, you're also a bit fuddled by this war psychosis. *I* am not looking forward to the first day of peace. I fear this day. Neither do I believe that this war will be the last . . . I'd just like to leave Europe . . . Is that not possible, during wartime? One more thing: will Pippa come too? Please write back and tell me what the present situation is with regard to emigrating to the USA. Because you don't seem certain that I *absolutely must* get away from here in June 1940. I cannot and do not want to stay here any longer. There's no way I can wait until war breaks out.

PS If you fancy it, could you and Musch write Herr Strøm a birthday card (1 October)? You have to keep your fingers crossed for me on 7 October.

Did you know that Sigmund Freud died yesterday?

MONDAY, 2 OCTOBER 1939, LILLESTRØM

A quarter to ten.

Dittl, I have a favour to ask you. Please don't make mention of bombing raids etc. in your letters. *You* may find it easy to joke about your own demise and behave all nobly, but I can't . . . Yes . . . politics is changing . . . It used to be you who would chirp nervously, 'Ruth . . . don't joke!'

Do you know what drives me mad? I'm not receiving any money! This sensation of going around with an empty purse! Whenever I get 'my' five kroner (five schillings) I'm so happy I could stroke, fondle . . . kiss the money. Not because I love money. *Fy da!* (Norwegian = Ugh!) No. These five kroner contain so many small pleasures. I'll buy a postcard with good copies of French pictures. I'll buy a couple of grammes of chocolate. And I can mumble to myself, 'If I wanted to I could buy myself a cigarette now.'

Dittl, about cigarettes. Yesterday it was Herr Strøm's birthday. Lots of people, typically Norwegian. Candles on the tables and food . . . So much food that the table was bowing (in spite of rationing!). Oh yes! Tobben came too. Frau Strøm's brother. You know, in rare moments he's the one person I feel slightly close to. And when are these rare moments? Answer: when he offers me cigarettes. He does it so openly and with such . . . grace. While looking into your eyes. And I feel so childishly happy . . . Whenever he comes I make these secret signs to him (smoking gestures), then with this graceful movement he offers me Blue Master or Frisco. Then he takes out a box of matches, lights my cigarette, and I . . . draw in . . . and for those few minutes that I'm smoking I actually feel . . . happy . . . actually.

You know, my life is relatively perfect . . . relatively. *I* am a free person, even if Herr Strøm has suggested that I should turn out my light at eleven o'clock. But . . . my God . . . Strange, I'm so footloose and fancy free that sometimes I long for a bit of: 'Ruth, you must be home by eleven o'clock at the latest.'

Crikey! Reputation! . . . a few weeks ago . . . (Days? Months? Years?) I ended up in a pub from another world. Just men. I was in such low spirits, I was fed up, and I thought, 'Well, so what?' I had no qualms about it, so I ordered a lemonade. In quite a roundabout way the waiter asked me to leave the pub. For a while I thought that everybody imagined me to be a harlot. It was fantastic.

Dittl, is it Pippa who has instilled this loathing of Trotsky in you? Maybe you're more enamoured of Stalin? If it's correct to use the word betrayal with reference to politics, then Stalin has betrayed socialism. But the Russian people are behind Stalin, and that's the worst thing. In England you are fed illusions with regard to Russia. Be sceptical. It is not improbable (actually, it's very probable) that Russia will enter into a military alliance with Germany. Oh yes. Of course Herr Strøm predicted the whole thing. (By the way,

unfortunately Herr Strøm is 200 per cent more stupid than I first thought!
He said something about the Russian Revolution . . .!) Yes, Dittl . . . I think
you should read Trotsky . . . instead of Conrad. I think the fact that Stalin has
exiled him is good enough reason to hold him in high esteem. And Trotsky is
a *socialist*, you know, who believes in world revolution . . . and you simply
have to share his belief. And how he writes! Oh yes, he writes beautifully. You
enjoy every sentence as if you were a child. You enjoy the melody, the wit, the
intellect. He has a talent for characterising people by their views. With a
single sentence he can deal with such 'resonant' names. One chapter,
'Lessing's arrival in Russia (Petersburg)', is so . . . exciting . . . that your pulse
doesn't stop racing. You have to read Trotsky.

And then you say that you're not a Zionist. Dittl, I don't believe you.
Moreover, I sense Pippa's influence here. I'm past wrestling with the ethics of
whether socialism contradicts Zionism. No, Dittl, I'm absolutely convinced
that the only home the Jews have today is in Palestine.

I'm only 'assimilated' as long as people appreciate my assimilation and
understand that I don't adapt out of cowardice but that, in proud recognition
of my particularity and my Jewishness, I'm doing what I consider to be right.
But if you want this acknowledgement of *sacrifice* that accompanies our
assimilation, you can go and look for it on the moon.

To put it harshly, it's undignified to talk of assimilation at present. Tragic,
if you want to be old-fashioned. Today, at a time when racial hatred is
flourishing in Germany – and to a tiny extent in Norway *as well* – you can't
just close your eyes and say, 'I want to assimilate, even if others spit on me and
curse me as a "Jew",' can you? You've got to understand that!

To assimilate as quickly as possible, only so that I can finally stop being a
Jew – I call that undignified.

Dittl, not long ago it occurred to me that when you're dead you stop
being a Jew. I was far away, lost in my thoughts. Can you imagine that?

Well, Dittl, it's got late. Your letter is in front of me. From cigarettes and
Trotsky to Zionism. And the war . . . yes . . . the war . . . Please write and
tell me whether there's any chance that we could go to the US in wartime.
It's incredibly important to me.

Yes, tell me about the English preparedness for war, which is much discussed here. About London in wartime. What does London look like, anyway?

Differences between Paris and London? Are the English nervous, excited, 'heroically' enthusiastic, resigned? The revised aim should of course be: Hitler's destruction. I think this aim is very high . . . too high . . . I don't believe that England will be victorious. By the way, have you considered that if England won, we *could* return to Germany? No, Dittl, I don't believe in an English victory, but I *want* to believe it.

TUESDAY, 17 OCTOBER 1939, LILLESTRØM

Dearest Dittl. Always the same headlines, always the same words. It is dark outside and on the desk there's a heap...

I'm not exactly in a good mood today. What's more, you've slightly fallen in my favour at the moment, as I don't have a letter from you in front of me. It's strange, you know, sad when there's no letter from you. You seem as distant as if we were two strangers. I get such a strong feeling that it's only the few lines we write to each other that keep us together.

So what do I know about you? So awfully little. Sometimes you seem such a stranger when I look at you in the photographs. No, Dittl, it is unbelievable that we were ever together, that every night before going to sleep I could admire your tummy.

Actually, it's not just me who is an admirer of your well-formed . . . yes . . . tummy. There are others, too. As far as this subject is concerned, here is my situation: having spent about a month chasing after all sorts of boys in my mind, I've turned into a man hater. That's to say I act as if I'm surviving off books and I'm already fairly well accomplished in 'playing the lofty woman'. I need not explain where this leads to. But as I said, should the 'barren years approach' without my having been active in a particular area, I don't know what will happen to me. It's no joke! I can't think of anything more abhorrent than an untouched body . . . You're embarrassed. You also find my style pompous. You're right, of course. It's because I only get the opportunity to *write* German, but not to speak it. You cannot appreciate what that means. By the way, I've discovered such a beautiful poem by Heine. Wait a minute, I'll write it out for you and you can learn it by heart.

I once had a beautiful fatherland.
The oak
Grew there so high, the violets gently nodded.
It was a dream.

It kissed me in German, it spoke in German
(One can hardly believe it,
It sounded so good) the phrase: 'I love you!'
*It was a dream.**

Beautiful? More than beautiful. And now Heine lies in Montmartre and Papa at Döbling cemetery. Oh well.

Since I've been here I've also written four or five poems myself. On the whole I think it's quite disagreeable to write poetry if you haven't a talent for it. You just dirty yourself. Do you know what Goethe said? Either a poem ought to be outstanding or it should not exist at all. I haven't quoted that word for word, but it's pretty much the sense of what he said.

The well-worn question: what have we done, undertaken, embarked upon since the last time? We've commuted by train between Lillestrøm and Oslo, learned Latin vocabulary, read the newspaper, and meanwhile we've realised that autumn has arrived. Autumn in Norway . . . Sometimes, you know, when I step outside the front door in the mornings, and the cool air brushes against me, I think that this is what it was like when I arrived. Of course, it was winter then, everything was close and everyone was nice . . . No, you don't understand what I mean. In a nutshell, sometimes I feel (inspired by the weather) a trace of the same atmosphere that was prevalent in my early days in Norway. That was a time when the idea of having to leave here made me shudder. I felt at home here. And now?

The day before yesterday I had a splendid argument with Herr Strøm. He asked me why I can't settle here properly. Why I've shut myself off from them. I gave him all sorts of answers. The result of this is that communication with the family has become ever so slightly easier. I can smile a little more openly when I talk with Frau Strøm. Frau Strøm has a sweet habit of ignoring me. She does it without noticing.

* Hal Draper's translation of 'In der Fremde' ('Abroad') by Heinrich Heine.

Ludwig Maier, who died in 1933, was buried in Döbling cemetery in Vienna.
Later, his wife Irma was laid to rest here. The gravestone also carries the inscription,
'In memoriam Ruth Maier'.

Have you received my long letter, Dittl? In it I made a Zionist confession
to you, which I stand by.

Dittl, there's not much to tell. You know that the leaves have turned yellow. You also know that I'll soon be entering my twentieth year. But there is
something that's changed here, strangely enough. I always used to tell myself,
'Heavens! How old I am already!' But now I say, 'But I'm only just nineteen,
I'm actually still young.'

When I was on the train recently, I looked at all the powerful, strong
Norwegian men before me, so tall, and with their candid looks, and I thought
that I'll pine for them later on when I'm in America. At *present* I'm pining for
the small, crooked-nosed Jew with inward-looking eyes.

I actually live in the countryside, you know. I'm only aware of this
when I'm on the train and see all the trees, the fog and the sky (with all its

accompaniments) race past. Then I feel very happy and think that I'll long for these things, too, later on. You remember that the first thing I noticed in Norway was the pure clarity of the sky.

SUNDAY, 22 OCTOBER 1939, LILLESTRØM

With your tremendous astuteness you will discover that I sent this letter much later [postmark 28 October] than when I wrote it. The reason is quite simple: I've no money! I mean, I do have rather a lot of money at the moment, coincidentally: thirty-four kroner!!! From Musch. But I'm not going to spend this money on stamps. I want to use it to buy something fantastic. Either a pair of shoes, or a skirt, a belt . . . or . . . Trotsky.

Oh yes, Trotsky. Goodness me, what has Pippa been telling you now? You really must let me know. I'm sticking by the following facts. First, Trotsky was Lenin's best friend and loyal colleague. And even Stalin and Co. think a lot of Lenin, don't they? Then, Trotsky was in charge of the entire October uprising and founded the Red Army. And he is supposed to have betrayed the Revolution? . . . Dittl, I'd also really advise you to read some history. Not about the Greeks and Romans, but about the age we live in. I'm at present reading a book by Edvard Beneš about the foundation of Czechoslovakia.

My future! Yes. Well, that is a funny thing indeed . . . And I really think that the 'future' will come into this world as an abortion. 'Future' is a stupid word . . . everything is the future; it's just also the present. Gibberish and more gibberish. But one thing is certain: I must leave here after my Matura!!! I don't believe that you'll be able to get an English visa for me, so I ask you to separate the American affidavit so that I can travel to the USA on my own. Please, Dittl, don't think that I'm writing to you in a 'good mood'! If you just consider it for a moment, you will conclude that my proposal is the only right one . . . Here in Norway, nobody has made any commitment to my further education. Right from the start the line has been that I'll only do my Matura here. Then I have to disappear. One little fact that's kept this very much in my mind: if I make a pledge to leave Norway after my Matura I don't have to take the exam in Nynorsk (this repulsive, second Norwegian language). If I do not make that pledge, then I'll have to take Nynorsk as a subject. Herr Strøm *will* act as my guarantor. Frau Strøm says, 'It's an absolute certainty that Ruth will leave after her Matura.'

Look, Dittl, you understand my situation. I beg you, therefore, to do everything so that I get my affidavit. Obviously it will be very embarrassing to arrive in the USA without even the slightest hint of practical work. I think that around Christmas (when I've done my Chemistry and Geography exams) I'll ask Herr Strøm if he'll allow me to do a typing course.

SATURDAY, 28 OCTOBER 1939, LILLESTRØM

What happened to Hildegard is so horrific. It's completely incomprehensible because Hildegard belongs to our generation. For a moment the whole world started to wobble and I looked in vain for something solid to grab on to. Did you feel the same? So pointless. Not because she's dead, but because nobody will look after her later on, because none of her longings, her dreams, was ever fulfilled.

Perhaps in this respect you've become a worker of *life*. Whenever I'm standing by a perambulator, looking at the tiny thing inside, at that moment I venerate life, or when I see a tree in blossom. But in general you lose this reverence. It was only when Hildegard was able to (allowed to, supposed to, had to) die that I understood what it actually means – *living*! I instinctively looked at myself in the mirror. And goodness! You really feel so alien.

In spite of this I would very much like to die for a cause. Perhaps I'm just saying this because I'm sitting in Norway, because there's no danger of Lillestrøm being bombed . . . and yet. I don't feel the slightest doubt when I say I believe it is our *duty* to meet our end on the Western Front. Dittl, it *is* our duty. Even if you must have such unconditional reverence for life, you have to admit that there comes a moment when it is worth sacrificing one's life. These are *not* just words . . .

For a time here, I must say I *toyed* with the idea of suicide. Everything was so pointless. I only feel happy when I look at the sky, when it's autumn, when the leaves fall etc.

THE ATHENIA

LIST OF 93 LOST PASSENGERS

50 BRITISH AND 30 AMERICANS

The Donaldson Atlantic Line last night issued a list of 93 passengers of the torpedoed liner Athenia, who are now officially reported missing. The list includes 50 British subjects, 30 United States citizens, seven Polish, and four German. Previously 19 members of the crew had been reported missing, so the total casualty list is now 112.

The following are the names:—

William ALLAN, British, last abode Northfield, Queen Street, Alloa; Georgina ALLAN, 51, domestic, British, West Croydon.

Harriet BARRINGTON, 52, housewife, British, Sandfield Road, Gateacre, Liverpool; John BERNARD, 23, student, U.S.; Peter BIRCHALL, 49, librarian, U.S., Hawberry Street, Bedford; Nancy BISHOP, 36, housewife, British, care of T. Eaton Company, Regent Street, London; Frederick BLAIR, 60, musician, British, born Chatham (Ont.), Savoy Court Hotel, Portman Square, London; Herbert BOWN, 79, retired, U.S., born Birmingham, England, Fairview Road, Dartmouth; Henry BRAUNSCHNEIGER, 33, lawyer, German, care of Cunard White Star, Liverpool; Elizabeth BROOKES, 60, widow, British, care of Scott, Highholm Street, Port Glasgow; William BROWN, 60, teacher, U.S., born Scotland, care of McMorland, Belmont, Barrhill Road, Gourock; Sarah BURDETT, 51, housewife, U.S., Broughton Astley, By Leicester; Helen BURROWS, 50, housewife, British, care of Coleman, York Lodge, Antrim.

E. CAMPBELL, 37, teacher, U.S., Ederston Road, Peebles; Helen CHALMERS, 46, table maid, British, Restalrig Circus, Edinburgh; Isabella CHALMERS, 51, nurse, British, Edinburgh, same address.

Ina May DUNCAN, 30, nurse, British, care of Davidson, Craighall Terrace, Edinburgh.

Hildegard EHRLICH, 16, German, Woodgrange Drive, Thorpe Bay.

Arthur FISHER, 16, U.S., care of R. Hancock, Tunbridge Wells; Mrs. A. B. FLETCHER, British, Kildare Terrace, Bayswater, London; Helen FLOWER, 45, housewife, British, Cromer Villas Road, Wandsworth, London; Alexandrina FORBES, 52, housewife, British, last address Frederick Street, Aberdeen; Muriel FRASER, 54, secretary, British, Cockspur Street, London.

Anna GACH, 13, schoolgirl, Polish; Cora GILROY, 41, housewife, U.S., Lockend Road, Leith; John GILROY, 7, U.S., born Detroit (Mich.), same address; Martha GODDARD, 52, housewife, British, Oldham Road, Manchester; Sarah GOODMAN, 31, Secretary, British, Northfield Road, London, N.; Nellie GRAHAM, 34, housewife, British, Collier Street, Carnoustie; George GRAHAM, 2½, U.S., same address.

Hildegard Ehrlich was one of the 112 people to die aboard the Athenia.

Recently I've had the ability to 'depersonalise' myself. I view myself as a wholly detached individual; I hover outside my own body, so to speak.

I've just been to fetch milk and cream; I was completely torn away from my very interesting observations.

Do you know that I bought myself the Trotsky? This will give you the chance to read him later. It cost twenty-five kroner (one and a half pounds). But now I have the book (two volumes) in my room, I can stroke the spine and leaf through its pages. It's mine . . . First I wanted to buy a pair of exquisite brown shoes, but then I bought Trotsky. I'm also reading, in English, those little 'educational books'. They don't cost very much and you do learn things, but one of these books means a whole month of reading English. At the moment I'm reading *The Jewish Problem*. I can send you *The Treaty of Versailles* (full of lies!).

This time I'm sending you a cigarette. I hope it arrives. Smoke it in secret. I tell you it's absolutely wonderful to smoke in secret.

TUESDAY, 7 NOVEMBER 1939, LILLESTRØM

I really think that Uncle Emil has been sent to Poland. It's all such a pointless waste of effort. So much misery. The people here in Norway have no under-standing of it at all. They visit their friends, water their flowers, eat crabs and lobster. Think of them all, one by one, they do so much. When I read the various letters from emigrants that come into my possession . . . ! They're all clinging to each other. Even the most intelligent ones can find no other words apart from: 'I honestly believe we will see each other again' and 'Be courageous!' etc. etc.

Enough of that . . . What I wanted to say was that it snowed today. You know what it's like, don't you, when you look out of the window in the morning and see that everything is white? I get a little impatient when I look out and see the roofs shining. The Northern Lights will be here soon. And everything will be as it was. Do you understand? Time just flies by! You're right: it's as if the days consisted of nothing but getting up and going to bed. I have an absurd anger at having to go to sleep. Sometimes I throw myself on the bed, fully dressed, and go to sleep like that. Anyway, 'bed' is a bit of an exaggeration for the frame I have to sleep on. It's soo narrow and *hard*, you see! No mattress, just wood.

Oh well, you get used to everything.

When I go walking along Oslo fjord, you know . . . I think I find my 'better self'. I start stepping in all the puddles, walk in a zigzag, stop at every crate and think of you when I read the words: 'Packed in Norway'. I haven't yet seen an English ship. But I have seen a German one – *Lotte* – which I'd have absolutely loved to have sent Churchill a quick telegram about . . . I often wonder how I might feel if I see a Norwegian ship in America. Wistful memories will 'wash over' me. Wistful, you understand? Everything will be bathed in the light of a halo. Even the idiotic Salvation Army hymns at my window on Saturdays. You see, if I consider my stay in Norway as a bundle of memories, then it doesn't look that bad. But looking at it from other . . . viewpoints! The only thing of use I've achieved here is that I can read Ibsen. As far as my future is concerned . . . uff! (uff is a Norwegian interjection; I apologise if it sounds affected).

Norwegian Matura!! Ha, ha! If only . . . if only I'd taken a typing, stenography, or English course! I learn French every day with the head-master, an arch fool who corrects my Norwegian (and French) pronunciation. These French lessons are torture! I'm amazed that I haven't run away from them. I have English twice a week . . . a tall, lanky and pale individual who wears a wedding ring. He's the virtuous secondary school teacher type. He thinks I'm undernourished. We're supposed to buy a new English book (*The Citadel*), so at break time he comes up to me and whispers that if 'it's difficult' for me, a collection will be organised. That's along the same lines as the secretary 'slipping me an apple'. Once I was at the German teacher's house, Bjerkelund. This episode was so typical, you know, that I have to tell it to you. It's a long time ago now, so I can write about it more 'loftily'. Anyway, she lives in an idyllic little house outside Oslo. Flowers in the garden, fruit on the walls (only symbolically I mean). The teacher is a white-haired, chubby-faced virgin. She reminds me of an 'apple dumpling'. Really, she does! She tried to tease a number of things out of me. Asked me why I go around on my own, whether the other girls aren't nice to me, whether I'm on my own here in Norway. At the end she started to cry. Honestly. It's terribly moving to see other people 'weep' for you. I immediately started to feel sorry for myself. But I was also ashamed of having told her anything. As I left she generously put some fruit in my bag (something exquisite this time).

There's a whole heap of boys in our class. The loveliest array of the most different types. But I have no erotic allure. I'm quite certain of that. If I were to go around with my bosom 'half-exposed', then maybe men would eye me up, but in my usual dress! . . . (You ought to know that I've a fabulous body: magnificent! I admire myself every evening in front of the mirror.) Yes, so I wanted to tell you that I have no sex appeal at all – I found this out immediately thanks to that intuition which is unique to women. (What do you think of this comment?) You mustn't get the idea that the dock-workers *don't* wink at me. But they only do it out of habit . . . Anyway, we have this whole heap of boys in the class. From time to time I try to convince myself that they're all idiots, but I only do this to comfort myself because I never come into contact with any of them. My female dance school self is crawling up to 'Nancy'. A truly 'charming' creature. A millionairess, apparently. What a talent for dressing up! What a smile! Her eyes are partly light and partly dark. Her hair is blonde (that's the general hair colour here). Apart from Nancy there are two other girls. One is called Solveig. I mention her name to create a bit of a Norwegian 'atmosphere'. Here the male names are: Arne, Oddvar, Åge, Henrik. All of them have connotations with Nordic bravery, virtue, honesty. The Latin teacher is great; we learn a lot with him. It's just that he's very, very short, and when he sits on the teacher's chair his feet dangle in the air!

The atmosphere in the school is . . . to put it mildly . . . terrible! The idea of collegiality is non-existent. Tell teacher? Useless! The moment you say anything, the moment you get involved, your fellow pupils yell at you (not just me). If you stay in the classroom even though you are supposed to be shuffling around the playground, your fellow pupils scream at you (see above) that it is forbidden. 'Lend me a pencil.' 'Why didn't you bring one?' If you come unprepared, your fellow pupils give a hurt smile. Then I have to tell you about my 'neighbour'. His name is Per (like *Peer Gynt*, which we're reading in school, by the way – I'll tell you about it in the US). He gives me long stares . . . in astonishment. He thinks I'm an oddball. When he learned that I didn't belong to any religion he said, '*Det er derfor du er så rar*' (Oh, that's why you're so strange). It's not just in school, but everywhere that people think I'm an oddball, whom they stare at to begin with, but who loses her appeal in the end.

My gabbling must have given you a headache by now. I could also tell you that Turid is having a good look through my chest of drawers (yes, I've reached the stage where I have a chest of drawers) for 'sanitary towels'. That's not interesting in itself, but it's quite good as a spicy detail in a letter. I think so.

Gabble on a bit yourself next time. I actually wanted to convert you to Zionism today. But you won't escape me. My hand is hurting at the moment.

PS A few minutes later:

How on earth could I write a letter like *that*?

THURSDAY, 30 NOVEMBER 1939, LILLESTRØM

Ugh, I'm in a filthy mood today. I could sit down and howl, if it made any difference. A combination of disgust, tedium, longing. I don't know . . . I saw a brilliant film yesterday. French (the Norwegian title is *Som kom natten* = *Then the Night Came*).* I was in a real state of 'excitement' when I came home from the cinema yesterday. Pierre Fresnay plays the lead role. The film is about a murder etc.

Well, the film still makes me shudder now. And then I'm furious, you know, because . . . ugh, when I think about the war, my heart starts to throb with shame. It's stupid to try to write this down. But I'm doing it anyway. Now consider this: this morning Frau Strøm passed me a charming note from Herr Strøm. Its content? Please leave the WC (ha, ha!) as you find it. Wait a moment. (Apparently some blood had dripped somehow and one sanitary

---

* The film was released in the English-speaking world as *The Puritan* (*Le Puritain* in French).

towel didn't flush away!!!) He didn't write that, but I know. I could *kill* myself. *A man* (who not sooo long ago put his hand on me) has to remind me to . . .

Oh well. On the train my thoughts switched between my stupidity and Pierre Fresnay (it's just occurred to me that letters are being censored. Interesting content!). Then I go into school, read that Russia has cut off diplomatic ties with Finland. At school, the Latin teacher says he'll have a word with Herr Strøm about me. I don't know what I'm supposed to have done wrong. Then come the special editions with the news that Russia is bombing Helsinki.

My conclusion is that there's no way I'm going to be able to put up with this for much longer. Everything is becoming a blurred jumble and I'm tripping over myself. Yes, that's the issue here. I'm getting in the way. I know myself inside out. I know exactly how I'll react to the attack on Finland; I know that after three hours of despair *at most* I'll calmly start studying Chemistry. I know that I know that I know etc.

By the way, there's this boy at school I *almost* fell in love with. He's about sixteen! What do you think of that? He's English, maybe Jewish, too. At least he looks as if he is. Actually it's nonsense that I almost 'fell in love' (what a stupid expression!) with him. I just have this slight pang in my 'heart' whenever I see him (or in my 'chest', I don't know which). He has an incredibly pure and noble face. He has the body of a ten-year-old. But I know nothing else about him. Once he raised his eyebrows nervously. I liked that.

The only reason why I'm writing about him is to be able to tell you something man related. At the same time that the Russians are bombing Finnish cities. People here are also saying a number of worrying things about northern Norway. After all, the northern part of Norway shares a border with Finland . . . There are potential consequences for us, too.

By the way, my respect for Nordic solidarity has sunk considerably. Of course Sweden and Norway must fight side by side with the Finnish soldiers. The Scandinavians now have the opportunity to show that they can defend their lofty ideals with actions and not just words. They ought to demonstrate that Nordic solidarity is a reality! All that the various Nordic foreign ministers have done is to talk in platitudes. And now the whole of Scandinavia is looking on comfortably while Helsinki is being bombed. Repulsive!

MONDAY, 18 DECEMBER 1939, LILLESTRØM

Eleven o'clock at night.

A boy from the past has turned up again. Pale and revolting. Slimy smile and really ugly clothes. I went to the theatre with him. Even though I felt disgusted by his hands, I was *young*. I hardly recognise myself when I speak with other people . . . even then . . . I think I was intoxicated somehow. I behaved very funnily and I thought I was pretty. The day before I tried on clothes and stared at the mirror for ages. When we were together he bought me chocolate, and I felt like a poor wretch because I was so delighted by the chocolate (chocolate costs money . . .). I was happy . . . and yet I said that it would be better if we finished . . . I felt like a harlot because I thought I'd only gone with him on account of the chocolate and cinema tickets . . . perhaps also so that a boy would look at my hands, eyes, lips. He thought I was sixteen (at most!). He asked me if I'd ever kissed a boy before. I went into a rage.

Why am I telling you this, Dittl? The whole thing is a problem for me. A question which comes up again and again: ought I to be together with a boy if I don't feel close to him *emotionally*? Should I let Herr X stroke my body just because he has trousers? Sometimes I yearn for physical caresses, even if it were from one of those 'dark' figures in Jenbarnetorget.* But when it gets to that point I just wince; for example, when Herr Strøm accidentally touches my finger. It's all more complicated than you would think.

Last week, I went to see a man who had placed a classified advertisement in the newspaper: 'Seeking girl for twice-weekly cleaning of *hybel* [furnished room].' I'd earn fourteen kroner, and I would definitely take the job if he ever got in touch again. I'm desperate to earn some money. Work! Do something. Tomorrow I'm giving my first German lesson to the cloakroom lady from the Deichmann library. One krone for two hours. (Peanuts!) The Strøms know nothing about this, of course.

It's horrible when you don't know anybody. The Strøms have disappeared into thin air. We smile at each other in passing. My relationship with Herr Strøm has become very spiky since the sanitary towel incident and since I

---

* A large square in front of Oslo central station.

Postcard showing the Deichmann library
and the city library in the Hammersborg district.

forgot to say hello to him one day. School is so ghastly that I'm sure I won't last out till June. I read Churchill in class. The only person I like is an English baby boy who makes fun of me. (But I couldn't care less.)

Apart from that I bury myself in the Deichmann library. Today I almost read the whole of Arthur Schnitzler's *La Ronde*. If there's any way you can get your hands on this book then do it. It's remarkable. It's made up of love scenes: 'The harlot and the soldier', 'The soldier and the maid' etc. Dialogues. Read it! Perhaps I'll copy out 'The harlot and the soldier' for you tomorrow.

So here I am, heaping all my 'worries' on to you. But all this tripe is boring and banal. I'm craving one thing: someone who will 'impregnate' me. I'm very grateful for every kind word, every nice gesture. Instead of that I get beaten up by . . . Turid . . . I know that, after a while, children always start hitting me. What was the name of that little girl in Brno? . . . Well, she hit me once, too.

It's very sad. Well, it doesn't matter . . . I'm talking myself into a sour mood. There's no point in that. The truth is that I'm young. I even feel it sometimes. Now it's winter, snow . . . the Norwegian winter is very pure.

Chaste. The Norwegians are good people, too. When I travel to school in the mornings and all those tall, strong Norwegian men sit opposite me, I love them very much. I've even had a few 'love escapades' on the train. One or other of them fixes their gaze on me . . . I sense that they like me. Once, a man (with two children) even gave me a couple of yellow narcissi. I've probably told you that already . . . it was in May. Now it's December. Christmas soon. Silver glittering in the shop windows etc.

You're at war. And it's very, very unlikely that we'll see each other again.

Nineteen-forty

JANUARY—MARCH 1940

Ruth is having a difficult time. At school, one of her classmates writes on her desk, 'Jews not wanted here!' Her host in Lillestrøm says, 'You just don't fit in with the way people think around here.' She starts questioning her mental health and considers finding a doctor. 'I'm living here as if I were a shadow! Grey in grey. I can't stand it any more.'

Yet her self-esteem at times remains intact: 'No, honestly, I do think I have an excellent figure. Slim and lithe.'

She gives German lessons in order to earn money. After school she goes to the university library. She starts attending a socialist evening class. She writes about the Altmark affair in Jøssingfjord in February. And about Finland's surrender to the Russians in March. At school they are knitting shirts for Finland. She reports that the Norwegians are hostile to the Germans.

She longs for somebody, longs for a man, longs for her sister, her mother, her grandmother in England. Looks gloomily into the future. At New Year she writes, 'Dittl, what will this year bring us? I think 1940 sounds so . . . horrible.'

The letters she exchanges with her sister represent her greatest contact with the outside world. For Judith's eighteenth birthday on 27 March 1940 Ruth writes a long letter. Her first poems start to appear. A new development is that several letters are now typed. The German invasion of Norway on 9 April 1940 puts an end to the ongoing correspondence with her family.

Dag	Navn	Stilling ell. studium	Dag	Navn	Stilling ell. stud

*From January 1940 onwards Ruth Maier is a frequent visitor
to the university library. Her name appears forty-three times in the
visitors' book — the last time is in 1942. She signs herself in as a 'student'
or 'schoolgirl'. On the page for 23 February 1940 her signature can
be seen ten lines from the bottom on the right.*

WEDNESDAY, 3 JANUARY 1940, LILLESTRØM

I'm so happy to have received your letter today! You know . . . my dear. Anyway, I've got to tell you something straight away. Look, you know I've always been mad. But for the last few days I've felt really crazy again. I've tried to tell myself that, in the same way that other people get physically ill, I have these funny turns from time to time – that's to say my brain gets ill. All I can do is wait until they pass. Do you understand me? I'll also explain to you my eccentric tic in detail. It's liberating to talk about it, you see. The first thing you have to realise is that I'll soon have been here for a year on my own. I mean alone . . . nobody close to me, who loves me in any way. No, please. That is a fact. Look, if you wander around on your own then you start to develop your very own philosophical systems.

You're alone with all your thoughts, with your yearnings, your dreams. On the *outside* you're still the same. You smile, talk, but only on the surface, so to speak. Inside you is your world. This means that there is a dual nature in everything you do. You say 'Please' and 'Thank you', and meanwhile you agonise over the following questions: is it me saying this and that, writing out vocabulary, straining to get to sleep at night? Sometimes while walking in the street I've asked myself, 'Who's that walking there? Fräulein Ruth. Interesting.' In the beginning these ideas were quite amusing. But then I woke up once in the middle of the night and found myself outside my own being, so to say. Do you understand that? I felt such a stranger to myself. My whole body started to tremble out of fear. It was horrible. Now I just go around, and behind everything I do is fear and the question: who are you? It sounds absurd. I'm only telling this to you because it's cathartic to discuss it with you. I might go to see a doctor, too. I don't know yet. Another question is, 'How can I get out of myself, must I always be me?'

These are all fruitless, unhealthy thoughts. There is a magnificent winter outside. I ought to go out and 'drink up' the snow, the sun. Ought to be happy.

But for the last few days I've even been afraid of going out for a walk. I don't like being alone. Dittl, I fear your sister has something that runs in the family. Perhaps Papa was like this, too, when he was young.

Dittl, just consider how awful it is for me to have to think that I'll be here until June. And how especially terrible for me to have to think that it's not yet certain I'll leave in June.

Look, Dittl, you've really got to seek out an English visa for me. If you haven't understood that yet, then I'm very sorry.

Yes, we had Christmas and New Year too. Christmas was lovely. We ate mounds of food, trudged around the Christmas tree and sang various Christmas carols. I even got two ski sticks and two volumes of Ibsen.

New Year was like a funeral. We held hands, Frau Strøm wept . . . and I almost did, too. You know, Dittl, recently I've been missing you so terribly! I could have cried just remembering Musch's hands. When I remembered your blue dress with the white collar . . . when . . . Well, you know that all these countless tiny things have significance when you think about them. Dittl, Dittl . . . I've read something beautiful: 'Will there come a time in life when you feel that experiencing something and being part of it coincide?' Look, when we were all together . . . were we part of it?

The other thing, Dittl, is that I know how futile my being here is, studying for my Matura. Fortunately all that Chemistry and Geography nonsense is behind me now. This means that the only subjects I'm taking for Matura are: Norwegian, Latin, Biology, French and English. I could take my Matura in any of these subjects today and do equally as well.

Dittl, what will this year bring us? I think 1940 sounds so . . . horrible.

Be good. Do send me a photograph. Just your face (otherwise, it'll be confiscated you see). I'm going to start counting the days . . . until June.

My coming to Norway was the most imbecilic decision of . . . the century.

FRIDAY, 5 JANUARY 1940, LILLESTRØM

I should tell you about Christmas. Yes, we did have a tree. Everything was a bit dull, obviously . . . I am nineteen, after all, and that golden lustre has passed. There was no quickening of the pulse, no secret dashing around the place. We all decorated the tree together quite leisurely. We dipped the branches in plaster and covered them in silver glitter. We also bought candles

ᵍ₌ₒ ÅRETS JÜLEGRAN

Julegranen kom til Universitetsplassen i morges. Ennå mens fotografen forerigel den, hvilte kjempa horisontalt, men reiste seg snart til glede for byens fattige. (Venskap mv.)

Ruth enclosed this cutting from the Norwegian paper Dagbladet *with her letter of 4 December 1939.*

and silver thread. On *lille Julaften* (23 December) we sat down together, and it was cosy. On Christmas Eve we visited both Frau and Herr Strøm's parents. I was given *A Doll's House* and *Love's Comedy* by Frau Strøm's brother. That was incredibly sweet of him! He's the one who gives me cigarettes, you know. He's the only *person* I know here. (That's a fact.) We ate frightfully large amounts of food. For New Year we were in the Telegraph, where Herr Strøm works. But as I'm not really one of the Strøms it was very boring. It was also sad . . . Here's something sweet: the Norwegians thank each other for the old year before they wish each other a happy new one. So typical.

There's nothing else new. Actually, it's incredibly sad. Everything. But particularly the fact that I'm here on my own in Norway . . . for no purpose . . . what I *really* need is people. Just a single one. There's nobody here. Herr Strøm is quite, quite horrible to me. We had an argument, which ended by his dismissing me with a tired wave of his hand (and with the words: 'It's impossible to talk to you'). What's more, over the course of this conversation it emerged that Frau Strøm reads my letters!

I do not belong here. That is the point. There are little things that remind me of it. Everything is tired here; one day is like another. Turid asks me whether I'm paying her father?! . . . Turid, well, she's really another story. On the one hand she is as common as they come, always nagging and with this ambiguous smile. She steals sanitary towels from my chest of drawers and looks at my underwear. On the other hand she can be sweet and has a charming laugh. Frau Strøm keeps on smiling and sometimes she gives me an orange. At the same time she is reading my letters. What am I to do? Whenever there are guests round I have my dinner in my room. Herr Strøm is still terrified of touching my hands.

That's all the news. Or is it of any interest to you that we've got a new bookcase?

You might find it interesting to learn how the Norwegians behave with regard to the outside world. There are many who think it outrageous that Norway is not helping Finland. These are the so-called activists. It's just occurred to me that I'm an activist, too. After all, Finland is fighting on behalf of the whole of Scandinavia. So why shouldn't we help them? Yes, of course! We are sending rucksacks to Finland, and doctors and nurses. And some have enlisted as volunteers. (If I were a boy, I'd do the same! Without doubt.) But to be honest, we should be fighting 'side by side' so to speak with Finland. Ibsen was quite right, you know, when he mocked the 'small' countries for not wanting to fight for a great cause, using their 'smallness' as an excuse.

Anyway I can quite clearly see you're yawning! I'm so looking forward to our seeing each other again. Do you know how it will be? . . . Three tiny people will come running to another tiny person. Viewed from a distance, all three people look the same. One of them is called Dita. This Dita, an ordinary girl with a red coat and fur trim, glasses, and hair curled up at the ends, is my sister. I won't recognise that you're my sister at all. I won't not notice that this red-coated creature has written all the letters which were so often a 'tonic' for me . . . I can see you with your small nose, no, I beg your pardon, your nose which turns gently downwards, and your pretty hands or legs. Dittl, tell me honestly: when do you think we will see each other again?

Listen. You must find out when we can go to the US. Perhaps you ought to fly. Find out, in any case. I hope you are aware that 1. I have to leave here in June, 2. that June is only five months away: January . . . February . . . March . . . April . . . May . . . June!

The reverse side of the cutting on page 205. In the left-hand column
Ruth has written: 'Can't you picture the man and the woman? The Danube.
A damp evening, you know, and so quiet. Are you looking forward to the next one?'
Above reads: 'If you like "The whore and the soldier" write it out and send me my copy
back! Next time you'll get "The whore and the parlour maid". I think these scenes
are very atmospheric. Very Viennese, too. You remember when the soldier says, "Well,
that would be best," and the whore says, "Who knows if we'll still be alive tomorrow?"
— That's just wonderful . . .' The scenes are from Schnitzler's La Ronde
which Ruth refers to in her letter of 18 December 1939.

MONDAY, 22 JANUARY 1940, LILLESTRØM

Now I'm sitting here by the typewriter (hmm) and just daydreaming . . .
having a bit of a think, yearning, being alone . . . You're far away, just a little
dot, a small world . . . and you often think that you're a 'world', that everything, everything exists for you alone, that *your* opinion is always right . . . for
the simple reason that it is your opinion. Honestly, Dittl, I think you're very

close to me . . . It's true, we almost never discussed problems. I teased you, 'separated' you from me. I used to whisper secretly with Käthe, and you with Rosl. There was one occasion, a single occasion when we spoke totally frankly. Do you remember it? I think we were discussing a book. I can remember exactly the strange, excited feeling I had afterwards. And then I gave you 'advice about life in the future' as we walked along the Obere Donaustraße. Ha ha!

I miss you. On the way home from school I pass a shop window with 'petit art'. Ceramic objects, vases and things like that. The shop also has a wonderful blue bowl. Blue and green, too. When I look at this bowl I think of our future home. So I'll buy the bowl! We'll put it on the chest or the table and all three of us will enjoy this little piece of beauty. Of course, the blue bowl itself is insignificant; what's important is that we can enjoy something beautiful *together*. You understand me. You have a tiny room where Musch is. You go there when you feel sad. Everybody should have something like that.

It's sad that I'm alone. I'm giving German lessons now, you know. To a boy who's about fifteen. So I go along there. A mother opens the door. The daughter is sitting by the fire, reading a book. And I feel like a supernatural being. Put dramatically (sententiously): I feel like somebody who was expelled from a very beautiful 'country'. (But Ruth!) And if this somebody sees other people in the beautiful 'country', he says 'pity' and shrugs his shoulders. I'm absolutely convinced that you would have understood me even without this *idiotic* analogy. The blue bowl thing was more original anyway.

My relationship with Herr Strøm is nothing but friction. I come home at six o'clock. School finishes at half past two. Then I go to the university library. There I read *Mein Kampf* and lots of other things. In fact, you ought to read *Mein Kampf* (as a child of the twentieth century). By the 200th page you'll start to get bored.

Do you know that I'm going to a socialist evening class (it's free). It is fantastic. We're learning about socio-economics and a lot about the trade union movement. In my opinion, the very important role of the trade union move-ment is typical of Nordic socialism. You know, of course, that the socialists are in government here. They're very moderate. The communists here are totally dependent on Moscow. They even defend the Soviet attack on Finland etc.

The most important topic here is Finland. Volunteers are even being sent over. Soviet Russia has felt moved to send 'us' a note of protest. I'm sure you know that already . . . The Norwegians are very friendly. How to put it? Yes, they are a democratic people. Debate takes up an inordinately large proportion of the newspapers.

So, a 'democratic people'. Does this mean that anti-Semitism is unknown here? Sadly not! In Latin I sit further to the front, at a desk where another boy usually sits. He felt moved to write on the desk: 'Jews not wanted here.' So I went and sat somewhere else . . . Look, Dittl, here we are again. You refuse to grasp that Zionism is a moral solution to the Jewish problem. Your argument that socialism makes Zionism unnecessary does not hold any water. The first thing is that you could just as easily replace 'socialism' with 'democracy' here. Democracy also demands the equality of all citizens before the law, doesn't it? So mix in the socialism! Now I ask you: do you think that the situation of the Jews in a democratic state is acceptable? Do you think that the sacrifice the Jews make in trying to assimilate is recognised? Do you not think from a moral perspective that it is degrading to be thrown out once, join another cultural community, only to be thrown out again? Look, if we could be allowed to 'assimilate' in peace, it would be the simplest solution. But they torture us, they don't like us! You were German until '38, then they threw you out, they said, 'You're a Jew!' Listen, don't you feel something akin to pride, pride that you're Jewish? For myself, I know that to the very end I will be as conscious of my Jewishness as my Americanness.

> *You give your orders and I will obey . . .*
> *Yes . . .*
> *I will fall to my knees, I'll lick spittle*
> *And I'll gobble the filth you shit out!*
> *Your filth!*
> *But do not strike me!!*
> *For I am so weak and frail.*
> *Nobody has ever struck me.*
> *I'm cowardly . . . a Jew . . .*
> *Your hands are so hard when they strike.*
> *It hurts.*
> *I want to crawl away, never more see the sun.*

But I . . .
I want to laugh, smile when you command.
But do not strike me.
For I fear your hands . . .your hands,
    Which are just like mine, when they strike
    They burrow into an open, bloody wound.
I am cowardly.
This you know.
See me weep. Kneel. Now clasp my hands. Scream in pain:
Have pity, do not strike me.

For if you strike me, I must slaughter you.
Your hands, your eyes, these I must kill.
Eyes that watched as hands struck me.
And I fear this slaughter . . . for I am cowardly.
So do not strike me.

Ditz, my dearest. You aren't angry, are you, that I give you so much bother? I do know that it's been a real torture for you to have to read this tripe. Am I right? Good, dear, strange, close Ditapunkterl. There's so much more I wanted to tell you. Such as the fact that I cannot speak German properly any more. I get into a muddle etc. I spoke Norwegian to a Jewish emigrant from Germany. I often long for you all. I had a dream about you recently. Your hair wasn't curled up at the ends any more. And your face was small and delicate, as I remember it from our 'childhood'.

You wrote so beautifully about London. Thank you! I've seen a brilliant film with Jean Gabin: *Le jour se lève*.

I think we should tell each other about the books we've read in all our letters.

This letter is only stupid because I wrote it on the typewriter!

WEDNESDAY, 7 FEBRUARY 1940, LILLESTRØM

I'm staring straight ahead as if in a daydream and . . . thinking of you. Yes . . . we will see each other soon, won't we?

Dittl, it's not nice here at the moment. School is making me feel really unwell. I'm a sort of pariah. I get the feeling that I'm only there so that all these revolting snobs can insult and abuse me. And then it's really nasty with the Strøms, too. Sometimes I make an effort; I go to Herr Strøm and say, 'Why can't we be nice to each other? What's the reason for it?' Than we chat for a while, and he says, 'You just don't fit in with the way people think around here.' I say . . . he says . . .

And there's also my tic, Dittl. I *am* going to go to a doctor, Dittl. I'll give him a false address so I won't have to pay anything. Ha ha! It's yucky to have to write about it . . .

Perhaps this happens to everybody who at some point in his life wonders, 'How much am I *me*?' But what's ridiculous in my case is that the whole issue assumes such large proportions. Listen, I feel as if I'm at the edge of an abyss . . . one that is incredibly deep . . . I must watch my balance the whole time to avoid falling in. All that I do from day to day merely covers a hole, a hollowness. When I try to uncover this 'hole' my chest starts to burn.

It's possible that what I'm saying here isn't rubbish. And because it isn't rubbish, because I feel it a thousand times a day, it's become a 'tic'. Let me say it once, twice, three times: I believe that I have some sort of 'inherited handicap'. Horrible word, but that's irrelevant.

Listen, tomorrow I'm going to the doctor who treats the 'emotionally disturbed'. No, I won't be embarrassed. His name is Bernstein, by the way.

Darling, you see I'm degenerate. Yes. It's obvious, quite plain. If I were healthy I'd work, I'd enjoy life . . . but I'm ill . . . degenerate. Ha ha! If only I were with you! Sometimes I think of you and cry! Yes I do. What a brilliant thing this 'crying' is. A tear rolls from the eye. At first it is very hot; it is a pleasant feeling and quite comforting . . . *uff da* . . . then it starts to run down your cheek and it becomes colder and colder . . . vile and disagreeable.

When in the past I became moody and emotional I used to laugh at myself: the emigrant is trying to make herself look interesting! Recently

I've been indulging myself: I've let myself become obsessed with particular memories; I suck on them . . . suck.

My sweet Dittl, let me say it once, twice, three times: I am not happy at all. Admittedly, I do go skiing on Sundays, yes, with young people. 'Young Socialist Workers'. This is great. You get to meet *workers*, you see . . . for the first time ever you talk to a worker . . . you have contact with his mind, you understand? You notice that this is a class of society . . . which . . . has nothing to lose . . . but everything to gain. I can see the *contrasting issues*. In the mornings at school there are all the mollycoddled pupils, each with his own fancies. And then you've got the young workers. How *ashamed* I am that I'm still going to school! . . . Last time I went home with a building labourer. He's unemployed . . . he talks . . . I ask questions. It's all so unfair, I think . . . so damn unfair . . . Herr Peter E., one of my fellow pupils, well, he has new clothes every day and white, manicured hands. And the other boy tells me that his rent costs fifty kroner and he doesn't receive any unemployment benefit because he's been living in Oslo for a year. Dittl, you should try to get to meet some workers. There's no point in being a socialist if you only mix with so-called 'intellectuals'.

Waffle, waffle . . . But I know the International Peace League already! That's where I met Øyvind . . . who last summer . . . walked arm in arm with me . . . ha ha! Don't you remember? After that I was on a skiing course with him. How people change . . . on a Norwegian summer's night in a short-sleeved shirt, at twilight when the air is balmy . . . and then in ski wear when air comes out of your mouth as white smoke. So, so different!

Talking of 'white smoke'! It's *incredibly* cold here at the moment. Minus thirty-four degrees. Well, I got fed up with the IPL after that, because they come across as so self-important and do nothing but waffle. They call themselves 'absolute pacifists'. If Russia were to invade Norway, they do not want to offer armed resistance, but fight with what they call 'mental weapons'. Mental weapons against concentration camps. Ha ha! Oh yes, Dittl. I envy you your happy heart. *My* heart is still in winter hibernation. It's very sad. What was it that Goethe said? Something like you *win* a lot when you're in love. You become terribly rich. Isn't that right, Dittl, that you've a wealth of joy and dearth of pain? When I'm happy, everything comes closer to my soul. Everything is reflected in me . . .

Dittl, my good, *sweet* sister, I have to sign off soon. I have to study. I do. Latin. I want to read a little, too. Have I told you what I'm reading? At the moment it's Irene Harand's *Sein Kampf*. I think it's stupid. She only deals with the 'Jewish question' and this in a pretty uninspiring way. It's all so crude, with no hint of humour and no new ideas at all. And I've also read Hitler's *Mein Kampf*. What he writes about the Jews is grandiose. Everything, every word, every line is an assault on all that you consider sacred. You ought to read it.

Then I've read a fantastic letter by Konrad Heiden. Just a minute:

Every lover of freedom must help to ensure that the end of fascism is not the end of Europe, but the beginning. If her day in history is to dawn, this Europe must be ready in our hearts and minds. Until then, we must act in a way that future generations can say of us: 'You had a fine life. You could fight for the freedom that we can only enjoy.'

There it is, Dittl, in black and white. Now permit me one little question: how am I to fight for freedom?

Someone like Konrad Heiden can 'fight' with his mind. All an insignificant Jewish emigrant can do is to enlist as a volunteer in the British army. He may fancy he's 'fighting' against fascism, but in reality he's merely helping Mr Chamberlain and his cronies. Another tragicomedy.

Tell me, what do people think over there about Finland? Here everybody is beside themselves. At school we're knitting shirts for the Finns. Ha ha! The headmaster has photographs taken of himself for the newspaper, surrounded by knitting pupils. And then, wrinkling his brow, he says, 'This means I'm in the danger zone.' Obviously the Russians cut out these sorts of photographs and make a note of the individuals concerned for later.

Ditta, Mitta! Thank you for 'chatting' so kindly to me. You sat there so still. And sometimes you moved your head like that. Do you remember?

SUNDAY, 25 FEBRUARY 1940, LILLESTRØM

Do you know what completely flabbergasted me? The fact that you don't read the paper! Here, somebody who doesn't read a paper is a rarity. Have I already told you about all the newspapers, periodicals and family magazines that there are here? Simply phenomenal! The Strøms take about fifteen. The three biggest daily newspapers (conservative, liberal, social-democratic) and then a huge number of family magazines. And it's not just the propertied classes who are so obsessed by magazines. Edla, the maid, also subscribes to a very interesting monthly publication. Strange! . . . I cannot understand how there can be nothing in the English newspapers! They're always referring to English newspapers here. *The Times* said this and the *Daily Herald* said that.

Tell me, is the interest in Finland still so great over there? Volunteers are being sent from Norway, and from time to time it looks as if we might be dragged into the war. After all, Finland did turn to Sweden for military assistance. But it was rejected. Whether this was a foolish or smart move I'm absolutely sure we'll find out very soon. Here people are also talking about the military assistance that England is allegedly going to give the Finns. That would be nonsense in my opinion. An expansion of the theatre of war can only be a disadvantage for England, can't it?

Overall the mood here is very sympathetic towards the Allies, although the 'Jøssingfjord affair' has cooled attitudes somewhat.* Personally, I really don't know who was in the right and who in the wrong. But psychologically it was a stupid thing for the English to have done. People are very hostile towards Germany here. About 300 people have died from the torpedoing of Norwegian ships. And every day there are new reports of '*krigsforlist*' ships.† Norway cannot give up her shipping yet! In my opinion, those seamen who 'sail on the ocean day by day' are truly admirable. *They* are really doing their *duty*. The Norwegians are generally very friendly anyway. If you wish to pay a Norwegian a compliment, tell him that he is very *grei*. *Grei*: straight, simple,

---

* An incident in 1940 in which sailors from a British destroyer boarded a German supply ship, the *Altmark*, and liberated the 300 British merchant seamen who were being held prisoner. The skirmish took place in Jøssingfjord, giving rise to Norwegian objections that their neutrality had been violated.
† Ships destroyed in war.

clear, uncomplicated (that's what it says in my dictionary). Being *hyggelig* [welcoming] is another attribute dear to Norwegians. As I'm neither *grei* nor *hyggelig* it's very difficult for me to attract much sympathy from the Norwegians.

They are all very proud of their democratic traditions. Recently a sort of law providing for emergency rule by decree was proposed in the Storting (like the one passed in Sweden). But they rejected it.

(Herr Strøm has also started typing; it makes me very nervous. Each time I type a letter, he types five.) Hey, I've read a fantastic book: *Through Two Decades* by Theodor Wolff. It has a very delicate, German, bourgeois and artistic sensibility, and a wonderful style. You ought to read it. I'm reading Hamsun's *Redaktør Lynge*. In it you can recognise the Nazi he was later to become. Yesterday I borrowed a 'new' book. About the situation of the Jews in Germany. Oh well.

By the way, Dittl, I was delighted by your comment that the poem I wrote was 'powerful'. I have no ambitions to become a writer. Really I don't. I know that I'm incapable of constructing a plot.

Dittl, it's got late. It's time for the radio news. I had wanted to tell you a little about the spring, which sits in the air like a very faint, faint memory. I haven't had my period for such a long time now, you know, and I think it's connected. It really gives me the creeps when I think about it. *Uff da!* (Sounds affected, I know.) *Write.*

I'm living here as if I were a shadow! Grey in grey. I can't stand it any more . . . Go!!! Idiot!

WEDNESDAY, 13 MARCH 1940, LILLESTRØM

Let's deal with your birthday first. My mind is not up to saying anything witty to you, so I'll make do . . . with offering you my . . . con.gra.tu.lations. Those three full stops in the middle make the word look strange. Three telling beauty spots. Hmm . . .

You're eighteen years old if I'm not mistaken. I'd never have thought that possible. Neeeever!!! . . . When I think that it was only yesterday that you

would crawl under the bed when Musch was angry, only yesterday that . . .
no, let's leave it. I'll just get all miserable and frightfully angry. At myself, at
you and especially at the repulsive, invisible ghost that haunts us all.

And I'm going to be twenty. That's the very obvious conclusion. When I
look at myself in the mirror *in the morning*, I can see two lines. One under the
right eye; another in the right-hand corner of my mouth. These lines are not
normal ones, you know. No, they're completely wicked, really distinct. I
don't understand where they've come from . . . I mean . . . of course the
'ageing process' thing . . . is another proof of my increasing calcification or
wrinkling. It's going to be spring here soon, you know, and children will start
playing hopscotch in the street. In secret I tried to hop five boxes in a row
. . . I was exhausted afterwards.

By the way, do you know how many kilos I weigh? Fifty-five, and I'm
1.62 metres tall. The ideal weight, as they say. Ha ha! No, honestly, I do think
I have an excellent figure. Slim and lithe. Shall I tell you what happened at the
women's doctor? Well, it's been some months now since my last period, so I
went to see a doctor for . . . etc. The funny thing was that she told me I was
probably pregnant! I felt on the one hand terribly chaste, but also very
pitiful. Poor Ruth! . . . So afterwards I confessed a few things to her. No, that's
not so appetising. She asked, you know, whether I didn't have a bad conscience about being pregnant. I felt the same as that time when a communist
came up to me and asked whether I was in Norway with *my husband*!

If you only knew how I sometimes yearn. For a man. Quite right, too.
The way I live here is quite impossible. You can't imagine how dreadful it is
here. I'd so love to find a quiet little place where I could vomit out all this
revulsion. It's simply indescribable 'at home'. About a week ago there was a
typical exchange of letters between Herr Strøm and me. If I had the time I
could translate his two letters for you. But I'll make do with a few characteristic excerpts:

'I get the impression that you wish to impose your personality on
everything that happens . . . You are the most egocentric person I have ever
met.'

Oh Dittl, what a stupid idiot I am! I know that I'm talking straight past
you. Everything is meaningless at a time when we're separated by a terribly
large green sea. (Look, although I've seen the North Sea I still imagine it to

be green.) Such a huge number of ships sail the sea and . . . You can see that my brain is melting.

There's all sorts of nonsense at school. I have this silent delusion that everybody there enjoys upsetting me. Every time I open my mouth, even at break time, one of the boys says, 'Be quiet!' at which the whole class bursts into laughter and the teacher, whoever it happens to be, just rubs his or her stomach. So I don't dare ask any questions. Strange. All my fellow pupils are frightfully rich and their mental attitudes are in accordance with this. There's no hint of collegiality. But on the other hand they are incredibly honest. Cheating and lying are almost unheard of. Most boys sign up for voluntary military service, and one of them, his face beaming, recently told us how they'd been taught the best way to stick a bayonet between a man's ribs.

Darling, they're playing the Finnish national anthem on the wireless at the moment. Today Finland signed a 'peace' with Russia. I'm sure you know that a number of countries feel obliged, on days of national mourning, to play the relevant national anthem to soothe their consciences.

But it's so strange, the effect that such a song can have on your nerves. Don't you think? The Finnish national anthem begins 'Our land, our land, our fatherland'. It has a really lovely tune. Whenever I hear the Finnish national anthem I think of all those men and women who, with sad eyes and bent over . . . No! Enough!!!

A while ago the president of the Norwegian parliament (or whatever you call him) delivered a quivering speech. He also had a bit of a bad conscience. But only a bit. You lot over there must remember that if Sweden and Norway had let your troops march through then the whole of the north would have become a theatre of war. But there were many interventionists here, too. For a while I counted myself among them, then I opposed them (ha ha!) and finally I just wavered between being an absolute pacifist etc. Now, 'peace overnight' means I no longer need to struggle with my conscience. But one thing is clear. All the Scandinavian states must now join together in a *forsvars-forbund* (military alliance). This piece of wisdom which I offered up days ago – why am I saying days? I mean *weeks* ago – this piece of wisdom has been stolen by the *Svenska Dagbladet* in Sweden. I always said that my future lay in the field of diplomacy.

Darling Dita, Dita, Dita, it's your birthday. I'll send the camera with Miss

McLachlan and . . . a book with pictures by van Gogh! You'll have to tell me which you prefer. One of the pictures is an almond twig in blossom, which hits a nerve in your chest. Really it does!

I don't have the book yet; I'll have to buy it.

SUNDAY, 24 MARCH 1940, LILLESTRØM

The first day of Easter.

Well, here we are again. I'm sitting here; you're sitting there. Nothing's changed on my side, which means I'm rather at a loss as to what to tell you. I live without actually *living*. By that, I mean without having any profound feelings, any nice experiences. I don't even have a boy I can apply lipstick for. I bought myself some silk stockings . . . that was a waste of time, because nobody's interested in my legs, even though they're really not bad.

Yes, my 'erotic' experiences are measly and it's absolutely no consolation that a young Norwegian lad who *wanted* to take my arm said, 'I know, you're an untouched flower.' I really don't understand myself. Look at Edla, for example! She has an unlimited number of admirers, or to put it better, 'boys'. As soon as her supply runs out she only need 'look around'. I'd really like to ask her whether she kisses all of them etc. Not long ago, I was coming home from the theatre with a young boy and a girl. She leaned on him, nothing more. And he held her round the 'waist'. You can't imagine how much that hurts sometimes. I just love drunk people. Not elegant people when they're tipsy . . . but the inebriated underclass. Whenever I see a ragged drunk like that, how he philosophises . . . I can see that, deep inside, all people are hurt. When they are drunk they . . . disclose their hurt. They are more 'themselves'. And they're easier to tolerate, you can . . . excuse them, if you like. One of them once said that there was nothing around him but a hole, you know, and that the only thing with any meaning was his self, his 'I' . . . I had such a lovely conversation with one of them about Finland, about the serious 'problems'. At the end he said in bewilderment how strange it was that we 'knew each other so well' even though 'we didn't know each other at all'. He asked me whether I had a *gutt* (boy), and I replied, 'No.' That really was strange. Oh yes, and then there was the English boy I was terribly fond of. I met him on Karl Johan and . . . he raised his hat and . . . I mumbled 'Morning' and . . . he turned round and was swept up in the throng of people. He had such beautiful black eyes. Looking into them you felt as if his gaze would never set you free.

Shall I write something sweet about 'love' for you? I was watching a very nice play, *Johan Ulfstjerna*. It was about Finland under Russian rule. But that's not important. A girl appears (Agda, lovely name?) and says something like: men have to fight for love . . . but the woman, she just waits, she does nothing, one day 'love' falls into her lap. For no reason. She is loved because she is what she is. Do you understand? Because she is what she is, she is loved. I find that so sweet. I think that when you're in love the wonderful thing is that the other person is so close to you. You can see the 'soul' of the other person in every smile, every tiny movement. That's how I loved Williger. When he laughed I felt *him* behind it. When he stroked me it was *he* who was close to me. And when I yearn, it is for this very, very profound, naked *he* who is close to me (or was).

Could you send me a photograph of Grandmother?

Anna Grossmann (1867–1942) with her granddaughters Ruth (left) and Judith.

Ruth Maier's diaries from Norway.
The second volume, covering 1941 and 1942, is 350 pages long.

III

War

DIARIES FROM NORWAY

1940–1942

A facsimile of the title page of Dagbladet *from Monday, 8 April 1940.*
The headline reads: 'In the night Western Powers seal off Norwegian territorial
waters with three minefields.'

In an occupied country

APRIL–JUNE 1940

From wartime in Norway we have two of Ruth Maier's diaries, which were saved by Gunvor Hofmo, and a few letters. The first diary begins with the invasion of Norway by German troops and ends in summer 1940. It is a quarto writing book containing about ninety pages filled with cramped writing. It has a soft cover that carries the inscription, 'skal ikke brennes!' (do not burn!).

On the morning of 9 April the airfield in Kjeller, near to Lillestrøm, is bombed. The air raid siren sounds. A little later that day the Strøm family take flight in their car to Seterstøa, in the Romerike region, where they stay on a farm. During a brief visit to Lillestrøm they pick up rumours and false rumours. After a time they return permanently to Lillestrøm.

In her diary entries Ruth recalls Reichskristallnacht.

School starts up again, but sporadically. Ruth continues to visit the university library. She does her Matura, but writes nothing about school. We only read about it retrospectively, a year later. Ruth remembers her Latin teacher in Vienna.

The fighting continues in southern Norway until the British fleet withdraws from Åndalsnes on 2 May. On 10 June all Norwegian divisions lay down their arms. On the Continent, Holland and Belgium have been conquered, while France is on the verge of defeat.

WEDNESDAY, 10 APRIL 1940, SETERSTØA

These two days have passed very quickly. Wait!

On 8 April we knew nothing. The headmaster came into our classroom, his face white. Putting on an important voice he said, 'You heard . . . in the seven o'clock news?' 'No!?' Well, then he told us that the English had laid mines. And then in the playground the boys started fighting over special editions of the newspapers. *Dagbladet* has the boldest headline. I sacrifice twenty øre to buy a newspaper. And afterwards I go to the university library. I revise some history. I sit next to the Jew with the black frizzy hair and the fine, pale mouth. I'm fond of him and sometimes I can feel him looking at me.

From time to time we talk 'at home' in Lillestrøm. Herr Strøm thinks the English are right, as do I.

And it begins the following day. I don't want to understand what's happening. I don't want to believe that it's worse than if I were back in Austria. No! . . . I hope. But I don't know what for. And then in some moments I'm aware of everything. All of a sudden.

Onwards. The next day begins at half past five. And it will be a day to remember.

Oh God! I'm sitting here again. A year has passed since I sat at the desk with the gravest of expressions . . . and wrote, 'These are the worst days of my life!' And now it's happening again. No difference. I'm alone. That's all; it's quite a lot.

Frau Strøm yelled out, 'Ruth, air raid. This is serious!' I jump out of bed. Then I think I've been dreaming. Frau Strøm is in a pink nightdress, Herr Strøm in a dressing gown. Both of them look distraught. They stand by the window and ask, 'That was an air raid siren . . . wasn't it? Should we pack our clothes . . . what's happened?' I smile to myself: hysterical people talking about evacuation and yet they don't even know if there was an air raid siren. With Edla we stand by the kitchen window. Outside there is snow and the yard with the car, as ever.

Then Frau Strøm rushes into the kitchen, shouting, 'Into the basement! Bombers!' . . . I take a brief look around the basement and think: my first time here. Women are crouching in every corner. Many of them are crying. They're all huddled together tightly, holding hands. It's comforting that there are lots of us; that's why I'm calm. My knees are trembling, but there's nothing I can do about that. I squeeze Edla's hand whenever the bombs 'blast' outside.

Yes, we could actually hear the bombs 'exploding'. It was horrible. The machine guns have a more delicate sound, like sand being thrown against the window. Frau Strøm faints. She sits there looking very pale, her eyes closed. Turid buries her head in her mother's lap. Hjørdis sinks gently to the floor. The men's voices are quiet and it is good to be able to see them. When you hear the machine guns and bombs it is terrible. Then the light goes out. Frau Gulbrandsen, the failed singer, calls out, 'This may be our final hour!' She asks us to pray to God. Lilleba, her blonde daughter, weeps.

Thinking back on it now, it was a dream. The Germans are all over me again. I think of the Germans more as a natural disaster than as a people.

Herr Strøm is very quiet.

Then we hear a little more noise. I stand at the window with Edla and we watch as people stream out of basements and crowd together in the streets, with perambulators, woollen blankets and babies. They sit on lorries, horse carts, taxis and private cars. It's like a film I saw: Finnish, Polish, Albanian, Chinese refugees – or to put it more elegantly: evacuees. It is so simple and so sad: people are 'evacuated' with woollen blankets, silver cutlery and babies in their arms. They are fleeing from bombs.

That's how it was. We went back up to our rooms, too, and packed our suitcases. We were amazed that nothing seemed to have changed. It really was as if we had returned from a long trip.

The mirror is hanging there, the bed hasn't been made. The air seems newer, even the dull view from the window has a new charm.

So we pack. Then we begin our evacuation. Herr Strøm drives the car. On the wireless we'd heard that the Germans had occupied Bergen, Trondheim and Oslo.

We drive to a farm in Rælingen. The sky is blue, there are cows, a pig and a very young kitten. The boys are tall and strong. They have not been called up yet. They do the milking, cart manure around and all is very peaceful. There is no reminder of the war. The lines in the sky are clear and straight. A calf licks my hand.

THURSDAY, 11 APRIL, SETERSTØA

Onward!

Planes with black crosses fly high above us like horrible birds of prey. They are bold and black against the blue sky. The boys in the stables go to the window and blink at the sun. Their dirty hands in front of their eyes. Nineteen have flown past. Germans are sitting up there piloting them. I cannot even bring myself to hate them. In resignation, I note: here they are again . . .

Frau Gulbrandsen wanted to go to Lillestrøm, so we drove back. Lillestrøm now looks completely different. Foreign, with its many factories and the red church. Our ears are keen, we search the skies.

We drive through Lillestrøm. Stand in front of the house and Frau Strøm rushes up to fetch my boots.

Many people are on the streets. A teacher comes over to the car and tells us gravely: Kjeller has been taken, the *Bremen* has been sunk with 30,000 people on board and the English have taken Bergen. The 5th Norwegian division is on its way to Lillestrøm.

Then we go on to Seterstøa. On the way some Norwegian boys stop us: 'Any news?' There are clusters of them on the road. They haven't been called up. They're waiting . . .

FRIDAY, 19 APRIL 1940, LILLESTRØM

Back 'home'!

At first it was strange, Lillestrøm and 'my home'. No pages had been torn from the calendar in my room. It still read 8 April. It was moving; I had the feeling that time had stood still in here.

People are walking very quietly through the streets of Lillestrøm and very demurely – I almost think too demurely. On the street corners you can read public notices. Printed in Norwegian, they request the people to behave loyally. Those who do not will be shot. That's how the protector speaks to those he is protecting.

Sometimes you see men standing there reading the notices, their expressions blunted. They have no weapons . . . Today they have been forbidden to wear Norwegian military uniform. Just now a few soldiers stationed in the telegraph office crept out without their uniforms . . . They looked to me as if they were naked.

Strips of brown paper have been stuck on to the shop windows in Lillestrøm. Sand boxes stand in front of the windows.

And life goes on . . . as usual . . . and me . . . what's going to happen to me? . . . Don't know.

Sometimes I think of Seterstøa. I yearn . . . Images come before my eyes.

I recall seeing the Germans for the first time, close up . . . very close up. It was raining, gloomy, the sky grey. I'm standing by the fence with Leif and Folberg, the farmer. Germans are standing in grey uniforms on the clayey, softened path, separated from us only by a wooden fence. Their faces are harsh – 'German' – I tell myself. In canisters hanging round their necks they have hand grenades. They talk . . . and I feel just how much I hate them. They say 'Get back!', 'You can't do that'. And as, in my fury, I have to strain my ears to hear them talking German, I hate them with such passion that I could shoot them, one after the other, without batting an eyelid.

I squeeze Leif's shoulders very hard. He is so young . . . and I am so sad. Leif has blond hair, a childlike boyish face . . . with his narrow lips he looks at the grey uniforms very seriously. His face is so angelic that I want to kiss him.

On another occasion I saw two Germans whizz past on motorbikes. They had grey helmets . . . Muck sprayed up . . . I only saw their backs, which got ever narrower and then vanished . . . I had leaped out of the cowshed, I stood in the doorway and watched them go.

The farmer sits at the wireless. He is very tall and strong, and has a sharp nose. He is such a good man. He stands with the others by the animal sheds . . . and talks. He digs into the snow with his feet. Pipe in his mouth. He says, 'I cannot work . . . I'm just staring into space . . . Normally I'm a devil at cutting wood . . . All I'm doing now is looking after the animals.' He always has something new to say, he's always hopeful and he has a soft heart. When the two Germans speed past he says, 'I feel sorry for them . . . They're young, handsome boys . . . They won't be going back home . . . Up there the Finns and Norwegians are waiting . . . They'll shoot them dead.' A discussion follows in which I try to convince him that it's stupid to 'have sympathy with the Germans'.

It's strange that I'm always meeting people who say, 'I feel sorry for them.' Karin, an evacuee, says, 'My God, how hungry and tired they look. I really do feel sorry for them.' Edla says, 'My uncle saw ships coming into Oslo fjord with German corpses: My God, I feel sorry for them . . . Twenty-year-old boys . . . Some of them haven't been home for three years. They have to fight the whole time. If they don't they'll be shot.'

Whenever I hear of German deaths I think, 'That's good.' All other human feelings have deserted me.

We're standing at the station in Seterstøa . . . Frau Strøm, Strøm and I. Strøm is going back to Lillestrøm . . . we're staying behind. We talk about the books that Strøm ought to burn, we assume that the telegraph station has been occupied by Germans. I think: It's just like it was back in Vienna. We've got to burn books again and agree on secret words that Strøm should use on the telephone (in case the Germans have occupied the telegraph station) . . . All around it is very quiet. The sky is full of stars . . . I think of how sad it is that people should have to fear each other.

WEDNESDAY, 24 APRIL 1940, LILLESTRØM

I've been to Oslo, too. There are many German soldiers there. They speak in German and that hurts. For I love the German language, but I hate the Germans. Not enough, I know.

One of them was standing at Jernbanetorget station, buying sweets, and I heard him say 'chocolate'. And the word 'chocolate' hurt me, it touched a wound and I had to be very strong about it.

The Germans walk around in light-grey uniforms and have thick, brutal necks. When they go past I look at the ground.

Many Norwegians are going for walks, too. The streets are unhealthily full of people . . . it seems to me.

Behind the university captured Norwegian officers pace up and down in their uniforms. They look like troubled children. Two stunted Germans with rifles stand guard.

'Captured Norwegian officers in the university gardens.
Drawn from Nisseberget by Thorolf Kloumann.' Dagbladet, 22 April 1940.
From Ruth's collection of newspaper cuttings.

FRIDAY, 10 MAY 1940, LILLESTRØM

I'm crying a lot at the moment . . . I think about Musch, about Dittl. Then the thought hits me — will I ever see Grandmother again?

It's so terrible now. I have to wait again . . . wait . . . all alone.

When I cry I have to open my mouth wide to avoid screaming. I'm so miserable.

I often go walking on the quayside in Oslo. There are lots of people there, gaping at the warships, which dazzle in the sun like monsters from a dream.

Today Germany marched into the Netherlands and Belgium.

TUESDAY, 14 MAY 1940, LILLESTRØM

There are lots of Austrian soldiers here in Lillestrøm. They have an edelweiss on their caps. They speak softly. One stops by a sweet child in a perambulator. He says, 'Murzl.' His voice is kind. I think: Perhaps he has a child at home . . . Then he puts his hand into his pocket, gives the child a sweet and says, 'Sweetie!' The mother laughs.

Two soldiers are standing inside the grocer's. One of them is young . . . with cheerful eyes. He's buying beer and because the lady at the counter doesn't understand how many bottles he wants he says 'two'. . . Then I can hear that he's from Austria.

Many of them are billeted in the school opposite. They're playing ball . . . They hang out their underwear to dry in the sun . . . Sometimes they sing, play harmonica: '*Muss i denn, muss i denn . . .*'

Unemployed men stand at the fence and stare.

I can hear commands being shouted through the open window.

There are also a large number of soldiers on the quayside in Oslo. They're lying on a supernatural warship in white swimming costumes, sunbathing. They wink at the people gawping at the ship. A loudspeaker is playing 'We're flying against England'.

The soldiers look well fed. When they march by their faces are just brown blotches, their legs in step. I think of Rausching's comment, 'A people has found its melody, the German people are on the march.'

A German soldier and a Norwegian man talk to one another on the jetty. I wait where I am. The Norwegian looks Jewish. His face is pale and he has dark, sentimental eyes. The German has a brown, open face. He is over thirty. His eyes are a clear brown colour. They talk in German.

I can't remember everything they said. The Norwegian points to the *Dagbladet* newspaper in his hand. 'What do you think we feel when we read a newspaper like that? . . . It's not good.' He speaks slowly and in an accusatory tone. 'And what are we to think of your Führer . . . he makes promises . . . but he doesn't keep them . . . He says, We don't want the Czechoslovak Republic, we don't want Poland, we don't want Norway . . .'

'We don't want them either, we don't want them either,' says a blond man with sky-blue eyes and the first hints of wrinkles. Then the one with

brown eyes says, 'Look, we just want peace, but if a little runt like Czechoslovakia is so impertinent, well . . . we're not to be trifled with.' As he says
this he raises the corners of his mouth.

About Poland he says, 'Look, I was in Poland, too, see? And there, the
Poles shot 60,000 German civilians. Before the war. They did.'

I can't help laughing.

He turns to me and says, 'Are you laughing, Fräulein?'

'Yes!'

'And our Führer!' He goes all misty-eyed. 'Obviously, he's a human being
like the rest of us, but he's the best, the best we have in Europe.'

The one with the sky-blue eyes – also misty now – nods: 'The best . . .
the best . . .!'

More people come over to listen.

The Norwegian says, 'Are we really to believe that you've come over
here to protect us? . . . That's what it says here!' He points to the newspaper
again.

'Protect you? No, we're not doing that.'

But the blond interrupts him. 'Yes, of course that's what we're doing.'

The brown-haired one thinks for a moment and then says, 'Yes, actually,
if we're honest about it . . . we're protecting you from the English.'

The Norwegian: 'And you believe that?'

A fat gentleman butts noisily into the conversation. He bellows at the
pale-faced Norwegian, who really gives the impression of being a bit soft in
the head, 'Don't think you speak for all Norwegians. You're foolish and
stupid!'

Then the German screams, 'Watch it!' The fat Norwegian disappears.

Now conversations begin on other sides. A tall, thin, 'chaste' schoolboy
looks with fiery eyes at a broad-chested German wearing spectacles, who
wants to explain to him just what German protection means.

A small soldier, who looks as if he's just been hauled out of a bakery,
repeatedly churns out the usual German arguments and when he finally feels
cornered he says, 'I'm a soldier and I have to obey my orders!'

A lot of the people around here view this sort of comment as synonymous
with: 'I'm against the invasion of Norway, but if I don't obey I'll be shot.'

But that's wrong. The German who says 'I'm a soldier and I have to obey my orders' uses this phrase as a final excuse if his brain is incapable of finding a justification for his actions. For this reason it's always the least capable ones who say, 'I'm a soldier.'

Lorries are driving through the streets. Sitting on top are men with tanned faces in work clothes. They're prisoners who have been freed and are now on their way home. They're smiling and look very cheery.

It sounds ridiculous, but I'd like to write down almost every word that I hear the German soldiers saying. I actually do not hate them when they're standing there in front of me: 'Fräulein, where can you buy salami around here?' But if I could, of course, I'd shoot them without thinking twice about it.

One of them is standing by the post office. He's tall and wears a wedding ring. A farmer from Lower Austria, I think to myself. He buys a set of stamps: 'Fräulein, is that a set? . . . Please give me another stamp – this one is damaged.'

Strange. He has a revolver on his hip. Tomorrow he'll be off to defend the Norwegians' fatherland, to kill – and today he's buying a set of stamps to stick in an album.

The sailors are singing on the warship in Oslo. They look so ridiculous in their sailors' caps and their blue 'bibs'. One of them is playing the guitar, the others are laughing . . . they're drinking wine . . . they're singing with their powerful male voices. The cannon at the end of the ship is pointing at the very blue sky. Seagulls are screeching . . . A small group of Norwegians stare at the Germans as if they were exotic animals. The girls have red lips . . . they're waiting . . . they're ready.

As she swayed her hips, Bjørg in Seterstøa said with saucy and childish pride to a Norwegian boy, 'I only go with Germans . . .'

FRIDAY, 17 MAY 1940, LILLESTRØM

It's the 'national holiday' again. The sun is shining as brightly as it did last year. But a lot has happened in the meantime.

There weren't even any flags hoisted today. Edla bought a 'Napoleonskake' and put on a pretty dress. And Herr Strøm is bringing custard: 'Because it is 17 May, after all.'

In the *Aftenposten* there is a photograph of a blossoming cherry tree, a snowy mountain and a lake. The caption reads: 'God protect our beautiful Fatherland'.

Somewhere, out there on the Western Front, lots of people are murdering other people.

17 May!

SATURDAY, 18 MAY 1940, LILLESTRØM

It is of course stupid to howl just because Kurt has sent me a telegram: 'Is Ruth safe? Cable.'

And yet! I cry. Because I am so alone and because somebody is worried about me . . . a long way away . . . in America.

I hate Lillestrøm. I want to travel . . . travel!

Spring . . . I yearn for the few people I love, who are very far away and who sometimes think of me, too. I'd like to have Dittl here beside me, Musch . . . Kurtl . . . Susi . . . Egon . . . all of them who are my friends. Perhaps Kurtl would squeeze my hand . . . because it is spring, after all. We'd wander together through these dreamy spring nights. And we'd forget about the horrible bombers and the war on the Western Front. Together . . . nice, familiar faces who look at you . . . who are kind to you. People . . .

My God! How modest I've become. In the past I dreamed of challenges that awaited me, of services I would perform for humankind . . . of work that would fulfil my life. Oh! And now all I desire is a home . . . four walls, a few books and a little sky through the window and . . . kind people to live with. Yes. And I want work, so I do not have to starve, so I can buy coal in winter. I will happily wash floors and clean windows to earn money . . . that's enough. Oh, my dreams!

What other people possess – a home – I have to work for. I don't have a home here with the Strøms. I'm a foreigner. Oh, so foreign!

And I'm not doing any work, either. I'm reading. I'm learning English, French. I'm nineteen years old and still I haven't had a . . . lover. Oh!

It's no use trying to console myself with the thought that this is a time of high drama we're living in. It is true — what's happening right now is world history. People are fighting for pitiable ideals, obsolete ideals: humanity, personal freedom etc. These sound wistful, bitter. But they do have the power to convince Germany's opponents of the justice of their fight.

As I've said . . . it's spring . . . I go for a walk. There's a boy. He has an ordinary face. He comes up to me and says casually, 'Let's go for a walk in the woods Fräulein?'

'No, thank you!'

He smiles: 'Don't you want to, or what . . .?'

'I don't want to!'

'Hmm!'

He continues to walk beside me. We go down a busy street. So I'm not afraid.

Then he says, 'You've got a cunt, haven't you?'

Well, I don't know what 'cunt' is. I say, 'I don't know what that is.'

He gives me a friendly smile: 'When did you last have your period?'

'Shut your mouth,' I say, irritated.

But now he really starts and I don't believe anybody's talked *so* shamelessly to me before.

In a very friendly way *he invites me*, shall we say, to go into the woods with him, because he wants to do me a favour. It's the last 'chance' I'll have. When I'm alone in bed this evening I'll regret it if I don't . . .

I didn't regret it, but I thought how much I'd love to have a child . . . why not? I'm only human . . . I'd like to 'copulate' . . . I'd like . . . I'd like . . . to give birth.

Lots of soldiers march past our windows. The horses' feet clatter on the ground. Then the soldiers start to sing. They sing with the fresh voices of boys.

Spring is terrible when you're all alone and when the nights are so light.

SUNDAY, 19 MAY 1940, LILLESTRØM

I've also seen prisoners in town. They were in yellow trousers and jackets, woollen blankets under their arms. They whistled as they marched. Germans in green uniforms with loaded rifles accompanied the platoon. This is war.

German sailors are standing on the quayside with bare torsos. They look so healthy, so young, standing there in the sun. 'Cannon fodder!' I think and go on my way.

The fjord is silvery blue. Iron-grey cars are loaded off a transporter. Akershus fortress still looks as it did. The tower stands out brightly against the blue sky. A swastika is flying on top.

A soldier calls out, 'Fräulein!' I don't turn round, just saunter on slowly. But I think, 'Why not?'

I can only love men to whom I can unfold my personality. Without having to fear rivals. I can really love old men and young boys such as Leif.

TUESDAY, 28 MAY 1940, LILLESTRØM

German 'reports from the front' on the wireless. A lieutenant talks about the capture of Boulogne. He has the voice of a boy from Berlin. He says, 'They had to storm a fortified wall. It was shot down in two places. Then they went up to the ramparts.' And . . . now comes the nice bit: 'We used hand grenades to clean out at the top.'

He says all this with a calm, cheery voice.

I'm writing while Mozart is playing on the wireless.

TUESDAY, 4 JUNE 1940, LILLESTRØM

I've realised that Williger might be at the front now, in France. That he might be killing now, and might be killed himself one day. It all goes so quickly. A splinter from a shell, a shot in the lung . . . and a life is finished. When I was mulling that over I thought it would be nice to write it down as it was. I want to write it like a fairy tale. An episode, if you like. When I think of him I don't even feel any warmth, just a distant sorrow. No perfume . . . just emptiness.

It's now three years since I took Latin lessons with him! He was recommended by Dr Brauchbar...

I was very shy at the time, I think, and very pure. I didn't put on any lipstick when I went to see him; I was only sixteen. I just wore a sky-blue knitted blouse and would briefly arrange myself in front of the mirror before I left. I had a side parting . . . and didn't know what 'flirt' etc. meant. I remember that I went to my first Latin lesson after an afternoon gymnastics session. With a satchel under my arm. In it was Sallust – no, in fact it was Caesar we were reading at the time. He lived high up on the fifth floor, in the building next to the Colosseum Cinema in Währingerstraße.

When you open the tall door to the building you are greeted by a friendly, balmy blast of air. There is a mirror on either wall. I take a contented look at myself and remove my spectacles. The five flights of stairs are horrible. He lives at the top. A small piece of paper stuck on the door with a drawing pin reads 'Ring three times for Williger'.

I am greeted by a tall, blond man in a white tunic. I am to wait. The Herr Professor is not at home. I am taken into his room. It's bright and very spacious, like a studio. Tall windows giving the view of a few grubby houses, some roofs with open chimneys, and a bit of sky. The walls are bare save for a few drawings loosely pinned to them here and there: some derelict ruins, the head of a woman from antiquity, a bust of Caesar.

The photograph of a young man: a handsome face . . . perhaps this is him . . . There's also a divan to the right of the window, a sort of table-tennis table covered in rulers etc. Books? A small bookcase: *Alice in Wonderland*, Tolstoy's *The Living Corpse* (later he told me that he once had a wonderful library, but it burned down). In a dark corner there is a table with some bread and a little tea. I pour milk into the tea and feel like an unearthly spirit. I smile wickedly and feel pleased.

And then he's there. Well. I now picture him with grey tufts of hair creeping out from under his hat. But my memory is mistaken. He has a bald patch . . . which I saw when he took off his hat. He is tall and thin, his hands are narrow. His thinness, I sensed, was not 'natural', no he is thin because of

'sheer age', as Grandmother says. His face must have once been handsome
. . . because his features are 'refined'. But his bald patch is repellent and his
teeth look as if they're rotten. He acted as if he were very busy . . . he asked
my name . . . set a time for the next lesson and sent me home.

He starts tutoring me and I become very fond of him because he is
a good-hearted and noble man . . . and because he understands how to be
kind to me. The two of us sat up there in his room . . . and we felt that it was
lovely to be alive . . . perhaps he felt young again.

He didn't kiss me on the mouth. He would just sometimes place my arm
on the armrest of my chair. Then I could smell his hands, his body. He was
warm. He would press my teeth together so hard that it hurt. This was his way
of showing affection. Afterwards he would ask, 'Don't you like that?' He was
a good man. When he spoke to me he would often kneel or relax and support
himself on the floor with the palms of his hands. It was natural and it was good
because it was part of him. I would often smile, smile about something sweet,
lovely that I had found in him. Then he would ask, 'Why are you laughing?' I
didn't answer.

It was so lovely up there in his room and I felt that he loved me as nobody
before. Once he decorated the table with flowers. He said, 'I've put some
flowers on the table. See?'

'Yes.'

And he asked me, 'Don't you want to say something nice to me, Ruth?'
I went red.

He would look forward to my arrival — oh yes, like children looking
forward to their birthdays. 'When are you coming back, Ruthle?' Oh, he
called me Ruthle. And when I think about it I still get a warm feeling inside.

Sometimes he would telephone our house. He said, 'You've forgotten the
Sallust . . . and how are you? . . . Oh, well, thank you!' He had a good voice.

He sometimes walked me home: 'Would you mind if I walked you
home?' 'No!' The houses would pass us by and we were the only two people
in the world.

We discussed many things. He asked, I answered; he told, I told. At the
Feuerbach monument, that grey stone column with a naked man, it was there
that I told him I wanted to buy a book: Werfel's *Class Reunion*. And up on
Aumannplatz, by the green park where children are always playing and old

men dozing, he pointed to a window that was red, because it was reflecting the evening sun: 'Look! Beautiful! Isn't it!? One shouldn't pass by the small beautiful things in life.'

He said many lovely things to me. He told me how much he had suffered because women hadn't understood him; they'd 'given up' all the ideals they'd had when young. But I was not to do that. Yes, he was a good man. And I listened and listened. I sat there in silence and let his words fall into me; I absorbed them and was happy. He asked me (in the course of one conversation) whether I'd prefer to be alive in prison or die. I said, 'No, there's no way I'd like to die.'

And he stood there, tall and thin; his face looked a blur. He said that he would rather die. 'Think about it, I'd never see Ruth again . . . never again. And you, wouldn't you miss me a little?'

I made the correct response to his confession, I know that now. I remained silent, I listened and listened . . . so as not to frighten him. And he said to me, 'Somebody who's never met you said that you're the first woman who treats me properly.'

All of a sudden my cheeks were very flushed.

But I wanted to please him. I know. I ran straight out of the room to look at myself in the mirror. Oh and I was happy.

When he invited me to go to the theatre with him I couldn't say yes. I felt ashamed and I wanted to torture him. We were standing at the door to the corridor and he said, 'Ruth, why shouldn't we always tell each other the truth? Why shouldn't we be truthful to each other?' I didn't reply and he was sad.

I have a very precious memory of him. I do. A memory that is deep in my soul and which shines when I recall it. I was wearing a golden bracelet – perhaps it was to 'say something nice' to him. I wondered, 'Will he notice it?' He asked, 'Did you have this bracelet before?' And I said, very matter-of-factly but terribly happy inside, 'No!'

I don't think I ever said much when I was with him. I would say 'yes' or 'no' – I'd laugh for no reason. And if he asked me a question I would remain silent. Once. Oh yes, once there was somebody playing the piano very badly. And I thought that the notes rang out so purely in the air . . . it was ugly . . . but also beautiful *because* it was ugly. He said, 'Stupid! . . . This piano.' 'No,' I

said. And he asked, 'What do you mean "no"?' But I couldn't answer him . . .
I just felt happy.

Then a sort of maid turned up and asked how much milk and bread she
should buy. And when she had left I couldn't help laughing, because I found it
so ridiculously sweet that he, the kind old man, had to worry about bread and
milk. He asked, 'Why are you laughing?' Again I was unable to say anything.

Once I coughed during our lesson. He was making tea, which was
sweet of him. He put the cup on the table. I could see that his nails were
yellow from smoking, his hands smelled of his pipe and soap. Not unpleasant,
oh no.

Then once he came to visit us in Hockegasse. I'd sensed that he wouldn't
fit in there and I was anxious about his visit. I met him on the stairs. He'd
bought me some chocolate and thrust it into my hand. I was very shy in those
days. He sat in our dining room, talked to Musch, and I didn't want to go over
to him. I was afraid. When he was sitting there on his own he said to me,
'Come and sit down, Ruth . . . I've been looking forward to seeing you all
week.' And I could feel that he wasn't lying. He *had* been looking forward to
seeing me all week. And when I thought about that, it made me happy. I lay
on the bed in our room. Then he took my hand and kissed it. I think it was
still a child's hand back then . . . I look at my hand that's writing now . . . He
kissed it, he's still alive.

I showed him books. I stood on top of the ladder and fetched a book, and
deep inside I could feel him looking at me. It was a good feeling . . . I didn't
move.

There was another occasion when I felt him looking at me. I was standing in front of a shop; he had walked me there and was now standing behind
me. He fixed me with a soft, smiling look. In the glass door I could see him
standing there. Then he stepped aside . . .

There's so much more to say. But it's only the small details that I can
recount. Up in his room it was his clear, beautiful personality, his eyes and
mouth that were there for me alone. His words came to me from a world
close by. I knew that here was a human being who wanted to be good to me,
who was a *human being* in the noblest sense. And I was able to make this
human being happy just by being there. He noticed my thin bracelet and there
were wild flowers on the table for my pleasure. He showed me a yellow

pencil stub and said, 'You left it here, you'd been biting it . . . I'll keep it.'
What was I to say?

I broke his fountain pen. I was mortified, but he said, 'It doesn't matter!'

I was a bright spot in his life: Ruth. On his calendar I saw he had marked
the day that I was supposed to come. It said 'Ruth', nothing else . . . If there
was more than a week before my next visit he would get very sad. He really
would. He would say, 'It's a long time until I'll see you again. Can't you
understand how awful it is for me that you have to *pay* me for these lessons?'

I did understand.

Whenever he told me something about himself, something that allowed
me a very profound look into his 'self', he would say, 'I've never told anybody
that before.' And then, 'So why am I now telling it to a young girl?' I was
sixteen at the time.

And then it was time for the last 'lesson'. We were translating Sallust. He
said, 'No, don't translate any more. I'm too nervous now.' I put my things
away. Took my coat . . . was about to go. 'Do you know that today is your last
lesson?'

'Yes.'

'Goodbye, then!'

And I skipped down the stairs.

Yes, I skipped. And now I remember that whenever he used to walk along
the corridor with me he would gaily say, 'Go on, skip!' And when I went
down the stairs and looked up, I would see him standing at the top, looking
down at me. Yes. Softly and with a smile. Yes.

And there was something he once said: 'Look away, Ruth. If you look at
me I cannot think.'

Thinking about it, it's only now that I realise how wonderful it is when a
man says to a woman, 'If you look at me I cannot think.'

The Germans take Paris

JUNE–JULY 1940

Wherever Hitler's troops advance they are victorious. Italy enters the war on the German side. After the invasion of Norway, Ruth's correspondence with her family is barred, as is the hope of being reunited soon. Her diary is full of hopelessness in view of the course the war is taking and anxiety over who will win: 'Oh, I'm terrified of the day when I read: German–English peace signed'.

Ruth detects Austrian voices among the soldiers in the streets of Lillestrøm. She writes about incidents on the quayside in Oslo.

Ruth also describes a persistent young Jewish man whose advances she pains-takingly rebuts. Her concerns about the future and worries about her upcoming choice of career grow. After finishing school she looks for work – at the end of July she finds a job on a farm near Lillestrøm.

A high point of the summer is meeting a young girl with whom she walks arm in arm: Agnes. On Agnes's sixteenth birthday Ruth buys lemonade and a cream cake. The housemaid Edla bakes waffles.

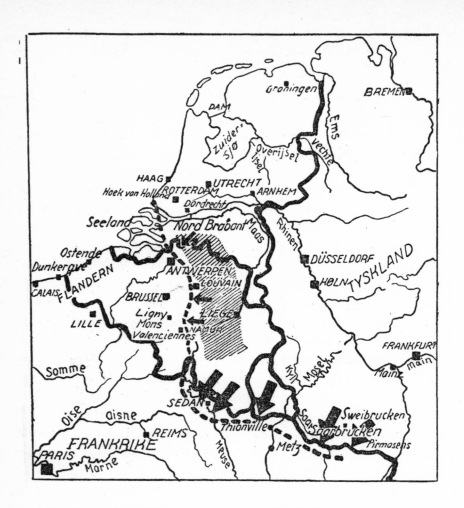

The German troops advance. A map from the Dagbladet, *17 May 1940,
which Ruth had amongst her collection of newspaper cuttings.*

FRIDAY, 14 JUNE 1940, LILLESTRØM

Today the Germans took Paris. An historic day.

I'm getting flashes of future history books. Here I am, small and ordinary, and eating sausages. Herr Strøm breaks the silence of several weeks between us with the question, 'Have you heard?' My face is filled with horror. First I think of the Champs-Elysées, German uniforms . . . then: It's going to turn out badly for us . . . turn out badly.

I'm very pessimistic. If America doesn't join the war, if Germany wins, then . . . Oh, I'm terrified of the day when I read: German–English peace signed.

When I hear about the battles on the Seine, Oise, Aisne . . . my head is so empty. I picture people dying, young bodies bleeding, hands twitching and then becoming still, eyes that will never see again. War.

Italy has also entered the war, which will bring victory to one or other ideology. The Duce's declaration of war met with 'endless rejoicing'. Oh yes. I know it: this rejoicing that starts by cutting into the heart and later is accompanied by a tired smile. They rejoiced in Vienna. My question is simply: *why* are they rejoicing? What are they looking forward to? There's only one answer: May the world ever stay young.* The time that has passed since our grey ancestors battered each other to death with stone axes has not changed the members of my species. Concepts such as humanity and love for thy neighbour are nothing to them but masks to tie round their heads in order to hide their chinless, barbaric faces.

Or not! People are evil *and* good. They're good when the curtain rises in the theatre and they're standing there, made up, and . . . acting. They're good when they paint pictures and write poems, they're good when they make music, a violin to the chin, the eyes closed.

They are evil when they murder each other.

I want to try to come to terms with the fact that people are not angels, but they are not devils either – this is how I want to try to view the Germans. They are evil people. So evil that I want to shoot them, all of them! I hate them, hate them profoundly when I see them before me, in brown uniforms,

* A quotation from a poem by the eighteenth-century Norwegian poet Henrik Wergeland.

trampling around Sacré Coeur, in front of the Arc de Triomphe, up by Montmartre. They've brought their cameras with them. They laugh, they grin – oh . . .! But I don't want to say, like Herr Strøm, 'This people ought to be exterminated.' The Germans are stupid and today they're evil, today they're roaring at their Führer like animals . . . later . . . later . . . another Goethe will rise among them.

Not even Heine in his grave on Montmartre has peace from the Germans. He's lying there so still.

THURSDAY, 20 JUNE 1940, LILLESTRØM

I could cut up all these blue-eyed, optimistic Norwegians à la Herr Strøm into tiny pieces. They've dismissed all shy 'buts' with a smile. What nonsense they spouted about the impenetrable Maginot Line . . . about the excellent French soldiers! Today these optimists are consoling themselves with the fact that the Germans haven't broken through the actual Maginot Line, but the extended one.

There's nothing more ridiculous than a disappointed optimist and nothing more hopeless than an optimist who becomes a pessimist.

France is suing for an armistice. The British Empire stands alone. A tragic moment, a great moment.

I don't think that Great Britain can keep going. I think this: The small island is a magnificent target for the German bombers. The Germans have a delightful mass of air bases. From Norway, Holland, Belgium, France and Germany they swoop down over the 'splendid isolated'* island like birds of prey. The Germans will not shy away from bombing civilian targets, defence-less towns in order to bring the war to a rapid conclusion. They'll land troops in England, and even if the English can bomb and sink transport and supply ships, a sufficient proportion of them will still reach the English coast . . . As a Swiss Jew told me quite rightly, the English flagships are obsolete, so to speak. All they are now are marvellous bombing targets for the German

* *Sic*. Ruth wrote this in English.

Heinkels and Messerschmitts. Then a German admiral said something on the wireless that sounded quite right: the theatre of war will be the Channel. It's impossible for the English battleships to operate there, as they were built for the wider spaces of the oceans. Although I'm no maritime expert, I get the feeling that this sounds about right.

About right! Oh my God! Just think of the prospects facing the world. Hitler annexes the whole world. Well, the English dominions, at any rate, the French colonies etc.! But do not say that if the tiny British island were to be turned into a heap of rubble, the rest of the Empire would continue fighting the war. No! We can see how useless the French colonies have been in their help towards France. There's no Reynaud, no Gamelin* who's thinking of resettling in North Africa or America.

No, if England is occupied, then farewell, sweet British Commonwealth!

This is what I think and I'm worried that my bleak hunches will come true. The German people will be victorious because they are a 'young' people. I believe this. A 'younger' people because they are closer to barbarism. The English youth, raised in a democracy, and poisoned by pacifist, humanitarian and democratic ideas, lacks the *élan* of German youth, its dynamism, its obsession with running wild, for whom 'marching' is the rhythm of life. But this dynamism will be able to do nothing against the future uprising of the oppressed and enslaved peoples. This uprising will come. I know it will.

A German soldier comes up to me. He asks, 'Fräulein, do you know where the hospital is?' Beside him limps another one in green uniform with silver braiding. 'No,' I say.

'Are you not from here either?'

'No!'

'Pity!'

Oh, they ought to be shot, these uniformed men with their robust consciences and mouths always wide open to sing. If you could see history from an artistic perspective, you'd cry out, 'What a fantastic play!' The German soldier, the herald of the new order, the child of an ascendant great power, the conqueror of France and Belgium, faces the British Empire, which

* Paul Reynaud (1878–1966), French Prime Minister in June 1940; Maurice Gamelin (1872–1958), French Chief of Staff and Commander-in-Chief of the Allied armies in France in 1940.

is assembling all its forces, standing there in its 'splendid isolation' and calling out fearlessly, 'Posterity will say of us: This was their finest hour.'

And it is possible that this hour *is* the finest of the British Empire. It is a question of to be or not to be, not just for England, but for the whole of European civilisation.

SUNDAY, 23 JUNE 1940, LILLESTRØM

There's nothing to say about today apart from the fact that I'm wearing a red dress because it's Sunday, I wanted to go swimming and I picked flowers! Picked flowers! Only lonely people pick flowers, or widows, orphans – think of anaemic girls with pale lips.

I was in Oslo yesterday. For the most part it's a pretty city. You can do what you want, and I know that nobody's paying any attention to me.

I sat on the quayside reading Jacob Wassermann. The ships were shining so brightly in the blue water. The sky was shimmering. German soldiers sat down and asked, 'Can you read German, Fräulein?' I stood up and left. I thought: No, I haven't got to the stage where I'm going to get involved with them. No, no, I haven't sunk that low yet.

But I am aware that German soldiers have a certain attraction for me. Perhaps the conqueror in uniform is appealing to my basic female instincts. Sometimes in the evenings I have this preposterous desire to dress up elegantly and go for a walk up to Kjeller airfield, just to walk past in elegant clothes.

I'd resolved that I wouldn't speak to any of them. But yesterday I did. I was listening to a conversation between a nondescript blond Norwegian and an older German soldier with a wedding ring. I butted in and, by the end, it was just the two of us in discussion. I was amazed by how easily I was able to refute the arguments of these Nazi fathers. These were no intellects, but they were so perverted by German propaganda that I felt very, very miserable. On my way home I just mumbled, 'My poor people.' This wasn't an affectation. I feel the same today: my poor people! And yet I'm forgetting that the Jews are my people.

My God! What rot they talked! And when they no longer knew what to say they started to grin innocently.

We also spoke about the Jews. At the end, one of them with a narrow face and pointed nose, whose uniform vanished in the fog, started – wonders will never cease! – doing some Jewish impersonations: 'Take my former boss, I can only write him a good report . . . My wife also . . . fought at the front . . . With all respect! . . . But when things have to be sorted out!'

The other one chips in: 'They used to have all the warehouses, the Jews, didn't they?'

You poor people, I think! You poor people. One of them wanted to shake my hand, introduce himself. I recoiled. No, not my hand. Not yet!

WEDNESDAY, 26 JUNE 1940, LILLESTRØM

I'm alone. Of course I'm alone. In the evenings I get this mad desire for a man . . . any man. I go for a walk in the evenings. It's light, everybody glows and looks peaceful. I walk and walk.

While I'm sitting by the fence with my head in my hands, a girl comes up and talks to me. She says 'You poor thing' and she thinks I'm crying. We start talking. She's a slut. She has a vulgar laugh, but it does have a certain charm, and her hair is garishly blonde. It's not her mind that exercises any attraction, but her young sensuality and the promise of pleasure in the way she moves.

She asks, 'Got any cigarettes?' Then, 'Hey, lend me some face powder.' Then, 'Got a mirror? I need to take a look; mine's so small.'

She tells me about the German soldier she 'got to know' yesterday. He asked, 'Shall I take you on my bicycle?' She replied, 'Yes.' Funny! She replied, 'Yes.' She's already got a photograph of him. He's a lieutenant.

Dreamily she whispered, 'They're dashing!' I try to warn her: 'But you're forgetting that they've come over here to kill!'

She nods in agreement: 'That's *true*, but . . . ' Yes. I cannot be angry with her. Because I do understand her, I understand everything, for I'm hypnotised by anything in trousers.

THURSDAY, 27 JUNE 1940, LILLESTRØM

I went for a walk. I met another girl and we ended up walking arm in arm. She's sixteen years old, blonde and fair. She radiates chastity and sweetness. She has a bright laugh. Her name is Agnes.

I feel dirty in her presence. A boy, who's perhaps nineteen, walks alongside us. When he vanishes suddenly she says, 'That blond boy, you know, he clings to me like a limpet.'

I smile. I'd thought he was walking with her because of me.

'Well, he looks nice, doesn't he?'

'Yes, but I don't like him. He's not my type . . . I've got a nice boyfriend, you know.'

She smiles dreamily. Again I feel dirty. I think: What happened to the time when I was on the lookout for my 'type'? Now I just want a man . . . nothing else.

One more thing. It's wonderful to walk arm in arm with somebody: it feels warm and good!

SATURDAY, 29 JUNE 1940, LILLESTRØM

A dream: Williger is German ambassador in Russia. He's on the telephone, saying, 'I cannot work any longer; I'm ill.' He's haggard, lanky, he leaves the room without greeting me. I run after him, saying, 'You could have at least said "Hello" to me!' But he starts berating me, he looks disgusted and he shouts about how I've tormented him with my stupid letters.

I go for a walk with Agnes in the evening. She's pure and very sweet inside. Sometimes she has a very womanly smile, yet she's still so young. She's fond of me. We pick flowers, look at the trees and people in the evening light. Her arm is in mine and I can feel her warmth. She only says sweet things: she says I have nice hands and that she's sure everybody is just as fond of me.

Her face is like that of a German Madonna. She talks like a child. When I get home in the evening I think about her . . . Cannot write any words. I'm happy to have found somebody . . . I'm terrified that I'll wake up and realise that I've only dreamed Agnes. That it will be like those occasions after lovely dreams when my body is all warm from dreamed love and tenderness, then I wake up and see the nasty room I'm 'living' in, and the awful truth hits: it was just a dream again!

And then I'd like to write about the two times I said 'yes' and, with that little word 'yes', 'betrayed' myself.

The first time it was because of a boy. I'd seen him a few times in the university library. I saw he was a Jew, with black, frizzy hair, horn-rimmed spectacles, high forehead and an incredibly delicate mouth. His hands were short and too fat. I gave him many looks.

So I was standing in the Deichmann library. Next to the cloakroom attendant I'd taught German to. He arrived. When he spoke Norwegian I detected a German accent. I stared at him. When he saw me looking at him he raised his eyebrows, his mouth twitched in slight astonishment and after a few seconds this changed into a broad smile. Grinning, he asked me, 'Can you tell me where the Technical Reading Room is?' I was totally baffled, and in German I replied, 'I'm afraid . . . I don't know . . .!' But where was he from? I asked. I was from Vienna. Still with a melting grin he started a conversation . . . Obviously we had a lot to tell each other. He was an emigrant, I was an emigrant. He'd been a secretary in Geneva and had (I believed this at the time) heard of Papa's name there. He was very skilled at paying me compliments . . . deviously, so to say. Here and there he would slip 'my friend' into the conversation. In the beginning, his melting smile and twitching eyebrows made me think he was shy. Well, I soon discovered that he wasn't very shy at all. So we went for a little walk. I showed him Wergeland's grave etc. When he saw I was freezing he rubbed my back and he occasionally stroked my arm. He talked uninterruptedly, told me about episodes, experiences and adventures in which he'd played a starring role. While he speaks his mouth dissolves, his eyebrows twitch, and he's practically spitting at me.

When he tells me that Norwegian girls can be chatted up because they promise a bit of fun, whereas girls in Geneva first have to be convinced, I say the most obvious thing in reply: 'You must have a lot of practice in chatting up girls!'

'Yes . . .' He raises his eyebrows.

He's handsome when he's not grinning, I think, looking at his few grey hairs.

And now the conversation takes the most extraordinary twist imaginable.

He says, smiling, 'Are you so frightfully inexperienced?'

'Well . . .' (I'm ashamed when I think of my 'chaste' existence.) I grin and reply, 'I've never reacted to being chatted up.'

He grins. Then: 'You don't look that . . . inexperienced . . .'

'What a nerve!'

'No, it's a compliment.'

It goes on in this way. By the end he seems to be implying: don't be so sure that I want to seduce you. He says, 'The most important thing is whether the seducer wants to seduce the object?'

I ask, 'Are you identifying me with the object?'

'Yes.'

'Do you not believe that it's just as important that the object wants to be seduced?'

'Yes.' A grin.

Well. I think to myself that if there's the slightest bit of pride left in me I must never see him again. His manner of suddenly staring into my eyes for a few seconds with a slippery look starts to get on my nerves.

I tell him just how unpleasant I find this corny look and that it makes absolutely no impression on me whatsoever.

'So you have to fight against it making an impression on you?'

I just feel a bit sick.

Then it's time for us to say goodbye.

He says, '*May* I see you again, then?'

I feel gloomy. We're standing in Henrik Ibsen Street, at the entrance to Folket Hut [House of the People]. I always have a horror of answering yes to such direct questions. I slip away from him a little. I smile . . . mumble, 'Maybe!'

He swings his coat and walks away.

I feel so awful, miserable and limp. I go up to the AUF.* They've got a club evening on and I want to join in. As it's been a long time since I paid my

---

*Youth organisation of the Norwegian labour movement.

subscription I'm not allowed in. In fury at the entire world and angry at myself I amble back to the Deichmann. God! What an idiot you are! What a conceited fool! A smart, intelligent chap, a German emigrant, like you a Jew, someone you've seen hundreds of times in the Deichmann library, of whom you've wished: if only he were mine! This boy wants to see you again and, although inside you're rejoicing, you play hard to get just because he's not some small-minded angel. You idiot!

I sit in the paved area outside the Deichmann. Just stare in front of me, thinking of him . . . And then, o joy of joys, he walks past me again. Inside I turn frosty once more. I say, 'You think I've been waiting here for you, don't you?'

I don't know how I could have said '*du*' to him; I'd really promised myself that I wouldn't. He accompanies me to the station. We talk about politics . . . put all vulgar topics aside. I tell myself, if he asks you again, say yes! Say yes! Yes! Yes! Stupid: instead of saying 'yes' I could have answered with a whole sentence, a second question. But no. I didn't think of it.

You have to answer 'yes' I told myself.

At the station he did ask me: 'May I see you again, then?' I know now that he only asked it out of politeness; at the time I didn't know it . . . I went weak at the knees. My heart started to throb . . . I closed my eyes and after an 'inner struggle' that only lasted a few seconds I replied softly, mawkishly: 'Yes!'

I opened my eyes and saw him standing there, bowed, with a satisfied smirk. Then, with a smile that looked joyful, he said, 'Yes?'

I gave a determined reply, my eyes directed bravely at his: 'Yes!'

At that moment the train whistled. Suddenly his face looked troubled and without trying to hold me back, or arranging a time and place, he let me get on. I sat at the window to give him one last chance. But he just swung his coat round. Turned on his heels and vanished with a smile on his lips, the archetypal Don Juan!

There was one other occasion when I humiliated myself by saying yes. This 'episode' is quickly told. As I want to become a nurse I'd written to Vår Frue Hospital and asked them for some documents. The reply came back that I should go and meet the prioress in person. I went into town. Once I'd reached Vår Frue Hospital I was shown into a small waiting room decorated with roses. I looked at the religious pictures on the walls . . . soon afterwards the prioress came in, wearing a black nun's outfit, a crucifix round her neck. Her face was pale, shrivelled and exuded renunciation. Her skin was lustreless; her eyes dead and expressionless. She questioned me in a colourless voice. She turned the discussion to religion. She asked, 'Do you believe in God?'

I was somewhat prepared for this question. I'd planned to meet it with a barefaced lie.

My lie was not barefaced, however, but cowardly . . . and for that reason I'll never forgive myself for my answer. My eyes started to look uncertainly for some support.

Then I said, softly and disheartened, 'Yes . . .'

I felt like Jason Philipp in *The Goose Man*, who comes to the station to stare at the deposed Bismarck and, when the latter fixes him with his eyes, shouts, 'Hurrah!'

A QUARTER PAST ELEVEN ON THE SAME EVENING – SATURDAY, 29 JUNE 1940, LILLESTRØM

I fetch Agnes every evening at seven o'clock. When she smiles at me in the distance with her Madonna-like face, surrounded by flames of light hair, it is as if I hadn't seen her for years. She could have died, I think . . . Now she is risen again from the dead. She gives love to everybody who comes into contact with her. That's why everybody loves her. I've been in Lillestrøm for more than a year now and she's the first person who loves me . . . She's been living here for three months. When I walk with her, people are constantly coming up to say hello, a smile on their faces. A child calls out, 'Agnes.' A boy stops what he's doing, another one walks alongside her, talks to her. There's a small blond boy she adores; his eyes shine brightly whenever he looks at her.

She walks past all men in a pure and chaste manner . . . whereas I am consumed by desire. She always says, 'I don't want to get married.' When we're alone she says, 'I *dare* not get married!' I understand. Her senses are still alive, she doesn't want a *man* yet.

As we walk together we pass a soldier who is standing guard outside the kitchen. He's got a helmet and a rifle. He has a good face, stony. His mouth twitches a little scornfully. The blond boy walking beside Agnes stops and begins a conversation. With a gesture of his hand he indicates that the soldier should chuck away his uniform and put on civilian clothes. The soldier replies with his twitching mouth, 'We'd *jump for joy* if we were allowed to wear those again. We've had enough of all this.'

The Norwegian points to a leather bag. 'What's that?'

'Hand grenade. Wait!'

He takes a photograph from the bag: a house in ruins; in front of it a crowd of German soldiers. 'Poland!' the German says. He smiles sarcastically again. He looks nice, I think . . . My people, I think.

MONDAY, 15 JULY 1940, LILLESTRØM

We've been on holiday. We hung around a cabin in Nittedal, stuffed ourselves with *syltetøy* [jam], *kaker* [cakes] and *pålegg* [cold cuts], and now we're back in Lillestrøm. I did a few nice drawings. Frau Strøm burned them. Oh well.

Now I'm sitting back here, pleased to be seeing Agnes again this evening, but I'm feeling empty. I keep on contemplating what sort of work I should do. What on earth am I going to do with myself? I read books. That's good. But it's not enough. My reading is thoroughly disorganised. That doesn't matter . . . but what kind of work should I do? Since I finished my Matura in May I've been unemployed. I've been endlessly considering various possibilities, talked it through with myself etc.

At first I wanted to concentrate on languages. There's no State Examination here. I wanted to take a German–Norwegian translator's exam. My feet were sore from walking all over the place and I ended up in the Ministry of Trade. There I was told that – unfortunately – people under the age of twenty-five are not allowed to take the translator's exam. Oh well.

I badger the hairdresser in Lillestrøm, plague her with the question as to whether she'd take me on as an apprentice. Apprentices have to pay and anyway there's little business in summer; I should come back in the autumn.

I read the classified advertisements in *Aftenposten*. Write to an artist who wants a model, a photographer who's looking for a copying apprentice, a lady who's looking for a dressmaking apprentice. A young girl is being sought for some light housework on a farm in Hedmark. I write.

I don't get an answer. I sign on at the Norwegian labour service. I'm looking to be taken on as a trainee nurse.

Nothing stirs. And I'm already quite desperate. I'm nineteen years old, I must do some work.

This is what I'm thinking:

1. It can't continue like this. I will get work, I must. I cannot go to England because movement between Norway and England has been stopped for the time being due to the war. As this war may or will last another two-three years, I have to look for work.

2. This work ought really to be unpaid, because I don't have a Norwegian work permit. Things could possibly get unpleasant for Herr Strøm if I were to act in violation of local regulations. I'm not worried about this as I think there's very little reason to believe that people will keep a watch on me. In any case, I've already given German lessons for payment in the past. So I want to take on paid work.

3. Better than taking on work would be practical training. But that costs money and Herr Strøm would not pay. Nonetheless, I can look around for training possibilities.

4. What should I learn?

(a) I've requested to work as a nurse. The chances of that are slim. I'm not twenty yet and do not have any housekeeping training. Were I to be accepted I'd find it very hard to pay the fees. I might be able to get it from my folks in Brno.

(b) Read the different classifieds in the various newspapers. Look around for apprenticeship posts. This would cost money, too . . . i.e. travelling to Oslo and back.

(c) Learn to become a hairdresser: costs thirty kroner per month.

(d) Put a classified advertisement in the newspaper: 'Young girl wants to learn housekeeping. Without payment.'

(e) Sit in on history lectures for a term at the university. Travel costs to Oslo.

5. What work should I do?

(a) Possibly as a home help. This wouldn't work as there's practically nothing I can do.

(b) Labour service.

6. What do I do?

Ask Strøm whether he could pay the train fare if I wanted to sit in on lectures at the university. If he agrees, I'll start on 15 August. If he says 'no', I'll put the advertisement in the paper.

(To be continued on Tuesday.)

Why should it be just Williger who has a place in my diary? Why not the others, too? Musch and Dittle, Egon, Susi.

THURSDAY, 18 JULY 1940, LILLESTRØM

It was Agnes's birthday yesterday. She came to 'my' room for the first time. I laid the table nicely, and bought lemon soda and cream cake with the rest of my money. Edla had made waffles and splashed out. We drank coffee and smoked cigarettes.

The whole room shone because she was there. She's now sixteen years old. When she stood in front of the mirror and combed her blonde hair the sight totally captivated me.

Then we sat on the ottoman. My head was in her lap and I was so happy. She talked to me with her bright voice. I did not hear the words; I just looked at her . . .

Even the bitterly cold days are good
if only they end like this . . .

SATURDAY, 20 JULY 1940, LILLESTRØM

Lillestrøm is now quite insufferable. You bump into German soldiers at every turn. They wink at all the young girls with the same self-confidence and the girls are always smiling back, infatuated by the uniforms. It's so painful to watch.

Two Norwegian soldiers appeared. They were still in uniform. Dark green, with green caps, slightly unrecognisable. They were carrying suitcases, no doubt on their way back from Sweden where they'd been interned. They remind one of the days when there was still something like a Norwegian government.

Even the newspapers are a reminder, those poor, mutilated newspapers. *Dagbladet* has disappeared completely.* Maybe there's the odd sigh from a good old patriot.

But, in general, people are getting used to it . . .

Because I now have a 'friend' again – a girl I love – I want to think about other young girls who used to be my friends, too. I want to think of Käthe. I find Käthe touching. She has so much desire, so much love, so much devotion, that there's little room left for intelligence and rational impulses. Her common sense is so drowned out by a sentimental exuberance of feeling. Perhaps Käthe has changed since I last saw her. She's got older. The last memory I have of her is associated with a conversation in the hallway in Obere Donaustraße. It was getting dark. I knew that her departure was looming. She stood opposite me and we talked about how she expected her future to be. She spoke in a whisper, saying, 'You know, I'm so terrified that I'm going to forget all the nice things when I get older. That I'll just blindly ignore all the things I believe in today.' As she said this there were real tears in her eyes. She was embarrassed, she squirmed.

It's sweet that she really cried because she was worried about becoming worn out in the future, about becoming 'used to everything'. It shows that behind her enthusiasm for art and music, for 'noble deeds', for 'socialism' etc., there was the real her, an inner being. Or does it in fact show that her premonitions of anxiety, like the artificially cultivated exuberance, will not be able to stand the test of time?

---

* The liberal paper *Dagbladet* was banned by the German censors in summer 1940.

There was nothing Käthe couldn't get enthusiastic about! At the Burgtheater she watched with bated breath *Medea*, *King Lear*, *The Sunken Bell*, *Hannibal*. Huddled close to one another we used to stand in front of Dürer's pictures, our eyes like saucers. We overflowed when we looked at Michelangelo's busts. And yet, there was something sickly, unreliable about her enthusiasm. Her intelligence could not keep pace with her heart. For this reason she made a slightly limp impression. The nice thing was, though, that she was fully aware of her lack of intelligence. But with a smile of self-denial she devoted herself to profound art and a variety of ideals. Her overflowing enthusiasm would sometimes put me in a difficult position. But for the most part we used to get each other excited about things. I spent some lovely times with her. We used to queue up together outside the Burgtheater. We would stand for six, seven hours in front of the large entrance door, books to hand. We read, learned and in-between times looked at each other with expectant eyes. In front of us was the Ring in the midday sun; opposite, the Rathaus, grey and graceful . . . the Rathauspark . . . people – very small – walked back and forth. Then the door would open, we'd be standing inside between the iron bars, young people in front of us and behind us. We would get our standing tickets, rush into the standing area of the stalls – in front of us the safety curtain with faint painted images of Schönbrunn and Stephanskirche – we would look up at the red boxes with ornate golden railings, see the people talking softly in the stalls: then we were happy . . . very happy. We breathed in an air that had no hint of political discussions, the Jewish question, Latin vocabulary or homework . . . but which was full of the things that made our life good: art, culture. Our hearts would pound when the iron curtain was raised, when the bell was rung three times, when the light went out, the noise died quite suddenly, and we were there all alone in the dark, to hear, to see people acting for us alone, just us alone. I think that the hours I spent in the Burgtheater were some of the loveliest in my life. I feel miserable when I think about it because I know it will never happen again. I even say to Dittl, 'Those were the days!' . . . If I think of the Burgtheater I also think of Käthe . . . If I think of the Kunsthistorische [Museum of Fine Art] in Vienna I see Käthe . . . She's always beside me, podgy, with a wide bosom and very short. Her curly hair all the way down her neck. Her face pronouncedly Jewish. With high-drawn black eyebrows, white skin and a fine mouth. Her face is a little too round, I think.

In the beginning we seemed to give the same to each other. But it soon transpired that I was her superior. I think she has a lot to thank me for, because I 'educated' her quite a lot. I worked on her poor taste, lent her good books and through our conversations showed her the way, I think. There were times when we drifted apart and times when we got close, very close. We were in the same class for four years; later Käthe attended the school of applied arts. There she was able to concentrate on work that she loved and she developed a more solid character.

When Hitler came to Vienna, we were close again. Just occasionally there were moments where she would go on at me about her life so much that I instinctively drew back.

To the very end Käthe continued to feel ashamed of her background. She was as ashamed of her father as she was of her mother, both of whom were very unintelligent and ran a shop that sold spirits in Hackengasse. They were Jews and painfully dim-witted. Käthe knew this and . . . was ashamed . . . I never liked that about her.

Käthe left Vienna before me for England. She didn't write to me much. I know that she's continuing to attend a college of applied arts and that she's being supported by a family. Once she wrote, 'Later this stay here will seem like a bad dream.' Maybe she's feeling the same as I am.

I've forgotten to say that Käthe suffered from inferiority complexes. And to a frightful degree. Boys didn't find her at all attractive: inferiority complex. She was very conscious of her stupid parents and her own less than impressive intelligence: inferiority complex. She always felt outshone and became a little eccentric. She developed a few tics, which she would disclose to me.

Käthe coincided with a portion of my life. Agnes with another. I've had enough of tics, ideals and eccentricities. I just want warmth. And this is what Agnes has. When I lay my head under the blonde hair of her neck it smells warm and 'intimately' feminine.

A picture from Ruth Maier's photograph album: 'Me after leaving school, aged 18'.
Ruth was due to sit her school-leaving exams in spring 1940. Because of the war
the examinations were cancelled. On 10 May the students were given
certificates based on their average marks.

TUESDAY, 23 JULY 1940, LILLESTRØM

This is the last time I'll sit in my room behind the darkened curtain. Funny.

The fact is, I've found work on a farm. A fragile, gouty, very ugly-looking old woman. The farmer is old, too, with rotten teeth. And then there's a blond son whom I like . . . Well, the farm is called Nyland. I've often been there and bathed. That's when I saw the son.

I'm going to have to work very hard. Feeding pigs, milking cows, washing floors and windows and so on. But there's other things I can do!!! Deep down I'm so happy – I'm not at all sad at the thought of having to leave Lillestrøm, Frau Strøm and her husband. No, I'm happy, for I'll be working and in the evenings I'll be tired from all the work.

And now I can look Musch, my dearest Musch, boldly in the eyes and say: I've achieved something, too – I've milked cows, I've washed up. Thank you.

On labour service in 1940. Ruth is the third from the left.

WEDNESDAY, 24 JULY 1940, LILLESTRØM

So, today I'm starting a new life. For how long I don't know. It's true that I'm pleased!

But there's a shadow looming over my happiness. It's the thought of Musch, Dittl, Grandmother. They're in England. Hitler gave a speech and I believe things are going to get tough. They're going to bomb cities . . . They're going to bomb cities.

Mama's smiling at me . . .

Be brave, Ruth. Head up.

I'd rather be in England. Much rather.

They're going to bomb English cities.

Meeting Gunvor

JANUARY—FEBRUARY 1941

The last — and most voluminous — of Ruth's diaries is a hardback book with 334 quarto pages filled with small writing. The book has a green marbled cover and the inscription reads, 'Ruth Maier's Diary 1941, 1942'. The diary begins at the start of 1941. At this point Ruth has just met Gunvor Hofmo at the Women's Labour Service, which began in late autumn 1940 at Feiring farm in Biristrand, on the north-western shore of Lake Mjøsa.

The diary begins with several pages of poems and the comment, 'Here are some of the poems of Olaf Bull, Gunvor's favourite poet.' We can see that the poem 'The Stone' (Norwegian 'Stenen') was started by Ruth and continued by Gunvor. 'Metope' (Norwegian 'Metope') was copied out by Ruth. She has crossed out the first three lines of the last verse: 'And I, a living man, at home in the world . . .' As a conclusion to the poem Ruth prefers:

> Embrace me, friend, and hold me! To squeeze each other thus
> is almost the last ray of hope that I know —
> the hurried, hot, glowing time, I might experience
> the waking inside me of another eternity.

In the various labour camps where she works, Ruth meets like-minded friends. In one of the camps she meets a young woman called Petter (in fact her name is Liv), while in Biri she meets the Danish-speaking Karen, who is married to a Norwegian fighter pilot. She is also a good photographer. It is Petter who introduces Ruth and Gunvor: 'Here is someone whose company you'll enjoy.'

Oppfordring til alle norske kvinner!

Alle norske kvinner over 14 1/2 år som kan komme fra, og som ikke har arbeid i jordbruket, oppfordres til å delta i frivillig arbeidstjeneste i år.

Landet venter nettopp din innsats. Matforsyningen må økes, men bøndene mangler arbeidshjelp, derfor bør alle de som kan ofre noe av sin tid, bruke den i frivillig arbeidstjeneste.

Deltakerne får fri reise frem og tilbake (fri frakt av sykkel og bagasje), fritt opphold i hus, fri kost og arbeidsdrakt, hodetørklæ og ulltepper i leiren. Har De sovepose, så ta den med!

Fri trygd. Dessuten i lommepenger 25 øre dagen den første måned, 40 øre 2. måned og 60 øre dagen 3. måned og senere.

Arbeidet varer i 7 timer daglig og består i lettere landbruksarbeide. Sport, lek og underholdning i fritiden. Fast læge og øvet kokke.

Deltakerne må binde seg for minst 14 dager. Aldersgrense nedad 14 1/2 år, oppad ubegrenset. Venninner som ønsker det, kan komme på samme leir.

Frivillig kvinnelig
ARBEIDSTJENESTE
Pilestredet 10, Oslo. - Telefon 12 888

AT-4119   HEROLDEN

After the end of hostilities in Norway a 'labour service' was set up for men which enlisted about 70,000 Norwegians. The women's labour service was voluntary. About 3,000 women worked in agriculture and the welfare service. We know that Ruth worked in at least three camps: in Svartskog, Biri and Tau / Ryfylke.

BEGINNING OF JANUARY 1941, BIRISTRAND

I cannot describe the warmth between myself and Gunvor. I so love her deep eyes. I love her manner of talking about things.

Gunvor is a precious human being. There is so much I would sacrifice to make her happy.

I get such an unpleasant sense of the filthy side of life whenever I think that she must earn money, that she doesn't have the time to set herself even the smallest of goals in life because she has to look for other 'work'. I feel so clearly that she would achieve a lot if she had the chance to study. Her thoughts do not fit any template. It's really hopeless when we try to talk about it.

Things aren't good at her house. Her father is so nervous that he has to live alone. The key question is how he can earn money to eat. She feels obliged to make her contribution in cash.

'Everything else is irrelevant. Don't you understand?'

It's intolerable. Yet again it causes you to look at our 'society' with particular bitterness.

Talented girl wears herself out with uninteresting clerical work because she doesn't have the money to study or for any other training.

Our conversations by the stove make all this so plain to me that I despair and sit with her there in silence.

LETTER TO HER FAMILY – FRIDAY EVENING, 3 JANUARY 1941, BIRISTRAND

The last letter I had from you was dated September 1940. Now it's January 1941. You are starting to become fairy-tale figures. That we four will be together again some time is too beautiful a thought to be true. Yet it's the thought of you that makes me hear the word 'future' with . . . feelings of such apprehension. Why all this endless moaning? You understand me. The four of us ought to be like a small island. Ha ha! I only hope that you're all well.

View over Lake Mjøsa from Feiring farm.
From Ruth's photograph album.

Relatively speaking, things are going really well for me at the moment. I'm at the winter camp in Biri. North of Oslo, next to a lake (Mjøsa). I'm sure you'll find it on a map. We spend our time here knitting and weaving, and as housemaids on the surrounding farms. The girls are very nice. I don't feel unhappy in the company of the others. Nobody is trying to offend me and I've even got some friends here. I really love one of the girls . . . as I used to Lizzy Kantor. She is so lovely: we chat . . . we often upset each other. Perhaps because we like each other so much. You know what that's like.

I tell her about you, Grandmother, about how you can rock your chair, how you tell nice stories. About 'Knillillipillilly' and about how brave you are, Musch! It sounds like a fairy tale.

Please write! So much is happening and I'm often worried. When are you going to travel? Please write especially with all the details.

Happy birthday to you, Dittl, and you, darling Muscherle. I wish you everything I wish for myself . . . and if I think about it . . . then even more. Think of me sometimes . . . and in those moments I'll be with you.

Write and tell me what you're doing. Dittl, are you still with Miss Griffith? And Musch, are you still cooking?

THURSDAY, 9 JANUARY 1941, BIRISTRAND

Everything is fine again between Gunvor and me. She loves me too. Sometimes she makes an effort and this makes me feel warm.

Gunvor's eyes are sky-blue. They are infinite.

I have never met such a *good* person before. She is good to me, as well. I have hurt her and hit her; she understands and her smile always remains the same. It's a beautiful smile, which always understands, or tries to. Because she is so good, I dare show her that I'm fond of her.

The days are longer when you love somebody.

When Gunvor is not there, something in me is missing. It is not until she reappears, far away in my field of vision, that I can let out a sigh of relief: she's back.

PROMENADE

There is only silence . . .
Like soft waves it washes the edge of my soul,
It soaks me,
Wipes away thoughts that make me weary.

Why, when I go on walking,
Do you, sweet silence, remain
Hanging between the white trees?
Will you hang between white trees for ever
Just to be silent?
Is it enough for you?

FRIDAY, 10 JANUARY 1941, BIRISTRAND

I can gaze at her face . . . for a long time! Her thoughts arrive like gentle mist on her brow. When she totally retreats into herself her face and eyes are distant. Then I love her a lot.

When she's away and comes back, I know just how much I've missed her.

I'll always remember her in that grey apron, standing in the doorway, and I suddenly go quiet and think, It's good!

She is good. She loves all people . . . because they are people.

I have a terrible urge to make her completely happy. When she sits there with her hands over her eyes, I want to take all her troubles away.

Now she is talking to Moss, who confided to Karen that she is a klepto-maniac. Karen passed it round and Moss is unhappy. Gunvor is comforting her, she speaks softly, her hands sometimes over her eyes. Then she smiles to herself.

MONDAY AFTERNOON, 13 JANUARY 1941, BIRISTRAND

Today, Quisling* is calling for all 'patriotic, responsible Norwegians' to volunteer for the German army.

This fills the average Norwegian with surprise and horror.

It's good – it will make people hate the NS party.†

Gunvor's on kitchen duty. That's why the days are empty. Yesterday we went across the Mjøsa together. It was sunny. The snow gave off a golden sparkle. Gunvor turned her head to the sun. And we walked. On the other side of the lake it was as if spring would soon be here. The grey boughs of the trees stood bare against the sky as if they were yearning for something. Gunvor was wearing her white jumper. I still love her just as much.

This is what I think: Why do people such as Gunvor, if they are not out-and-out fighters by nature, sink so often into resignation? It is so very sad

---

* Vidkun Quisling, Nazi sympathiser, collaborator and prime minister of occupied Norway, sentenced to death and shot after the war.

† *Nasjonal Samling*, Quisling's Nazi party.

to see her honest, resigned smile when I talk to her about her future. Her dull eyes when we discuss assurance, belief and ideals. *I* am no different from her . . . But I'm not including myself. I'm just incapable of life . . . When I see her listening to me so droopily, I have the irrepressible urge to set her a goal: *here* – this is what you ought to achieve . . . Then she'd be happy.

And yet, with her clever humanity as well as aimlessness, I prefer Gunvor to all these so-called narrow 'idealists' who are mad about so-called 'intellectual' things and who set themselves various 'ideals' = fixed ideas, which they use to approach all questions.

Why not count Gunvor and Williger and Papa among the idealists? They have the will not to do everything by the book. They are idealists.

Later, when the time is right, I will recall the conversation that we had together in her room. Gunvor was pacing up and down, just up and down. She spoke of 'succumbing'. She was quite serious. Among other things this conversation showed me that she is not as resigned as I am. I think that so few people have the opportunity to succumb 'mentally' that it's scarcely worth the effort of talking about it. Those who do succumb, who become deadened, they have *deserved* to succumb.

Käthe wept when we talked about it. Williger felt sorry. But in those days I was still full of belief. In what? I don't know.

WEDNESDAY, 15 JANUARY 1941, BIRISTRAND

Liv Bjørn = Petter.

A tall, well-developed girl with beautiful, noble-looking hands. Looking at her makes you feel good. There is always a small, ironic smile on her lips, echoed in her eyes and . . . her nostrils. This smile is quite enchanting and gives her otherwise unremarkable face a charming appearance.

I know little of what she's like inside, this seems hidden behind an ironic, astonished smile.

In the evening.

If you are like me it is difficult to love . . . girl or boy.

I spend the whole day looking forward to the evening . . . that's when Gunvor finishes work. Then perhaps she'll sit on the sofa next to me, stretch out her legs and say the odd thing.

Two days ago she went promptly to bed. Yesterday we were only together for a quarter of an hour. Then she vanished.

Today she asked me whether I'd like to go to the café with her and some other girls. I pretended to be indifferent to her suggestion but didn't do it very well. She asked me repeatedly and repeatedly I replied, 'I don't know.' Then I said 'yes' and then 'no'. I didn't go. I wanted revenge for the quarters of an hour that she's stolen from me by being with other people. And yet I so long to talk to her!!

Afterwards I sat down and couldn't help crying. I thought how much I'd been looking forward to this evening, and that she was now with Bjørg . . . without me, and that perhaps she'd be somewhere else tomorrow, too.

I do not think that my love for her is unnatural. I only love her for her humanity, just as with Williger.

I think how happy I am when I can darn her stockings, sit in her room. And when she asks me if I'd like to go with her for a walk I give a shrug of indifference. When she's gone, I cry.

Sometimes we walk along the path behind the house. It rises steeply and passes through the woods for a while. Then we come to a small stretch where it's flat. We stand there silently. Beneath us are the snow and the lake, and we have this very strong feeling of being 'as one'. The same ideas and mood envelop us.

Or we sit together in the café. It's a room with old photographs and pot plants. We drink coffee, we talk, and sometimes we just sit there quietly and I look into her face. I think: Later, when I'm alone, that will be a good memory.

I'm going to be here for the next course, too. It will be painful without Gunvor. Every place will remind me of her.

Pencil drawing from Biri: 'The bedroom'.
Found amongst Gunvor Hofmo's papers.

THURSDAY, 23 JANUARY 1941, BIRISTRAND

I'm drawing: a bright picture (*Alone*). In the foreground a naked woman with her hands over her eyes. A yellow, curved path leads on. In the background a house, tree, children. Petter has this picture.

A bomb attack: a black dot is the aeroplane. On the street (angular houses with black spots for windows) there are people, mostly women clinging to one another.

Two landscapes: one spring and one autumn.

I've done other pictures, too: Gunvor and Karen. Gunvor in her room crouching on an armchair etc. I gave this picture to Gunvor.

I don't think the pictures are any good. But I see a piece of me in them and that's why I'm fond of them. I really enjoy drawing with colours. It is as if I were making music. A yellow and a red next to each other make me feel happy inside.

Recently I've very much enjoyed listening to music. I can listen to Mozart and Beethoven for ages. I have to follow the music with my ear to identify the melody. Sometimes it's so enjoyable I almost feel like sighing.

Things are good with Gunvor. We sit together by the stove and talk. That's all we do. She talks about her family. All her mother's siblings apart from one girl have gone insane. They tell her that her mother was born out of wedlock. She never used to believe it and she was *frightened*.

I'm happy when she tells me things. I know it does her good, too.

She talks about Reidar, her boyfriend. It is the simple things that are so difficult: the fact that their relationship is becoming stale, that she doesn't love him any more, while he continues to think she does and so is counting on marrying her. She asks whether she shouldn't finish their relationship. I think about it and say, 'Yes.' And we go on talking. Aunt Klara comes to turn out the light. She's sympathetic and lets us talk a while longer. The room is dim. My roommate sleeps. Gunvor talks. And then she says, 'I'm an idiot for telling you all this. You must never, ever talk about it.'

Gunvor still demands a proper 'relationship'. I want somebody who will save me from masturbation. *C'est tout.*

FRIDAY NIGHT, 24 JANUARY 1941, BIRISTRAND

I've drawn a nude: Gerd-Marit, a jaunty, 'sweaty' girl with open, round lips and small, twinkling eyes has been my model. She has a beautiful body.

SUNDAY, 2 FEBRUARY 1941, LILLESTRØM

I'm back. I don't want to talk about the reasons. It's too horrible and it doesn't really matter. Anyway, why not take natural things naturally? The reason was some sort of illness: debilitas nervosa. (That's what happens when you choose the Latin track.)

Gunvor helped me when I was ill. I'll never forget that. She came with me to see the doctor. She comforted me with her good-natured smile. I'll always remember the time I've spent with her. She has shown me just how important it is to have somebody when times are tough.

I remember . . . remember every moment. Gunvor is standing there, radiant. I can see her in her white jumper . . . in her blue dress, grey apron. I can see her eyes, her nose . . . her nose, her mouth, her hair.

The last evening! Why can't I keep hold of the atmosphere in that small, narrow room? I had to go away!

When I felt ill I went to see her. It came over me quite suddenly. She was standing in the laundry room down in the basement . . . with soaking wet hands. Dear Gunvor. No, why not hide these moments, rather than sully them with words that could never describe them fully, for they do not know the fragrance, the warmth that *existed* on that evening.

The last evening! I looked into her face; just don't ever forget those lines!

It was dark. We talked. Talked about the future and said we must never drift apart.

'Maybe Karen will rent a furnished room. You can live with her.'

'Yes.'

Frau Heltene appeared and broke up our conversation. After she left, I slipped into Gunvor's bed. Like an intuition I could sense her body was there.

I was suffocated by the affection swelling up inside me. I was nervous, I started trembling. Now I was with her. Gunvor pushed a pillow under my head. I knew it: she *was* here! My nervousness was just blown away: it was like a good dream. We had turned off the light. Against the window my arms looked slender and light when they stretched out from under the blanket.

Gunvor laughed. I kneed her in the stomach. She laughed even more.

Then it was quiet. I remember saying, 'Now I feel well.'

She was around me. She was not afraid even though I had behaved like somebody who's ill.

I'll go to hospital the day after tomorrow. I'm heartened by the thought that Gunvor has promised to visit me.

I pine for her so badly. I didn't even feel this deeply for Agnes. Gunvor has given me more.

In the end I had sufficient courage to show her my love. It was Karen's birthday. We ate cake and cream. There was a particularly good mood in our room – the defenceless ones. Around eleven o'clock the girls went down to dance in the hall. The two of us stayed on our own, sitting on the bed, legs outstretched . . . I scratched at her belt with my nails, very gently.

On the evening before my departure I stroked her hand. And I thought: Everybody ought to be as good to you as I am. Everybody should have somebody they love as much as I do you. It really was true that everything was dark and the only light radiated from Gunvor.

Today I've been reading old letters. I've read what Dittl and Musch wrote to me before 9 April. I saw how much Musch loves me, what a fantastic person my sister, dear Dittl, is. Dittl is different from Gunvor. Gunvor is highly intelligent. When she speaks you can sense that she is thinking. And she's full of insight. Her eyes see. She is good without knowing it, without expecting gratitude.

Dittl, please excuse me for thinking about Gunvor. I love her in a special way. Should I tell you what Gunvor is like?

She is tall and strong. Her breasts are small. She makes no impression on you when you see her for the first time. You think her face is almost non-descript, blurred. Later you notice that her voice is 'pure', like a baby's, slightly inflected. Her eyebrows are restive. Her eyes, oh yes, it's only with time that you see how her eyes can change. Sometimes they have a distant look and at other times she looks so profound when she's thinking. The lovely thing about her face is that it's so twitchy, it plays. Other people would describe this as 'pulling faces'. I love her for it. Even her gait is strange. She walks bent forward, she swings her hips, and her arms dangle back and forth, kinked at the elbows.

You cannot imagine how good I feel to be able to write about this.

She has a way of smiling, even about things that are sad. It is a good smile.

In the beginning, when we used to go walking together, this smile was between us. This smile made us friends. Made us 'friends'! Well! If only I knew whether she sees herself as my friend. She's so strange. I'm always scared to get close to her. It was totally different with Agnes. I could lay my head in her lap, play with her hair.

Then we had to say goodbye. You know how it is. Time suddenly becomes a monster. The clock ticks. She asks, 'What time is it?'

'Don't ask!'

I look at her. She's sewing. Her head is bent forward. I just want to see. I draw you with my eyes. That's what you look like. Then we're standing by the stove. The smile is between . . . How much longer?

'Yes, yes!'

She and some others take me to the bus. I can only see Gunvor.

She squeezes my hand, for longer than usual. I cannot draw away. Only her eyes exist. I sit in the bus and watch through the frozen window as she turns away. She's wearing the brown coat I've teased her about so often. She throws back her head.

REUNION

Do you never think about how it will be
Our reunion?
Whether the sun will shine
Or the rain pound
On the windowpane?
Will you suddenly appear
On the street corner,
Like a dream falling to me in my emptiness?
Or will I expect you
Anxiously counting the hours on the clock
Until you come?
You.

Will life have carried you away,
Making you a stranger?
Will we greet each other quickly

With a patient smile, and then move on again in haste?
Or will it be as it once was?

TO GUNVOR

If I hurt you with gestures too swift,
with ugly smiles and harsh words, do not be angry and understand . . .
And if I slapped your face, offended you with feigned indifference and nauseating
  whims, do not be angry, and understand that it hurt me . . .
And if I sometimes came too close to you, stroked your hand, reached for your brow, then
  forgive me because I did it out of love.

Ruth gave this photograph the title: 'Gunvor reading Olaf Bull'.
The picture, taken by Karen Voldsgård Jensen, shows Gunvor in her room
on Feiring farm in Biri.

In hospital

FEBRUARY—MARCH 1941

In late winter 1941 Ruth is a patient on Ward VI at Ullevål Hospital in Oslo. Following a nervous breakdown in Biri she takes it upon herself to seek psychiatric help. Gunvor Hofmo visits from Biristrand. Ruth receives a couple of letters from her family in England. She answers them, but hides the fact that she's in hospital.

In her diary, Ruth describes her fellow patients and the dramatic happenings on the ward. Ruth tries to listen and comfort the other patients. She paints watercolours. Her favourite artists are Munch, van Gogh, Gauguin and Degas. She reads the letters by the Norwegian writer Camilla Collett to her friend Emilie Diriks — and finds the friend clever and more likeable than the writer. She discusses Judaism and Zionism with a Jewish woman. She reads Novalis and the Norwegain modernist, Claes Gill.

In her diary she describes dreams, and she analyses her own dreams and those of her fellow patients; she had been reading Freud in Biri. Ruth waits in anticipation for letters from Gunvor, she thinks about Gunvor, her relationship with Gunvor, the song that Gunvor used to sing so often:

> You were also once a child on the lap of a woman,
> but you cannot see the days that lie ahead.
> Hallelujah, Hallelujah!

According to Ruth's medical file, her stay in Ullevål lasts from 3 February to 27 March.

Pencil drawing: 'In the corridor', Ulleval Hospital, 1941.

TUESDAY, 4 FEBRUARY 1941, ULLEVÅL HOSPITAL

It seems as if I've been here for a long time. But I only arrived yesterday. I've been lying in this bed for an age, staring at the peaceful blue walls. The ceiling is white. A dull light shines up there.

I'm lying here with another woman. She's thirty-eight. She tells me her 'story'. Everybody has their own story. These are not jolly people.

It's tedious here.

The people look 'normal'. There are eleven of us on the ward in white beds. All the nurses are young and pretty. They go about their business very quietly. A doctor comes twice a day. Stands by the beds for a short while. The *overlege* [senior consultant], who reminds me of a razor blade, comes twice a week. Sweeps past with a procession of fresh-faced trainees, doctors and nurses who all stare at the patients as if they were exotic animals.

From two to three it's visiting time. That's when my roommate's son comes, fourteen and a half years old; he brings with him the scent of *outside*. He loves his mother and his arms are full of cakes, newspapers etc. He smiles.

During all the gaps in the day – and there are lots of them – I think of how it will be when Gunvor comes to visit. She'll sit here by the side of my bed. That smile will be on her lips. I'm looking forward to it. She's the bright spot in my life.

WEDNESDAY MORNING, 5 FEBRUARY 1941, ULLEVÅL HOSPITAL

Generally speaking, people have the touching urge to keep themselves occupied.

I cannot just lie in bed and stare at the blue walls. I draw:

Ward six: A girl sitting in an uneasy position on the bed. In front of her is the profile of an old lady. Her arms hang down and her face is tense. (Dr Munch has this picture). *The hospital garden*: A path edged by bare trees, where people are walking; most of them have their backs facing the viewer. *In the corridor*: Two women walking down the corridor in striped clothing, you see them from behind. One girl is standing by the window, the other is in the foreground. (Gunvor has this picture).

I've discovered my own 'style'. It's influenced by Edvard Munch.

Another drawing: *Longing*: an avenue of bare trees, a meadow, a large house. A person is walking across the meadow. Birds in the sky. When I get some colours I want to paint it.

SUNDAY, 9 FEBRUARY 1941, ULLEVÅL HOSPITAL

I'd so like to have my paintbox here with me. I'd like to be able to do proper pictures! To give other people a sense of the compassion I feel when I see the patients in blue and white.

The young girl with the large eyes sniffs the white crocus, surrounds it with her eyes.

Frank sits in gaudy clothes — because they're not white — next to his mother's bed. Whenever he moves there is a rustling sound; he's wearing a newspaper vest under his winter coat because it's so cold. He taps his mother on the shoulder. I feel very old, for he is only fourteen and a half.

Outside, people wander around in the snow-covered garden, in both fine and gloomy weather. The men wear blue-and-white striped trousers. I pity them.

And sometimes the sun comes out. Then people in the ward get excited; they are full of yearning. The nurses open the windows a little and sigh: 'Oh no! I can't bear it! Fresh snow. When I think of those beautiful cross-country skiing tracks in the woods.' I think they ought not to say that, because we 'can't bear it' either.

I'm getting to know people here. There's Frau Schmidt. She's thirty-eight. When her face shines peacefully from the white pillow you can see that it was once beautiful. Her mouth would have dazzled. Her eyebrows used to be finely curved, her skin pale and soft. Now it's been destroyed by life, by her illness. When she gets up and walks around she's just old. She's bent over and she moves carefully, as if she were afraid of falling. She talks about her life. She has two sons. One of them, Frank, visits her every day. She loves him dearly. Full of pride she tells me that she and no other is his girlfriend.

'We go for walks together. I have to get ready for him, look pretty. When I go to buy a dress, he has to come with me.'

Her second son had a personality change after an accident. She thinks about him day and night. He doesn't come to see her. He hates her.

She's separated from her husband.

'He's a weak man, a thrill seeker. He can't hold himself back. He hasn't got another woman; he loves me.'

She's always arguing with her mother. But life has not made Frau Schmidt bitter. She's a kind person, and this combination of tenderness and lack of intelligence reminds me of Aunt Ada. How she wants to be loved: '"You're born to be loved!" That's what a friend told me when I was young.' Her unhappy life has given her a smile that looks on things with mildness. Gunvor's smile is different: it's the convulsive smile of a woman who, because she cannot find any other way, goes back to *herself*, and as if by surprise . . . discovers a smile there.

It's strange that, no matter where I begin, I always end up back with Gunvor.

Then there's Fräulein Vik. She always wanders around in a sweet-smelling veil. She is old . . . relatively . . . thirty-eight. Although her face is full of lines, it radiates beauty. She moves as if she were pregnant, carefully, almost as if she were sleepwalking. Six months ago she gave birth to an illegitimate child. Her face shines when she talks of her Bjørn Roald. My son!

She doesn't know how she's going to bring up the child, as the father doesn't want to support it financially.

Sometimes she comes with her modest, graceful smile and 'visits' us here in our 'separate' room. She says, 'Yesterday I went to see my son. He was so de-light-ful!'

I watch her as she leaves and want to know if she's aware that her presence gives something to other people.

I feel that I have to do something good for these people. It's terrible to think that they're killing each other out there, when life is difficult enough already.

Then there's Hjørdis. She's afraid of death. She has these 'anxiety attacks'. I've seen one of them. I stayed calm and tried to help by stroking her and singing lullabies. And I saw that it helped her. That's why she likes me.

It drives you crazy to see her unwell and not be able to do anything. Her eyes are large and full of pain. There are deep shadows under her eyes. Around her mouth, which looks as if it's been filled in, there are marked lines like wicked fans. She has this yearning inside her for health, for happiness . . . the same yearning that's inside me. She tells me of her sad childhood, of her father who drank, of the dark apartment . . . of her lover. She talks about death, which she fears. I ask her whether she isn't comforted by the knowledge that she can have children.

'Yes. I've got a boyfriend and I pleaded with him to do it with me . . . But I was too young at the time.'

She showed me a letter her lover wrote her to console her. It was a good letter, revealing somebody with a good heart: he writes about the spring, the autumn, the fact that the leaves are wilting etc. When he comes to visit he's not handsome, but he does have a pleasant voice. They start whispering to each other. His deep voice plays with Hjørdis's silky woman's voice.

Sometimes she laughs and I can see her eyes gleaming as they scan him. Once I overheard one of their conversations. It was about life in general. She accused him in a severe, agitated voice; he tried to explain. It was already dark in the room. And there was a lot of silence between the words. I thought of all the young people who at that moment were talking about life.

Hjørdis's behaviour is often quite disgusting. And if she were well, I would probably find her insufferable. But I feel pity for her.

There's Nini: a blonde, eighteen-year-old girl. She ought to be called Doris . . . she has light, wavy hair and coffee-coloured eyes surrounded by the whites of her eyeballs. The upturned nose and the small red mouth make a striking impression. She has the face of a spoiled lady of leisure.

She grew up in a children's home. When she talks of the five years that she lived there she gets quite irate. She says with a nervous laugh, 'There are these waves that swell up right here inside me. And then I want to batter someone to death.' One of the people she has a deep-rooted hatred for is the woman who used to run the children's home. Various hints give me the impression that she's become obsessed by the idea of exacting revenge. The woman who ran the home made the girls call her 'Mother'. Her constant refrain: 'But girls, aren't you grateful?' Nini then decided to run away with two of her friends.

Her description of their flight is so dramatic that I can picture the whole thing in great detail. Nini is a gifted storyteller in any case. Although she speaks incredibly quickly, she knows how to paint the atmosphere so beautifully and to accentuate small details.

Their escape was successful and they spent a few jolly days with an acquaintance until . . . well, the police came on their trail. Nini was thrown into a women's prison. Her stories from this place are like a novel you'd read with a sceptical smile. The prison population was made up of whores. Before meals they had to say the Lord's Prayer. On the Sunday they were given a book in their cell – a book about the Franco–Prussian War. They had to spend the whole day doing the washing. There were iron bars in front of the windows . . . no stove in their room. Nini cried uninterruptedly for a week. Then she was brought to Ward VI, not here but to a sub-ward called 'Post I'. That's where the 'troubled' ones are kept. She didn't have a clue where she was until she was awoken in the night by the mad people screaming. Then things became clear.

It's sad to see the way Nini childishly despairs of other people and the world in general. She laughs and says, 'Such is life.'

Nina and Hjørdis had to move from the ward today. Hjørdis was in total despair and I saw that she really likes me.

That made me feel good. Nini was crying too; her face was covered in red blotches.

TUESDAY, 11 FEBRUARY 1941, ULLEVÅL HOSPITAL

How songs can reproduce a mood that only lives on in one's memory! This morning I suddenly thought of the song that Gunvor enjoyed singing all the time: 'You were also once a child on the lap of a woman, / but you cannot see the days that lie ahead. / Hallelujah, Hallelujah!' I sang this song and felt so miserable. I tried to imitate the sound of her voice. I saw her face before me, with the eyebrows that twitch and lips that try to hide a smile.

I'm expecting a letter from her. She's already written to say . . . that she's missing me: 'Everything here's the same as usual, except that I'm missing you.'

LETTER TO HER FAMILY IN ENGLAND – FRIDAY, 14 FEBRUARY 1941 [ULLEVÅL HOSPITAL]

I've now got your letter on the table in front of me. Your thoughts. My God, how can you be so far away?

Shall I write about me? As you know, I'm on labour service. And I'm really enjoying it here. I understand that I've become a 'better' person, for there are many people who like me. And I've also met somebody here. Gunvor. I've told you about her . . . in my thoughts. A friend! Yes, Dittl. You're right. It's just what I've been missing. You must excuse me if I write about her. She means so much to me. And then there are other girls here. From a 'practical' viewpoint, of course, it's a real shame that I haven't got 'further' in life. But you know very well that I've never been able to stand the word 'future'. And while I'm still young enough to enjoy the moment, you can keep your 'permanent job' etc.

I associate the idea of a permanent job with work that I do not like: maid etc. I'm certain that I want to study something, something that interests me. So from a 'human' viewpoint I've gained a lot from my time in the labour service. I earn 'just' enough that I can buy a small book now and then. And Gunvor is here. For a time I loved her so much that it hurt. But now I know that she likes me, too. She has a small room where we often talk.

As far as America is concerned, the consul doesn't want to give me a visa and Kurtl is trying his best to see that E. Fox guarantees me an affidavit. I'm waiting. I heard from Mattelin that everybody is keeping well. I'd love to have *regular* news of you. Kurtl is there!!! I scarcely need tell you that you mustn't worry about me. Neither do I need *any* money. I'm surviving.

Your first kiss, Dittl! Somebody kissed me once, too. But I let it happen only because I wanted to know what it was like. He was ugly and married. And I didn't look at him again afterwards. Yes, yes.

There are a few of your letters on my bedside table. My dearest Grandmother, Dittl and Musch. Happy birthday to you all! Time passes so quickly. If I know you're well, I'm happy. Please send my most heartfelt greetings to everybody. Kisses and so much love. What wonderful people you are!

Dittl, I'm very pleased that you like van Gogh. You really *must* read the letters to his brother. And you ought to read *The Grapes of Wrath*, too. By John Steinbeck!!! Brilliant.

MONDAY, 17 FEBRUARY 1941, ULLEVÅL HOSPITAL

The time has passed. Gunvor came yesterday. I waited for her the whole day. And as the clock ticked on, it became warmer. I looked. Occasionally I said out loud to myself, 'I'm so happy.'

I sat in the living room. She arrived in the brown coat. She stood at the door with a slightly wounded expression and very round eyes. Next to her was Bjørg, another girl from the labour service. I could only see Gunvor.

At first she said quickly, 'Listen, I'm sorry I couldn't come on my own as we'd arranged. I just bumped into Bjørg here.'

We sat. The atmosphere that evolved was distant . . . empty yet happy. She sat next to me. The brown coat. The blue dress.

'How large you are!'

'Didn't you know?'

And the smile is back. I feel so close to her that I shy away from looking into her eyes. We don't talk much.

When she leaves there is this unsatisfied feeling: not disappointment, just the thought that there ought to have been more, we love each other – that's why there ought to have been more – it was not enough.

I've always been tormented by this thought when we've been together. And yet it's this very dissatisfaction that has kept our relationship fresh. This is why we haven't got sick of each other in the three months we've lived together – our feelings have never been given free rein. There was something unspoken between us. Yes. That's how it is. We only really speak properly to each other when we sit there together in silence.

And I also want to remember the look that made me feel good. It's her mild look, when her eyes appear to be hiding behind a veil . . . and are slightly distant and squinting. That's when I love her the most.

MONDAY, 24 FEBRUARY 1941, ULLEVÅL HOSPITAL

Gunvor has just been. She comes frequently. When it's visiting time I pace up and down the corridor and wait. And it's good that she comes. It makes me happy.

And yet! There is 'something' that torments me: she has left; we sat there and felt that we had drifted apart. There is so much that can come between us: the atmosphere in the hospital, the people, the doctors, the view from the window, the flowers on the bedside table. 'Goldfish', my friend. Hjørdis who is being consumed by jealousy. Synnøve, who is lying silent and pale in her bed after a terrible attack. Everybody and everything separates me from her. It's so painful. And her gestures, her smile stir me like the memory of something that used to be. We sit and talk about this and that, but we do not touch on the things deep in our souls. It's enough to make you cry. I think about the times in the camp, about our final evening. She predicted that it would be like this. I laughed and called her 'lazy' and 'limp'. But how right she was in spite of everything. Oh! And what hurts is that I cannot bridge this gulf.

But it's worth developing our relationship again. I'll talk to her about it and, if she gives me a sceptical smile, I don't want her to come again.

MONDAY, 3 MARCH 1941, ULLEVÅL HOSPITAL

There's now a Jewish woman on the ward. She's forty-three, but looks much older. Her face is thin, emaciated, it's practically just bones. She is so strong and strident, with a protruding nose and shining, deep-set eyes. They remind me of the eyes of children who already know what 'life' means. When she talks about her illness she looks as if she has suffered a great injustice.

Her eyes burn and she nods her head as if she were certain that all the rest of us feel the same way as her. All of a sudden a triumphant smile comes over her face.

We talk together. She speaks Yiddish. As her Norwegian is very poor, I ask her where she came from. She answers with a beaming smile, 'But I'm Jewish!'

She holds my hand in hers, explores my features with her gaze, as if she were looking for Jewish signs in my face.

For her it's a matter of course that Jews can only feel comfortable in the company of other Jews, can only have Jewish friends.

'Do you have any friends?'

'Yes.'

'Jews?'

'No.'

'What do you mean "No"? I don't understand.'

When she learns that I live with 'Christians' she shakes her head in astonishment.

'I don't understand. They're not Jews but they feed you, let you live with them. No! You have to go to the Jewish community. You must tell them that you don't have any parents, that you're alone in Oslo and ask them who you can live with who's Jewish. After all, it's better to live with Jews than Christians.'

There's also an emigrant from Russia on the ward. She's small and colourless with age. Her face is quite grey, her skin sags loosely from her bones. Her eyes, hidden behind tear sacs, give a good-natured shine.

'Come and see me again, we'll have a chat. It will provide some amusement at least.' She speaks passionately of Paris.

'The shrubs are already green there. Sun everywhere. No snow! I hate snow.'

She talks about Russia as if in a dream. About the dark, southern nights.

'I hate these bright nights here. I wait, I wait for it to get dark.'

Her opinions are incredibly narrow and conceited. A typical representative of the 'better class'. She calls herself a 'cultured lady'. She sees the Russian people as a stupid, good-natured mass, who were ruined by 'culture'. I'm amazed that I can talk to her with such conviction about the socialist idea, amazed that she can't counter my arguments about socialism. The more she talks about the criminal communists, the more convinced I become that my viewpoint is right.

Private property! Socialism! Socialisation! These words buzz around the ward. I get excited, start to gesticulate. The old Russian lady sits there in bed like an owl and says, in her sing-song German, 'It's rubbish. All rubbish. It sounds very nice . . . in books . . . in books . . .'

TUESDAY, 4 MARCH 1941, ULLEVÅL HOSPITAL

I see many suffering people here. The thought I have is: help them.

Miss Vik, the terribly thin woman with the face that's both old and young, is crying like a small baby. 'I haven't slept a wink the last few nights. I must have a sleeping tablet . . . I can't stand it any more.'

The doctor has forbidden her from visiting her child and this makes her unhappy.

Hjørdis is standing by the window, looking straight ahead with her dark eyes, and the tears run slowly down her face.

FRIDAY, 7 MARCH 1941, ULLEVÅL HOSPITAL

A young trainee, whose job here in the hospital is to flit around in a white coat, has recently started to corner me and discuss various 'questions'.

He's a fan of van Gogh and, although he thinks that van Gogh and Edvard Munch are similar, I think he's a rather nice chap.

I like watching, for example, how he always needs to get to the bottom of a subject when he's in conversation. His large, grey-green eyes disappear into space while his brain slowly develops an argument. But his opinions are very shallow. Our exchange of views usually comes back to square one when, with a look of submission, he mutters an embarrassed: 'There's something in what you say. There is.' Then we change subjects.

Nini calls him 'Broom', for his hair sticks up in all directions, and his figure is as flat and hard as a broom.

Synnøve, our former roommate, has had to be transferred to the other section . . . Synnøve is fourteen years old, a well-developed and voluptuous girl. Her face is soft and when you get to know her she starts to remind you of a good Madonna. Her very being radiates youth, unfettered cheerfulness. But her moods are highly variable. After having wept bitterly for five minutes she laughs heartily, only then to start crying again suddenly.

In our room (I shared it with Hjørdis and Nini) there were many arguments. During one of these quarrels Nini hit her head. Synnøve began to cry. The crying turned into a convulsive sobbing. She dug her fingers into the pillow, into the blankets . . . her whole body shook, contracted. Synnøve sat on her bed. She held my hand and squeezed so hard that it hurt. Then she totally lost consciousness and started talking nonsense.

I'll never forget those few hours. It was evening. The sister had allowed us to keep the light on. We sat there tense, upright in our beds. Unable to do a single thing to help her, we watched as her poor hands tightened, her fingers became stiff. Her body doubled up and it was as if electric jolts were shooting through her. The doctor didn't arrive until later and, as expected, he couldn't do anything. In other words, Synnøve was given a powerful drug and calmed down.

But in the night, while I was sitting beside her bed waiting for the doctor, an anger rose inside me, such an immeasurable fury, because something like that could happen, because innocent people, children, become the victims of frightful diseases. Then I remembered that there are people who believe in 'God' and with this thought my wrath had found a target. It fell on this God, whom the Christians call a God of love. I'd never had such close contact with this God as on that night. This God that I do not believe in.

SUNDAY AFTERNOON, 9 MARCH 1941, ULLEVÅL HOSPITAL

Outside the sun is shining. The sky is a perfect bright blue. Melting snow is dropping from the roof.

I'd love to be outside. I think about the quayside. About the ships in the fjord, the jolly people who wander up and down . . . work. I'd like to watch the seagulls with Gunvor, sunbathe.

Whenever the sun shines I think of Gunvor. She worships the sun. Her features become languid and reach out to the warmth. Without Gunvor I wouldn't be able to tolerate life. I feel as if she is my link to existence. When I think of her being away from me everything turns grey and I get scared.

I'm reading a lot here. Today I read a fantastic book: *Foma Gordeyev* by Maxim Gorky. Each scene is so human and written in a manner that makes you think: yes! It must have been exactly like that and no other way. There is a character with a lot of feeling, and whose reason doesn't try to make sense of life. Feeling takes the place of reason and tyrannises this man, who is rootless in the world. Neither Yezhov the socialist, nor Maiakin, the egotistic materialist, can satisfy him with their views. He gets the first glimmer of a better world from being together with workers at a camp fire.

Foma is *better* than the others. Through this superiority he feels pointlessness, mercilessness and, if you feel the pointlessness of existence as Foma does, you're close to madness. Gorky might be using Foma's lack of direction and continual lack of restraint to represent the Russian character, specifically the Russian character of a certain class that has no right to exist. (Here Gorky is thinking of the merchant class.) In any case, what Gorky intended is irrelevant; Foma is immortal because he depicts a man who suffers – it is too easy to call his suffering world weariness. Scenes such as the one when Foma pushes off the ferry full of people from the bank, or when he sleeps with the first woman on the barge – these will stay in my memory.

MONDAY, 10 MARCH 1941, ULLEVÅL HOSPITAL

Days pass. And today it's almost spring outside: a fierce, blinding sun, a bright blue sky. Nini and I wander up and down the 'garden'. There are new sounds to be heard, which resonate with spring: trickling water, snow, icicles falling noisily from the roof, the first birdsong. I'm full of longing.

Gunvor came again today, even though she was here yesterday. We're good friends again. She says that I've no reason to despair . . . for I'm often in despair! In those moments life stands before me like a creepy monster against which it would be absurd to attempt a struggle. No, not that! It's like a black

Spill ved midnatt
Claes Gill

Magisk mørke din ...
du åpner ditt vindu;
sommernatten iler
hvitt henover din hud

og uro i ditt blikk
du ritrer; et kjølig
drag av himlens lys
grønne hav langt i vest

mot ditt hår; mot krattets mulm,
jett av dyrs pust. Nu!
Nei, du hasper ditt vindu
og ser ikke; o kval

A poem by the Norwegian writer Claes Gill (1910–1973)
that Ruth copied out in her diary.

night . . . and I don't have any light! And I can't do anything but stay in the same spot and try to be as little afraid as possible.

Then the doctor comes and says that I'm pulling faces and that I should endeavour to behave better. I sit there and think of all those people who have told me the same thing. I think of those who loved me even though they were aware of my faults: Williger, Gunvor and Sissel!

There's now a thirteen-year-old girl staying with us: Solveig. She has brown hair and large grey-green eyes ringed with dark shadows. Her light-brown, high forehead is childish, as are her mouth and nose – this reminds one of a duck's beak. And yet, when I look at her I think of the men she will love. There is an enchanting girlishness about her small, delicate and completely undeveloped figure, but she's not aware of this yet. This impression is only heightened by her nervousness: the shadow of a brief, agonising thought often flashes across her light-brown forehead; two small but distinct lines form on the bridge of her nose; her fine eyebrows move about; and her slim fingers nervously toy with things. Solveig is a very lovely creature.

TUESDAY, 11 MARCH 1941, ULLEVÅL HOSPITAL

A dream. I have this friend. He is terribly nice. Our friendship is Platonic, so to speak. We go for walks together and he says: I'd really like to meet some girls. I think: How funny! Here I am walking beside him and he wants to meet some girls; that means he doesn't think of me as a woman . . . Evening comes and we have to sleep near a loo or bathroom. He's in a different room from me. I think: If he doesn't come! During the night somebody comes into my room. I hear noises, I can feel the presence of a stranger, but I cannot look up. It is as if I am surrounded by a grey fog. This stranger is a man who resembles Lenny from *Of Mice and Men*. He approaches my bed. I think: He means to have me. Let him help himself. He comes closer and I think: He means to kill me. There's a knife in his hand. I'm terrified and start to struggle. I wrestle the knife away from him and drive it slowly into his neck, above his Adam's apple. I have to kill him slowly because the knife is blunt. The blood runs thickly and slowly.

THURSDAY, 13 MARCH 1941, ULLEVÅL HOSPITAL

A small old lady is pacing up and down the corridor, crying. She wants to go home . . . The tall, slim girl who smiles for no reason has a tissue in her hand that she presses gently to her eyes . . . Frau A. fell over in the corridor; we were awoken in the night by her devilish screaming. What's wrong? Frau A. has fallen over. Thank God, I thought somebody had gone crackers.

That's what it's like here. Someone who's gone about their business quite normally suddenly starts to cry in the corridor, starts to scream wildly. And we watch her with a profound empathy and understanding. Our blue-striped dresses make us comrades. We don't know when our turn will come.

Yesterday I was sitting here with Goldfish, teaching her German. We heard someone scream; it was wild and drawn-out. Then it happened again, and a third time. These were words shrieked in uncontained fury, in madness. We jumped up and raced to the door. The screaming, which was muffled by the door, now got loud! It was Gerd who'd had an attack. Three nurses were dragging her through the corridor, half unconscious. Her full head of red hair was almost touching the ground . . . She'd been raging throughout the day, and had been throwing glasses and bowls against the walls. And then in the evening her fury had reached a climax . . .

Gerd is a 'normal' red-headed girl. Her face is pale and delicate. When she talks she comes across as very self-absorbed. She had an operation a fortnight ago (and now can no longer have children). The operation took a lot out of her; she walks cautiously and slowly as if she were somehow afraid of shattering into tiny bits.

After the attack she was taken to Post I.

Standing in the corridor, still feeling quite warm and thinking about these cursed illnesses, a comment by Emilie Diriks, Camilla Collett's friend, comes to mind. In one of her letters she writes to her friend: 'There can be no greater misfortune for a mortal being than to love Welhaven.'*

Oh, these stupid, conceited women! How delighted Gerd would be to swap for this misfortune, or Synnøve when she's screaming in a violent frenzy, 'Don't want to! Don't want to!' and people flee from her as if she were a wild animal.

---

* Welhaven was a nineteenth-century Norwegian poet with whom Camilla Collett was unhappily in love.

LETTER TO HER FAMILY IN ENGLAND – THURSDAY, 13 MARCH 1941 [ULLEVÅL HOSPITAL]

A letter for you. How much that means, for you, for me! I send you thoughts that remain unspoken, love, tenderness, which are in some inaccessible place *within* me! I'm beginning sentimentally. But be patient, I'll endeavour to write normally. Dittl. Musch. Grandmother. I don't know what order I should put my words in. You just mean so much to me.

I'm back in Lillestrøm. Well, what can I say? Musch, ask Dittl what it means to live c/o somebody else (and yet have no employment). Oh well. But I hope that I'll also be beyond this stage soon. I really enjoyed the labour service. As you know I found a friend there, which has been so important to me. How can I describe this to you? She has made me aware of my 'better self' and the fact that she's *there* gives life much more meaning. Yes, I know I exaggerate, but you'd understand better if you knew just how lonely I was. Overall my future is tough and bleak. The only thing I look forward to is you. God, that sounds like the quivering words of an eighty-year-old. But it's true: I'm not expecting anything for myself! Should something nice cross my path, of course it would always be welcome.

No, I can't continue in this tone. I want to write about something nice. And this nice thing is a wish. So it's a 'nice' wish. In spring I intend to go hiking in western Norway. Together with four or five girls including Gunvor. I'm just so excited about it. If our plan goes down the drain . . . No, stop! Gunvor and I are always making plans that are such fantasies you'd never believe it. The funny thing is that we believe in our own plans. We're very similar. Sometimes people think we're sisters. Musch, if you love me then you'd have to love Gunvor too.

I also think that she'll come with me if the opportunity arises. I do. As you know, opportunities are pretty slim. Today Kurtl let me know that E. Fox has guaranteed me an affidavit. It's to be hoped that it will help me achieve my goal (my journey to the US). As you can see I've become very cautious. I no longer say 'I hope', but 'It's to be hoped'.

Anyway, spring will be here soon and in Norway that's when people put their worries aside. It's true: in spring, work, duty and energy are seen as ballast. People live for the moment in spring. You have no idea of what spring is. Think of us, you lot in the south. Although it's the middle of March there's still snow on the ground here. But just wait. Soon it'll be the middle of May and our hiking tour.

My darlings, please be more assiduous about writing. I could have post from you more often if you made the effort. My Muscherle, Grandmother, Dittl, our reunion *must* happen some day. Reunion is as 'delightful' a word as 'farewell'. It's sad. One ought to write a poem about reunion. Something that you write when you're in a state of yearning.

Well, I've been chatting with you for a while now. It pains me to have to put my pen down. But that's how it has to be. Yes, it's so long.

CONTINUATION OF THE LETTER – FRIDAY, 14 MARCH 1941 [ULLEVÅL HOSPITAL]

It's a new day. The sun is shining outside. And there's nothing to say, actually. The snow is still on the ground and the sky is blue.

I'm so looking forward to our tour and to Gunvor's first letter. She's leaving from Oslo tomorrow. We said goodbye yesterday. But Karen will come to visit me. She's a small, blonde Danish girl. She's very sweet and lovely, and she's already married. Then there's Nini, a blonde Norwegian girl. So I do have friends. I won't get any work etc. I find it really hard to imagine that one day I might earn a so-called 'livelihood'. At any rate, I've come to the conclusion that it's not so important. After all, most livelihoods are not based on a satisfying job. I'll abandon myself to a philosophy of *dolce far niente*. No, no. It's not that bad!

I need not say it again: you don't have to worry about me. There's also plenty to eat here etc. Your birthday has passed, Musch. Now it's your nineteenth on 27 March, Dittl. I'll buy some flowers and think of you. Next time. Who knows? *Qui vivra, verra*. Yes. Thinking of you lots!

FRIDAY, 14 MARCH 1941, ULLEVÅL HOSPITAL

When I was arguing with Nina just now, it occurred to me that Gunvor is very different from other girls in this respect, too. Gunvor doesn't know how to argue. I've never heard her utter a single improper, tasteless word. She cannot bicker or argue; her smile is far too animated. Very often *I* have argued with *her*. But that was always different. It was because I loved her and wanted to cause her pain.

Gunvor could never talk in such a vulgar way as Nina. Gunvor says she is too lazy to get into an argument with anybody. No, Gunvor is too clever, too good-natured.

Yesterday we said goodbye to each other again. She's going to Biri. She'll write. It will be empty here when she's gone.

I waited every afternoon from two to three. And I would get very uptight if she arrived five minutes late. I drew letters and played with my hands, out of nervousness. And then she arrived. I saw her brown coat in the distance. A feeling of warmth surged inside me. I went over to her.

It's true – it's a wonderful feeling to wish a better life for a friend rather than for oneself. What Gunvor has managed to bring to life is the goodness inside me. She's shown me, reminded me just what *living* should mean. Not by discussing her ideals in a quivering voice, but talking about life in a quiet voice, about how it is, about how she doesn't believe in anything any more. But between the resigned utterances I could hear her determination to avoid piece work. And to ignore her material livelihood when dealing with things you cannot answer for to your inner self. To hear that she thinks like that, too, has given me new courage. A courage which is of no use on Ward VI. What is of use here is human kindness. Whenever other people cry, I want to cry too . . . That's how it is. When I hear Fräulein Vik wailing, when Solveig cries, everything stops. All of a sudden I'm very small and I ask myself what I should do to stop them from feeling the need to cry any more. And the funny thing is that all of them calm down if you speak to them nicely. Even Hjørdis, who once had a terrible attack, became calmer when I stroked her and sang to her.

People are often in a mood here. One cries, another sits silently at the window, a third . . . You see so much misery. Nini has just been crying. She's had a very difficult life. Dragged from one children's home to another, she's now got to spend weeks or even months here because she ran away from her last children's home. She dreads the idea of having to go back to a home. The doctor doesn't want to give her any duties. And she says, 'Soon the nights will be light and I'll be here . . . No, I'll run away at night. Oh, I'm so sick of it all . . . I'm so sick of life. Right now I could hang myself!'

I get into a very bad mood when I think that I'll have to leave here soon . . . for Lillestrøm! I have a horror of going back there. I sense that I'll fall ill there again. That environment! Those people! The only consolation is that in summer I'm going hitchhiking in the Vestlandet with Karen, Petter, Bjørg, maybe Nini, too. If only I didn't have this cursed illness, everything would seem simpler. But it lurks in the corner. The only comfort I get is when I'm with Gunvor. She wasn't at all afraid when I clutched on to her in total horror. Once she said, 'You scare me.' But she took back her words and went with me to the doctor. I could feel her concern for me. On the last evening we were in her room. It was dark. She thought I'd like to have the light on. Casually, but with great tenderness, she said, 'We can put the light on if you like!'

SATURDAY, 15 MARCH 1941, ULLEVÅL HOSPITAL

Some people say that I'm a hard woman, that they can't imagine me crying. Other people call me *bløt* [soft]. And because time passes so slowly here, I'll try to recall the times I've cried in Norway. It hasn't been that often.

It was summer 1940. The Strøms and I were spending the holidays in a cabin in Nittedal. Frau Strøm told me to brown the liver while she went to fetch some water. I fried and fried, but the liver turned grey instead of brown. Frau Strøm came back and said in her sweet voice, 'You can't be trusted to do anything. And you're so . . . And food is so expensive.'

I cried a lot back then. I would go out in summer. The meadows were bright green. And I wept and wept, and thought: I must get away from here. How can I live here? I'll go to Sweden. I went and buried my head in the grass. At the time I had nobody to comfort me.

My God, how I hate Lillestrøm. What ugly memories I have of it.

I was supposed to take up a bright pink linen dress. I took it up further than Frau Strøm wanted. What an outrage this caused. She said, 'If you do something like this again, that'll be the last time I wish to see your face.' I had to sit there and listen to her talk like that. I thought, where should I go? Where should I go? I know that I'm a burden.

Those hours in Lillestrøm when nobody was doing anything but reading, and I didn't fancy going out into the streets, and I was suffocated by the air inside those rooms because I knew that we were one too many!

When somebody came to visit I would grin, offer my hand and mutter my name. In spite of it all I was happy to see people again. People who were completely indifferent to me.

When school started I didn't get home until about 6 or 7 p.m. I would spend the only pleasant hours of my day with half a dozen sandwiches in the Deichmann or university libraries. My greatest, loveliest experience at the time was to read Trotsky's *History of the Russian Revolution*. I would come back home in the evening, receive sideways glances as I gobbled down my dinner next to the stove in the kitchen. And then the evening would pass again with reading, or night-time walks picking flowers.

My loneliness at school turned me into a leper. I spent break times in the loo, for I was afraid of the looks aimed at me by people who always saw me alone, alone.

Painful, wicked memories! The caretaker – a repulsive, pompous man, who looked quite nasty – offered me hot chocolate because he thought I didn't have the money to buy any. I said, 'No, I don't like hot chocolate.'

Gassmann, the divinity teacher resembling a dwarf with a long beard, skulked in the corridor to give me an apple. I said, 'No, thank you.' He was offended because I didn't allow him the chance to be 'good'.

The small, red-cheeked German teacher invited me to her house, stuffed my pockets full of fruit and asked, 'Are the people you're living with in Lillestrøm nice?' I said, 'Yes they are, they're really very nice.'

And I cried when Hitler annexed Czechoslovakia. I was sitting at the table with Strøm. When I read the newspaper and saw the headline, I jumped up and went to my room. I threw myself on to the couch. All I could think about was the pain, pointlessness and pitilessness of the world. It was the same when I asked Strøm what I ought to do to get out and his answer was, 'You'll have to wait.'

I then realised that I'd have to wait again, like before, all alone. And I wept.

I don't actually know why I'm writing about this.

Today Gunvor's going to Biri. Perhaps I'll go there too.

SUNDAY, 16 MARCH 1941, ULLEVÅL HOSPITAL

I've now read Camilla Collett's letter to her friend, Emilie. I don't find this letter superior to many written by your average person. There's the occasional spark and nice idea, a natural, deeply felt emotion. But one is really struck by the pompous language, especially in the first few letters: 'Emilie, these tears implore you, write!'

This restlessness in her letters, so full of yearning, makes her proclaim things such as, 'Oh, if only I had been born in another age.' Had this been written by somebody else, I would have found it all very ridiculous.

I much prefer her friend, Emilie. She has reserve, lacks pathos and I like that very much. But my God, how modest this creature is. She gives herself entirely to her friend. Emilie is reflected in her and Camilla in Emilie. How sincere her warnings sound.

The two share a certain upper-class way of thinking. It's very funny that neither of them thinks for a moment beyond the narrow horizons of her class. They mix exclusively in society events and soirées etc. And during her stay in Hamburg, Emilie's thoughts do not once turn to those standing by the doors, starving.

On the other hand, these letters have shown me a close friendship, if not a model one. And as I read the book my thoughts were with Gunvor.

A dream that Camilla relates begins like this:

[Letter to Emilie Diriks, 24 July 1835]
> *I found myself in a large grotto with divans along the walls. The ground was covered in a type of moss which was finer and softer than*

*normal moss. A basin had been sunk in the middle of the grotto, I think it
was marble; but what made it so enchanting was that water trickled down
from countless water taps, beautifully arranged above the basin. This water
twinkled in the light from the lamps that studded the walls. And yet the
light from these lamps was pale, like the moon – giving all objects a silvery
glint. The trickling of the water produced a wonderful melancholic sound
and the echo in the grotto chimed in lovely harmony. Two of the three
supernatural figures around me were standing right beside the basin and
appeared to be preparing a bath, for they were emptying out large urns and
they threw something in afterwards. The third figure was standing beside
me and looking at me pensively. They were all cloaked in sea-green
gauze-like robes and were also wearing collars of white waterlilies. Their
facial features were no more regular than ours normally are, but they were
much more limpid. Yes, these figures were airy, almost transparent; I was
expecting them to dissolve into a mist. Their hair hung straight down and
was blonde, almost white. By earthly reckoning I assumed, therefore, that
these must be young women of twenty, maybe twenty-five. The girl standing
next to me was very pretty. I could not make out the other two so well; when
my wonder turned to curiosity, I reached for my pince nez, so as to look at
them more closely. Unfortunately I did not have it on me. Finally, they left,
pointing at the water. The invitation was only too clear. I stood up, but
walked across this mysterious ground with a certain trepidation. Soon I had
thrown off my clothes and I plunged into the basin. In this divine bath, a
new, indescribable fire flowed through me. Mixed into the water was a
sweet-smelling herb that I did not know. While my body rose again, as it
were, my soul became lost in rapture at the idea that a burning desire had
been satisfied. What even the wildest imagination could scarcely conceive
had been marvellously transformed into reality. And yet, while wondering
how this adventure might end, I could not rid myself of a tingling feeling
of disquiet.*

In the camp at Biri I read Freud and teased people about the meaning of their
dreams using symbolism. Now Camilla tells a dream that immediately reminds
me of Freud's interpretation of symbols. I'm struck by how easily his symbols
can be applied. The dream is easily understood, you see, if (following Freud)

you accept that three is the number of men and contact with water signifies being born. The *three* girls help C into the bath. When she climbs into the *water* she senses that one of her *most burning desires* has been satisfied. She feels as if her body has been remade. The fact that the girls throw something into the water while running the bath must, in this context, have a deeper meaning.

It also seems quite plausible that Camilla, who has such strong ideas about morality, love and sexual intercourse, should use symbolism in her dreams: the dream censor must – in her case – be extremely well developed.

MONDAY, 17 MARCH 1941, ULLEVÅL HOSPITAL

What a life this is! It's not enough that I should have no prospects of getting a job, earning money, standing on my own two feet; I have to drag this illness around which will lie in wait for me when I leave this institution, and which often assaults me here, too.

I've spoken with a doctor and I'm still without hope. Everything looks very black. In moments like this the thought of Gunvor is a sheer delight. And then I cannot conceive how I might survive without her.

Since she left I feel as if I've lost something . . . but I don't know exactly what. It's as if I haven't really taken in the fact that she's gone. So when I think of her I don't feel much pain, just unease.

I'm to stay here for another month. My only diversion is painting.

Park: Very good. Green meadows on either side of a path. Bright spots and flowers. People are walking along a path, which curves to the left. People are sitting on a bench. A woman looks into the distance.

Spring: A blue-black tree with white branches in the foreground. A little wall in front of the tree. Three bushes to the left of the tree in a bright meadow. Behind that, three dark-blue oaks. Two bare trees on a hill with houses.

Another *Spring*: Miniature people wander up and down a path. A few bare trees.

Bare trees: Five bare trees in front of a row of houses.

In my thoughts all my pictures are dedicated to Gunvor.

I'm in a wretched mood. However I try to imagine my future I feel sick!

If I think about another stay in Ward VI then a slight feeling of dread rises inside me. The sun is starting to shine, the snow is melting and my legs get wet when I go strolling outside with the Russian emigrant. A greyish-green patch has appeared where the snow has melted at the left-hand corner of the 'Rondeau'. And the days are getting long. It's still light at half past seven. Sometimes the light is not dazzling and we look at the silvery moon. When I think about it, the idea of another stay here is quite unbearable. If Gunvor were here, if she came at visiting time, we could wander up and down the corridor together! That would be something different. But! I think longingly of the jetty. Of the ships in the water, ready for adventure as if in a fairy tale. Of the quayside teeming with people and the clear sky arching overhead. And I feel a longing that burns inside me: out!

Whenever I think of returning to Lillestrøm it's like a huge weight on my shoulders. I see my room with its grey walls, the gold-framed mirror, the sophisticated dining room, those people I've nothing in common with. Anxiety inside, anxiety outside. The well-established walks: up to Storgate, to the bridge that crosses the river, under the railway crossing to the flowers – my friends of last summer. The days pass with the same grey monotony. And there's something hard inside me that wants to get out.

Why is it so difficult to live? Sometimes it seems as if nothing makes sense. Life is only good when I'm painting or thinking of Gunvor.

There's another prospect: to return to Biri. Do I really want to go back there? All the girls there know where I've been. With her sweet smile Frau Heltene would welcome me back like a dangerous animal. People would scrutinise me, analyse my behaviour, draw their own conclusions. I'd also be far away from the city, and if 'it' were to happen again I'd have to treat everyone to the same farce. But thinking about it more closely, I would prefer to return there. In spring I'd be with Gunvor. We'd see the spring through together. I can picture us absolutely silent as the first birdsong rings out and the snow squelches under our feet. And in the evenings we'd be sitting in our room. I'd paint, too, and show Gunvor my pictures. Oh, it could all be so lovely. But the damn thing is not the same in reality as it is in my mind.

Watercolour: 'Bare trees', March 1941.

TUESDAY, 18 MARCH 1941, ULLEVÅL HOSPITAL

I had such a lovely dream about Dita last night. She was very small, terribly sweet and beautifully dressed. She looked delicate, and in her face I could see intelligence and maternal feelings for me. I was with Gunvor in a landscape that represented the hospital. Then she arrived, I think she was carrying a bag. I introduced her to Gunvor. And Gunvor really liked Dittl. Dittl went to the doctor and asked in a very deliberate way how I was. She was expecting an answer when I pulled her away and said, 'You cannot say anything.' Gunvor and I were agreed that Dittl was a good person and that we could never make her unhappy.

Inside the room a blonde girl has been crying. Her hair is like straw and she's screwing up her eyes as if she were afraid of the sun. She holds something mercilessly in her hand and she squeezes ever more tightly until she throws herself on the floor. Then, all of a sudden, she goes rigid and her features ossify as if she has seen something horrific. She screams, 'Oh!' The nurse drags her off the ground and puts her in the bath. These are the kinds of scenes you witness here. I haven't got used to them yet.

WEDNESDAY, 19 MARCH 1941, ULLEVÅL HOSPITAL

The days are long now. When it's light in the evenings I feel a burning inside me. I walk around the lawn, still totally covered in snow, with Finn, a sixteen-year-old boy who suffers from shellshock. From Ward IV some girls slouching by the window call over to us in German. Their lips are red and most of them are street prostitutes suffering from venereal diseases. They call out, 'Haven't you gone mad yet?'

The bare trees look so hungry. It's evening already, but light.

I paint. A hungry tree in a colourful meadow. Houses on a crimson hill. A picture: *Alone*. An avenue with a blue path. Crimson meadows in the background, blue firs. A black man crosses the meadow.

Frau Stefens used to lie there apathetically in the room, not making a sound. She was thin, so skinny that whenever she got up to take a wash I feared she would collapse. There was never a smile on her lips, nor a word uttered from her mouth. With a terribly shrunken, colourless expression, she would just stare into the distance and tug at her lips. She's a human being, too, I thought. She was transferred to Post I. I'd almost forgotten her when she turned up again last week. It gave me the greatest pleasure to see her lying in bed, smiling. Her face had started to fill out and she was smiling. This person was entirely changed by her smile. She talked as well. And twice I said to her, 'My, how strong you've become.'

Later I see her wandering up and down the corridor. She's smiling and talking. When she smiles her face looks younger. Her voice is deep, calm, friendly. I'd like to do something nice for her.

AT THE WINDOW

*Outside in the garden, people who will soon be better walk back and forth. They look
too sad and pale against the blue sky. They walk slowly . . . they stop by the shrub which
will blossom, but whose blooms will then wither. They bend over the first brownish-green
patches in the snow.*

Outside, people who will soon be better walk back and forth.

THE JEW AND THE VIOLET

Are you still my violet, blue and fragrant?
Do you wave with innocent childish hands, so that I bend down to you?
You sweet, good friend, soon to be my only one.
You forgive my cursing, my cursing in despair.
Searching with my eyes for the human, for the horror, I forgot you.
I will break you off softly! Hold you to my breast and
On my knees, endeavour to pray.

THURSDAY, 20 MARCH 1941, ULLEVÅL HOSPITAL

Yesterday Nini said that Synnøve has gone to a mental institution in
Dikemark. I thought about her. About how horrified we'd been when she
started to writhe around in bed after she'd taken medication. The next morning she was wandering around as if asleep. With distant eyes. She was moved
into the main room. She was happy when I visited her there. Her magnificent
Madonna head lay softly on the pillow. Her clammy hands held mine. She gave
the smile of somebody who had just suffered a serious illness: weak, delicate.
She was taken to Ward I. She returned a week later. We strolled in the
'garden'. Whenever a dove fluttered its wings or an icicle fell from the roof
she shuddered. Before she left she said, 'I can't stand it any more.' Finn with
the deep-set eyes sings:

Diki-Diki-Dik, Dikemark
Diki-Diki-Dik, Dikemark

FRIDAY, 21 MARCH 1941, ULLEVÅL HOSPITAL

I had an exeat. I was in town. It was springlike everywhere. Sunny in Karl Johan. Heaps of dirty snow alongside the pavement. The girls looked extremely pretty. I was very taken by the people who were walking here and there, and ever onwards. I hadn't wanted to come back here. I thought it would be good if Gunvor were by my side. I didn't have time to go to the fjord. I was at the university library exchanging some books. Still the same pleasant silence in the reading rooms. Afterwards I went down to Karl Johan. It was as if everything were new. I stared at the shop windows full of cakes and tarts, at books, at a beautiful black dress. The girls who walked past were pretty. A few German soldiers here and there! There were some places, by bare trees and narrow streets, where I wanted to stop and draw. I bought two cards: Gauguin and Degas. Very beautiful. Then I went home. Nini greeted me with a cry of joy. She was sitting at the window. Visiting time was over. I slipped into my blue-and-white dress and – here I was back again.

SATURDAY, 22 MARCH 1941, ULLEVÅL HOSPITAL

I'm reading Novalis. A lovely, warm-hearted writer. Very profound.

The awful truth is that I can no longer imagine my life outside Ward VI. A painful feeling of unease comes across me when I think about life 'outside'. I see myself *alone*! (What a horrific significance that word has developed for me.) On wrong paths, which lead here and there, in the darkness, in the light, me, me. And my energy, the will to assert myself, has abandoned me.

I can really understand van Gogh, who writes to his brother that he's incapable of 'ordering his life' and seeks refuge in St Rémy . . . This place is a refuge, too. Peace paid for by my freedom of movement. But what good is freedom of movement to me when I'm *afraid* of moving? . . .

The best thing would be if Gunvor were with me and she ordered my life for me. I would paint and read. 'Photograph', as Gunvor says.

My God, it doesn't have to go wrong. After all, I'm not out of my mind. And anyway, spring is on its way. Light evenings that arouse the senses, the first foliage. I want to paint. Oh, sometimes I feel as if I could really achieve something with my splatters. Not that I think my painting could mean anything to *other people*. What I want, what I expect from my painting is to satisfy an urge inside me, to satisfy the urge to create. I used to be very different. I wanted to be an actress, a writer – not so much for me as for other people. I wanted to show people who I was, I wanted to become famous. Many a seventeen-year-old's head has become filled with dreams of 'becoming famous'. The fact that one later starts to distance oneself from this 'dream of fame' is, for me, the sign of an inner development. I've also distanced myself from the desire to 'become somebody'. All sensible people harbour this urge to become somebody. But behind this desire is not the idea of life as a ladder where the aim is to reach the highest rung. That's totally wrong! It's not about climbing the rungs of the ladder, but . . . well. That's the great riddle. Perhaps one should refuse to climb as a protest against the fact that the ladder has been put there in the first place!! Perhaps this idea I am consumed with has come from a 'sour grapes' complex. That's the truth, I expect.

MONDAY, 24 MARCH 1941, ULLEVÅL HOSPITAL

Nini's dream:

'I was together with a group of people on a trip to the woods in Fornebu. The landscape was made up of hills, clearings in the woods, mountains and trees. Three Germans appeared. We were terrifed of them, so hid behind some tree stumps. In the end we made friends with them and started talking to them. We shared cake. We saw some aeroplanes plummeting to the ground and ran over to see who would get there first. We counted the aeroplanes. Our task was to count the aeroplanes, so we were happy to have found some.'

Solveig's dream:

'I was going into a wood. At first the path was wide, but it got narrower and narrower. The wood was dense. Where the path stopped there was a small lake. It was very pretty there. Two pairs of birds flew straight into each other and fell down beside the lake. Then I could hear something snorting, roaring, and making even more noise. It was a rhinoceros. Suddenly it awoke. It began looking all around. The rhinoceros had long, pointed – very pointed – teeth on both sides of its mouth. Then it saw the lake. It noticed a seal which was popping its head above the water. The seal was small and very soft, colourfully mottled. The rhinoceros plunged into the water, creating a splash. Then it ate the seal. Inside the rhinoceros's mouth was very light, and I thought that my head would fit in there perfectly. Then everything turned sort of misty and vanished before my eyes. I woke up and was sitting on the steps.'

I've been astonished by the symbolism (according to Freud) contained in these dreams.

Dream 1: Woods, glades, mountains etc. signify the female genitalia. Three Germans are walking through these. Three is the male number. Nini is afraid, she's hiding. Then she befriends them. I see the second part of the dream as connected to the first. It gives her a sort of satisfaction to count the crashing aeroplanes, which have taken the place of the men.

After talking (to Gunvor) about the second part of the dream, I've come to the following conclusion: the aeroplane (engine) is drive, lust, sexual urge. She counts the aeroplanes as they plummet (plummeting signifies relaxation after the sexual act). She is counting the number of times she has been with a man. She was happy when she saw the aeroplanes nosediving.

Dream 2: The path which leads to a pond is the path to the secret that, for her, surrounds the issue of sex. The path enters a wood. The wood is the symbol for the female genitalia. The sexual act, which for her represents something horrific, terrifying, takes place at the pond. The sharp horns of the rhinoceros signify the male element. The very smooth seal is the female element. Afterwards the rhinoceros disappears into the water with the seal he has swallowed up. A mist descends.

Solveig also has regular dreams about men who pursue her.

Nini has left now. She looked very pretty in a cheap, rust-red dress, a white scarf and brown coat. She spent the last few hours just pacing up and down; her bright and perky eyes wandered nervously about the place. Her mouth was much redder than usual and firmly closed. Her hair was bright and shining – she looked even more beautiful. A short, plump woman, who's in charge of the home she's going to, picked her up at three o'clock. We squeezed each other's hands. She left us laughing, her cheeks glowing, her hands warm.

Nini is a lovely girl. She's full of life. She laughs, talks with her hands, with her whole body. I taught her how to twitch her eyebrows. Without her it's very quiet here. We had regular arguments and I was amazed by the vulgarity of some of the things she said. But then I understood: she'd never had an easy life and had been around many selfish people, some of whom had spoken like her. She has an irresistible way of flattering people. I flatter because I like you! She isn't stupid. On the contrary. She has great perception and is very alert. She lives with her senses open to everything. Like everybody, she was born to be happy. It's painful that her life has always been difficult.

She's going to visit me on Wednesday. And we'll get together after that, too. We'll sit in a café and sunbathe in the palace park. All will be good.

TUESDAY, 25 MARCH 1941, ULLEVÅL HOSPITAL

I'm waiting for a letter from Gunvor. I was hoping to receive one today. But none came. And a frightful bitterness is growing inside me. I know that the bitterness will be gone in a couple of hours. And that's painful, too. I'd like to write:

'Look! Perhaps my last letter was over-sentimental. I wrote about cherished memories and about how my pictures belong to you. Perhaps that hurt you; I tried to get too close to you.

'I'm always afraid of trying to get too close to you. It's hard not to become sentimental when life is so cruel; you're the only thing that gives me some light and my happiest hours are when I'm writing to you. That's why you have to write. You do not know how happy I am when I see your handwriting on the envelope.'

I think about how beautifully she writes letters:

'Now Åse's singing a song in Latin. Oh, how ungrateful we listeners are! It's casting pearls before swine. Face and eyes in convulsions, trying to suppress a laugh. And yet she sings beautifully!'

I can see her smiling and saying, 'And yet she sings beautifully!' It sounds like a story in itself. And it was created by somebody with a good heart.

Or: 'What I'll miss most of all are the small room, the café, and all those moments that we've sat there and been practically bursting with contentment. There's very little reason for it, almost nothing. A lit candle, the strange, bleak atmosphere of the café.'

I can picture her sitting in the café. She has such fine eyes that see, understand. The strange, bleak atmosphere of the café! How lovely that sounds. It's as if she's giving thanks for being permitted to experience a 'strange, bleak atmosphere'.

Well, the diary has fulfilled its purpose. In writing about Gunvor and her letters I feel better. And now I feel calmer as I wait until tomorrow – perhaps – brings me a letter from her.

Long evenings

MARCH–APRIL 1941

At the end of March Frau Strøm collects Ruth from the hospital and brings her back home to Lillestrøm. Ruth spends a lot of time reading and with her friends. She often thinks back to friends she used to have in Vienna. The diary also contains the drafts of letters to Gunvor. During March and April 1941 Ruth writes three letters to England; these have been inserted here between the diary entries. Ruth celebrates Easter with Edla in Enebakk, where the Strøms' housemaid hails from.

On the first day after her release from hospital Ruth meets up with her friends in a coffee house in Oslo: Café Ansgar in Møllergate. They are told that Karen's husband has been killed. Karen is not at the reunion. They talk at length about the fatality. Gunvor isn't there either. Ruth longs for her close company, her letters. She writes poems about her longing for Gunvor.

The friends are about to embark on a new spell of labour service on a farm on the west coast of Norway. Ruth is looking forward to leaving Lillestrøm. Before her departure she rereads the letters that she has received while in Norway.

This spring she writes a lot of prose poems.

Draft of a letter to Gunvor in Ruth's diary. Ruth learned Norwegian quickly, spoke it fluently and also had a good written command of the language.

SUNDAY, 30 MARCH 1941, LILLESTRØM

Frau Strøm collected me from the hospital. She's standing in the corridor, smiling sweetly, looking slim, a little too slim. I sit there, dressed in my ordinary clothes; somebody else will wear my blue-and-white dress. A taxi is waiting in the garden. Hjørdis stands up and watches as we carry the suitcases away. She is so sweet, the way she stands there all small and delicate. I squeeze her hand. I think: Would I have preferred to stay here? What will it be like outside? When will I come back? But I have to go. I get into the taxi. I think: Finn asked me to write to him. I will. The taxi reminds me of my childhood. Papa. Frau Strøm and I try in vain to have a conversation. It goes silent. Grey streets, bare trees go by.

I notice that my eyes have sharpened during my stay in the hospital. Things look much closer to me. Trees, people. Things are too close. Burning.

As ever, Lillestrøm makes me feel depressed. Strøm is there, and Turid. A visit is company. People eat and they're content. Smoke cigarettes and bask in their own views. I think: I'm not imagining it – there *are* people who are not happy in themselves, who in conversation show a different 'self' from you lot when you talk about England and pork. I know Gunvor. And I'm an outsider among these people. When Gunvor and I spoke about life, all that we discovered inside ourselves was pain and longing – and delight at having found each other. So I sit here and because I know she exists it doesn't bother me if I'm lonely.

Before I left the hospital, Nini visited me. She's so lovely. She was wearing red lipstick. And a red turban on her head. She's very fond of me. She is very cool, but affectionate at the same time. We wander up and down. I tell her I'm going to leave, and that I'll visit her. We wander up and down. I marvel at her red lips and red turban. She gives the impression that she's a pleasure seeker. I'd love to be able to buy her a beautiful blue silk dress. Take her out for tea. Her hands are cold from working.

The day before yesterday I was in town. A group of us from the labour service met up in Café Ansgar: Petter, Ingrid, Buster. Café Ansgar is Gunvor's favourite coffee house. It's a nice place. *Hyggelig* [cosy]*!* It was good to see the kind old faces again. Petter, with the tremulous smile in her eyes and her mischievous nostrils, still looks like she's at boarding school. She has a good figure and looks very 'erotic'. Heart-melting. Ingrid came with a colourful headscarf. She laughed as kindly as ever, with the same sweet French profile. Buster, full of laughter, part of her still a child even though she's eighteen. Buster is very lovely. She has a very nice laugh. We sat there, chatting. We talked about the Norwegian Nazi Party, *Hird* troops,* the war, our trip to western Norway, and England.

Where was Karen? Karen, that gentle blonde woman, didn't come. She's been informed that John has been killed in England. He was a pilot. It was a complete shock when Ingrid mentioned it.

We can't understand. How is it possible? John and Karen, who are like one person. John, who means the world to Karen. John, whose photo we'd all admired. John! John! What will Karen do without John? She was engaged to him when she was sixteen and at twenty she married him. When she talks about him her eyes sparkle. How can they have murdered John? We can't understand. Next time we see Karen how are we going to look her straight in the eyes?

So we talked, about John, about Karen. The time passed very quickly. Occasionally somebody would mention Gunvor's name. Everybody loves Gunvor.

Buster said, 'I really miss Gunvor. She used to sit here, waving her arms about, smiling and staring.' I thought: I miss Gunvor, too.

Only now do I know what it means to have a friend. Whenever I read or hear the word 'friend' now, I feel a light inside me. I think: Yes, it's good to have a friend.

I know that Gunvor doesn't feel so deeply about our relationship. That doesn't matter. Perhaps it's better like that. It makes me smaller.

---

* *Hirden* was the paramilitary organisation of Quisling's party.

SUNDAY, 30 MARCH 1941, LILLESTRØM

Dear Gunvor

I always think of you when I hear beautiful music. Like now. Something good rises up inside me. Something that wants to be released. And I achieve this release when I write to you.

The truth is, I think about you constantly when I see or hear something good. That's how it should be, shouldn't it? No, no. I'm not insisting that you should think of me when you're 'photographing', getting feelings of spring, or read Olaf Bull. By the way, I read a lovely poem by Øverland yesterday. I had to smile, because it made me think of you.

It's not exactly *nice* here, you know. It really isn't. That's why I think you ought to write a little more often. If you knew just how much your letters meant to me, I'm sure you would. I think well of you. And I recommend that you should think well of somebody, too. It's a truly wonderful feeling to think well of somebody. Yes, I do think well of you. I'd like to think well of you even if you hurt me or did something wrong. In that way it would be impossible for you to disappoint me. I'd like always to think: Yes, that's just how it is, she *had* to do it. Otherwise she wouldn't have done it. I also trust you. You see? When I'm feeling bad, I think of you. Then everything becomes much easier. I do not understand how people can survive without a friend. But it's probably the case that it's only those who are small and weak who cannot survive on their own. 'A wise man is never less lonely than when he is alone.' I read that somewhere. Oh, my God! I don't need a wise man if I've got you.

All the best. If I'm feeling bad, I think: Oh well, perhaps I have to struggle through here, so that you can have it good. And then it is easier to bear the burden.

Yours, Ruth

TUESDAY, 1 APRIL 1941, LILLESTRØM

There's snow on the trees, there's snow on the streets and roofs. The evenings are long, but the snow makes me doubt that spring is coming.

And no letter from Gunvor. What does she think I am? I'm going to get 'furious' with her.

Because waiting for letters that never arrive turns one into a slave. What happened to those days when I would get furious? Now I'm peaceful and happy. I think: I've got a friend! But that's all. Just as the light of Williger once glowed inside me, now it's Gunvor.

But there really ought to be a letter.

It is true that Karen's husband, John, has died. It's the women who have suffered most at this time. 'Young woman of 1940'.

You ask, 'Why?' Millions have asked the same question before me, and millions will ask it after me. Karen is one of thousands whose life has suddenly become meaningless because a bomb exploded or a shot hit its target. But people don't ask about that. People are too generous. They don't worry about life! The fact that John will never again be able to put his arm round Karen is beside the point. It's all about submarines, merchant shipping, strategic points.

Many have said this before me. Many will say it in the future.

But Karen is reality. Karen who smiles when she says, 'my husband'. Karen who dreamily says 'John'.

It's women who suffer from death, women who suffer from life. With their children they suffer from life; with their husbands they suffer from death.

WEDNESDAY, 2 APRIL 1941, LILLESTRØM

No letter. That sounds so simple. But how I yearn for her handwriting. I do not want to leave the house before a letter from her has arrived.

My dream last night: Gunvor was in Ward VI, too. Dr Munch spoke to her. He interrogated her, kept on shaking his head. And Gunvor was all agitated. She said, 'No, I'm not going to put up with that.' And I got furious with the doctor who had upset Gunvor. I ran up to him and told him. Full of passion and zeal, I told him without any ado just what Gunvor was like. That he was wrong to think ill of her. She is a calm person and a good one, too. I told him about Reidar and her struggles. Everything. I chatted to him for a long time. As I was in conversation I wanted to speak to Gunvor. But she was with other people. I thought she was angry with me because I had been talking about her.

I cannot help myself from feeling so strongly about her. I'm sure the doctors thought there were unnatural inclinations in my relationship with Gunvor. But that's wrong. My feelings for her are totally natural. I feel myself connected to her spiritually and mentally. There's not the slightest hint of a physical desire. But it may be true that I have a need to love and to express this. Gunvor is a most welcome target for this love.

THURSDAY, 3 APRIL 1941, LILLESTRØM

It makes me feel very strange when I hear lots of girls calling me their friend. One of them doesn't do that, but I feel friendship for her, a wonderful unique friendship.

Nini signs off her letters: your friend. Although I'm fond of her, it's not friendship that binds me to her.

Karen, who lost her husband, writes in a letter after my attempt to console her: Dear friend.

It's a good thing that I have these people. I want to try to help Karen, to give myself to Nini and to love Gunvor without any resistance.

FRIDAY, 4 APRIL 1941, LILLESTRØM

Dear Gunvor

I expect you've no idea how it pains me when I don't get a letter from you. I wait, and no letter arrives . . . Otherwise you'd write. Or, to ask you honestly, is it a burden for you to have to write to me? Are you worried that my responses will upset you, that they might penetrate the armour you surround yourself with? I don't know, don't want to know.

GERMAN SOLDIERS

When they go for walks with girls on spring evenings, the German soldiers laugh gently with their deep voices, too. When their hands ask for love they are not murderers, but boys who stand there smiling innocently in radiant nakedness. The girls smile bashfully, too, and dream fantasies. Being human has never been as obvious as now.

TO AGNES

When your face, which exudes such peace, merges with the light blue of evening, warmth radiates from each of your features into my heart. With the evening and your face as one, I grasp how lonely I was before I met you.

SUNDAY, 6 APRIL 1941, LILLESTRØM

Dear Gunvor

You're right. Don't spoil me. I could take it for granted that you'd write, write me letters. And that's bad. So I'll just have to wait . . . But I do believe that you would write if only you knew just *how much* I'm waiting for a letter. Last night I slept badly and I know why. Because you're not writing. Waiting is so horrible. Gunvor. From nine to five, from five to nine in the mornings. That's why I thought you'd write . . . I'd really love to see your handwriting. I like your letters.

But as you've decided not to write, there must be important

reasons that have led you to this decision. Or maybe not. Perhaps you just don't want to write. It's got something to do with spring, with the noise, the people around you, the new people. And so *writing* becomes something very complicated for you.

For God's sake, Gunvor, for someone who had the time to visit me every other day in Ward VI — now you've suddenly no time to write once a week? No. I'm very happy to spare you that. For it's much worse to think that you dread the idea of writing than that you're not writing because you don't have to.

There's so much I'd like to tell you, but somehow everything slips away from me because you're not writing.

Perhaps it's not so much that you dread writing to me as receiving a *response* from me. Every time I've sent you a letter, there's always something in what I've written that torments me, something that I'd like to unwrite. Small things, a single word that perhaps sounded too affectionate, too intimate, too silky. I wish that language were structured in a way that made it impossible to express one's feelings without leaving something in reserve within one's self. If I say I like you, then afterwards I am empty inside; the words have taken all my warmth away with them. But if I say, 'I can't bear the sight of you,' then I feel twice as warm inside, because I didn't say what I really meant. You understand that. I'm sure you understand that. Always. Gunvor, whenever I say something to you, something that I've never told anybody before, I get the feeling that you understand. And everybody needs someone who understands them.

That's enough for today. Just think about the fact that I'm waiting, that I'll try to make myself small and meek, even if no letter comes from you today, either.

Ruth

MONDAY, 7 APRIL 1941, LILLESTRØM

No, it bothers you not one bit that I'm sitting here, that I exist, that I am yearning. It was you who made things blossom within me. Our times together, which blossom inside me, these will never wither. But that does not bother you. Why is that? Are you not aware that within me there are thousands of things waiting to be said to you? Our life, our future, everything we spoke about only occasionally. Do you not know that there's a whole world inside me just waiting to be unfurled by you? I know you have delicate fingers; you will not cause me any pain. Everything is waiting. And you do not write. I'd love to see 'Dear Ruth!' I'm exaggerating. Let me exaggerate, let it be: I want to exaggerate. This feeling I have for you inside me, I want to make it bigger, I want it to shine in every colour. And it will be big and shine in every colour. It's already shining now. It shines whenever I listen to music, it shines when I smoke a cigarette.

I often ask myself: How can she suffer me? And it is so good that you do suffer me. You suffered my hitting you, you suffer my writing to you, my excitement at your coming. How long will you continue to suffer me? I can sense it: you will go away. Simply go away from me. And you'll go away because I annoy you. I understand that. Just as the little Jew, Cain, annoyed the others, I will annoy you. If I say I'm asking for nothing, that will make you mad. And if I say I'm asking for everything, that will make you mad. And if I say nothing, that will make you mad. For perhaps what's inside you is sufficient. And you cannot understand that I want to share. I want to share. That's what my letters say and my words say: share!

And you don't want to share.

Dear Gunvor, perhaps I'm doing you an injustice. You are different. But how should I look you in the eyes, when I've spent so long thinking about you? Writing letters to you that you will never read. Oh. It will be all right. I tell myself that it's just the longing that is making me write. The longing for . . . I don't know what.

My friendship with Karen is weird. Gunvor and I were together, but she was on the side. It was we two and she was the third. She was jealous, too, because she loves Gunvor very much. She has a fondness for me, which I returned faintly, very faintly. I was with her so that Gunvor would sense me saying: it's not just you! There are others, too!

There are also certain things about Karen that do not appeal to me. She thinks too highly of herself. Her self stands before her like something incredible, unique. She attaches too much importance to the intellectual. She looks down on the person as a *person*, untouched by literature, art etc. Because *Kristin Lavransdatter** makes her shudder, and because she buys books by the tonne, she thinks herself superior to other people. And yet she makes a very favourable impression on everybody. Her bright eyes, her beautiful open mouth, the untamed blonde hair kept to one side with a clip – all these give the impression that this person is clever. But she disappoints when you get to know her better. You expect to be meeting a 'special' person. After I left Biri, she visited me, with a beautiful, radiant smile (Gunvor's smile is not beautiful). She said, 'I'm fine.' Always in motion, full of her own existence, and of John, the man she loved above all else, she gives the impression of being a happy person. She has 'ideals' she wants to 'fight' for in a vague way; she has the idea that *she* is like that, not like the others. (She tries to have some sort of Masonic relationship with those people she thinks are 'important'.) She has John.

Nini is well. I visited her on Friday when I was in town. She's in a children's home in Holtegate in Oslo. She showed me around a fairly well-ordered house. Young girls passed by in silence. Her pretty brown eyes sparkled. Her blonde hair shone. She didn't have much time. I left quite soon afterwards. She wore a bright blue pinafore which pressed very tightly against her bosom. And that pained me. Because that pinafore which is too tight, is just so typical of Nini. She ought to have pretty clothes, eat chocolate every evening. Oh well.

On Friday I got together with the girls from the labour service again. Petter, Buster, Ingrid. We sat there together. The four of us aren't bad looking. When I see Petter with her half-open, delicate, bright mouth, her large, dreamy eyes and the fresh colour of her skin, I always feel as if I'm looking at a bud that's just opened, that's about to open, will open again. The men look

* A trilogy of historical novels by the Norwegian writer and Nobel Prize winner Sigrid Undset (1882–1949).

at Ingrid. Bjørg is a quiet girl with a resounding laugh. Bjørg is very fond of Gunvor. She has got used to her manner of talking with her hands. She utters Gunvor's name with a certain delight.

I feel very happy when I'm together with these girls. We have the feeling that we're young. All four of us. We talk about bread coupons, the new bread, America. Sometimes we say, 'Do you remember?'

We also talk about our forthcoming trip to the west coast. We make plans. Occasionally somebody says, 'So strange that Gunvor's not here.'

We part company at half past nine. Frau Strøm greets me with a tart smile: 'You're late coming back!'

I'm writing about myself a lot. While there's a lot going on outside — history, this pretentious name that people are wont to call the outrages being perpetrated right now. When Hitler marches into Prague they call it history; even when a Jew is beaten up it's history. John's been killed, Hildegard Ehrlich drowned on the *Athenia*. History! History!

Here, the German spirit is producing shoots. Stunted, linguistic shoots. But the *Nasjonal Samling* is still the Norwegian offspring of the NSDAP.

Hirden, which is roughly the equivalent of the Hitler Youth, is making itself unpopular with vulgar uniforms and even more vulgar behaviour. They diligently wield their truncheons, they feel important. The *Nasjonal Samling* is trying to acquire members by using blackmail etc. The Gestapo is on guard. (Beverfjord, an acquaintance, has been arrested.) Others are in prison, too. You can't write much about it. But we're well used to it now. Discord. People are encouraged to inform on each other.

In spite of the propaganda pressure etc., the Norwegians are behaving well. You often meet people who would rather risk their job than prostitute themselves. That's why I like the Norwegians a lot. There's something upright in their character. I've never shaken such good hands as here.

Nini, drawn by Ruth in her diary.

MONDAY, 7 APRIL 1941, LILLESTRØM

I'm not keeping a diary to put down my 'reflections', to immortalise profound ideas. I'm writing in order to resolve my feelings, which would otherwise get stuck into me and dig into wounds so that they would stay open.

I remember how Gunvor smiled when I asked her, 'Are you going to write?'

She answered, 'No! I shan't.' She smiled.

At Easter 1941 Edla, the Strøm's maid, invites Ruth to her home town of Enebakk.
The picture shows Ruth, Edla and Edla's sister.

FRIDAY EVENING, 18 APRIL 1941, LILLESTRØM

Gunvor is back in town. I am so happy. Now she is close to me. I can see her
waving with her arms. Grinning . . . Sorry. I'm going to see her again next
Friday. Everything within me is waiting! Waiting for the sight of her. For her
gently muffled laugh, her slightly deep voice.

It doesn't matter that I'm just writing about Gunvor. I have to write
about her. For I haven't *told* anybody how much I love her. I do not feel the
urge to write that it's spring, or that the Yugoslavian army has surrendered
today, but I have to write that I'm happy at Gunvor's return, because I have
to communicate to somebody the joy I feel within me.

SATURDAY, 19 APRIL 1941, LILLESTRØM

'If you are struck by a higher idea of human nature, do not doubt that this is the true one.'

Bettina von Arnim

SUNDAY, 20 APRIL 1941, LILLESTRØM

I'm rereading Bettina's letters to Goethe. I've never read such heartfelt letters before. How much love there is in them, how much spirit, what a sensitive soul!

She says lots of very lovely things about music:

'Soul becomes through music a feeling body, each tone touches it; music works sensually upon the soul. Whoever is not as much excited in playing as in composition will not produce any thing witty.'*

MONDAY, 21 APRIL 1941, LILLESTRØM

I've remembered that whenever I rang the bell, a chair would shift inside, and soon afterwards I would see through the letter box his long, thin legs come to the door.

And I also remember that when he was hurt he would use the formal '*Sie*' when addressing me, and call me 'Fräulein'.

If a memory like that still has very happy colours and perfumes because I haven't recalled it so frequently, it sometimes burns into my heart and my heart starts to beat faster.

My love

It's times like this that cause me to write, whether I want to or not. What's the point of resisting? I've such a yearning for you. A

*Translation by Bettina von Armin, 1837.

yearning that I can only control by lifting up my pen. Then I become quite peaceful and my mind bows to yours. Nothing more. What else could I say? And yet I don't do anything else but 'say'. Words just come sighing from my mouth and you call that garrulity. Well, let me be garrulous so that I may call you mute, let me be small that I may call you tall, let me be stupid that I may call you clever. What am I saying? You. You, whom I will see tomorrow. Tomorrow already. Tomorrow. Tomorrow. I bet you're not as excited about it as I am. I say out loud that I'm going to see you and I can scarcely believe it. Whenever I see somebody I love I always think they've come back from the dead. That's how it will be tomorrow, too. The very sight of you will make me pray. Thank God that she hasn't died.

I prattle so much that I could sit like that for hours. You don't find me puzzling. That's why I feel comfortable in your company. The others say that they can't understand. But you understand me. And I used to fear that people would just pass me by until you came along straight into my arms.

Now I'm very happy.

LETTER TO HER FAMILY IN ENGLAND – TUESDAY, 22 APRIL 1941, LILLESTRØM

I was at the American embassy yesterday. Well, they told me that I won't be able to get an American visa before the end of the year. That's all right in the sense that I know now where I stand.

I received news of you yesterday through the Red Cross. From December! It's April now. So why *do* you not write any more? I find it quite puzzling. After all, I guess you're in contact with Kurt etc. And is it really because of the cost that you so rarely write to America? That was a Norwegian sentence construction. But so what? You have to consider that, in my mind, *every day is one day.*

That's right. Anyway, you don't have to worry about me. I'll keep on going until . . . until. Well, perhaps I'll just have to keep on going until it's all over. The fact that I'm in the state I'm in — that's all part of it. Ha ha! 'A pearl of truth,' Gunvor would say. Gunvor! Yes. I've told you that she's my friend. An unusual friendship where the emotions are not at all the same on both sides. I was with her yesterday. Perhaps you'll meet her soon. That would be a pleasure. Well. It's funny that for you and for me there is a yesterday. A tomorrow. That you've had a different yesterday from me. A different 'today'. My God, I'm getting philosophical and yet there's so much real stuff I want to tell you. I could write reams about Gunvor. And about this: on Sunday (it's Tuesday today) I'll leave this delightful town of Lillestrøm again. The faces, so dear to me, of the Strøm family will have to do without me for a while. Now, I could preserve the illusion for you that I really mean it about these faces being 'so dear to me'. But I'm wicked so I won't . . . You're dying to know where I'm off to. 'All right'. I'm returning to the labour service with Gunvor, Petter and Bjørg. This time to the west of Norway. And then we'll move on from there. So by the time you read this letter I'll be with three adolescent, no, young Norwegians somewhere in Norway. *To put it mildly*, I'm sick to death of Lillestrøm and the honourable Strøm family!

It's true that in the labour service I'll have some sort of opportunity to 'make progress', as it says so nicely in the textbook. But I have to admit: I couldn't give a damn about making progress. Recently a friend of mine called Karen gave me some money. Although it's very unsavoury, it's also very useful. As long as I have a bit of money for a little book or a suspender belt, it's fine. Yes, yes. I know one ought, I ought . . . What ought I to do, actually? That's the big question. Even Gunvor shakes her head when we talk about it. But it's better if two people shake their heads.

Well, my darlings, I'll sign off now. I've really been cuddling up to you, but I've said nothing of how much I love and miss you all. But you'll read that between the lines.

FRIDAY, 25 APRIL 1941, LILLESTRØM

On Sunday morning I'll be leaving Lillestrøm. That's great. I'm going to Stavanger to do labour service with Petter, Bjørg and Gunvor. We'll be there together for the entire summer. I really hate Lillestrøm. It's a dirty, ugly town, which has caused me much pain and still does. It's a liberating feeling to think that I'll be leaving it. I won't be seeing Strøm and his wife any more, either. These people are a horror for me. Frau Strøm still feels she's inferior to me. It's wholly incomprehensible that we don't mean anything to each other any more. There are so many reasons why people fall out that it's impossible to understand how the relationship between two people becomes unfathomable. But one thing is for certain: if people start to fall out then there's no way of salvaging a relationship.

I'm feeling slightly uneasy because I don't know what's going to happen and because this life of uncertainty, which I basically love, is unfortunately starting to annoy me. But for God's sake! I'm so excited. Gunvor's going to be there and that's almost too wonderful. I saw her again on Tuesday. When I was in hospital there were things about her appearance I'd sometimes find unpleasant. I would notice a spot on her nose and get annoyed. I don't get this feeling any more. I think she's become more beautiful. Her face is tanned from the sun. And sometimes, when she turns round like that, moves her hand . . . Well. I'd better not write about it. It's just too wonderful.

I saw Karen as well. Her behaviour hasn't changed. The same beaming smile, sometimes a little sigh, which she immediately suppresses. I really like the way she is dealing with John's death. I compare her behaviour with Mama's when Papa died. Musch's way of bursting into tears in front of any old person at the mention of Papa's name alienated me from her. Karen does nothing like that. She doesn't give any sign that she's suffering. Besides, she was very lovely and looked pretty. In a charming blue kaftan and delicate golden chain. Her hair is long now and makes her look much more feminine and dainty. We talked about the future. She proposed that I should live with her in a furnished room in autumn. That would be nice. Much too nice ever to become reality. Then I'd have something like a 'home'. That's what I need. I envy those people who can live without it.

Today is also a good day because I received a letter from Musch and Dittl.

They love me very much. This love of theirs compels me to . . . I don't know what. I think that I'll never, *never* be able to do justice to their love. I get quite sad when I think about it. Anybody who is loved as much as I am by Dittl can only disappoint.

It was so lovely yesterday! Statsråd Lunde (*Nasjonal Samling*) delivered a speech in the market square in Lillestrøm. The *Nasjonal Samling*, the only authorised party, had expected a large turnout . . . The number of those that actually came was minimal. There was a small collection of people gathered around the speaker's chair. It was ridiculous and very uplifting. We thought: This is how the liberated cheer on their liberators. And then we went from one room to another, rubbing our hands.

LETTER TO HER FAMILY IN ENGLAND – FRIDAY, 25 APRIL 1941, LILLESTRØM

It's awful that we love each other and yet cannot be together. But there's nothing we can do about it. Just be good and watch out. I'm living only for the day we'll see each other again. But enough of that.

There's no point in spending too much time thinking about me. If you think about me a lot you'll be quite disappointed when I arrive. Because I'll have great difficulty in satisfying your expectations. Right now you're absolutely correct to call me an idiot. I am an idiot; I'm always seeking out what's 'difficult'. You ought to have seen how much I loved Gunvor. How I struggled and always found something in our relationship that ought to have been different. By the way, yesterday she came from Biri to Oslo. We walked through town and it was very nice. It really was. And the day after tomorrow we're leaving here for labour service again. I couldn't bear to stay here in Lillestrøm any longer. It's a ghastly town. Anyway, let's talk about something else.

Dittl, you asked me whether I talk about you to anybody. I talk to Gunvor about you, Dittl, and tell her that you're such a good and strong person. That you're so you. I say a lot more besides. And everybody knows when I get news from you. Gunvor looks at me with round eyes and says, 'Aha!' And she asks how you are. I say: They tell me they're fine. Karen says: That's what John wrote, too. And John is her husband and, well . . . Why bother writing about it? I'm out of my senses, you see.

I received a letter from Egon. He's the same as ever. Sends his regards. Wishes you happy birthday, Dittl. A little bit late, eh?

And what do I say about Musch? It would be too complicated to explain. About Grandmother? Well, Grandmother, I've told Gunvor a whole host of things about you. About how we used to come home and you'd read out loud and repeat each word ten times. I told her so much. About the bickering and . . . well. And I've talked about Thimig. We went for a walk in the snow, and I told her about the violets and your letters, Dittl. And Gunvor said: 'You've got a very strong sense of family.' But that's rubbish. Because my love for you all has nothing to do with sense of family.

Oh my dearest Musch, make contact with some film directors. No, please excuse me for laughing. *Those* times are past. And even if I sometimes write a poem or paint: *those* times are past. I would really like to go to art school. But Musch, my opinion of this school would be quite different from how you imagine. I really like painting. Sometimes I produce some pretty colours. I've done two things that are beautiful. I want to frame them later and hang them up in *our* room. One of them is called *Spring* and the other *Bare trees*. I've got a lot of photographs of the labour service. It's going to be lovely when we look at them all together.

And in autumn I might live with Karen, a small blonde girl who's a widow. That would be fantastic. There I'd wait for my great voyage. It's still going to take some time. I've been to the American consulate about it. I've got a second affidavit, which doesn't help, unfortunately. I'm sure to get a visa after the war. But not before then . . . So we need to be patient. Write to me. Tell me you send me a kiss on the forehead. That Dittl loves me . . . Yes, yes. Sometimes I dream about you too, dearest Grandmother. Be brave. A thousand kisses to you. On your hands too. And to you, Musch. Just please write.

When are you leaving? Please send me precise details.

SATURDAY, 26 APRIL 1941, LILLESTRØM

Yesterday I was leafing through some old letters . . . I imagined myself to be somewhere totally different. Those words were like a sophisticated poison, written by loved hands. I heard voices, I saw people come and go. Friends who are scattered everywhere.

There's a marvellous letter written on blue paper, light-blue paper. I can recall receiving it. I trembled, put it under my blouse, went downstairs, and nervously looked at the handwriting over and over again – *his* handwriting – before I opened it. Then I did open it. There was nothing 'particular' in it, but every letter was a gift, because it was meant for me. And he also wrote, 'Now I have the aspect of seeing you.'* I clutched at this sentence, imbibed the whole of it. His handwriting! His characters were chopped off in the middle. There were so many pauses in his words. These words were written so earnestly and so powerfully. Not at all 'sentimentally'.

Then there's the letter from Dr Brauchbar. His handwriting is so easy, quick and delicate. This letter of his really helped me. He was the first one to say that I was in love with Williger. And he didn't shake his head disapprovingly or wag his finger. He said, 'Love is the only undertaking.' He wanted to give me strength, even if he did put it a little pretentiously.

There were other letters…

Dittl! How she writes. With as much goodness as strength and her letters are endearing. Such a passion for life. For living life. Life as it is. And although internally Dittl tends to 'inflate all values', she has never slumped into resignation. Her heart is still young, it beats rapidly. And she says: My hands, my heart, my eyes! This virtuous self-consciousness speaks from her entire being. Just as people ought to be . . . At school she was known for saying, 'But I'd rather be Judith Maier.' Her letters are the best I have ever read. Because everything is so natural, because she writes without inhibition or complexes, without any ulterior motive. Perhaps it's only to me that she writes like that. Her letters have been like a refreshing bath to me.

Musch, with her regular, feminine handwriting. An unending wealth of love and concern on the pages in front of me. My God. I feel as if I will *never*

---

*This sentence is in English in the original.

be able to return the love and care that Dittl and Musch have shown me. It makes me feel quite disheartened. I brush off those who love me. Or they have to become unhappy with me. It's wretched not being able to love. There's the letter from Williger, from Jenda, from Gunvor. How I've resisted, resisted any feelings of love when they swelled inside me.

Here are Polina's intelligent thoughts laid out before me. Her letters were so full of longing, passion, tears, and often real despair too, that I couldn't find the courage to continue our correspondence. I lacked money, as well. But I can see Polina. Her slightly nasal voice, her black, curly hair, her good figure. I can see her sitting with the Bettina von Arnim book, absolutely riveted. Only smiling when Stein ran down Heine. We were very fond of each other.

There's Käthe. Her handwriting reflects her character perfectly. A little extravagant (intellectually), lacking discipline, much imagination, slightly too much feeling, no clarity! She lives in London. At the moment she's in America.

Then there are Kurt Pollack's letters. He's still got childish handwriting. His style somewhat roguish. He does put together some impressive words from time to time, but they're diminished by the wisecracks he inserts throughout. We're very good friends now. Even though we weren't at all in Vienna.

There's Egon, too. I always feel a kind of pity when I read his letters. Even though he's managed to establish some sort of life in Holíč. But there's something demoralising about his letters. Something tired. As if he were already very old. He's always coming out with wise sayings. Last time he wrote, 'Everything points towards an eternal convergence.' That's nonsense, but I've given up teasing him. There's no point. That's his character. His letters remind me of those really *lovely* times in Hitler's Germany. Of how a friendship developed out of misery and horror. The friendship with Egon. With Taubers. My God. I can see him before me. I can see everything.

And Susi! I remember how I used to love him. When he sat there at the table looking so strong and healthy in a white shirt. He was so strong and so good. Once he spoke so beautifully. Apart from that he was silent. There's one letter from him. His handwriting is so childish. I'm all alone and that's why I want to revive old memories. Susi is sad.

Reading his letter was so strange. It reveals a new side to him. Susi is sad . . .

Oh, there are many other letters. Gunvor's four letters are together with other Norwegian ones. I handle Gunvor's letters delicately. I'm terrified I'll break them if I hold on too firmly. There's so much I have to read without changing the expression on my face. So I don't upset her. And while I read I often have to make myself small so that she doesn't take fright. It was like that in Währingerstraße, too. When he started talking I would make myself small so as not to scare him, to make him forget that I was there.

Første kvinnelige arbeidsleir iår.

Igår reiste 11 friske jenter avgårde ned Vestbanen til den første kvinnelige arbeidsleir iår. Den ligger ved Thou i Strand kommune ved Stavanger hvor jentene skal plante skog. De 11 får forsterkninger underveis i Skien og Tønsberg, og noen deltagere kommer også med fra Haugesund, slik at det i alt blir 30 i leiren. Reiseleder igår var Tullemor Johansen, og leirleder er Jarli Brundhansen. Hendriksen fra Haugesund. Det var fint vær ved avreisen, og humøret var på toppen.

In spring 1941 Ruth travels to another labour service camp.
This photograph from the Morgenposten *of 28 April 1941 shows, under the*
headline 'First women's labour camp of the year', the girls' departure from
the western station in Oslo. On the left are Liv Width (known as Petter),
Gunvor Hofmo and Ruth Maier.

Travelling around

APRIL–JULY 1941

At the end of April several friends from the camp leave for another stint of labour service on Tjøstheim farm in Tau, which is in the municipality of Strand. Their journey starts by train to Kristiansand, then they take the bus to Flekkefjord, then another train to Sandsnes and further on to Stavanger. Ruth describes the towns of southern Norway, the Norwegian coast and later the landscape of the fjords in Ryfylke.

The narrative takes a dramatic turn when a police sergeant arrives at the farm and arrests Gunvor Hofmo, who ends up in prison in Oslo. (Her arrest is probably connected to a suspected attempt to flee to England. In a letter to her sister, Ruth had mentioned that Gunvor and she were planning to visit 'Mattelin', although Judith does not know anybody by that name.) But Gunvor returns after only one and a half weeks. The friendship between Ruth and Gunvor becomes closer than ever. During an argument in the camp, in the course of which Ruth is insulted as a Jew, Gunvor very publicly protects Ruth. Both of them leave the camp.

At the beginning of June, five of the friends set out on a walking tour in the Gudbrandsdal. In return for their help working on a farm they receive a few weeks' board and lodging in Kvam. The tour ends when Ruth and Gunvor accept work from a farmer, weeding carrot fields in Melhus, south of Trondheim. The remaining friends join another labour service in Gyl, near Tingvoll in the Nordmøre region.

TUESDAY, 29 APRIL 1941, STAVANGER

We left Oslo the day before yesterday. Spent the night in Kristiansand. Kristiansand is a pretty town. Typical of southern Norway. The houses are painted bright yellow, grey and pink. The roads are straight. A very beautiful quayside. The Wergeland statue by Vigeland is in the centre of town. Beside the church. Very beautiful. The next day we took the bus to Flekkefjord through the Sørlandet [southern Norway]. It's hilly with pale colours. Grey, blue, brown, green. The towns we passed through looked homely, with narrow lanes and striped, crouched houses. The sea lies gently beside the coast, for it's divided by skerries and scattered cliffs. Mandal was so beautiful with its narrow lanes; Flekkefjord has a white bridge which reminds me of a song that Gunvor sings: Under the white bridge . . .

We then continued our journey by train to Sandnes. We crossed the Vestlandet [western Norway], Jæren! Jæren is quite unique. Particularly its colours: an ochre-brown beach, dark-blue sea, light-blue sky. We went quite silent. Only a few girls were bold enough to shout out, 'wonderful!' There were houses laid out on this expanse, brown, green. The first buds were on the trees. The Norwegians have a gift for making their houses fit the land-scape. We spent the night in Sandnes on a boat.

The next day we continued to Stavanger. What a contrast. Narrow streets climb up the mountainside. The houses are real and unreal at the same time. In their pale colours. These streets are picturesque, offering up new perspectives by the second. The harbour is particularly beautiful. Only the front part of the cathedral is how I like churches to be. Gothic inside, striving upwards, the ornate glass windows decorated with such curves that it makes you think of music. Stavanger was like a picture book.

TUESDAY EVENING, 29 APRIL 1941, TAU

Petter, Bjørg, Gunvor and I are staying on a farm with two other girls. The landscape is magnificent. The narrow Ryfylkefjord far in the distance. The mountains made of stone, brown fields, green-brown grass, the blue fjord, bare trees reaching out into the countryside. White gulls fly over the fields.

FRIDAY, 9 MAY 1941, STAVANGER

There are nice girls here. But it's still a good thing that the four of us are together. I love Gunvor very much. I think that all true feelings are limitless. That's the case with my love for Gunvor. I also know that she deserves limitless love.

Gunvor and I go for a walk. The trees are slightly green already. I say, 'Look, the trees are coming into leaf.' She smiles . . . I . . . and the world turn silent. The trees are green. It's always like that. When the two of us are together.

I also get the feeling that I mean something to her. We were going to work. I'd stayed behind the others. Walked on my own. I saw her shape sitting beside the path. Sunbathing. She was waiting for me. When I got there she stood and asked, 'Why are you so late?' And we walked on together.

I had a dream last night. I was telling Musch that I had to leave at half past seven. For the north of Norway . . . I was really looking forward to the trip. Petter, Bjørg and Gunvor were coming with me. The time of our departure drew nearer, I arrived too late . . . I was unhappy when I arrived on the platform and couldn't see anybody. But Gunvor was sitting there on a suitcase and she said, 'We waited for you.' I was happy and grateful.

FRIDAY EVENING, 9 MAY 1941, TAU

I find it almost painful that Gunvor has become so much more beautiful, that she's so good. Too good.

Today she said, 'I like dogs. All dogs, not bulldogs . . . But then, if I got to know bulldogs better I'd like them too.'

I can't stand the woman who does the cooking here in the camp.

Me: 'She's obnoxious.'

Gunvor: 'I'm sure there are many people who don't find her obnoxious.'

WEDNESDAY, 14 MAY 1941, TAU

We were assembled in the prayer house. When the village policeman came for
Gunvor it was like a thunderbolt. He said he had to talk to her. We suspected
that this did not augur well. Gunvor is very well liked here. We stood in a
circle around her. She smiled and nervously twiddled her fingers. When she
left us we were scared. Petter and I sat in our room and waited for her to
return. Outside the weather was as horrible as in autumn: fog, rain. The
policeman's red car was in front of the house – small and boding ill. I thought
that the 'new era' had to tackle people like Gunvor. I reflected on our friendship. Wondered: Will they take her away and lock her up? And everything was
quite ghastly. Then her heavy steps came up the stairs. She said, smiling, 'Oh
yes, my children . . . I've got to go away now, for three years… ' I could feel
myself turning very pale. My mouth gaping open. I said, 'No, Gunvor, don't
talk nonsense.' As I said this I could see that she was fooling me. Nothing had
happened, not yet. We went off to work together. It was raining. The path was
green. Gunvor, in a black raincoat, her arms swishing around, looked like a
bird flapping its wings. Deep within my soul I could feel that we were friends.
We spoke about the possible consequences of the conversation she'd had with
the policeman. We decided to leave on Tuesday.

    The following morning Petter woke me and said, 'The village police-
man's come to fetch Gunvor again.' I waited for her. When she came I realised
that they intended to lock her up. She packed her suitcase. Everything
happened quickly. The policeman was waiting outside. They'd only given her
half an hour. I was still half asleep. I sat in my sleeping bag, spectacles on my
nose. I couldn't say anything. What would be the point? She knew what I was
feeling. We squeezed each other's hands. There was a half-smile on her lips.
Yes, I asked her, 'Write.' She replied, 'I'm sure that won't be allowed.'

THURSDAY, 15 MAY 1941, TAU

The days are now very empty, because her voice is absent. Her smile is missing. I hope she'll only get a few months. These months will pass slowly for Gunvor and me. I find it of some consolation that I can say: I'll wait. She might have gone away, and then 'waiting' would have been pointless.

I think: I have to put up with it, I mustn't be too sad. Then, perhaps, in her loneliness she'll feel my strength and joy. It will help her a lot.

It's stupid to lock people up. However dreadful it is, it's especially stupid. It just makes people bitter if they have to sit there in a cell without any air. Alone. Now they're even locking people up who are fighting for their beliefs. Incredible! Nothing will astonish me any more. Nor am I surprised that they've locked up Gunvor. I only wish I could be with her. Whom is she to smile at now?

FRIDAY, 16 MAY 1941, TAU

How bizarre it is that scribbling words down with pen and ink makes the heart lighter. When I sit here and write, my longing crouches over the lines, it lingers there and I cannot feel its pain.

Since Gunvor left what is around me only touches the surface. The girls that are here, the sun outside – it's as if I don't need them any more. I look straight past the green buds that were so dear to me when Gunvor walked by my side. When I smile to myself I miss her smiling back at me.

I may complain now, but I'll be stronger for it when I sit here without a pen in my hand. Dear God: we will see each other again.

SATURDAY, 17 MAY 1941, TAU

It's Norway's national day today. But there's no festivity. We go around with the Norwegian colours in our buttonholes and we're sad. It's something of a mockery that, in spite of all that's happened, the egg custard still tastes good. The fact that Gunvor's seat is empty makes everything even sadder.

LETTER TO HER FAMILY IN ENGLAND – SATURDAY, 17 MAY 1941, TAU

With my being so miserable today your letter arrived like a wonderful gift. (Your letters are always like that anyway.) Oh, when I write to you I always want to write something a bit more relevant to all of us. Then I sit here with the pen in my hand and think: That cannot be enough. That's idiotic! I'm afraid I have to tell you why I feel sad today. We're now on labour service. A long way from Oslo, near Stavanger. We thought about travelling on further. Gunvor and I also wanted to visit Mattelin. But the visit was prohibited. Two days ago Gunvor had to go to Oslo. That's why I'm sad. And going around in my head are the images of her packing her case, our holding each other's hand to say goodbye, her smiling again. Don't say that I'm just feeling sorry for myself, because I really do miss her. Everything is frightfully empty without her. If you could see us discussing music, the Jewish question, our favourite writers, a nice book – if you could see us you'd probably say: Ruth is very happy at the moment! Even when we're just together. It's true. Two days ago she left. I don't have a clue how she is and I cannot help her.

Everything is all quiet around me now. The girls I'm sharing a room with have gone for their evening meal. I'm alone and so my thoughts are more deeply with you. Overall, it's very nice here. You know how good it is to be together with other people. We're also doing some good work: sowing potatoes and planting woodland. But we don't intend to stay here for ever. We're going to walk to the south of Norway. When we're out of money we'll take work on farms. Everything would have been so completely different with Gunvor. I'd rather go to Oslo if I thought it might be of assistance to her. Oh well.

Musch. When you talk of your daughter who 'faces up to the hardships in life', these are grand things you're writing. It's not that dangerous, it sounds rather nice. What else is one to do? . . . Outside, a bird was just tweeting and when we go to bed at night there's such a beautiful twilight in the room. But now there's just an empty space where Gunvor used to sleep. And although I don't really like to gush too much, I'm sure you'll forgive me. Also for writing about Gunvor when my thoughts are very much with you.

And Musch, I'd like to say from the bottom of my heart that you should not think about me too often. Time will pass anyway and some time, somewhere we'll see each other again. When I think of you, sometimes I think: Perhaps what Kurtl calls life will then really begin. But that is so far away. Until then I'll just be part of the labour service. And there's nothing more to say. Once Gunvor said I ought to work as a painter. But when I merely laughed in reply she understood me perfectly, even though she loves my pictures. But it's not *that*. I must keep the nice things for myself.

If Gunvor is able to come back here, we might pay Mattelin a visit. But it could take a long time.

Dittl, you're still the same as I remember. You got a perfume bottle that looked so 'precious'. That was wonderfully put. This thing about being 'precious' is quite singular, isn't it? You often say, 'Beautiful!' And every time you do it I know that you understand 'beautiful' to be very good. But you don't say 'beautiful' about those things that are 'beautiful' on the surface. Because that way you'd ruin the beauty. Oh, I'm prattling on and on. And my grandmother must think I've lost it.

Shall I let you into a secret, Grandmother? I don't just darn my own stockings but Gunvor's as well. And I do it with pleasure. Gunvor says '*Takk*'. That means 'thank you' in Norwegian. When I feel good inside me, then things themselves are generally good. But when things are generally good, things are often not good inside me. That was a cryptic saying you'll excuse me for.

A kiss for you all.

On 17 May the girls in Tau celebrate Norway's national day. The two birch branches
make a gate, with the letters AT standing for ArbeidsTjenesten (labour service).
Ruth Maier is crouching in the front on the far left.

It's not working with the Strøms. In any case I shudder whenever I think
of Lillestrøm.

WEDNESDAY, 21 MAY 1941, TAU

It's now a magnificent spring day outside. The trees that stood there so bare,
their branches grasping out for something beyond their reach, no longer
evoke any longing or pity. For like a dream they now gleam with green buds.
I just wander around and think: It can't be possible that spring has finally
arrived. And it pains me very much to think that Gunvor's sitting in prison.
'Prison' – it's another one of those words without end. It's quite incomprehensible that Gunvor is sitting there right now, in this sunny moment. Gunvor
was not made for it – nobody is made for it, but Gunvor really is not.

Christ! Every day I see her so many times. She sits beside me at the table.

She walks beside me down the path. Calls out to the dog, 'Look out! Look out!' Puts her hand into its mouth and says, 'Bite it! Bite it!'

Although I've suffered much because of her, I also know that there have been few better times than those I've spent together with Gunvor. Within me there's often a great seriousness, a deadly seriousness, which can watch the others laugh without laughing with them. Gunvor is the only one who can penetrate this seriousness, with a single word, a smile. Oh well.

Yesterday we got a letter from her. She was in custody in Stavanger for three days. Then she was transported to Oslo. She wrote her lovely phrases: 'It's so pointless.'

SATURDAY, 24 MAY 1941, TAU

Gunvor will be coming back at the end of this week. She called from Oslo. Her voice sounded good on the telephone. She'll be here soon. She'll see the cherry trees blossoming and the blue violets. I'm happy. Our plans will blossom again. Everything looks better now.

PRAYER
I'm praying to feel at peace. When the fjord shimmers so blue outside, brown fields stretch afar, mountains reach into the distance, I'm praying to feel at peace. Oh I wish I could finally feel at peace.

SUNDAY, 8 JUNE 1941, LILLESTRØM

After a lovely trip I'm in Lillestrøm, from where I'm off again tomorrow. I'm excited.

These are times I want to cling on to. And it's a pity that they're over already.

Gunvor and I sitting in a paddock in Stavanger. In the evening! People, children playing before us, a pane of glass shining in the sun. We just sit. Two

Watercolour from Tau, May 1941, with the dedication: 'For Petter from Ruth'.

old women walk past. One points at an empty spot, where there's just debris now. Says, 'We had many good times here. Here were the steps down to the cellar, that's where the garden was.' And points at a place where there's debris. She's almost in tears. Gunvor and I become melancholic, we can feel the hours passing. And the old woman who is tearfully thinking back to her childhood walks up close to us.

Yes, in fact we were driven out of the camp. Gunvor and I. The reason for it was stupid. It began with the cook's dislike of us and ended in a dramatic scene in which Jarli (the *leder* = supervisor) and Gunvor were the main actors. We were accused of being insubordinate, they made an issue of my 'racial affiliation', of Gunvor's political beliefs, our discussions etc. I got to see a new side of Gunvor. She was highly agitated and spoke very intelligently, carried away by her feelings. With her hands in her trouser pockets she went on the attack and I thought what a shame it was that her energy was so wasted. Something else I'll never forget is when Maud, who cannot stand the sight of me, said, 'You cannot deny your race.'

In response to a comment by Jarli and with reference to Maud, Gunvor said with utter conviction (it was almost a threat), 'I wonder who the simple one is here?'

I'm grateful to all people who take a humane stand on the Jewish question. So I'm grateful to Gunvor, too.

Day one, Monday, 9 June.
10.30, Sinsen tram stop / To Jessheim / Jessheim / Studying the map / Gjøvik park /
Overnight in Gjøvik, The Strange Party *[title of the book in the picture].*

Day two, Tuesday, 10 June.
Woods near Gjøvik / Stallion fight, Vinstra / Stallion fight (us waiting),
11.30 / In Vinstra, barn.

Day three, Wednesday, 11 June.
Café Vinstra / Gunvor picking lilac / Staying in a barn.

Day four, Thursday, 12 June.
*Country road / Potato soup on the banks of River Lågen / At a communal
grave for five English soldiers / We camp down in a hut.*

To Trøndelag and back

AUGUST—NOVEMBER 1941

At the beginning of August, after their walking tour, Ruth and Gunvor get jobs in Iris's flower shop in Trondheim. The shop also runs a nursery. Until the end of the month they stay in the Young Women's Christian Association (YWCA) hostel in Prinsensgate. After that they rent a room on a farm in Nedre Søberg, probably near Ingrid Gimse, for whom they had once worked. Ruth and Gunvor spend two months in the area. At the beginning of October they take the train to the south: Ruth to Lillestrøm, Gunvor to Oslo. That same autumn they both do clerical training in Oslo, which includes language and stenography courses.

There is a crisis in Ruth's and Gunvor's relationship. Gunvor wants to end their friendship, Ruth does not. The heated arguments end in reconciliation. Ruth becomes pensive.

Many of the entries from late autumn deal with dreams and their meaning. Ruth demonstrates how incisive she is in analysing her dreams, which include various scenes where both Gunvor's and her parents crop up, as does Gunvor's former boyfriend, Reidar.

The letter that Ruth writes at the end of August 1941 is the last one to her family that we know of.

Watercolour: 'The red bridge', Trondheim 1941.

LETTER TO HER FAMILY IN ENGLAND – SUNDAY, 24 AUGUST 1941, TRONDHEIM

First of all, I'm angry. Very angry. I'd prefer to say nothing to you at all, but just sit here in defiance, absolutely refusing to reply if you ask me anything, because I'm angry.

What kind of behaviour is that not to write? There's always plenty of ink and paper. So there's no excuse. I think I've already been far too patient with you and that's why you've become so neglectful. And then you want to try to persuade me that you're thinking of me 'day and night'. No, thank you. Think less of me, but write at least every fortnight. You're strange people. And you expect me to tell you things? You, who don't write at all? What do I know about you? That you live together in a flat, with hot water, and that my beloved Dittl works in an office.

Grandmother, Dittl, Muscherle. Oh well. Everything is going to be all right.

I'm very well. At the moment. So well, it's as if it were a dream. I've got work. Something similar to street work. I earn a pile of money. Something like seventy schillings per week. I save a little and buy books, not too many. I'm living with Gunvor in a room in Trondheim. It's a *very* long way from Lillestrøm. You know that we (five girls) did a walking tour from Oslo. Well, we ended up here. The three other girls are doing labour service; the two of us found work. There's a lot of work here, you see. Gunvor and I have a good life together.

We are very fond of each other. We still cannot believe that we're earning money, that we're independent. There's no Strøm to rebuke me, I don't have to ask for money.

I *live*, I *work*. I could tell you of our life as two settlers, of the pretty town we live in. In the evenings we come home tired from work and sometimes we're happy. We do whatever we like, read books, I teach Gunvor German. I go for walks. Sometimes I paint. On Saturdays and Sundays we have lunch, at other times we live off sandwiches and milk. It works very well.

Frequently, however, Gunvor is sad. It's part of her character that she's often sad. Then she creeps into my bed. And I have to be like a mother to her.

But there's none of what you're implying. And even if it is good, it's not

*Gunvor's application form, dated 12 August 1941, to the Trondheim welfare office
for a flour and bread ration card. Gunvor and Ruth worked at Iris florist's, owned by
Forbrigd (whose name appears on the form). As they were doing horticultural work
outside they were 'instructed' to eat bread.*

so good. Because a human being is not a simple thing. Even if things are good
around me it's not necessarily the same inside. I'm getting carried away.

It's now evening. Sunday. Gunvor is getting undressed. There's a grey sky
outside. It's rained all day long. We went to the café, and had cakes and lunch.
I did the washing and darning. I've bought some grey skiing trousers out of
my wages. O my dearest ones. You really ought to see me sitting like this in
the evenings.

An aeroplane is roaring outside. I think of times past. Nobody can understand it. Even Gunvor, who understands so much. Now, goodnight to you all.
And do I have to say it again? *Write!*

Addendum 28 August:

IRIS BLOMSTERFORRETNING

NAVN: *Ruth Maier*   UKEN:

	Timer à		Kr.
akkord	25 %		"
opgjør	50 %		"
	75 %		"

Kr.

Kr. *76.57*

IRIS BLOMSTERFORRETNING

NAVN *Gunvor Hofmo*   UKEN: *18-24/9-41*

	4/5 Timer à *1.50*		Kr. *67.50*
	25 %		"
	50 %		"
	75 %		"
TREKK *Skatt 13.—* *Trygd 2.90*		Kr.	*67.50*
		"	*15.90*
		Kr.	*51.60*

Ruth and Gunvor's wage slips from Iris florist's. Ruth did not have a work permit in Norway, so neither tax nor health insurance was deducted from her wages.

A letter from 'you' today. I'm very upset because my mother has not written. I assume that Muscherle has a reason for not writing. I have to know this reason. I'm not a child, after all. And no greeting from Grandmother. Oh well. You're becoming scarce. You will not get a reply from me until I get a long and detailed letter from you all!

SATURDAY, 13 SEPTEMBER 1941, SØBERG

I've been away from Lillestrøm for five months now. Spring has passed, as has summer, and now there's a cool, dark autumn evening outside. It's raining on the black windowpanes. It's warm inside.

We're living in a house in the country. About thirty kilometres from Trondheim. We've rented a room on a farm with little furniture. We like it. We're free. It can get very cosy, homely. In the evenings, on Saturdays, Sundays. It's a home. But it won't last long.

WEDNESDAY, 17 SEPTEMBER 1941, SØBERG

There is a deep melancholy within Gunvor that sometimes engulfs her in a very sinister way. On those occasions she needs me. There she is, the big girl, like a small child. She's told me certain things that I do not intend to write down. As somebody once said, a secret is no longer a secret if you tell it to your own skirt.

I've never met a person who has so suffered from life. Who asks with such unfathomably deep, sad eyes: Why? . . . And then? These eyes, when they dilate like those of a child who has been done a bitter injustice, often pain me. Yet there's nothing I can do but to stroke her softly across the forehead or kiss her. Then I feel the heartbreak of a mother who has an ill child but cannot do anything to help.

THURSDAY, 18 SEPTEMBER 1941, SØBERG

We are such good friends. We've been living together for a month. For a fortnight we stayed in Trondheim in a hostel room at the YWCA. The view looked out over a grey backyard. The room was grey, three beds, a table, we didn't feel at home. Gunvor would lie on the bed, the white bed, drinking milk and eating fat yellow waffles with butter and sugar. While I buttered eight slices of bread. Eight sandwiches. Sometimes I went for a walk in the evenings. On one occasion my goal was a red bridge that crosses the Nidelven; another time it was a green, slightly dusty park where red summer roses glow and children's voices sound muted. The quiet streets where lights flashed were twice as quiet. I came back home and Gunvor smiled at me.

That was in the YWCA.

Now it's even better. Here we are totally free. In a large room with two beds, a table and a stove. View over an autumn landscape. We don't have to worry about landladies who ask us sweetly when we're finally going to 'move out'. We no longer have to hop up the stairs anxiously to avoid meeting the manageress. Here we are free. And if Gunvor isn't sad, life is good. When we have coffee and cakes, or herring and potatoes, a smile crosses Gunvor's sometimes pale face. As she slurps her coffee, the fire crackles, it's evening outside and in here a white twilight softens the sharp forms, she says, 'Not bad at all.'

Then I can feel myself smiling inside and the fact that I'm *young* comes over as so strange.

MONDAY, 22 SEPTEMBER 1941, SØBERG

Autumn has suddenly arrived as if overnight. Last week we were astonished as the trees were still green and the evenings still light. Now we're just as astonished because the leaves have turned totally yellow as if overnight. When we ride past in the tram, the trees in the park sway gently. The nights are now dark, and at night-time I cannot see Gunvor when she lies beside me like a small child. In spring and summer I saw her eyes watch me at night, so deep, so inscrutable, often so unutterably sad, too. Now I can only feel her mouth and her soft skin, and hear her say, 'It's so wonderful to have you lying beside me.' Softly: 'So secure.'

WEDNESDAY, 24 SEPTEMBER 1941, SØBERG

Our cosy days here will be over soon. We've already become a little wistful. Like a separating couple we look melancholically at our 'home' here which, although it may be rather primitive, we are very fond of. On some evenings, by the stove, we have experienced that lovely atmosphere people like to associate with the 'golden era of youth'.

Yes, this golden era of youth. Who on earth invented it? I once read Hjalmar Söderberg, a Swede, who wrote, 'It's wonderful to grow older; it was too bad to be young.'

If only Gunvor were happy. Recently her fingers have become no more than pink edges. She looks so tired, but let's not forget – the golden era of youth.

FRIDAY, 26 SEPTEMBER 1941, SØBERG

I'll just jot down a few lines on those days I'm here. I'll say: We were in town today, it was a golden autumn day. We went over the red wooden bridge that shines from afar and crosses the Nidelven. Very pretty, snug lanes looked autumnal from the other side of the river. We climbed up to the castle, an ugly, very rectangular construction. From there we had a wonderful view over the whole town: the church, the river, lots of roofs and the fjord outside the town. Where an oil tanker is burning there are flames and a lot of smoke. The leaves lay yellow at my feet. Trondheim is a town I like, even if I would not wish to live here for ever.

TUESDAY, 30 SEPTEMBER 1941, SØBERG

The days here are approaching their end. I sit on Gunvor's lap under the electric light in the middle of the room. It's evening. Outside it is dark. It's with dread that I contemplate the days that are to come . . . in Lillestrøm.

In autumn 1941 Ruth and Gunvor learn stenography at a business school in Oslo.

MONDAY, 13 OCTOBER 1941, LILLESTRØM

It's been a long time since I last wrote in the diary. Since Gunvor and I lived together in the large room with practically no furniture. In between times there has been a long succession of grey days: the journey from Trondheim to Lillestrøm. We left on a clear autumn morning, left our room, took the pictures from the walls, packed up our books and the room was completely empty when we left. Then, at the small station in Søberg, a final argument with Gunvor.

I tried in vain to convince her how stupid it was for us to go, to leave our 'home'. Then came the train journey. Lillestrøm approaches, I grab my suitcase, we arrive in Lillestrøm and suddenly I'm standing there at the station, even more alone, in the dark . . . Frau Strøm greets me with a startled smile. Strøm sits and reads, shakes my hand and welcomes me with an interminable discussion of his difficulties at work in the telegraph office. Nothing changes.

I'm now going to Oslo every day to learn typing, and Norwegian and German stenography (using the money I saved) with Gunvor. I love Gunvor very much. I can't imagine my life without her. So it goes on. But the money I saved will soon be all gone and then things won't be so pretty. I won't be able to bear living here in Lillestrøm without work, without Oslo, without Gunvor.

TUESDAY, 14 OCTOBER 1941, LILLESTRØM

I'm always astonished at how I keep on getting older. Twenty-one. I say it out loud, and try to make sense of the sound of that word: twenty-one. I've achieved so little. I did a so-called Matura, and that's all. Well, I'll say it as Gunvor did in a lovely short poem she wrote as a seventeen-year-old: 'From now on I'll wait for my hair to turn white.' Yes! I will wait for my hair to turn white, and I'll eat crispbread.

FRIDAY, 17 OCTOBER 1941, LILLESTRØM

I'm so sad. I do not recall ever having been so sad before. There's a sadness within me that I'm trying to cry away.

I cried on the train, in town, on the bench. All around me a cold autumn, yellow leaves and people who rush around, and I think: Is everything still the same? Gunvor and I were standing together at the door to a laboratory that had advertised in the newspaper for two young women. I was fooling around. In some way I was feeling bad, so I was fooling around. Gunvor was as she always is: she couldn't help smiling, she gave me such a lovely and good-hearted smile, stroked my hands, and her eyebrows went up and down. And yet! All of a sudden she said, 'You're as much a stranger to me as the next

person and I couldn't care less about you, couldn't care less at all.' I replied,
'If it's like that, well, if it's like that . . .' I went completely pale, or red, I don't
know which, but I was looking for words. I wanted to say, 'Then let's
separate, we never knew each other.' And she understood what I wanted to
say. She replied, 'That's what I think, too.'

'How did this all come about?' I ask. 'Just like that?'

'No, it's been going on for a while.'

And there's silence.

I remember how she said to me that morning, 'This is the last day I'll
walk through town with you.'

I feel so wounded and hurt. But I understand that she's serious. And I
walk away from her, even though she holds me back. I go, go down the stairs,
go on to the street . . . expect her steps behind me. But nobody comes. So I
continue to walk, sit on a bench, then I'm in the library. From time to time
I'm in tears and many ideas go through my head . . . Now I'm sitting here in
Lillestrøm and I still cannot understand. I find it all so incomprehensible. I
think that it cannot be true. And when I write this I also feel that it cannot be
true. I've dreamed it and it's unreal.

I cannot think her out of my life. If she's absent, nothing has meaning any
more. What's the point in learning stenography, going to the theatre, looking
for a job? She, yes, Gunvor, she gives me the . . . I ought to say strength . . .
to . . . endure it all. It sounds very sentimental and very crude, but that is
how it is. Inside me is this idea that something has been torn away from
me, something I had used for support . . . Oh, what's the point of all this
scribbling? It doesn't help.

Last week I was with her, at her home. She was as nice as ever. Showed
me her poems. And she leaned against me. She lives high up, in a tiny room.
Her brother and sister came, both of them good souls. I was grateful to her
for inviting me into her home, even if I didn't show it. And we walked home
together in the evening. She showed me the eastern part of Oslo. The streets,
the squares of her childhood, the school, the *løkke*, a small recess in the light
shaft where, aged three, she had a sexual encounter with a small friend of
hers. We spoke together. I felt secure.

It cannot be that all that is *over*, that she'll never be with me again. I feel
dread, great dread if I contemplate a winter without Gunvor. I must have her.

I'll see her again tomorrow, at college. It will be difficult for me to behave proudly when I want to spit at myself and kiss Gunvor's feet so that she stays with me.

I cannot do anything else with my mind save think of her continually, of the times we spent together. Never before have I been so at one with somebody. I know everything about her, I adore her every single gesture. How secure I felt when she comforted me, convinced me that it would be all right. And all that is now past? The times when she lay sobbing, twitching at my side, clutching at me, haven't these bound her to me? A year living together with her – for I was constantly in her company – hasn't that brought me so close that she can no longer leave me alone? Hasn't she understood what it means to me to be alone, lonely? Is she deaf and blind that she cannot see or hear that it's she who gives me the courage to endure life here in Lillestrøm? What am I to do, now that a 'tomorrow' or 'day after tomorrow' without Gunvor smirks back at me? When I'm with other people, with Karen or Nini, there's a Ruth who talks and laughs and knows how to get up to mischief. With Gunvor I find my own self. And she cannot understand that? Cannot understand that I need her? My God, who's going to hold it against her that she doesn't understand any more? If her love for me suddenly disappeared like that. That's right. For *she* loved me too. She often told me that. She used to cuddle up to me, she . . . well, she loved me. And it's over. On Tuesday she was saying, 'Oh, if only we could live together again.' We were hungry together, laughed together, wept together – does all that mean nothing? No, I will not believe it, *will* not, even if something within me says she was being serious. But I want to console myself: she was also 'serious' once before. I will recall this time. Want to write about it, for I cannot turn my mind to anything else.

At the time we were staying in the YWCA. We'd been given notice by our landlady, a fat, cross-eyed woman. We'd been searching in vain for a flat in Trondheim. We were feeling morose. The prospect of being without somewhere to stay in three days was not an attractive one. It was also terrible autumn weather at the time. It rained endlessly, the sky was just grey, and there was a horrible wind. We froze at work, we got soaking wet and we had to work hard then, too: digging to a depth of fifty centimetres in stony ground. Gunvor had got sick of staying in Trondheim. We made one last attempt: we enquired about rooms on farms in Søberg, about thirty kilometres from Trondheim. On one farm, near Gimse, there was an unfurnished room for rent. I went for it straight away and promised the people that I'd move in within two days . . . Gunvor then decided to go to Oslo. She didn't want to live so far from the town, she was fed up with the work, fed up with Trondheim. I recall very well her telling me all this in great detail in a small café in Melhus. I felt just as wounded and hurt as I do now. We'd ordered cakes and suddenly there was silence between us. I tapped my fingers nervously on the table. All at once I was overcome by so much pain and tears that I got up and walked out . . . out . . . out. Gunvor came after me with my coat over her arm, with her kind features, her smile: 'Come on, be serious.' I didn't say anything, I ran away from her, hailed a lorry and went back to Trondheim without waiting for her. The next 'scene' took place at the YWCA. Gunvor was still determined to go back to Oslo. I made no response to her excuses, her attempts to discuss it with me; I just asked her to shut up. She tried over and over again to talk with me. The room was getting dark, I was darning stockings, I listened to her, and a fury was rumbling inside me. I hated her; I thought it rotten on her part to abandon me in Trondheim. Every word she uttered hurt me, and yet: when she wasn't speaking, I longed to hear her talk, even if just to be able to shout back at her, 'Shut up!' Then, all of a sudden, my rage took hold of me; inside me everything went red and dark. I'm convinced I could have killed her at that very moment. I was *completely* beside myself. I felt the anger surging inside me, I yelled, no, actually I hissed, 'Shut up!', threw her on the bed, went for her neck and started to strangle her. Then I ran out of the room and slammed the door behind me. I went to my dusty little park in Erling Skakkes gate. I sat there and wept. Just as now, I was dreading the days to come in a strange town with nobody for company. After a while I made my way back. Gunvor was still at home. She looked at me in astonishment with her large, deep eyes. Then she went downstairs to settle the bill with the landlady. When she returned I felt that a change had taken place inside her. She was sitting silently on the edge of the bed. I started to darn my stockings again. I couldn't help smiling. Then I felt this certainty: she's going to stay, she's going to stay! There was such a long silence. Then suddenly, Gunvor's voice: 'When are you going to Søberg?'

I forced myself to give an angry and matter-of-fact answer: 'You know very well I'm going tomorrow.'

Silence again. And both of us almost had to smile. Then: 'Pray tell me, Fräulein . . .' She was embarrassed, now she was smiling broadly: 'Would it be permitted to accompany you?' Inside me I was rejoicing. I said, 'Stop talking nonsense.' But from that moment on, everything was fine. And I was so joyful, so happy. Then Gunvor told me when I asked her why she'd been thinking differently. She gave me an answer. And she was very close to me. The look she gave me was even more profound than usual: 'Don't you understand that I love you far too much to just leave like that!'

I'll recall more things . . .

First of all those wonderful days in Biri, then her lovely visits to me in the hospital. And finally, our trip to Tau. The gorgeous trip by train. I remember how she mothered me, how good I felt in her company, how we went through thick and thin together in Tau, how we were both chucked out of the camp together. At the time it was just Ruth and Gunvor, Gunvor and Ruth. Never only Ruth, or only Gunvor on her own.

How she was then arrested. I've suffered a lot on her account. When I had to leave her in Biri and then when she was arrested. I felt so much pain at the time because of her. I didn't believe that she would be able to cope with being locked up in a cell. When they drove her away it was raining. Then when she came back. First the telephone call, a lovely voice saying, 'I'm free!' Oh, then her return. I was lying in the cherry orchard, reading. Out of a feeling of loyalty towards Gunvor I'd detached myself from the other girls. I was lying in the garden, reading, when the small, blonde woman called out to me, 'Gunvor's arrived!' I went up the stairs, she was sitting on Petter's bed and I just looked at her. I didn't even hold her hand. Just looked at her.

There are so many images coming to mind. And all of these will be mere memories if we never share good times again. But that simply can't be possible!

Nᵒ· 00234   Trondheim, den

K. F. U. Kˢ HJEM
PRINSENS GT. 10 - TELEF. 2529

Mottatt av *Frk. Hofmo og R. Maier*

for *Losji for 11 døgn à kr 1,25 + 2.*

Kr. 27.50   *Anna Graae.*

K. F. U. K.
Hjem & Hospits

One of several extant receipts for a room shared by Gunvor and Ruth at the Young Women's Christian Association hostel in Prinsens gate in Oslo.

SATURDAY, 18 OCTOBER 1941, LILLESTRØM

Things are good again between Gunvor and me. It was difficult this time. But I am so happy. And yet I harbour this feeling – it's now a hunch – that our friendship will not be long lasting. For this reason my intense love for Gunvor is now bound to such pain. Whenever I see her I want to cry, stroke her softly, hold her, press her to me.

I felt so miserable yesterday. The tears kept on welling up although I don't normally cry very often. In the evening when going to bed, and in the morning when getting up, I could only think of Gunvor. And of how suddenly our friendship had come to an end. Many thoughts came to mind: perhaps there was a secret reason for it, that's why she wants to keep me at a distance. Perhaps . . . she intends to commit suicide . . . on her *own*. Many thoughts entered my head and I resolved to ask her: Tell me the reason, tell me why you don't want to know me any more.

I met her at college. She came up to me, smiling, wearing a red jumper and blue skirt. I immediately went weak at the knees, went terribly dizzy and couldn't contemplate asking her the question. In class I sat a long way from her. On one occasion I had to leave the room to wipe away my tears. I couldn't help crying afterwards, either. It was awful to have Gunvor sitting so far away from me, diligently following the lesson and chatting with her neighbour. I had to make a real effort to stop myself from doing something rash.

When the class was over I followed her into the corridor.

'I want to talk to you.'

'What?'

'I want to know the reason and I want to know whether you were being serious.'

She let out an embarrassed laugh. Childishly, she made a grab for my hands.

'I don't know . . . Yes, perhaps it was all a load of nonsense.'

'Why are you teasing me like that? Do you imagine I find it amusing?'

'I'll wait for you after stenography, we can talk then.'

I waited for her in the corridor. We were supposed to be having a chat. But what was I to say? It was so sad. Gunvor stood there and I asked, 'Shall I go?' She replied, 'I don't care,' and then, 'No, don't go.' 'It will pass.' 'I can't help being like that.' And so I stood there. She laughed occasionally and said, 'You like a scene, an argument, it reminds you of the theatre, of festivals, doesn't it?' I stood there, still uncertain of how it stood between us. A sign said: 'Alms are only given out in agreement with the Kristiania charity organisation.' I read it. It was raining outside. And Gunvor reached out for my hands. I asked, 'Can't you say anything at all? You're torturing me.' Every now and then one of us said something. I said, 'I don't want your charity.' And with her childish look Gunvor said, 'It's passed now, that's the truth.' And then, 'You know I'm mad. Why do you have to behave stupidly?' This sentence hurt me deeply and my whole body suddenly froze: 'You know I'm mad.' That's so sad. I repeated to myself, 'I know she's mad. Why do I have to behave stupidly?' And, as always, I forgave her everything. I said, 'So that's settled.' Then we shared some chocolate that I'd bought her.

From now on my love for her will be even more painful. I was too sure of her and now my punishment is due. Everything, everything about her will cause me pain, even her embraces, because I'll always be thinking: She'll leave. Now she loves me. Tomorrow she'll go. I feel as if I have to cry whenever I see her.

FRIDAY, 31 OCTOBER 1941, LILLESTRØM

Dreams (mine):

1. I want to buy a lipstick. I'm standing in the shop. The shop assistant shows me different quality lipsticks. I try out the colours on a white cloth. None of the colours suit me. Eventually, however, I apply a red one to my lips. I become very ugly, I want to get rid of the red colour, and wipe it all off my lips. I have to hurry to catch a train. The train has not stopped in the usual place but on the opposite side. A small path through the grass leads to it. Mama and Papa are also on the train. I'm delighted that Papa's there and I want to sit next to him.

Analysis: lipstick = the male sex organ. I try out the lipstick *colours* and I'm not happy with any of them: I'm unsatisfied with the opposite sex. It doesn't satisfy me 'mentally'. In the end, however, I do put on lipstick: sexual intercourse. Afterwards I'm ugly and try to wipe the colour away. I have to hurry as the train is waiting for me. So: I have to satisfy my sexual urge before I die. That means: time is flying and I'm still a 'virgin'. I see Musch and Papa on the train. Association: Papa is dead and I wanted Musch to die, too.

2. I'm sitting in a café. Gunvor and a lot of boys are there. There's excellent jazz music playing on the wireless . . . Suddenly I realise that we shouldn't actually be sitting here. The café owner must be a Nazi because he has a wireless.

Analysis: café = room + music = sexual intercourse + desire. Gunvor! is taking part, hence the feeling that it's forbidden.

3. I'm sitting with Gunvor. There's a boy at another table. I like the look of him. I think: If only he wanted to have me. Suddenly he makes a sign with his hand: he wants to meet me at three o'clock. I'm very happy.

Analysis: 3 = the male number. I'm happy that he wants to give me the opportunity to satisfy my sexual urges.

At this point some pages have been torn from the diary. The next text begins without any recognisable connection.

We stood there and asked: Should we each go our own way, or should we stay? I don't think we arrived at any conclusion yesterday. But this morning we got up with such cold eyes and I felt with such certainty: it's over. And yet inside me I loved her just the same as when we said goodbye to each other in town. Just like this: 'Bye bye!' It was as if I'd had her torn from my heart, and in her place were just pain and tears. And behind these a ghastly emptiness. When I put down my pen and think how she's been wrenched away from me – it's so horrific. Pointless, pointless. There's no point in anything any more. Nothing. I feel like I did back in the hospital, when everything was in the dark.

And I'm always thinking of her, how she lay there unconscious, helpless. Of how she's feeling pains and I cannot comfort her. No, I cannot bear it.

Gunvor und Ruth on a trip to Kolsås ridge in autumn 1941.

SUNDAY, 2 NOVEMBER 1941, LILLESTRØM

Back from a magnificent autumn excursion with Karen and Gunvor. Gunvor is behind everything I do. My love for her fills my entire existence. I do not believe I've ever loved anybody as much as her. Well, perhaps Williger and Papa.

TUESDAY, 4 NOVEMBER 1941, LILLESTRØM

Gunvor's dream:

There's a party at Reidar's house. There are more rooms than usual. Reidar gets up and sets the table. Decorates the walls with flowers. Reidar's sister enters one of the rooms and asks her to stay. She goes. Reidar asks Gunvor to stay. She says: I cannot.

Analysis. More rooms than normal: sex life offers more opportunities – homosexuality. The sister enters the room: sexual intercourse. Asks her to stay. She goes. Gunvor goes. Reidar asks her to stay. She cannot.

My dream:

I'm sitting in the theatre. I'm meant to be listening to a Beethoven concert (music). The curtain rises. Horst is standing at the front of the stage. I think: What's he doing here? He disappears behind the scenery. The concert begins and turns out not to be a concert, but an opera cobbled together from various tunes. First of all there is a snow-covered landscape. A girl starts to sing. A tune from *La Bohème*. I'm disappointed; I was expecting music by Beethoven.

Analysis: I imagine sexual intercourse to be like magnificent music (music = desire). But I'm disappointed by the trite melodies, which don't sound right. Horst, who disappeared into the opera house, didn't give me what I was expecting.

Gunvor's mother's dream:

'I dreamed a man came after me and threw knives!'

Symbol: Knife(point!) Knife-throwing: symbol for sexual intercourse.

MONDAY, 10 NOVEMBER 1941, LILLESTRØM

CHANGE
(For Gunvor)

Even the small café is cruel to you today. For you know the white, spotted tablecloth on the table and chubby waitress smiling. You also know the dusty grey flowers and the sky outside. The smell of cakes and freshly cooked waffles suddenly fills you with disgust. You want to be sick. And this same café once gave you a peculiar, slight pleasure. Now you sense: that was long ago.

PRISON

Here the trees are yearning for me, and the snow. Here every black has a red for me, every blue has a yellow. The tree trunks look at me with large eyes and the birds sing my songs that have long slumbered, unloved, within me. Everything turns towards me until I think: Things wish to come to me because I cannot go out to them.

TUESDAY, 11 NOVEMBER 1941, LILLESTRØM

Dreams (mine):

1. I'm with Gunvor, at her house (they've only got one room and a kitchen). But now somebody's living next to them who has lots of rooms. I sneak about over there. There's a wireless in the corner. I think: They must be Nazis. Somebody turns the dial on the wireless.

2. I've got a job in a shop. It's dark there. I'm supposed to be selling clothes. Supposed to be earning two and a half kroner per day. Gunvor arrives. I think: I've got a job now. Now that'll be the end of our friendship as she doesn't have anything to do. Dita appears with a pail; she's meant to be cleaning the floor. She looks terrible. I go around touching the clothes. One of the items is a sort of bathing suit: top and bottoms. I take the bottoms. I'm sent away to do housework: dusting, scouring pots. I don't like it. I don't want to work as a housemaid.

'Don't like being on my own', Ruth writes in a form dated 7 November 1941 for Ullevål Hospital. She receives forms like this every six months following her discharge in March 1941. Each time she writes, 'I feel in perfect health.'

That same night: I'm walking with Gunvor to a station. A few men are standing there wearing women's clothes. I say, 'They must be Russians.' We wait there and listen to them speaking Russian, very cultivated. A Russian is sitting on the roof of the train, which is right beside us, and turning the dial on a wireless: Russian is being spoken.

In a weekly newspaper, a teacher writes about an 'unexplained experience' he had when he was small. He was with his father when, suddenly, he

heard some unearthly music. His father didn't notice anything. He had never
been able to explain where this music had come from. Music is well known
as a symbol for desire.

We were at Karen's yesterday. We played a game. One person says a word
to her neighbour, who then says two words that can be associated with it. I
said to Karen, 'ladder' (symbol of sexual intercourse). The two words that she
associated with ladder were 'suction' and 'relief'.

I don't think there can be any better proof that this symbol really is
anchored in the unconscious.

Karen und Gunvor on Kolsås ridge in 1941. From Ruth's album.

An Artist's Model

NOVEMBER 1941 – MARCH 1942

The Strøm family now treat Gunvor and Ruth as a couple and invite them together for birthday parties. Ruth earns money by modelling for the painter Aasmund Esval (1889–1971), who that autumn has a large exhibition in the artists' hall in Oslo. His studio is at 30 Tollbu gate. Ruth can spot parallels in her relationship with the Oslo painter to that with her Viennese Latin teacher. While she takes off her clothes, Ruth thinks of Esval, 'Do you know that you're the first man who's seen me naked?'

Ruth is still living in Lillestrøm. Her correspondence with England has stopped. After the Japanese attack on Pearl Harbor in December 1941 the USA enters the war. There are memories from Trondheim, where the Germans insulted a Norwegian man in the middle of the street. Ruth's friends tell each other their dreams and try to analyse them. On Christmas Eve, on the train back to Lillestrøm, Ruth meets a distraught Finnish soldier. He's been in the war and there are tears in his eyes. 'My people, every man!' Ruth listens to him.

The registration of Jews in Norway takes place by means of a questionnaire that has to be filled out. We see from Ruth's answer of 4 March 1942 that she'd left the Mosaic faith to which she belonged by dint of her birth. And that she has finished her stenography course. Now she is doing a six-month course at business school.

Gunvor Hofmo's first poems are being published. The relationship between the two of them has stabilised. Although Ruth is worried that it won't last. In late winter she writes, 'I'm sleeping. I'm longing not to be awoken.'

*'After swimming'. Gunvor's father, Erling T. Hofmo, took this photograph
in April 1942 on Drammensveien in Oslo city centre.*

FRIDAY, 14 NOVEMBER 1941, LILLESTRØM

I'm now an artist's model. I want to write about that because it's easy to write about. I don't think it's difficult to capture the mood when I'm standing naked and still in that small, square studio. Most of all, being a nude model is an . . . erotic experience and when I write about it I experience something akin to lust. Perhaps it's wanton to write about it . . . perhaps.

I got an answer to an advertisement: 'Would you please come to my studio, etc.' I went along. Gunvor came with me. My heart was beating fast. I was greeted by a short, very short man, all ready old, with a tired, quite shattered face, shy eyes that wept, and something twisted about his figure and gait. I was to begin immediately.

'Do you know what it means to stand there without any clothes on? Does it bother you?'

'Oh, I'm sure it's not going to be that dangerous.'

Feeling flushed and very distant I tore my clothes off my body. Finally I was standing there, naked. Very white. And I wasn't ashamed. Then I stood on a piece of brown paper. I thought, 'Do you know that you're the first man who's seen me naked?' And I felt something like pride. Pleasure. Shame? I don't know. I modelled for an hour. With brief pauses. On occasions I thought I would pass out. I was very tired. And my mind was totally empty as I stood there. Just like that. Naked. I tried to compose a poem, something. Nonsense: 'In the small square area, me naked, radiant, my own self and yet not me,' etc.

Last time. I want to write it down because thinking about it is still so painful and awful. I had my period. I didn't say anything because I was afraid of losing the work. Money! My knickers were only a little bloody. I thought: It's not a problem. He won't notice. I cannot understand now how I could have thought like that.

I got undressed. I stood there for the first half-hour. Totally still, not moving a muscle. From time to time I would go rigid with horror, terror, I froze inside. I thought: It's going to come . . . It was ghastly. I thought of Maria, I don't know why. When we had a break I wiped the blood away. It was even worse in the second half-hour. I was totally steeped in it. I'd hate to have to relive that experience of thinking: Now and now! If only it had already happened.

I could feel it coming. I froze. It was as if I were made of stone. It was like a tale of woe. I thought: It's over. Then he said, 'Do you want to rest?' I asked, 'Is half an hour over?' He replied, 'Yes, almost.' While I spoke I continued to stand there like a statue. Then I bent backwards and went to have a rest. There was a spot of blood on the brown cardboard.

I was with Gunvor today. We did a little excursion. There was a weekday peace in the woods. The colours are still autumnal. But it's cold already. Gunvor is beside me. The person who, today, is the most beloved and close in the whole world. I've never wept so much as when I thought that it was over between us.

We walked, we looked. We drank coffee in a small, quiet café. There was nobody there. She kissed me. There was a twitch in her eyes that said, 'Come!' I love her eyes. They have such depth that one could fall into them. They are so sad and so good-natured. If I could write poetry I would write about Gunvor's face. We went home. There was a good atmosphere between us.

When Gunvor came to me the day after we'd decided to break off our friendship, and told me she'd thought everything over and that everything we'd said was nonsense, I was so jaded from all the tears and the pain that I almost couldn't feel *happy*, but a sort of peace and calmness came over me. And a mild sadness. I thought: How much will I have to suffer for your sake? Now everything is fine again and we've killed everything we said that night with our words.

SATURDAY, 15 NOVEMBER 1941, LILLESTRØM

Sometimes I think I've finished with this diary. I think I've grown out of it, I've grown older. I've said what has to be said. I'm through with myself. I'm so lacking in any illusions I could be forty years old. Why bother writing in that case? There's no richness or excess of feelings that need a release. All that remains of my good and young sides emerges when I'm with Gunvor.

I have no idea what purpose these pages might still serve. The fact that I continue to write is more habit than anything else. Capturing a few nice hours to fill the time. So I can say to myself later: I can still write something, about myself, about me, my life. Writing, writing. There's a lot that can be written.

But what exists between Gunvor and me is too sacred to be touched by words. Besides that, there's nothing particular to note. Apart from the fact that I still have no home. That's old news. When I think of how homeless I am, think of it as an onlooker, then I almost feel sorry for myself.

There's something else I've been meaning to write about for ages. It was in Trondheim. We were coming back from work. We were tired and drawn. We walked down Prinsens gate, boring old Prinsens gate. We were already standing by the entrance to the YWCA. People were crowding around a few German soldiers . . . and? We approached them. Well, a small German soldier in a green uniform was standing there, railing at a drunken man who couldn't even stand any longer. He was just smiling mischievously, while the German kept on abusing him.

The soldier became irritated. He let the drunken man fall to the ground, who ended up flat on his stomach. The people standing there and watching moved uncomfortably. A young man, slim and with a clever face, stepped forward. I won't forget the expression in his eyes. He said: 'But please . . .'

The soldier got even more annoyed. He went over to the young man. 'Now just move on.'

The Norwegian man understood German. But he didn't leave. The soldier took another menacing pace towards him and started waving his hands around in front of his face. 'Don't you understand German?'

The other man opened his eyes wide: 'No. I don't.'

The soldier was fuming now. I thought: No, he won't do anything to him. But he did do something. He hit the man in the face. Wallop!

I could hear a quiet sigh from those who were standing around. But they stood there stiffly, seriously. There were lots of them. The solider was just one against many. Just him on his own.

The Norwegian's eyes now had a pained expression, and he looked young and gentle. All he said was: 'But please . . .'

The soldier was led away by other Germans who had arrived.

I found the whole scene terrifying. I cannot recall that anything of this sort has upset me as much as that incident. It was strange: Gunvor didn't find it as terrible as I did.

Another typical occurrence these days. The son of Frau Heltene, our
'leader' in the winter camp in Biri, died on the Eastern Front. He was sixteen
years old. I've read his letters: he totally misunderstood National Socialism
and idealised it in such a childish manner, and with such enthusiasm, that you
can't help but smile. He volunteered for the Waffen SS. He was Frau Heltene's
only comfort, her great love.

Hildegard, John and now that. That's how it is every day. Nonetheless it's
idiotic to report it as anything but fact. It would also be quite wrong to start
thinking in terms of 'holy murder'. I think that it's the same for everybody
who reads the daily tally of dead and captured soldiers at breakfast. Feelings
are lost. Only from time to time do you think things like: They're
murdering each other. Yes. And when is it going to end? . . . But that's all.
We've become so blunted. We're not surprised any more. That's why we're
closer to what happens here in Norway.

Even outrage and enthusiasm (?) over some death sentences (and again it's
the workers who are being sentenced to death) don't last longer than an hour.

WEDNESDAY, 19 NOVEMBER 1941, LILLESTRØM

Facts!

A short list of facts, a Norwegian daily digest?

The food situation.

Bread: few people manage with the ration cards. Those undertaking
physically demanding labour get additional rations.

Milk: not rationed until October this year. Now adults receive one-
quarter litre, children under ten one litre per day. All the milk goes to
Finland, Germany etc. Milk rationing led directly to a number of strikes in
Oslo factories, with the result that two Norwegians (Viggo Hansteen, Rolf
Wickstrøm) were shot and others sentenced to 'life' imprisonment.

Butter: goes to Germany. Impossible to find dairy butter. Margarine
getting ever rarer. People are using whale oil for frying.

Meat: you need cards. (Almost) unobtainable. Probably goes to
Germany.

Fish: getting rarer and rarer.

Potatoes: difficult to buy. But people have hoarded them, so it's all right.

Eggs: none.

Chocolate: none (queues).

Cigarettes: none.

Coffee: very little, with ration card. Soon there won't be any coffee ration cards.

Cocoa: none.

Sugar: little, with ration card.

Clothes: clothes card of 300 coupons (a pair of mittens costs 10 coupons).

Shoes: have to apply for them. Application usually approved.

SATURDAY, 22 NOVEMBER 1941, LILLESTRØM

Concerning loneliness. I'm no longer lonely. I have Gunvor. I've staked everything on her. That is why I felt so dreadful when I thought I'd lost her. I cried. I've rarely cried like that. And yet sometimes I long for a man. Without Gunvor I'd never be able to cope without a man. So this man-less-ness is just a gentle pain inside me.

I remember every snippet of conversation I have with men. I love many of the faces of men who walk past. Those that I see in the Deichmann and university libraries.

At the moment Tobben is sitting in the dining room. Frau Strøm's brother. I would love him very much if he only gave me the chance. When he offered me his hand his face felt like a pain to me and I look at him as if he were my lover. Tobben is a very good man. He has such a lovely, calm way of talking, as if he didn't want to hurt people, get too close to them. He said, with a slight singing in his voice, 'So . . . how are you?'

At that moment I loved him very much.

Sometimes I see Jewish people and they have this completely – how shall I put it? – erotic effect on me. They awaken a feeling of love within me. I feel myself drawn to them. Today I saw a small, tiny Jew. He was from Germany and spoke Norwegian with a German accent. He was talking with a blonde girl who was twice his size. I think he was very lonely because there was a thin, coy smile on his lips. A little soft. He was very ugly. Spectacles, big nose and so short. He said, 'I'm a bookworm.' A crooked smile, then: 'Yes, I am a little nervous.'

Oh, you little Jew. It's an unappealing habit of Jews to say of themselves, 'I'm slightly nervous.'

Another Jew in the library. Also from Germany, tall with a bent back, his whole face turned inwards. Eyes deep below the forehead. Looked somewhat blind and moved nervously as if he had poor sight. Nodded his head.

I love Jewish people. I'd like to go up to them and say, 'I love you.' I'd like to kiss them.

There was another Jewish man in the library. He used to be in my class. In the Frogner school. He's from England. His face is also somehow painful. A finely curved nose, a delicate mouth, deep eyes. He looks so young, as if he'd just turned eighteen, and so Jewish, so fine looking, so painfully fine looking. I used to see him at school a lot. Once he said 'Cheer up!' to me. And to his brother, 'She is always so sad.' I'd really love to have kissed him today, but he just gave me a fleeting glance.

Those are the men in my life. Then, of course, there's the old man I model for. I'm just waiting for my love to be consecrated. He's so short and has a hunchback. He's the first man who has seen me naked. Today I passed out. When I leave him I always feel as if I'm parting from a friend; there's something that binds us. I'd love to know what's hiding behind his face. We speak very little.

'Is it cold?'

'How dark it is today!'

'Hold your right arm a little further to the left.'

SUNDAY, 23 NOVEMBER 1941, LILLESTRØM

It's totally unjust not to have a home. It's totally unjust to have to take a mean comment from Frau Strøm.

MONDAY, 1 DECEMBER 1941, LILLESTRØM

It's very interesting working as a model. You have contact with so-called artists. You learn things: ah, so these are the select individuals who produce works of art. But very often these 'works of art' turn out to be anything but art.

Esval, the short, hunchbacked man, is very sweet. I think that deep down he is a very good man. He has a haggard, wizened face. And yet there's something childish in his eyes and his smile.

He draws me with a pencil on ordinary newsprint. Sometimes he captures a position excellently. But no individual perception, no individual *style* ever emerges in his drawings. His pictures that hang on the wall are very poor. Not art. But he's sweet. Today he gave me five kroner extra and said with his sweet smile, 'I've sold such a lot.' That was nice. Not just because of the five kroner.

Another painter drew me recently. I believe his name is Refsum. He drew me and then coloured in the drawing superbly. Once I had one arm over my breasts, the other hanging down limply. His drawing was wonderful. Perhaps wonderful is an exaggeration. To put it better, there was an individual *charm* about his drawings, especially in the colours. Today I sat for three women. Two 'painted' appallingly. On canvas. One of them used completely lifeless colours (Jensen) and made serious mistakes in her composition. The other one's composition (Nordahl-Lund) was even more inaccurate and she kept on coming out with profound comments, especially about art. The third one (Refsum) painted the human figure fairly well. It was lovely to listen to them talk about their work. Another thought I had was: I imagine it won't be long before I'm fed up with the so-called artist's crisis.

1. A few days ago five more Norwegians were shot: sabotage.

2. Politics is now mixing with the food issue: unwilling and lazy people don't get as much as hard-working individuals, etc.

3. Rostov was evacuated by the Germans.

4. The Norwegians are continuing to hold out. I love them. They are a brave people. They won't be forced to support the NS.

TUESDAY, 9 DECEMBER 1941, LILLESTRØM

It's funny that the newspapers don't mean anything any more. All that's in them, 'advance, retreat, number of deaths, bombing raid', doesn't concern me any more. I stop myself from thinking about it . . . it won't make any difference. I also avoid anything that makes me feel even more impotent. Either one ought to do 'something' or, if one is not in a position to act, one ought not to concern oneself with politics at all.

I heard the so-called Olavsguttene* singing in the Trefoldighetskirke. It was very beautiful. At the end they sang '*Ja, vi elsker*'.† Everybody stood up. These were pure voices singing, never before had I felt just how much I love Norway. I had to stop myself from crying. I've never felt like that for Austria. I heard a man behind me breathing deeply. A woman was sitting with him on the bench, weeping. Her whole body was trembling. Three German women were standing next to me. I felt that we were all as one. They sang, '*Når dets fred, dets fred slår leir* . . . [When its peace, its peace will be one]'. It was painful.

Gunvor's dream:

'I'm walking down a hill. Reidar comes up to me. He asks me to go with him. I tell him I cannot as I have to go into town.'

* A boy's choir in Oslo.

† The Norwegian national anthem.

FRIDAY, 12 DECEMBER 1941, LILLESTRØM

My life is playing out very peacefully between 'business school', modelling and Gunvor. The days spent in her home are the best. A childish dream has started to stir inside me again: to draw, paint, live for 'art'. If I could bring this to fruition my life would not be in vain.

Sometimes I crave a home. A place where I know I wouldn't be a burden to anyone. Musch is sitting there and Dita. But that's very far away. As America has also joined the war I won't hear anything from them any more . . .

I wanted to write more. But there's nothing but emptiness in me.

Oh yes: Thorolf, Gunvor's brother, took me out. I cannot stand him. He has a naked face like a baby's bottom. On the one hand he fancies himself terribly, very pleased with his banal opinions and bad jokes; on the other he's very uncertain when faced with the opposite sex and he cannot assert himself – I'm sure he suffers from an inferiority complex. When I accepted his invitation to go to the cinema, he of course immediately felt on top of the world. He sat next to me and pressed his knee against mine. I found it so repulsive and yet pleasant. As with Reidar, I couldn't look Thorolf in the eye either. I didn't like him enough.

MONDAY, 22 DECEMBER 1941, LILLESTRØM

A dream (mine):

Esval is in a room. He's small and hunchbacked, as in real life. He writes me a letter, opens the door and puts the letter on the threshold. From the letter I can see that he loves me. Among other things he writes, 'I don't have enough paper and pencil to write any more to you.' I'm happy that he's written to me. I want to show that I'm kind, so I give him paper and a pencil.

Analysis, discussed with Gunvor She analyses it quite correctly (as ever she's very sharp). Esval, who's much older than me and yet does not come across as masculine, says: I'm not man enough. Paper and pencil (very clever symbol if you think about it). I give him (I'm still young) his virility.

WEDNESDAY, 24 DECEMBER 1941,
LILLESTRØM – (SO-CALLED CHRISTMAS)

I'm alone this time. But that's not why I want to write. There's a war going on outside. I've often thought it, but I've never felt it as strongly as today. So dreadfully close.

I took the train to Lillestrøm to celebrate Christmas with myself. An old Norwegian and another man got on. He didn't look Norwegian, more Slavic, with slightly slanted eyes and a very good face. I think he was drunk, for he just talked to himself. Incoherent words. Gesticulated with his hands. He didn't talk Norwegian either but a totally foreign language, sometimes a few German words. He laughed, smiled.

The man with him said, 'We come from Finland. You believe he's drunk, but he's got mental shock.'

Nothing happened . . . But he still sat there . . . talking nonsense, hid his face in his hands. He straightened himself, saluted, then laughed scornfully. Occasionally he looked around wildly, anxiously. Then he looked upwards with begging eyes.

He said, 'My people. Every man.'

His face was lifeless. He acted as if he were loading a gun, then he fell backwards with his arms stretched out.

The most awful thing was when he started to cry.

I just thought: war.

I wouldn't part with the memory of this Finnish solider, not even for a nice, cosy Christmas Eve. How a wet streak ran down his nose when he said, 'My people. Every man.' How he beat his chest and said, 'My people, my people,' then laughed laconically; his eyes were so dead from sadness.

I'd like the image of him to engrave itself on me like that of the Jew who had attempted suicide and become blind as a result.

I'd so love to have kissed him.

It's this feeling of helplessness: who are you and what can you do? Outside they're committing murder, letting each other die, being killed. Young men, sixteen-year-old boys who have never touched a woman. They're being killed. Those with soft hearts are going mad, pleading towards the heavens and weeping. It's inconceivable. Each time this feeling of helplessness causes the same pain. Perhaps it's worse the older you get.

There's one thing I know: I'm a socialist. I'd like to have told him this when he was crying: we must 'fight' for socialism. 'Fight' is an old word.

Even the feeling of helplessness is good if you feel it deep inside you. This helplessness becomes strength if you're aware of it at your very core. What isn't good is that this feeling of helplessness, like any other profound feeling, also passes. That the image of the weeping soldier will fade, after a day. What makes a person great, what makes him capable of action is this: the ability to sustain a feeling for years on end with the same intensity, to feel an injustice bitterly even if it is not new. Such people have to become fighters. But we, who when we feel a pain, an injustice, console ourselves with the fact that it will disappear within a week at most, we have no right to open our mouths and complain.

Yes, we're far more affected by a moving war book than by a terrible report in the newspaper. 'A thousand dead.' 'Hand-to-hand combat. Many men died.' What does 'hand-to-hand combat' say to us, what do '10,000 deaths' mean? Even if it was printed that there were 1,000,000 deaths we'd just open our eyes wide. We would try to count – 'One, two, three . . .' – but we'd soon give up. Even one and two are just numbers. It must be that we have too little imagination. That we're too lazy to think through what's printed black on white. And also: we're used to it. Oh, this cursed habitualness. For as long as I can remember we've been served up death for breakfast. Should we let ourselves get grey hairs over it? What do I care about other people? I am me, my own world. I don't know them. They're shadows.

Then somebody comes along and says, 'Comrades, every man.' And he weeps. And then it passes through me like a happy certainty. No, I am not just me. To be 'me' I have to endeavour to include all the others in my heart. All those who hold out their hands and fall to the ground. They've all just succumbed to a madness. Deep down they're good people. Otherwise they would not be capable of crying.

I'm getting emotional and that doesn't suit somebody of my age. I ought to be disillusioned because that befits our generation. Now, be quiet.

My God, the things they've perpetrated against us! Everything,

everything, they trampled every tiny belief until it became so cold and deso-
late within us. They haven't left us a single ideal. If you don't have a heaven
you ought to believe that it's because life is for living on earth. We've all
become resigned at twenty-one. Resigned to life as it is, resigned to violence,
injustice, war. It's there between every line. Nobody should have suffered like
that, not even for an exceedingly good cause. How pointless, how base, that
one's life is of no use. People suffer because Germany wants colonies, because
great powers are used to scrambling for raw materials. Because . . . because
. . . because . . . It's the same as ever: there is sorrow in the world because of
suffering. The Jews have suffered in Germany, they have not understood the
reason for their suffering, because there is no sense in suffering. Sorrow can
never be a justification for suffering. And the highest goal is: not to cause
suffering. Rather suffer with the sufferers than cause suffering to others.

THURSDAY, 25 DECEMBER 1941, LILLESTRØM

Better to recount dreams about our conflicts than write diary entries.

Dream: I'm together with young boys and girls. The boys are very
feminine. I like one of them and he likes me. He looks very gentle and girl-
like. A good relationship develops between us. As we get to know each other
better we become physically closer. He kisses me. I think it's marvellous. Our
mouths cling together, they don't come apart. In my presence people talk of
us as 'engaged'. I say to him (as the dream develops he looks almost like a
girl): 'If you hadn't come along I'd be with Gunvor.' I only say it to see how
he will react. He replies, 'I know.' I tell him that I have homosexual tendencies. He is not surprised. He says, 'Now you have me and so you must end it.
We'll see how things go. If you last a month we can get married.' Then
Gunvor appears. She puts her arm round my shoulders. I love it and I think
that I have to tell him that it's not right. I can't just end it because I've found
a boy.

Dream: I'm naked. I'm very ashamed. People are everywhere, but I'm
naked. Finally I manage to dive into a bush so that nobody can see my nakedness. But somehow I have to get away from there and so I say quietly to Dita,

'Fetch a cab.' A sort of carriage pulled by two horses drives up. We leave. We go along an avenue, with shrubs left and right. A girl staggers around the carriage, she wants to sit on top of it but she can't manage. I think: Just sit, for goodness sake! A drunken man stands in front of her. He sits on the carriage. The girl takes a bicycle and cycles off. I notice that she has my watch round her wrist. I say, 'Give me my watch.' We keep going. I'm still naked and I ask the coachman to stop so that I can get dressed in the bushes. But he keeps on driving. We arrive at a sort of cave. There are a few girls there. One of them almost falls into a chasm. German soldiers appear and say that they will blow up the cave, which is in a cliff. We're very worried, I fear for my life. The Germans say, 'There will only be ten bangs.' We count three. I'm scared. I run down some steps to a room where girls are reeling around a machine that makes sparks. (A spark flies with every explosion.) I stray between this room and one higher up. Each time I try to enter this room above a dog bites me.

I think of the soldier in the train. I love him. It's terrible to see a man crying. I'd like to have the opportunity to demonstrate my love to him, to kiss him. I can still see his wet face.

He was sitting opposite me. Suddenly he went very quiet, made himself comfortable, folded his arms, screwed up his eyes . . . and looked at me. He shook my hand to say goodbye.

SATURDAY, 27 DECEMBER 1941, LILLESTRØM

I was with Thorolf. There was one bit of sexual rubbing. I can't stand Thorolf, although it feels good when he touches me. That's how desperate it's got. So, in addition to all the other setbacks, now there's this.

This is how it must be when one's in love. Like my feelings when I think of the soldiers in the war. I long for him.

ORDENE

Ordene, lysende stille
skal jeg finne
gi dem til deg,
hamre noen øyeblikk sammen
inn under evighetsrammen
så aldri du glemmer meg.

Billeder, ånd og jord
det som er deg,
smerte, uro og håp
det som er meg:
Vidne ved ordenes ord
som vi aldri skal finne,
vidne ved våre øyne
søkende i blinde
at ilden kan ikke dø!

GUNVOR HOFMO

Tegn. av Trygve Mosebekk.

*'Ordene' ('Words') was one of Gunvor Hofmo's first published poems.
It appeared on 19 July 1941 in* Magasinet For Alle.

SUNDAY, 4 JANUARY 1942, LILLESTRØM

Feelings between people move around so erratically. I still love Gunvor. But I'm worried that soon I won't love her any more. It's dreadful. I've already had these feelings before. I saw her face – it looked as nice and good-natured as ever with those eyes, that mouth – but it was only a memory of something that used to be. And I looked at her and looked at her, stared, but it was no use. It's worse to look at a person and to want to love them but not be able to than to look and suffer with the feeling that my love is unrequited.

It had got so bad that I told her yesterday. But when she was sitting there in the kitchen, suddenly everything fell away and her eyes, her eyes were serious. Then I was in love with her more than ever. It's true, I've never been so in love as yesterday. I was filled with such brightness.

At the moment I love her. But I sense that I don't love her enough.

Nobody has ever been to me what Gunvor is now. She's my friend and beloved. She is all life, goodness itself . . . Say nothing about it. Gunvor's also writing poetry.

EARLY 1942, LILLESTRØM

[Esval is like] a friend. He shows me his pictures and we talk about all manner of things. He is also fond of me and I 'flirt' with him; I like it because I'm in charge and because with him it's out of the question.

Esval/Ruth really reminds me of Williger/Ruth. The only difference is that Williger was obviously taller. And I loved Williger. Why did he not kiss me? He was tall, after all. The most Esval dares to do is to put his arm round my shoulder and he has to stand on his tiptoes to do that. And then his breath smells. *C'est ça.* But it's nice to discuss pictures with him.

A dream of mine analysed by Gunvor:

Uncle Oskar, Strøm, Papa and I are sitting at a table. Frau Strøm is there but out of sight. The table is in front of the door. We're all embarrassed because the table is bigger than the door. We push it in front of the door and put it lengthways. Fossli (the neighbour here) appears and we don't know how to hide this great shame from him.

Analysis. Table bigger than door: obstacle. Strøm (married), Papa (my father), Uncle Oskar (my uncle) are sitting at the obstacle. The three men in question sit with me at a table that is bigger than the door = entrance = sexual intercourse.

SATURDAY, 21 FEBRUARY 1942, LILLESTRØM

Esval's dream:

'I'm wearing skis and want to take the lift. But I find it embarrassing, as I only want to go to the first floor . . . Then I go into the street with my skis and try to get on to the tram. Everything happens very slugglishly, I don't

Skjemaet utfylles i 3 eks.
Helst maskinskrevet!   *Dato* 4/3, 1942.

Spørreskjema

for

jøder i Norge

fra

.... Romerike .... politidistrikt.

```
Etternavn .....................        Maier
(For kvinner også pikenavnet)
Samtlige fornavn ..............        Ruth
(Bruksnavnet understrekes)
Født (sted, datum, år) ... Wien 10/11 1920 ............ I hvilket land ... Østerike.
Privatadr. (gt., nr., by) ..... Storgaten 7, Lillestrøm
...................................................... Privattlf. ....2
Nuværende religionssamfund ..... Intet ............ Siden når ... 1926.
Tidligere religionssamfund ........ Mosaiske ved fødslen.
Familieforhold: (Ugift, gift, enkestand, skilt) .......... Ugift.
For- og etternavn på ektefellen ...............................
(For kvinner pikenavnet)
Ektefellens fødested, datum og år ...........................
Har ektefellen jødisk innslag i familien? .....................
Antall barn: .................................................
                        (Navn)                (Alder)    (Oppholdssted)
................................................................
................................................................
................................................................
Nuværende erhvervsyrke ............ Intet.           Selvstendig? Ja/Nei
Yrke av fag ..................................................
Event. biyrker ...............................................
Teoretisk og praktisk utdannelse . Artium. Eksamen i stenografi. Går f.t. på
.......... ½ års handelsskole.
Militær utdannelse .................. Ingen.
Offentlige tillitshverv .............. Nei
Medl. av fagl. organisasjoner før ..... Nei
Medl. av fagl. organisasjoner nu ....... Nei
Medl. av andre foreninger og organisasjoner ..... Nei

Har De vært frimurer? .. Nei..... Fra.................. til.............
Hvilken grad? .................. Hverv ....................
Nasjonalitet .......... Tysk.............. Statsborgerskap .... Tysk.
Når kom De til Norge ...... 30/1 1939.
Siste oppholdssted utenfor Norge ..... Tyskland.
```

2. 42. nelson trykk, oslo

Early in 1942 all Jews in Norway received a questionnaire from the police which they had to fill out in triplicate. Ruth Maier's form, dated 4 March 1942, was sent to the police headquarters of Romerike district.

manage to get on. In the end I go to a ski repairman to have my very battered skis mended. He says that he can repair them. He bends the ski tips upwards, but then breaks them off.'

It's all very clear: Ski with ski tips – the ski is a symbol for the sex organ. With his skis he wants to get on to the tram, which is the symbol for sexual intercourse. But he cannot. So he goes to the ski repairman. The skis are battered. He says that they can be mended, but he breaks off the tips. Makes them completely unusable.

It's understandable that he wants to take the lift with his skis. But why does he think it embarrassing that he's only going to the first floor? Doesn't that really mean that he finds it embarrassing that he cannot get past the first floor anyway?

SATURDAY, 14 MARCH 1942, LILLESTRØM

Sometimes it just turns up as if from afar. My relationship with Esval reminds me of the relationship with Williger. Sometimes it's so similar that I can't help smiling and I think I'm dreaming. Recently, for example, Esval said, 'You've been chewing this pencil . . . It's a reminder of you . . . I almost feel like keeping it.' Williger would stand a bit further away at his desk, and with the stump of a small yellow pencil he would say, 'I have to keep this pencil. You've been biting it.' The thought of Williger can still give me a little warmth sometimes.

I'm an artist's model. That's my life now. I also harbour a small, innocent dream: to become a painter. Will it come true? It will soon be spring, but why should I be looking forward to that? No. I'm afraid and I'm quite happy that it's still cold. When spring arrives so do all those indefinable yearnings, that great dissatisfaction. Move out! But where to? Staying all summer in Lillestrøm? How inconceivable. Then I'll be without a man as well. That's why I'm happy that it's still winter. I am sleeping. I do not long to be awakened.

Watercolour: 'Alexander Kielland square', Oslo 1942.
On 27 March 1942 Ruth writes, 'Gunvor really likes this picture.'

Spring is upon us

MARCH–JULY 1942

Ruth Maier writes more seldom in her diary. She is still living in Lillestrøm and travelling to Oslo to work as an artist's model, now also for the sculptor Gustav Vigeland, whom she admires: 'His hands are still young. But I get the impression that he's a wise man.'

It is spring. Ruth is in high spirits. On the train she allows a stranger to kiss her. She is sexually provocative towards Aasmund Esval. In her diary, she hardly mentions her relationship with Gunvor.

Ruth paints watercolours of urban scenes, often cemeteries. One watercolour from March 1942 is of the Christ cemetery, near the Deichmann library and the Swedish Margareta church. Another watercolour shows two female figures by blocks of flats, which can be identified as opposite Alexander Kielland square on the way to Gunvor's place. Ruth is teaching Gunvor German. In her textbook next to the last 'homework' it says: Nesodden, 15 August 1942.

The Hofmo family take a holiday in a summer house in Nesodden. Ruth sometimes spends the weekend there. All the 'unspeakable pain' of summer is condensed into a few prose poems that Ruth writes here. Ruth misses the solidarity with Jewish people she used to feel in the past.

In spring 1942 Ruth modelled for Gustav Vigeland.
The photograph shows the plaster figure 'Surprised', a work that Vigeland had
begun way back in 1904. The face is probably that of his model at the time,
Inga Syvertsen. In 2002 the sculpture was cast in bronze
and is now in Oslo's Frognerpark.

END OF MARCH 1942, LILLESTRØM

Spring is now coming, very gently. Today it almost made me drunk. The air is so mild, everything is incredibly black: the trees, the people. I just move along and drag my legs with me. And I feel as if I were nothing but an eye . . . All things make me rich . . .

Introduction: on the train. I'm standing and looking out through the open carriage door. Outside the landscape is white and mild . . . it's already twilight. A man, tall and broad, is standing next to me. He says, 'Lovely weather, nice breeze.' I say, 'Yes, fantastic!' Then I can feel him getting closer to me. I feel: spring is upon us. There was desire within him and me.

Then he kissed me. I kissed him. It was very nice. Unfortunately it just wasn't enough. Sometimes I have such a strong desire . . .

There are even some moments when I'm modelling for Esval that I think: Why don't you kiss me, take me? But he's not man enough. And yet he loves me so much. He sits there with his hands hanging by his side and looks at me so sweetly. But all I can do is ridicule him. That's how I am. Because this Saturday is the last time I'll be modelling for him (I've now got some other work: varnishing or God knows what), perhaps I'll kiss him then. But his breath smells and his forehead is so dry and wrinkly.

I'm also modelling for Vigeland. The man whose work I really love: his *Mann med kvinne i fanget* (Man with woman on lap), *Mor med barn* (Mother and child), 'Camilla Collett monument', 'Wergeland' etc. He's old, fat and his hair is totally white. But his hands are still young. He's working on a female figure for his controversial bridge in Frognerpark.

He's nice to me. Tells me sweet stories from his life: from snails he ate in France to a Christ model who cheated him. And yet I've never got the impression that he's a wise man.

FRIDAY, 27 MARCH 1942,
LILLESTRØM – (DITTL'S BIRTHDAY)

I was frightfully dizzy today. The spring is to blame. I went up to Esval. I was angry with him. I couldn't bear the sight of him. I sat there on the chair and he drew a nude. I felt terribly uneasy. My whole body was prickling. I could scarcely control myself: I wanted him to make approaches to me and more. I breathed heavily. And yet at the same time I couldn't bear him.

I provoked him. Appealed to his male instinct: 'You're not the type of man who gets anywhere. One doesn't ask women for permission.'

He sat there and got smaller and smaller. I went further. I smiled. I laughed at him. In the end I told him about the man on the train who had kissed me without seeking my permission.

Suddenly he put down his sketch pad on the table and rushed towards me. I was naked. He took my head in his hands and wanted to kiss me. He succeeded in kissing me a bit. He kissed in a voracious way. Finally!

I pushed him away. He began drawing again and said, 'That was your fault.'

I was satisfied. He shone like a newborn baby. I felt very calm. I'd got what I wanted. I didn't tease him again.

Edla said, 'You like being alone, don't you. You're as lonely as you were in the first couple of years. A normal person couldn't stand it.'

I remember . . . People used to consider me very peculiar. I picked flowers in the evenings. I stood naked in front of the mirror and yearned for a man. Oh, and how I yearned!

I would go for walks. Alone. I talked to myself. No, not to myself but to somebody who walked beside me, whom nobody could see. Whenever a car came I would run to the edge of the street. I remember. Once a car came and woke me from my thoughts. The tears flowed. I felt lonely.

These memories! Perhaps it's spring that brings them back.

I really must write. Even if the window is closed and the blinds are down. It was damp and cold this evening. I must write. About my pictures, perhaps. I've painted a black cemetery with a church in the background. There are black trees between the gravestones. The church is yellowy-brown, the sky blue. I really like it.

Watercolour: 'Churchyard behind the Deichmann library', March 1942.

I've also painted Alexander Kielland square (watercolour). Gunvor really likes this picture.

TUESDAY, 31 MARCH 1942, LILLESTRØM

Gunvor said to me with narrowed eyes: 'The more I think about it – becoming something – the more foolish I feel. I mean, you cannot become something . . . well, perhaps a better person.'

As she said this I was suddenly aware as perhaps never before of how stupid the impertinent demand to 'become something' is. As if that were decisive: this or that career, such and such an income. As if human beings were all the same size and shape . . . As if we could stop at some point and be satisfied with what we had achieved. As if we didn't have to go on any further, ever further. As if the 'becoming something' had any meaning for us, our *inner* selves.

Spring is taking its time. The evenings are cold, but nice and light already . . . 'tender'. Perhaps spring is responsible for this new emotion developing inside me. It's good because it's so new.

SATURDAY, 9 MAY 1942, LILLESTRØM – ON THE TRAIN BETWEEN LILLESTRØM AND OSLO

THE STRANGER

And suddenly a stranger reminds me of you. The eyes, the mouth, and your mouth, your eyes. The hands doing and leaving, with woeful memories, which touch, touch me as if I'd once loved you . . . So perhaps that's why I love you, you sweet, dead man.

We ought to have told each other more.

Oh, I forget. You see. I forgot how much divides us, and I'm starting to see you as one of the living again.

'We ought to have told each other more.' That almost sounds like hope. And I'm not hopeful.

So be good. Perhaps this is the last time I'll write. Perhaps there will come other times.

MAY 1942, LILLESTRØM

I saw a film not long ago. It was like it used to be: the next day I went around wrapped in something warm, something indescribable, as if in a dream. The memory of the film which made me feel so good. Such an experience.

It was a Swedish film. It was called *Ett brott* = *A Crime*.

I've just been thinking of the scenes that I particularly enjoyed. When the murderer, in a shattered voice, suddenly says to his father, 'Shall I pardon you?' and weeps.

When he touched his wife's hands when she visits him and says, 'More.'
Then the fantastic love scene between the murderer and his wife.
It didn't seem at all as if it was acted by people. Or, by *people*.

JUNE 1942, LILLESTRØM

BRIGHT NIGHTS

*For me, these bright nights are as if somebody has opened my eyes wide and
I cannot close them again. They're dreadful, crazy, as if I had been born
blind, in vain. I always yearn to get away from this endless, dreadful, bright
darkness; to the other, black, merciful nights. Only there will I inhale the
austere, long-wished-for peace, that I may sleep blissfully on your breast.
Oh night. And to see nothing.*

SATURDAY, 20 JUNE 1942, LILLESTRØM

I was in a synagogue. It was very strange. The Jews arrived, well dressed with
hats on their heads. One, with a white scarf and black cap, was praying before
a sort of altar. He prayed and sang. The Jews would frequently join in, half
singing and half speaking. (It was like the inside of a beehive.) When I closed
my eyes it was like being in the Orient. Occasionally I could make out
'Adonai'. That's Hebrew for 'God'.

I didn't feel as if I belonged there. I was a stranger. The Jews had black
hair, they were short and dark. I saw them as Jews and myself . . . as . . . a
non-Jew. There was something inside me that held me back from them. It
used to be different.

I was very close to the Austrian soldiers again. I wanted to talk to them.
My people, I want to be able to say. And yet they're not my people at all. Their
language stirs deep in my soul. On the train I consoled one of them. He was
talking to a Norwegian girl. She asked him where he was from. From
Austria, he said. It made me feel so good. Afterwards I saw lots of them with

their green peaked caps. They were so familiar to me. Their language is like a lullaby.

I've come to the remarkable conclusion that I don't know the Jews after all. It's very sad. I'd like to be with them again. To love them unconditionally. Like when I was with Dita in the Zionist Union. They sang Hebrew songs. Back then I had a sense of where I belonged.

JUNE 1942, LILLESTRØM

I've read a good book. In English. *The Life of Oscar Wilde* by Frank Harris.

JULY 1942, LILLESTRØM

It's now a year since we went to Trondheim.

SUNDAY, 12 JULY 1942, LILLESTRØM

NOTHING EXISTS

Nothing exists save for the emptiness that trembles here in my breast. Oh, those grand words that you gave me, where are they now? The window over there that faces the bright summer, the reddening clouds that spread out over the golden crown of a quivering tree; if not that, then what do I wish for? What else have I wished for? And yet, omniscient one, this emptiness — from where did it come, if not from a bright summer of unspeakable pain?

From Ruth's photograph album: River Gudbrandsdalslågen near Kvam.
View from Forbrigd farm on the eastern side of the valley towards the south.

Ruth, Gunvor and Karen in August 1942 in Rondane. Ruth titled the last page of her photograph album: 'Climbing the Storronden'.

Her own place

AUGUST–NOVEMBER 1942

In autumn Ruth gets a small room of her own in a hostel for young women at Sankthanshaugen, in the centre of Oslo. She earns money by decorating souvenirs and takes drawing classes at the art and crafts college. Gunvor visits sometimes. Many of the entries are written in Norwegian, including the last four prose poems. There are a few short pieces in French.

In her diary Ruth describes the huge round-up of 25 October 1942, when Jewish men were arrested throughout the country. Ruth mentions that Terboven* has been checking who is staying at the hostel. Ruth's diary entries continue until 12 November.

The second round-up of Jews begins in the capital at dawn on 26 November. This time women and children are arrested as well. On the Donau, 532 Jews are deported from Norway to Stettin, from where they are sent on to Auschwitz in goods trains. A prisoner number is given to 186 men and these are made to do forced labour. Nine of them survive. Women, children and those incapable of work are killed in the gas chambers immediately on arrival.

Gunvor Hofmo later said that she had wanted to accompany Ruth on board. She was stopped by a German soldier who shouted, 'Stop there! Go away!' As she was being driven away, she yelled, 'Is she your friend or mine?'

* Josef Terboven, Nazi commissioner during the occupation of Norway.

TUESDAY, 18 AUGUST 1942, LILLESTRØM

I really will be moving away from here soon. Then life will 'begin': the struggle for one's daily bread, as it's so nicely put. It's different from how I imagined it when I was young. I'm twenty-two now . . . I work with these souvenir things. Although I did sense back then that I might be able to do something with my painting.

It's not that long ago that I was going around as if in a dream. Every hour I heard this whispering in my ear: I will paint pictures. It was as if I was experiencing a new spring. I wasn't sure whether I could paint, whether I had the talent; but I was convinced that it would occupy me, somehow justify my existence. But that was a long time ago. When I look at my pictures now I recoil. I feel sick.

To fill the void that has appeared I throw myself into my books. I'm reading like a demon. And then I'm 'working'. Yes, yes.

I just wish the war were over. Then I'd leave here. Travel. See things. But depart from oneself? Who's capable of that?

And then I had the idea of going to university. But I haven't even done that. What use would it be? To sit there, poring over books. What I want is life. And yet. I'd like to know more. Oh, I'm sure I'm too old for it.

TUESDAY, 1 SEPTEMBER 1942, OSLO

RAIN

I walk along the street, I walk because it is raining and my hair will get wet. While others stand anxiously, umbrella in hand, stand by the wall, watching, I walk in the rain. Just a tree reflected somewhere in the puddle. Everything else is blurred. Oh well. I remember different rain when I was a child, when there was just one window in the living room. The rain was so different, more like salt.

Pencil drawing of a street scene in Oslo.

AT THE HOSTEL

Finally! In your room. Shut the door. Like that. Shut out the world when you shut the door. The world is outside. Here, you are here. Do not weep because you are finally alone. There are your books! They stand like candles, stand like holy candles, smiling. Oh, the eternal smile of books. Here is your window. With the cross, the ever austere accuser that wants you to bear this suffering without complaint. So be silent. And do not start when a door opens. Nobody is coming to you. To you nobody is coming!

Untitled watercolour from 1942.

SEPTEMBER 1942, OSLO

It's been a while now since I moved from Lillestrøm to Oslo. Here I'm living in a small room with a view on to a backyard. I'm right down at the bottom. Opposite there's a yellow, windowless wall, no sky at all. There's a small bookshelf by my bed. It's dark in here and the lamp, a white hospital lamp

Watercolour: 'Longing', 1942.

high up in the ceiling, doesn't light it up adequately. Gunvor sometimes comes in her grey coat. I sit and read.

I'm reading a lot at the moment. I work until three o'clock . . . decorating souvenirs . . . wooden things. At four o'clock I go to a drawing class. Six o'clock I'm back home. I attend drawing classes. Why? Within me there's a dormant dream: to become a painter. An artist! Is it vanity, a frantic attempt to salvage something from this general collapse? I have a white smock. But do I have the strength in me to create, endure, sacrifice? Oh, I could sacrifice, I could sacrifice for all sorts of things: for socialism and peace, for knowledge and beliefs. But sacrifice for art? For the *sake of art*? Not for the sake of sacrifice! And do I have the energy, the strength to put everything into painting? *To see the world with the eye of a painter*. That's hard. And you have to be bursting at the seams with your art. Oh, I feel I'm so small and I don't know how I have the nerve to think about it. And yet: if I have paints, and I paint, and I succeed. A blue and a red! And it blends. A mood develops. Then I feel happy.

I walk down the street. See a house, a tree. Sky. I think: I'll paint that, later . . . But that's what gives me doubts, this later. Why do I say later? If I were an artist (for I must be an artist now already if I'm ever to be one), if I were an artist I ought to paint everything I see, everything that grabs me. But I'm afraid. Yes, I'm afraid. I set my whole future on each watercolour that I begin. And if it goes wrong, then . . . Oh. It's not as if there's a fire within me, consuming me with the idea of painting. I have a small talent that I'm carefully nurturing, gingerly nurturing.

And yet! If my talent were a thousand times smaller than it is. And if nobody had told me that my colours are nice. That's not what concerns me. What concerns me is the ability to be totally saturated by one's art. To paint as another might eat and drink. Because he needs to. Not to sit down, force oneself and say: I've got to make an attempt now, I've got to prove that I have talent. I'll paint now. No, I was not born for art.

I think this a lot at the moment. I'm one of a type. I've read about myself in books. I'm one of those who . . . oh yes, they've got talent, they write poems, short poems, and read books, and in the past they wanted to be actors. They're interested in literature. And they paint small pictures in pretty colours, they love pictures, are interested in literature and poetry. God knows what they're not interested in. It's easy to think of them too highly. Perhaps they look a little interesting. As if they've overexerted themselves reading. Some say these people are intelligent because they wear glasses. And from time to time in conversation they say something . . . good. They like discussions, you see. But not anything with a serious basis. All told it's superficial.

Oh, in the past I seriously believed that I had the *talent*, at least, to enter into something. I believed I had the will to get to the bottom of something. To study, maybe. To get to the bottom of something. I'm discovering that I don't even possess that. I'm attending drawing school . . . perhaps just in a frantic attempt to preserve an illusion. Oh, how I sometimes loathe myself because of this blasted drawing! Why are you vain? I think. You're still doing small watercolours and you think that gives you the right . . . yes, you feel you are being 'summoned' to become an artist. In the same way that another sets out to become a shoemaker.

Watercolour: 'The palace park', 1942.

I ought to be able to do just as much as other people. I'll succeed in drawing just as well as thousands of others who live from selling their pictures. I don't doubt that. What I doubt is my ability to *experience*. To experience the world through the eyes of an artist. And it's not just that I must be able to experience, to see it as a painter, I must also feel the need to express my experience. If only I didn't like colours so much, if only I had never painted those small watercolours that I do like. Sometimes I feel that the longing to become an 'artist' makes me tired, it drains me. The awareness that a picture must be created from what I see takes away from me the ability to experience.

Oh no! First I'm starting to analyse, then . . . It's a curse to be so self-absorbed.

Gunvor's brother, Thorolf, will most likely be sent to Dikemark Hospital. That's the way it is.

FRIDAY, 25 SEPTEMBER 1942

There was an air raid today. In honour of the Reich meeting that was to be held today.

During the air raid I was in town. There was a strange atmosphere. Little old Oslo had changed so much. People crowded together on every corner. Broken panes of glass on the street. Smoke rose from a house that had been hit. Another house had been totally bombed out. The floors were hanging on top of one another, the windows had been blasted out. It was a terrifying scene. Many people were killed. The fire brigade and ambulances were racing along Drammensveien.

Later, the *Hird* troops turned up: bumpkin farmers with bent knees, brainless cripples, square-shouldered boys with apathetic faces. They try to imitate the Germans: they march, sing . . . Karl Johan is jammed with people. Some thrust their hands in the air, some wear the badge of the NS, the Norwegian fascist party. But most just stand there and stare.

I like the Norwegians. Not only because they are *actively* combating Nazism. They're different from how I imagined. I'd lost all hope of coming across people again who, without orders from above, can think and act independently. Almost every day things happen that demonstrate the Norwegians' attitude to the 'New Order'. Assassination attempts took place at the state police headquarters in Henrik Ibsensgate and at the eastern and western railway stations. Teachers as well as priests have refused to pay a subscription to a so-called 'union' established by the Nazis. (As a consequence, many hundreds of teachers have been sent to the district of Nordland.) Several priests resigned in protest against the new government. Non-Nazis were dismissed etc.

The Norwegians are not giving up. They're not making a big thing of their 'struggle for their country'. Same as ever they sit in the commuter trains, dirty after work, woollen jumpers under their coats, their eyes somewhat tired. They've used up all their bread coupons, they stand in queues from early morning till late evening. They are not giving up.

I particularly like them when they come back from work. And I like the worn-out working-class women who stand in queues. They have far too many wrinkles. They talk of rationing, potatoes and vegetables . . . 'Oh, I remember what it was like before the war.'

I feel as if the war has always been with us.

SUNDAY, 27 SEPTEMBER 1942

Terboven has written to our hostel requesting to know who lives here. I'm now just waiting to be thrown out any day.

I will try to remain calm. I will not be seen crying, nor begging to stay here. In such moments I feel solidarity with all those others around me who are 'suffering' for their country. It's a shame it's the mere fact we are Jews that makes us martyrs.

FRIDAY, 23 OCTOBER 1942

Time is passing very rapidly. There's nothing much else to say. I take refuge in my books.

Christmas will soon be here. It's a year since I saw the Finnish soldier. Two since Biri. I'm so tired. I'm going to smoke a cigarette. So that this emptiness passes.

I'm going to bed. Will I ever arrive at a clear understanding? Will I ever stand face to face with myself? Will I always be fleeing from myself?

J'ai envie de commencer écrire en français. Le jour passe si vite. Je me lève à sept heures et demie. Je déjeune et commence à travailler à huit heurs et demie. Je décore des boits, des cervettes etc. Je n'aime pas mon travail. Mais je gagne bien, 70–80 kr. par semaine. Après avoir diné je vais à l'école. La classe commence à quatre heurs et dure

deux heurs. A six heurs et demie je suis chez moi. J'apprends le français, le suédois et lis
des livres. Je me couche à onze heurs. C'est toute ma journée.

THURSDAY, 29 OCTOBER 1942, OSLO

They're arresting Jews. All male Jews between the ages of sixteen and seventy-two. Jewish shops are closed. That doesn't surprise me. I just feel sick. I'm no longer 'proud' to be a Jew. I can walk past a Jewish face without going wild. But when I hear 'the Jewish question' I get a nasty taste in my mouth. I'm tired of hearing that Jews are being arrested again. I think: Why do they *bother*? Zionism, assimilation, nationalism, Jewish capitalism. Oh! Just leave us in *peace*! It's so horrible to hear about the yellow badges and the Jewish martyrs. It's so repulsive. It reminds me of disgusting worms, slippery, foul worms.

People oppress others because of their views. People kill other people to defend their fatherland. But you don't punish, you don't strike other people because they *are* what they are. Because they have Jewish grandparents. That's moronic, idiotic. That's madness. It runs counter to all reason.

I cannot understand that the Jews can withstand this. That they're not going insane. I no longer love them with the enthusiasm of a seventeen-year-old adolescent girl. But I will stand by them. Whatever happens.

If you shut yourself away and look at this persecution and torture of Jews only from the viewpoint of a Jew, then you'll develop some sort of complex which is bound to lead to a slow, but certain psychological collapse. The only solution is to see the Jewish question from a broader perspective. As forming part of world events of today. Within the framework of the oppressed Czechs and Norwegians, the oppressed workers. Then Zionism becomes unimportant, it gives rise to just itself, it becomes uninteresting. We'll only be rich when we understand that it's not just we who are a race of martyrs. That beside us there are countless others suffering, who will suffer like us until the end of time . . . if we don't . . . if we don't fight for a better . . . Oh no! I'm too old, too tired to believe in this.

This Jewish martyrdom creeps up on me like a repulsive worm. Eating away at my thoughts. There's something absurd about it. I thought I'd been more blunted. Why does it not affect me as much when they arrest Norwegians, shoot them by the dozen as happened recently in Trondheim? Am I too egotistical? Can I not see far enough? I think it's the absurdity that pains me so much. Norwegians are fighting for their country. They're socialists, *Jøssinger* [Norwegian patriots]. They torture us because we're Jews. I'd like to be able to destroy this boundary that makes Jews into Jews. I'd like to see Jews without wounds. Without *any at all*. They should not weep any more. They should walk upright.

Oh, my Muscherle. It's now four years since Vienna. And still there's the same pain. The same inner turmoil. It's being Jewish.

This continual beating of defenceless people disgusts me. It's like hitting into something soft. It's disgusting. Perhaps they'll fetch me too. *Qui sait?*

NOVEMBER 1942

At some point everything comes to an end and then everything will be all right.

There's a sort of uneasy trembling in my breast. A gnawing. What are you? Why are you living?

I've failed in everything I've started. I feel as if it's too late now, as if my life were missing something fundamental.

My only comfort is to place my hand on my forehead. To seek peace in one's own pain.

NOVEMBER 1942

J'ai décidé d'écrire en français. J'ai encore de m'exercer en écrivant français. Je vais écrire de petits notes chaque jour. Je vais raconter ce que je fais comment je m'occupe toute la journée. Si j'ai vraiment besoin d'ecrire je vais écrire en allemand.

Aujourd'hui nous allons voir Vildanden par Ibsen. Je me rapelle ces jours à Vienne quand nous allons au théâtre. Je me rappelle si bien.

THURSDAY, 12 NOVEMBER 1942, OSLO

From a stroke of poetic 'inspiration':

AT WORK

In the pale light of the window, the coloured tins stand beside the empty bottles, they grin at you: a perfect expression of the irretrievable, definitive emptiness of your life. Behind, curtains made of pink crêpe paper . . . boxes . . . boxes. No sun, just a lamp — white, round like a ball — that wants to shine and bring reconciliation. And the smoke from the cigarette, which knows that it is not happening.

TO A COLOUR

The Jew will bleed red if you strike him.

Tilt the head to one side, look elsewhere with timid eyes. Wipe the blood away with the back of one's hand. Walk on, without turning round. It will bleed red from the wound you will tear open when you fight for the fatherland, for justice and freedom.

It is nothing more than a red stripe, running from the heart or the forehead, which shows where you struck. Nobody asks after the one who is dead. He himself is silent, so you can feel safe. He who has found his peace by applying his own hand to himself bleeds red.

Exhausted grey men and women fall from benches in the small parks, while drops fall from a maltreated wrist. Nobody says you are responsible for his death.

A MEMORY

I remember one evening. Twilight in the room and you are standing in front of the mirror, younger, yes, young. You were wearing your dress, Mother, the one with the white spots. We snuggled up to your long legs and said, 'Mother, how beautiful you are now!' You smiled and Father was standing behind you. Tall and very different from when he was dead. He was waiting and you, you were standing in front of the mirror. I remember that we were to stay at home and you were on your way out. To the theatre. How we

enjoyed that word. It was dark outside . . . the lock clicked. And we were
alone. You had gone.

TO MAMA

I sometimes wait for you. I with my tiredness, my empty desire for something
quite different from this life of mine. And you come. You have always come.
A curtain has moved in the wind, a smell, similar to rain, has reminded me
of my childhood. Soft voices have drifted up to me from the street. A girl
who laughs, a child crying weakly. I see that a shimmer of red has spread in
the east. Then it is over. You have gone and I sit there startled. My brow
feels so cool.

The Donau *leaving Oslo harbour on 26 November 1942.*
The photograph was taken secretly by Georg W. Fossum.

EPILOGUE
. . . who disappeared

The diary of Ruth Maier ends at this point. The hefty book she had been writing in since January 1941 was full by November 1942. If she did begin a new volume she probably took it with her when she was arrested.

We know that Ruth Maier declared herself to be Jewish in the 'Questionnaire for Jews in Norway', dated 4 March 1942 in Lillestrøm. When she moved into the hostel in Dalsbergstien 3 in autumn 1942 she was living in the Sankthanshaugen police district in Oslo. It is unknown whether she informed the police authorities of this.

As late as 15 November 1942 she was not yet on the list of Jews in this police district. Her name does appear on a list that was drawn up five days later. The round-up of Jews took place on 26 November and 300 policemen and Gestapo took part in the operation. Taxis confiscated in the capital were used.

Nunna Moum lived in the same hostel as Ruth. She remembers that the arrest happened quietly. Two Norwegian policemen led the young Austrian woman down the stairs to a car waiting in the street. She was ushered into the back seat of the car, where two other women were in tears on the floor. The girls in the hostel woke each other up and watched the events unfold. Someone said, 'We'll look after your gold wristwatch until you come back.' Ruth replied, 'I'm not coming back, ever.'

This eyewitness report contradicts an earlier description, which claimed that Gunvor Hofmo was with Ruth Maier when the arrest took place. In any case, Hofmo must have learned of the arrest soon after.

Those arrested were taken to Oslo harbour and put on board the troop transporter *Donau*, which had been converted into a prison ship. There is a photograph, taken from the quayside, of a silent crowd watching as the *Donau* is towed out of the harbour. On the right of this group there is a figure who may well be Gunvor Hofmo. The ship set sail in the afternoon and reached open sea in a heavy storm, which delayed the crossing by a day.

The last words we have from Ruth Maier are a few lines cited by Gunvor Hofmo from a letter that was smuggled out to her from the *Donau*: 'I think it's just as well that it happened this way. Why shouldn't we suffer when there's so much suffering? Don't worry about me. Perhaps I wouldn't even change places with you.'

Oslo, 3. mai 1947.

Dear Judith Suschitzky

Several times I have tried to write to you,
but always in vain.It is so difficult to write in this case,because
words seems to be nothing.

In a way I think I know you very well, because
Ruth has told me so much about you.She loved to talk about you.
About the rest of her family too,but especially about you and your
mother.She talked about your mutual childhood,about the school,
your passinate love for theatre,your enthusiasm for the actors(Thimik?)
I dont remember his name.

I cannot say anything to help you. But I
want you to know that Ruth was not so lonely in Norway as you perhaps
think,she had friends who were very,very fond of her,friends who are
full of thankfulness that they have known a such human being as Ruth.
Ruth was a such great personality,full of understanding and goodness.
Of course she had her "faults" as some persons love to say.Her distrait
negligence of things which meant nothing to her,brought her several
times into troubles.

First time we met each other was in 1940 at the
"Arbeitsdienst"which at this time was not " nazistisch". After we left
this,we worked in the country,then we took a job together in a flower-
shop i Trondheim,and the last year we were busied in Oslo as
ornamental painters. The afternoons Ruth spent at "Kunst og Hånd-
verkskolen"i Oslo,to learn drawing.And she loved to go in the streets
to find out things to draw and paint.I have some Water colours of her,
perhaps you will like to have some of them?

Ruth lived in a boarding-house,she left Strøms,
as you perhaps know.She could not stand to live upon peoples charity,
without work,without money,you know how that is.

November 1942 she was sent away together
with the other Jews in Norway.It was on Thursday,I remember it too well.
She was very calm.It seems to me ,that she had chosen her way:I must
be with the Jews.And she wrote in her last letter,when they still were
on the ocean:Ich glaube dass es gut so ist wie es gekommen ist.Warum
sollen wir nicht leiden wenn so viel Leid ist?Sorg dich nicht um mich.
Ich mochte vielleicht nicht mit dir tauschen ."

These words,so full of characteristic,beautiful maturity has followed
me these years as a light.

A letter from Gunvor Hofmo to Ruth's sister Judith, 3 May 1947.